It wasn't too long ago, it seems, that Web pages contained text and images—and little else. The very concept of animation, of sound, of actual software programs embedded in Web pages, seemed revolutionary.

Times change quickly on the Web, and a number of new technologies allow you to create pages that move, speak, and react dynamically to user input and to the state of other objects on the page. These technologies have names like GIF89A, plug-ins, Java, JavaScript, Shockwave, ActiveX, and VBScript. If you're out to add new capabilities to your Web pages, or even just to add a little flash, chances are you'll explore many of these new concepts and choose the one that's right for you and for what you want to accomplish.

This book, then, will introduce you to Microsoft's ActiveX and VBScript technologies. Whether you're just interested in finding out what ActiveX and VBScript are all about, or you're a long-time Visual Basic or OLE programmer looking to move to the Web, or you're just interested in exploring new Web technologies, this book will help you get started. As with all the *Laura Lemay's Web Workshop* books, you'll get all the basics and explore plenty of examples so that you can get a feel for how ActiveX and VBScript can be immediately useful in your own Web pages. By the time you finish this book, you'll be fast on your way to creating the kind of dynamic and interesting sites that are so in demand on the Web today.

Laura Lemay

lemay@lne.com

http://www.lne.com/lemay/

LAURA LEMAY'S
WEB WORKSHOP

ACTIVEX AND VBSCRIPT

Dedication

To Deb, Russel, and Victoria.

—Paul Lomax

Overview

Contents

Acknowledgments

I would like to thank a number of people who have made my first project for Sams.net such an enjoyable experience. First of all, David Mayhew, who has had to put up with my many rambling e-mails, and who has done a brilliant job of keeping me on track. Also, Mark Taber, to whom I am thankful for having faith in me, and Fran Hatton and Ryan Rader, for their expert eagle eyes. Thanks go to Rogers Cadenhead for his work on Chapters 12, 15, and 21; to Dick Oliver for the use of his very useful HTML appendix; and, especially, to Laura Lemay for setting the standard to which we aspire.

I would also like to thank the VBScript team at Microsoft for producing another outstanding product. My thanks go to Andy Kington for his excellent Web resource on cookies (`http://www.illuminatus.com/cookie`), which provided much of the inspiration for Chapter 19. Also, I'd like to acknowledge the work of Dave Paris, Aries Solis, and Melvyn Myers, whose Perl script credit-card checker was ported to VBScript for the example in Chapter 11.

Thanks go to my co-directors in Mentorweb, Rick Armstrong and Alan Ashby, who persevered with my long periods of apparent inactivity while I was writing this book. Also, thanks to all our friends in Bahrain, for their help, support, friendship, and love. The past year was not an easy one for many of us, for many different reasons, but a special bond between us helped us through. We miss you all.

A big thanks to my in-laws, Mavis and Frank, for taking Deb and the kids off my hands for several months over the summer. Bahrain was never so quiet!

A special thanks to Mum and Dad for always allowing me to be me, and for giving me the confidence that can only come from unquestioning support and encouragement.

Above all to Deb, Russel, and Victoria, my motivation and strength.

—*Paul Lomax*

About the Authors

Paul Lomax is Technical Director of Mentorweb (http://www.mentorweb.net/), a leading Web design and hosting company. He has been a programmer for more than 12 years and has been a dedicated fan of Visual Basic since version 1—back in the days of DOS.

Paul has written systems for financial derivatives forecasting, satellite TV broadcasting, and the life insurance industry, and he has written a major materials tracking system for the oil and gas industry. He has worked for clients in the UK, Germany, Holland, Denmark, Saudi Arabia, and Bahrain. He is also responsible for the concept, design, and programming of the successful "Contact" series of national business databases.

Paul and his family—wife Deborah, and children Russel and Victoria—have recently returned to their home in England after three years of living in the Arabian Gulf.

Over the past two years, Paul has created and maintained over 60 commercial Web sites for Mentorweb's clients. Paul has also created a Web resource dedicated to VBScript, which can be found at http://www.vbscripts.com/.

Rogers Cadenhead (rcade@airmail.net and http://www.cruel.com/rcade) is a Web developer, computer programmer, and writer, who created the multiuser games Czarlords and Super Video Poker. Thousands of readers see his work in the *Fort Worth Star-Telegram* question-and-answer column "Ask Ed Brice." Rogers has developed Java applets for Tele-Communications Inc. and other clients, is the co-author of *Teach Yourself SunSoft's Java Workshop in 21 Days*, and contributed to *Java Unleashed, 2nd Edition*.

Tell Us What You Think!

As a reader, you are the most important critic and commentator of our books. We value your opinion and want to know what we're doing right, what we could do better, what areas you'd like to see us publish in, and any other words of wisdom you're willing to pass our way. You can help us make strong books that meet your needs and give you the computer guidance you require.

Do you have access to CompuServe or the World Wide Web? Then check out our CompuServe forum by typing **GO SAMS** at any prompt. If you prefer the World Wide Web, check out our site at http://www.mcp.com.

NOTE: If you have a technical question about this book, call the technical support line at (800) 571-5840, ext. 3668.

As the publishing manager of the group that created this book, I welcome your comments. You can fax, e-mail, or write me directly to let me know what you did or didn't like about this book—as well as what we can do to make our books stronger. Here's the information:

Fax: 317/581-4669

E-mail: newtech_mgr@sams.mcp.com

Mail: Mark Taber
          Sams.net Publishing
          201 W. 103rd Street
          Indianapolis, IN 46290

Introduction

by Paul Lomax

The Web is the single most important communication development since man first daubed the image of tomorrow's lunch on the wall of his cave. The opportunity is available to all of us to produce the very medium itself, to communicate our ideas and concepts to the rest of the planet literally within minutes of the concept forming in our brain. For the first time, a virtual world within a world has been created—one in which time races by and information distribution times are counted in seconds rather than days. For the first time, businesses have a flexible and instantly updateable medium, which they can use to communicate with potential customers, current customers, employees, shareholders, and the rest of us.

When Microsoft executives realized that they where in danger of missing out on the opportunity that the Internet and the World Wide Web had to offer (and, even worse, that a potential threat to the Windows platform was looming on the horizon), the virtual world as we know it was to change forever.

Microsoft's vision, and its strategy to become a serious contender in the Internet stakes, was to turn the Internet into an extension of the PC desktop. But the comparatively rudimentary interface offered by the Web meant that a huge gulf existed between the Web page and the Windows desktop. If the vision was to be realized, a revolution needed to take place—and fast.

What followed was an unprecedented frenzy of software development activity. Product after product was rolled out via the Web as beta copies, development followed development, and the "Internet year" was shrunk to the point where just a few days off the Web could leave you feeling like you'd just missed the boat.

The result of all this feverish activity is indeed a revolution. In a few short months, the face of the Web has been transformed to the point at which it is now possible to create applications held within a humble Web page that feel, act, and for all intents and purposes *are* Windows applications.

At the heart of the revolution is the technology known as ActiveX. The reason that the technological revolution on the Web has been achieved with such speed (apart from the instantaneous distribution the Web affords) is that ActiveX is not really new. It is actually an extension of the technology that makes up nearly all Windows programs in use today—the building blocks used by programmers to construct Windows (and now Web) applications. However, ActiveX controls and components need a glue to hold them together. Therefore, a programming language is needed that is easy to learn and use, safe to transmit across the Web, and able to interface with existing HTML controls.

VBScript is the glue that holds the ActiveX controls together and allows controls to interact and interface with each other and the outside world. Again, VBScript leverages several years of tried, tested, and trusted technology in the shape of Visual Basic, a language used by millions of programmers across the world.

ActiveX and VBScript are the foundation for future development of Web and intranet applications. Therefore, it is important that you understand the technologies involved and how they are implemented. But ActiveX and VBScript are not the only means of creating interactive content within Web pages, so why should you put the time and effort into learning how to implement ActiveX and the VBScript language, rather than say Java applets and JavaScript? Here are some reasons:

❏ Many corporations are now looking seriously at moving from a traditional network environment to an intranet. Large numbers of the applications used by these corporations are built using Microsoft technology. They have Microsoft back ends, such as SQL Server, and run on Microsoft Windows NT. They use front ends written in Visual Basic. So it makes financial and logistical sense to use these applications as the basis for an intranet application and thereby protect the large investment that has gone into the applications, rather than throwing them away and starting from scratch. ActiveX and VBScript will form the basis of these conversions.

❏ A less clear-cut scenario exists on the Web, with the Netscape and Microsoft browser wars. Because ActiveX and VBScript currently operate only through the Microsoft Internet Explorer (MSIE), Netscape's dominant position in the browser market at present would appear to suggest that the case for using ActiveX and VBScript is weak. But Microsoft is catching up fast, and the following recent developments ensure that a growing percentage of Web surfers will be MSIE users or have ActiveX- and VBScript-enabled browsers:

   ❏ Microsoft has signed deals with all the leading online services, whereby the online services will issue MSIE to all of their subscribers.

   ❏ Microsoft will include MSIE with the install of Windows 95.

   ❏ Netscape will almost certainly support ActiveX and VBScript with the next release of Netscape Navigator.

❏ With every passing day, the distinction between Web and desktop interfaces is becoming less and less evident. Soon, surfing the Web and using a desktop application will blend together seamlessly, and due to the almost universal use of Windows, Microsoft will be dominant immediately in this exciting new environment. This will bring ActiveX and VBScript to the forefront of Web application development.

There is a growing need for more interactivity within Web pages, a need to produce Web sites that are easy to navigate through and easy to use—in short, a need to go beyond what HTML has to offer. Furthermore, within the Web you have a great deal of competition. As a Webmaster, you must find ways to set your site apart from the rest, giving people a reason to visit your site and keep coming back for more. Using ActiveX and VBScript—collectively known as Active Content—is the way to achieve new, exciting, and intuitive Web sites. These Web sites capture an audience's imagination; users enjoy visiting them and find them easy to use. Such sites and applications perform more like Windows applications than like HTML Web pages.

Whether your background is in Web page authoring or application development, you can't afford to be left behind as the two specialties merge into one. Take the opportunity now to learn how to produce Active Content Web sites using ActiveX and VBScript. You'll find it rewarding and, above all, great fun.

How to Read This Book

The following examples show how this book's Tips, Notes, and Cautions help guide you through the information you will need to know.

TIP: Tips offer important (or at least interesting) hints and suggestions related to the topic at hand.

Margin notes tell you more about the current topic, as well as give you cross-references to places in the book where you can find further information about a specific subject.

NOTE: Notes provide you with interesting, added information about the subject at hand.

CAUTION: Cautions prompt you with gentle warnings to help you stay out of trouble.

I

Fast Track to ActiveX and VBScript

ONE

Getting to Grips with ActiveX

The combination of ActiveX and VBScript makes your Web pages more appealing and easier to use—features that are vitally important in a Web where thousands, even millions, of Web sites are competing for attention. ActiveX and VBScript bring your Web pages to life; you will soon see how quickly and easily you can create interactive, intercreative Web pages that Web users will want to visit and return to visit again.

ActiveX is the technology that will eventually bring together the Internet or World Wide Web and the desktop—whether it's Windows or Macintosh—as one seamless environment. One of the most exciting aspects of using ActiveX and VBScript to enhance your Web pages is that you help further the development of the Web in a direction that was merely a pipe dream only months ago.

In this chapter, you

- ❏ Learn how ActiveX brings your Web pages up-to-date with active content
- ❏ Obtain the ActiveX Control Pad and install it on your computer
- ❏ Create a new ActiveX HTML Web page using the ActiveX Control Pad
- ❏ Add an ActiveX control to a new HTML document
- ❏ Set the properties of an ActiveX control
- ❏ Edit the properties of an ActiveX control
- ❏ Create a simple script to interface ActiveX controls
- ❏ Use the ActiveX Script Wizard
- ❏ Create hyperlinks using ActiveX controls

Tasks in this chapter:

- ❏ Downloading and installing the ActiveX Control Pad
- ❏ Creating a simple welcome page in the ActiveX Control Pad
- ❏ Adding ActiveX label and command button controls
- ❏ Setting an ActiveX control's property values
- ❏ Editing ActiveX control properties
- ❏ Bringing ActiveX controls to life with active scripting
- ❏ Adding hyperlinks ActiveX style

In Chapter 21, "Advanced ActiveX Techniques," you will learn that you can even use standard, current Windows controls as ActiveX controls in your Web pages.

You might be surprised and even a little disappointed to learn that ActiveX controls are actually nothing new. Windows as we know it would not exist but for ActiveX controls, or as they used to be known, OCX controls. Although ActiveX controls are somewhat less bulky, they are really the same as OCX controls, which gives you a huge advantage when using ActiveX. Years of usage and development went into the underlying OLE (Object Linking and Embedding) technology.

This chapter gives you some of the basic knowledge that you need to get started using ActiveX controls: how you add them to the page and how you can customize them to suit your needs. You'll also take your first look at the *tool du jour*, the ActiveX Control Pad, which makes the job of interfacing ActiveX controls quicker and easier.

Downloading and Installing the ActiveX Control Pad

The ActiveX Control Pad and HTML Layout control that come together as a complete package are freely available for download from Microsoft's Site Builder Workshop Web site at `http://www.microsoft.com/workshop/` (see Figure 1.1). Simply follow the links to the ActiveX Control Pad download area. At the time of writing, Microsoft requires you to complete a very straightforward registration form prior to downloading the ActiveX Control Pad.

Figure 1.1.
The Microsoft Site Builder Workshop.

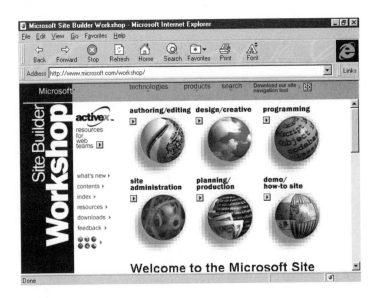

To install and use the ActiveX Control Pad, you must first have Microsoft Internet Explorer 3.0 installed on your machine. Additionally, your system must have the following minimum specification:

❏ PC 80486 or above

❏ Windows 95 or Windows NT 4.0

❏ 12MB RAM

❏ 10MB free hard disk space

❏ Microsoft Internet Explorer 3.0

The ActiveX Control Pad and HTML Layout Control are very easy to install. The single file containing them both is a self-extracting, self-installing archive. To set up the Control Pad, all you have to do is locate the file you downloaded (setuppad.exe) and double-click it to extract the contents and commence the installation procedure, as shown in Figure 1.2.

Figure 1.2.

During the Control Pad installation, you can accept the default directory or enter your own.

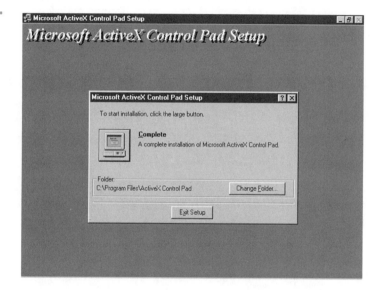

The installation creates a program group called Microsoft ActiveX Control Pad that you can access from the Windows 95 Start button. As with all software you install, the first thing you should do is read the readme, but you always do that anyway—don't you?

The ActiveX Control Pad is an HTML authoring tool with a difference. It enables you to add active controls and active scripting to your HTML pages. When I say active controls, I don't mean only ActiveX controls; you can embed Java applets, too. Active scripting doesn't mean only VBScript; JavaScript and Microsoft's implementation of JavaScript, known as JScript, are also supported. You can add controls quickly and easily using the familiar Windows point and click method.

ActiveX controls can be as simple as the buttons or drop-down lists you regularly find in Windows programs, or they can be complete stand-alone programs, somewhat like a Java applet.

You'll learn more about the theory of ActiveX controls in Chapter 21. But for now, create a simple active-content HTML page using one of the preloaded ActiveX controls.

 ## Creating a Simple Welcome Page in the ActiveX Control Pad

Open the ActiveX Control Pad as you would any other Windows application by double-clicking the icon in the ActiveX Control Pad program group. Figure 1.3 displays the ActiveX Control Pad as it appears when you first open it. You'll notice that it automatically creates a new HTML page, complete with a simple HTML template, ready for you to start creating your active-content Web page.

Figure 1.3.

The ActiveX Control Pad showing the automatic HTML template.

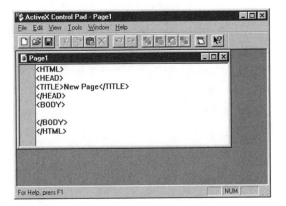

NOTE: In this book, I assume that you're already up to speed with HTML, so unless there are any new HTML tags or tags specifically designed to handle active objects, I won't waste your time detailing the HTML. If you need an HTML refresher or primer, you can consult Appendix A, "HTML Reference/ MSIE Extensions." As a bonus, the book *Teach Yourself Web Publishing with HTML 3.2 in 14 Days, Professional Reference Edition* by Laura Lemay is included on this book's CD-ROM.

Take a look around the ActiveX Control Pad window. You have a text editor but no WYSIWYG screen. WYSIWYG editing and control placement are the jobs of the HTML Layout Control, which I examine in detail in Chapter 14, "Using the HTML Layout Control." The goal of using the ActiveX Control Pad is to place code that implements ActiveX and Java controls and any associated scripts in your HTML Web pages with a minimum of fuss and trouble and even without any programming skills. The ActiveX Control Pad is where you start to build or edit your active-content HTML pages.

To try the text editor and start getting a feel for the environment, enter some simple HTML into the document.

1. Give the page a title, My First ActiveX Web Page.

2. Add a BGCOLOR="white" attribute to the <BODY> tag.

3. Add <CENTER> and </CENTER> tags below the <BODY> tag.

4. Now, between the <CENTER> tags, add a main <H1> heading, Welcome to my Active Web.

5. Save the document as welcome.htm in the directory of your choice.

By default, the Control Pad saves all work in the Program Files\ActiveX Control Pad\ subdirectory. In the Control Pad, the saved HTML page should look like the one in Figure 1.4.

Figure 1.4.

welcome.htm *in the HTML text editor of the Control Pad.*

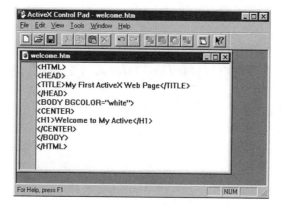

After you save the page, run it with the Internet Explorer either by opening the Internet Explorer and opening the page from the File|Open menu option or by clicking the filename that is now available in the recent Documents menu attached to the Start button—assuming you set Internet Explorer as your default browser. The page should look like the one in Figure 1.5.

Figure 1.5.

welcome.htm *in the Internet Explorer.*

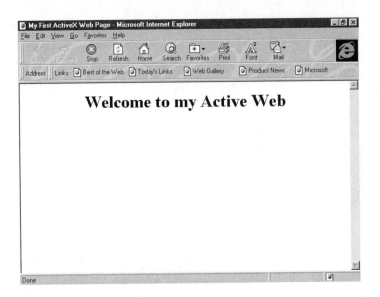

 Adding ActiveX Label and Command Button Controls

Now that you're satisfied that the ActiveX Control Pad can create normal flat HTML Web pages, your next step is the one you've been waiting for: adding some active content. Return to the ActiveX Control Pad, and if you've closed it in the meantime, reopen welcome.htm.

TIP: You can invoke the ActiveX Control Pad and open an HTML document in it by right-clicking the HTML document's icon in Windows Explorer and selecting Edit in ActiveX Control Pad from the pop-up menu.

Insert an empty line after the </H1> tag. Enter a <P> paragraph tag to add some space under the heading and press Return, making sure your cursor appears at the beginning of this blank line.

To insert an object, select Insert ActiveX Control from the Edit menu. The Control Pad displays a dialog box similar to Figure 1.6, which contains all the insertable ActiveX controls registered on your system.

You should at least see a number of Microsoft Forms 2.0 controls listed in the ActiveX Control dialog box; however, the number and type of controls available to you depends upon the software you previously loaded on your computer.

Figure 1.6.

The Insert ActiveX Control dialog box, scrolled to show the MS Forms 2.0 controls.

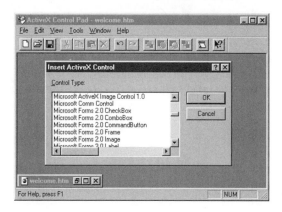

NOTE: If you installed Microsoft Visual Basic 4.0, you'll see a large variety and number of controls, most of which will be immediately familiar to you, confirming that the OCX custom controls used in development environments such as Visual Basic are in fact ActiveX controls and can be used as such. In Chapter 21, you construct a Web page using one of the Visual Basic custom controls.

Take a moment to scroll through the list of controls. Find the control named Microsoft Forms 2.0 Label, select it so that it is highlighted, and click OK. Figure 1.7 shows what you should see next.

Figure 1.7.

The ActiveX Object Editor and Properties window.

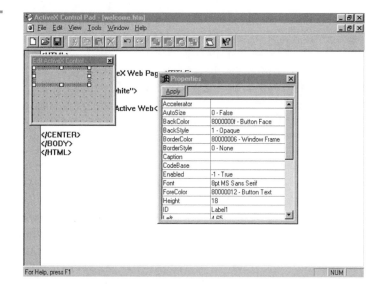

The small window on the left is the Object Editor (see Figure 1.8). This is NWYSIWYG, *Nearly*-What-You-See-Is-What-You-Get. The object you selected in this window is shown as it will appear on the HTML Web page but not in the place where it will appear. The placement is still determined by its order within the HTML source document. However, you can use the mouse to change its size and other properties, as you'll see shortly.

Figure 1.8.

The ActiveX Object Editor.

The larger window to the right is the Properties window (see Figure 1.9). Here, you can see a long list of attributes that this label possesses. Take a moment to scroll down the list of properties. Some are self-explanatory; others are somewhat more obtuse. All the property values listed here are the default values for this particular control. You change a property by selecting the particular property value next to the property name.

Figure 1.9.

The ActiveX Properties window.

Setting an ActiveX Control's Property Values

Some of the controls you'll use are just fine with their default property values, but most of the time, you'll want to customize the control in some way to suit your purposes. After all, customization is one of the really neat things about Windows controls. You can see from the list of properties that not only can you change the outward appearance of a control, but you can also change how the control operates. You can make the changes quickly and easily even if you haven't written a program in your life. Here's how you set an object's properties:

1. Put your mouse cursor over the value for AutoSize and click to select it. The default value should be 0- False.

2. Immediately, several things happen: The property value appears in the drop-down list, which becomes enabled at the top of the Properties window, and the Apply button becomes enabled.

2. Click the down arrow next to the drop-down list.

You see the choices available for this property. `AutoSize` is quite straightforward; you choose either `-1 - True` (the label automatically changes its width to fit the caption it contains) or `0 - False` (the label always remains the same width regardless of the caption width).

3. Select `-1 - True`.

The label automatically reduces in width. It's really as simple as that; some of the properties have many different values you can choose, and some rely entirely on your input, but customizing each object is very straightforward.

To save the current property values and return to the HTML page, simply close the Object Editor window. The relevant HTML code for this object and its parameters are then transcribed automatically onto the HTML document in the Text Editor window (see Figure 1.10).

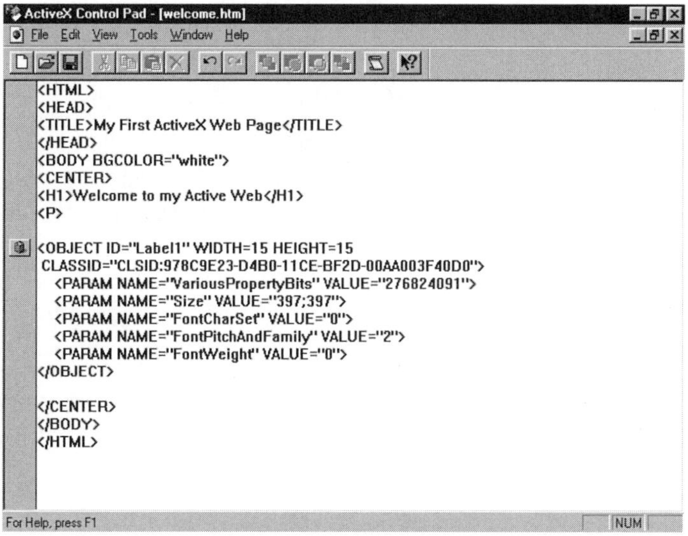

Figure 1.10.

The control's HTML definition is automatically placed in the text editor.

```
ActiveX Control Pad - [welcome.htm]
File  Edit  View  Tools  Window  Help

<HTML>
<HEAD>
<TITLE>My First ActiveX Web Page</TITLE>
</HEAD>
<BODY BGCOLOR="white">
<CENTER>
<H1>Welcome to my Active Web</H1>
<P>

<OBJECT ID="Label1" WIDTH=15 HEIGHT=15
 CLASSID="CLSID:978C9E23-D4B0-11CE-BF2D-00AA003F40D0">
    <PARAM NAME="VariousPropertyBits" VALUE="276824091">
    <PARAM NAME="Size" VALUE="397;397">
    <PARAM NAME="FontCharSet" VALUE="0">
    <PARAM NAME="FontPitchAndFamily" VALUE="2">
    <PARAM NAME="FontWeight" VALUE="0">
</OBJECT>

</CENTER>
</BODY>
</HTML>

For Help, press F1                                              NUM
```

All the code that defines and implements an ActiveX control is added for you, including the horrendous-looking `CLASSID` that uniquely identifies each type of control. You can now see just how easy it is to add ActiveX controls to your Web pages. At this point, you'll probably get a rush of adrenaline and want to start adding all types of controls all over your pages—so don't let me stop you. Here's how to do it:

1. Place your cursor at the end of the </OBJECT> line and enter another <P> paragraph tag; then press Enter again.

   This time, you add a command button to the page.

2. Select Insert ActiveX Control from the Edit menu, and select the Microsoft Forms 2.0 Command Button object.

3. Open the Object Editor and the Properties window by clicking OK. In the Properties window, select the Caption property, which determines the message on the face of the button. Click in the box at the top of the Properties window next to the button marked Apply, and type Click; then click the Apply button.

Your new property value appears in the property list and displays on the command button itself in the Object Editor window.

Editing Objects in the Object Editor

You can also change properties by using the Object Editor. Click the button that you created in the Object Editor window. A hatched marquee containing eight small, white drag blocks appears around the button. You can use the drag blocks at the corners of the button to increase or reduce the size and width in the same operation. You can use the blocks at north, east, south, and west to drag the button's height and width independently of each other.

Click in the center of the button. This gives you a flashing cursor, and you can see that the text on the button face has the focus. Using your arrow keys, move the cursor to the end of the word Click, press the space bar, and type Me. Notice that the change is echoed in the Properties window. Editing properties is that simple. To save the current properties and return to the Text Editor, close the Object Editor window. Your HTML page should now look like the one in Figure 1.11.

Save the file with the Save icon or choose Save from the File menu, and run the page with your Internet Explorer browser. It should look like the page in Figure 1.12. If your browser is loaded with the page from earlier in the chapter, simply click Refresh to see the amended Web page.

Figure 1.11.

The command button definition added to the HTML page.

Figure 1.12.

Your page with an HTML caption, an ActiveX label, and an ActiveX command button.

TASK Editing ActiveX Control Properties

Now you have two ActiveX controls on your page: a label and a command button. You probably think your ActiveX Label control looks far from appealing, more like a mistake than state-of-the-art active content! You can do something about that.

Return to the ActiveX Control Pad with your `welcome.htm` page open. Look down the left margin of the text editor. You see (and probably saw before) two blue cube icons. As you might guess, these icons represent the ActiveX objects you placed on your page. Click the cube icon next to your label control. Voila! The Object Editor and Properties window open, ready for editing.

Editing the `BackColor` Property

Now you can do something about this label. By default, the label's background color was set to the same color as a standard Windows button—gray. So follow these steps to change the label's background color to white so that the label blends into the page:

1. Click the `BackColor` property in the Properties window. At the top of the Properties window, you see two controls next to the Apply button. The standard drop-down list contains all the standard Windows colors you can choose, and a new control displays three dots, known as an ellipsis.

NOTE: The ellipsis button displays whenever you select a property that can be set using a separate dialog box for sample color or font.

2. Click the ellipsis button to the right of the list, which invokes the Windows color palette shown in Figure 1.13.

Figure 1.13.
The ActiveX color palette.

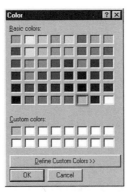

You can choose one of 48 basic colors or create any custom color you want for the background of your label. This color palette is available for most color properties. For this exercise, set the background to white:

Depending upon your system's color capabilities, some of the colors in the standard color palette might appear to be duplicated many times.

1. Click the white color box (bottom-right corner of the basic palette).
2. Click OK.

The BackColor property shows the hexadecimal value for white, and the label in the Object Editor displays white. Because the background of the HTML page is also set to white, the user will see only the text that is on the label; the rest of the label will blend into the background.

Changing a Label's Caption and WordWrap Properties

The main property of a label is its caption—the words that the outside world sees displayed on the page. It's about time you gave your label a meaningful caption:

1. Simply place your cursor over the Caption property and click.
2. Enter the words Active Content in the box at the top of the Properties window.
3. Click Apply.

If your label has all the right default settings, it might not look quite as you anticipated because labels are by default set to wrap words. This means that characters that do not fit within the width of the label are forced onto a new line; as a result, the words appear down rather than across the label. Change the WordWrap property as follows:

1. Scroll down to the bottom of the property list until you find WordWrap.
2. Change WordWrap to False.

NOTE: In effect, when you set the label's WordWrap property to True, the width of the label is fixed, and the height is variable. When you set WordWrap to False, the width of the label changes to accommodate the caption in one unbroken line, and the height is fixed.

Changing a Label's Font Property

The label should now have its correct proportions, but it's still somewhat small. You should increase the size of the font as follows:

1. Find the Font property and give it a click. The ellipsis button appears so that you can choose settings from a specialized dialog box.
2. Click the ellipsis button to see a complete font selection dialog, as shown in Figure 1.14.

   As you can see, you can choose from all the fonts installed on your system, along with all their corresponding styles and sizes.

Figure 1.14.
The ActiveX font selection dialog box.

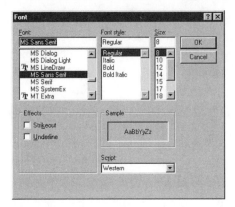

NOTE: Remember that not everyone has the same fonts that you have on your system. You can create a Web page with the very latest and greatest fonts that look stunning on your computer, but when a user with a standard set of fonts downloads the Web page with his browser, it might look very different indeed. It's therefore wise to stick to the main system fonts.

3. Select a font size of 24 points.
4. Click OK.

The label caption and the label itself should change size. If the label didn't grow to accommodate the new larger text, make sure that the AutoSize property is True.

Close the Object Editor or Properties window to save the properties you just amended. Save the page and look at it in Internet Explorer. You see your first ActiveX welcome page as shown in Figure 1.15.

Impressed? You've just created your welcome page; it is rather straightforward, but it's ActiveX without the *active*. To give the page some interactivity, you need to provide some instructions to the controls, which is where VBScript comes in. In the next section, you'll find out how to use VBScript to quickly and easily interface ActiveX controls on your Web pages.

Figure 1.15.

Your ActiveX Welcome Web page.

 Bringing Your ActiveX Controls to Life with Active Scripting

Active scripting refers to the technology of adding to your Web pages a script or program that interfaces with the active controls. Scripts download within the HTML page as ASCII text so that they are safe, meaning that a rogue programmer cannot write a hidden virus or other mischievous program within the script. Internet Explorer supports any scripting language that is written to the ActiveX scripting specification.

This book concentrates on VBScript, which has the full title Visual Basic Scripting Edition. Adding VBScript procedures via the ActiveX Control Pad is as easy as other point-and-click operations because of the Script Wizard. By default, the built-in Script Wizard generates VBScript code; however, it also has the capability to generate JavaScript (or JScript, as Microsoft now calls its implementation).

VBScript is a subset of Visual Basic for Applications (VBA). To ensure the safety of Web pages downloaded across the Internet, VBScript leaves out several major features of VBA that deal mainly with functions and procedures that interface with the hard drive and the underlying operating system. You can implement VBScript only to function within the context of the browser.

With VBScript in particular and active scripting in general, you can access a control's properties, methods (things a control can do), and events (things done to it), making the controls truly active. Above all, you can achieve very professional results in very little time with little or no programming knowledge. Of course, the deeper you get into using active controls and active scripting, the more you need to know about the workings and implementation of controls and scripting. In later chapters, you will learn how to produce complex programs with VBScript.

Opening the ActiveX Script Wizard

Add some life to the welcome page you created in the last section. First, open the `welcome.htm` page in the ActiveX Control Pad. You can open the Script Wizard in one of three ways:

❏ Select the Script Wizard menu option from the Tools menu (Tools|Script Wizard).

❏ Right-click anywhere in the Text Editor and select Script Wizard from the pop-up menu.

❏ Click the Script Wizard toolbar button (which looks like an ancient scroll).

The Script Wizard dialog box, shown in Figure 1.16, contains the ActiveX objects you placed in the HTML page earlier.

Figure 1.16.

The ActiveX Script Wizard.

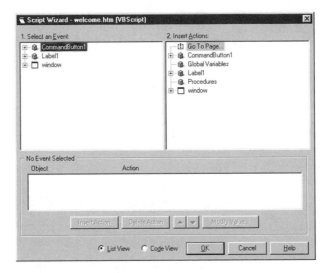

The Script Wizard has three main components. The left pane of the dialog box is the Events window. If you click one of the plus signs next to an object, a list of the events for the object expands under it. The diamonds to the left of the event names denote whether a script was attached to the event (black diamond) or not (white diamond). The right area of the Script Wizard contains the methods and properties for each of the objects. The properties are denoted by a white icon containing small blue lines. The methods icon is yellow and contains an exclamation mark (!). The bottom pane contains the scripted actions for the Web page; you see two radio buttons marked List

View and Code View. List View displays a general brief description of the code that was generated; Code View displays the code itself.

Attaching a Simple VBScript Procedure to a Button

Add a short procedure to the button so that when the user clicks the button, the caption of the label changes:

1. In the left pane (the Events window), click the plus sign next to the CommandButton1 object.

2. Click the word Click under the CommandButton1 object. This means that the code is attached to the Click event of the button.

   The next thing you must do is to link the event to the Label1 object; in other words, when the user clicks the button, firing the click event, the program acts upon the Label1 object.

3. In the right pane, click the plus sign next to Label1. You see a list of the properties for the label object.

4. Double-click the Caption property to display the caption entry dialog box.

5. Enter Hello ActiveX in the caption entry dialog box, as shown in Figure 1.17.

Figure 1.17.

Changing the Caption *property of the label from the* CommandButton *click event.*

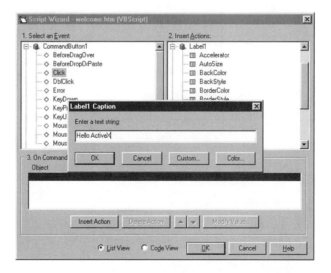

6. Click OK, and the event is registered in the Actions pane toward the bottom of the Script Wizard.

To view the actual code that is generated by the Script Wizard, click the option marked Code View. That's how easy it is to add active scripting to your Web pages. Before you rush off to try your new page, you must add code to one more event.

Collapse the events list by clicking the minus (-) symbol next to the CommandButton1 object. Do the same thing with the Properties list for the Label1 object in the right pane. Add code to the MouseMove event for the Label1 object that displays a message in the status bar at the bottom of the browser:

1. Click the plus sign next to the Label1 object in the left pane.

   You see a list of events for the label object. You might notice that the events for a label are slightly different from the events for a CommandButton.

2. Click the MouseMove event.

3. Move to the right pane and click the plus sign next to the window object.

   For this code, you want to interact with the browser itself. Scroll down the list slightly to find the Status property.

4. Double-click the Status property to display the text entry box.

5. Enter Goodbye Flat HTML Web Pages.

6. Click OK.

To generate all the required code and return to the Text Editor, simply click OK at the bottom of the Script Wizard screen. The Script Wizard places the code for the two events on your HTML page, which should now look like the page in Figure 1.18.

Figure 1.18.

The Script Wizard automatically generates the code for the two events and places it in the HTML file.

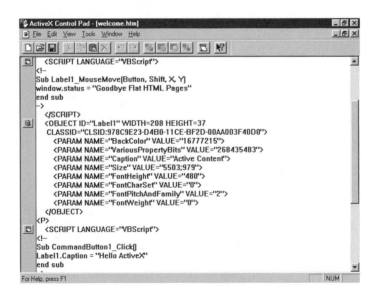

```
<SCRIPT LANGUAGE="VBScript">
<!--
Sub Label1_MouseMove(Button, Shift, X, Y)
window.status = "Goodbye Flat HTML Pages"
end sub
-->
</SCRIPT>
<OBJECT ID="Label1" WIDTH=208 HEIGHT=37
   CLASSID="CLSID:978C9E23-D4B0-11CE-BF2D-00AA003F40D0">
   <PARAM NAME="BackColor" VALUE="16777215">
   <PARAM NAME="VariousPropertyBits" VALUE="268435483">
   <PARAM NAME="Caption" VALUE="Active Content">
   <PARAM NAME="Size" VALUE="5503;979">
   <PARAM NAME="FontHeight" VALUE="480">
   <PARAM NAME="FontCharSet" VALUE="0">
   <PARAM NAME="FontPitchAndFamily" VALUE="2">
   <PARAM NAME="FontWeight" VALUE="0">
</OBJECT>
<P>
<SCRIPT LANGUAGE="VBScript">
<!--
Sub CommandButton1_Click()
Label1.Caption = "Hello ActiveX"
end sub
```

Save your `welcome.htm` file in the Control Pad Text Editor, and run the page with the Internet Explorer to make sure it all works (see Figure 1.19). When you pass the mouse arrow across the label, a message appears in the browser's status bar at the bottom of the screen. When you click the button, the label caption changes to read "Hello ActiveX." Congratulations.

Figure 1.19.
Your almost-finished welcome page.

 ## Adding Hyperlinks ActiveX Style

You now have an active welcome page. As a welcome page, it's lacking a major ingredient, though—links. Your welcome page should do just that: welcome visitors to your site. From the welcome page, your visitors then roam around your Web pages viewing, reading, and generally experiencing that which interests them. How are your visitors going to get from your welcome page to the rest of the site? In HTML, you use the good old anchor tag, `<A HREF=...>...</>`, and of course, you can use this tag in your ActiveX page as well. But what you really want is a state-of-the-art ActiveX hyperlink, right? Well, this is your lucky day!

ActiveX and VBScript enable you to use any of the controls you place on the screen as hyperlinks, buttons, images, and labels. You can script everything in such a way that clicking the control causes the browser to load a new page. In this section, you'll create a hyperlink menu that actively displays a short description of the linked page.

If `welcome.htm` isn't open in your ActiveX Control Pad, open it for editing as you saw earlier.

To place the controls on the page in a logical order, you need to construct an HTML table. The following code provides the framework you need to add to the page under the button control and just above the `</CENTER>` tag:

```
</OBJECT>

<TABLE WIDTH=80%>
<TD>
<!--The first pseudo hyperlink goes here-->
<TD ROWSPAN=2 VALIGN=TOP>
<!--The hyperlink description goes here-->
<TR>
<TD>
<!--The second pseudo hyperlink goes here-->
<TR>
</TABLE>

</CENTER>
```

The preceding definition creates a table in the center of the page with two rows in the left column and a single row in the right column that spans the two left rows.

Place your cursor under the first `<TD>` tag (the top left cell), and select Insert ActiveX Control from the Edit menu. Select the Microsoft Forms 2.0 Label control and click OK.

Amend the following properties to these values:

```
IDLink1

BackColor   White

ForeColor   Blue

Font Size   12 Point, Bold

WordWrap    False

Caption     My Links Page
```

You'll remember from the earlier sections that to change a property value, you simply select the property you need to change in the Properties window. Then, in the case of the `ID` and `Caption` properties, type the new value into the text box at the top of the Properties window and click Apply. For the other values you need to change, click the ellipsis button—which displays the relevant dialog for the particular property, either the color or font—and then simply select what you need with a mouse click and click OK.

TIP: A neat shortcut to save time when setting properties is double-clicking the property value in the Properties window, which immediately invokes any associated dialog box or toggles the property value in a selection list (such as True or False).

After you set these property values, close the Object Editor window to transcribe the object declaration to the HTML page.

Move your cursor so that it is under the `<TD ROWSPAN=2 VALIGN=TOP>` tag, which will contain the description of the link. This tag appears on the right side of the table, and as you can see, the cell takes up the whole height of the column. You're going to place a label control here. Select Edit|Insert ActiveX Control, choose Microsoft Forms 2.0 Label, and click OK.

Edit the properties for this label as follows:

```
IDLinkDescription

BackColor  White

Font Size  12 Point
```

There is no caption because it is added actively. Unless stated, all the other properties are left with their default values. The only other thing you need to do with this label is increase its size as follows:

1. First, increase the size of the Object Editor by dragging its lower-right corner.

2. Place your arrow over the lower-right corner of the label until your arrow changes to a northwest/southeast arrow.

3. Drag the lower-right corner of the label. It's not vitally important for the purposes of this exercise to get the dimensions exact, but you need the label to be around 70 pixels high and 140 pixels wide. You can check the current size in the Properties window; the property values change as you drag and release the label.

Close the Object Editor, and you're ready to add the last object. Place your cursor after the final `<TD>`, and insert another label as you did before. Change its properties as follows:

```
ID         Link2

BackColor  White

ForeColor  Red

Font Size  12 Point, Bold

WordWrap   False

Caption    My Fun Page
```

Close the Object Editor, save the page, and give it a test run with the browser. Your page should look like the one in Figure 1.20.

Figure 1.20.

Your welcome page complete with hyperlabels.

Adding VBScript Code for ActiveX Hyperlinks

It takes several steps to create a hyperlink that lets the user immediately identify what the link promises, both in terms of its content and also its filename. You need procedures that provide visual clues as the mouse is passed over the control, and you must also instruct the browser to load the new page when the control is clicked.

Add the following procedures to this page for each hyperlink:

❏ A MouseMove event that automatically places a text string in the LinkDescription label control.

❏ A MouseMove event that automatically changes the ForeColor (color of the font) of the LinkDescription label control to that of the link label (to provide an additional visual clue).

❏ A MouseMove event that automatically echoes the link filename in the status bar of the browser.

❏ A Click event that instructs the browser to load the link file.

With welcome.htm loaded in the ActiveX Control Pad, select Script Wizard from the Tools menu.

To create the script that places text in the description label, change the font color of the label and display a status message when the user passes the mouse over the first link:

1. Click the plus sign to the left of Link1 in the Events pane.

2. Select the MouseMove event from the list of Link1's events.

3. Click the plus sign to the left of LinkDescription in the Actions pane.

4. Double-click the Caption property from the list of LinkDescription's properties and methods.

5. Enter the following text into the Caption dialog: This link takes you to my link page where you can find loads of links to really cool pages—or words to that effect!

6. Click OK.

7. Double-click the ForeColor property, which is a few items below the Caption property.

8. Click a suitable shade of blue from the left palette and click OK.

9. Collapse the LinkDescription property list by clicking the minus sign next to LinkDescription.

10. Open the list of properties and methods for the window object by clicking the plus sign next to Window.

11. Scroll down slightly to find the Status property—in fact, it's a property of the Self subobject.

12. Double-click the Status property to display the Status text dialog box. Here, you enter a URL that is shown in the status bar at the bottom of the browser. You need to do this because the browser does not recognize the label as an HTML hyperlink and therefore does not display the usual "Short-cut to …." You are in fact replicating the procedure that usually happens within the browser for a hyperlink.

13. Enter the following text:

    Shortcut to http://www.anydomain.com/link.htm

    Don't worry at this stage that neither the domain nor the file exists; this is only an exercise, after all. Click OK.

You now have a list of three actions for the MouseMove event for Link1, and your Script Wizard window should look like the one in Figure 1.21.

Remain in the Script Wizard because you need to add the event that changes the page when the link is clicked:

1. Select Click from the list of events for Link1 in the left Events pane.

2. Scroll the right pane to the top and double-click the top item, Go to Page. This opens a dialog box in which you enter the URL of the linked page. Because this is only an exercise, don't worry about what you type here. After you enter a URL, click OK.

3. Click OK at the bottom of the Script Wizard to generate all the code for Label1, which should look something like what you see in Figure 1.22.

Figure 1.21.
Your Link1 MouseMove
event action list.

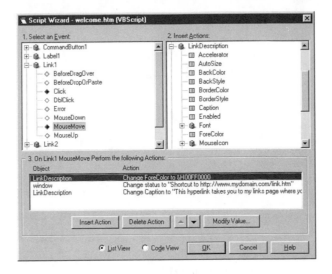

Figure 1.22.
*The code automatically
generated for the* Link1
object.

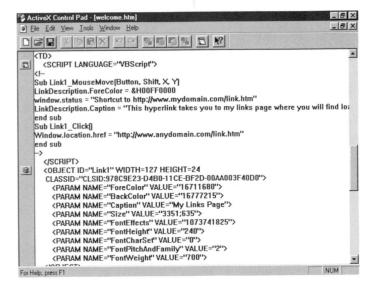

To complete your code for this welcome page, you need to repeat the preceding steps for Link2. For Link2, choose a green color for the LinkDescription ForeColor, and when entering the caption for LinkDescription, use wording that describes the fun page.

When you complete the code for Link2, save the HTML page and open it in the browser. When you pass the mouse over the link, two things happen. First, you see a description of the page on the right of the link in the color of the link, and second, the filename appears in the status bar.

Figure 1.23.

The finished welcome page with ActiveX hyperlinks.

Workshop Wrap-Up

You covered a lot of ground in this first chapter, and if some of the terminology and methodology is unfamiliar and confusing, don't worry too much at this stage. The goal of this first chapter was to stimulate your imagination. You can see how straightforward it is to create professional active content for your Web pages. ActiveX goes beyond animation applets and things that look pretty; it is about creating fully active content where all the objects you place on the page can be programmed in some way to interact with each other and with the browser, too.

Any programming language is just a beginning, an empty shell. As with an artist's canvas and a palette of oils, it's up to you to exploit the power of the language and add the creativity, and that is what I will help you do through the rest of the book.

Next Steps

Now that you've had a chance to use some ActiveX controls, use the ActiveX Control Pad, and write some basic VBScripts, you can delve deeper into the rest of the book.

❏ To learn more about using VBScript, see Chapter 2, "Using VBScript with HTML Controls."

❏ Chapter 12, "Using VBScript with ActiveX Controls," discusses ActiveX objects.

❏ For more information about the ActiveX Control Pad, see Chapter 13, "Implementing an ActiveX Menu Control."

Q&A

Q: Can I use other ActiveX controls that I've downloaded from pages on the Web?

A: Possibly. Some ActiveX controls that your browser grabbed from a Web site as part of that site's content show up in the ActiveX Control dialog box. However, you cannot use many of these controls unless you have the license agreement for them. See Chapter 12.

Q: How do I know that a user will have the controls I used in the welcome page example on his or her computer?

A: In order for visitors to use this page, they must have Microsoft Internet Explorer 3; therefore, they must be running Windows 95. As a result, they'll have the Forms 2.0 controls ready and waiting. When you use other controls, you might need to provide copies of the controls on your Web site for the browser to download them. See Chapter 12.

TWO

Using VBScript with HTML Controls

Adding active content to your Web site doesn't mean that you have to scrap the pages you've probably spent a long time writing, maintaining, and developing. In fact, you can do a lot very quickly and easily to improve your Web site with active content utilizing your current Web pages and HTML controls.

Your current Web pages are probably filled to the brim with HTML controls and objects. Submit buttons, text boxes, and so on—anything that you added to the page using the HTML <INPUT> tag (and more besides)—are known as intrinsic HTML controls, and you can interface them with VBScript using the ActiveX Control Pad.

HTML controls and objects don't give you anything that approximates the functionality of an ActiveX control, but they have the advantage of always being immediately available to every user, which means they will load faster. Anyone with a browser capable of handling scripts gets the full benefit of your Web page, and even those Web surfers with browsers that don't know an ActiveX control from a hole in the ground still see the complete page, albeit without the scripted functionality.

In this chapter, you

- ❏ Learn how you can use VBScript on its own within a normal HTML document
- ❏ Discover how to use the ActiveX Control Pad with intrinsic HTML controls
- ❏ Define HTML intrinsic controls
- ❏ Create a new active-content Web page using only HTML controls and implementing a simple VBScript
- ❏ Learn how to use VBScript with HTML hyperlinks
- ❏ Create a simple custom VBScript procedure with the ActiveX Control Pad
- ❏ Add VBScript to a current HTML Web page
- ❏ Add a global variable
- ❏ Create a simple data array

Tasks in this chapter:

- ❏ Making HTML controls interactive with VBScript
- ❏ Spicing up a home page with VBScript

As the Web continues its never-ending but ever-quickening development, you can avoid excluding certain visitors to your site by using a mixture of straightforward HTML Web pages, pages that combine HTML objects and active scripting, and pages that make full use of ActiveX controls. This chapter is devoted to the middle ground, helping you to recycle some of your current pages and bring them up to date using HTML intrinsic controls and objects linked to active scripting.

What Are HTML Intrinsic Controls?

If you've spent more than five minutes using HTML, then you've probably used HTML intrinsic controls—but you might not have called them intrinsic controls. HTML intrinsic controls are usually associated with a <FORM> tag and defined in the HTML page using the <INPUT> tag, although it is possible to use them outside the <FORM> tag. For example, hyperlinks can be treated as controls. HTML intrinsic controls are not as flexible as ActiveX controls; after all, they were never designed to do more than gather simple input from the user and pass this input to the server. For example, you can't change the font sizes and colors of an HTML intrinsic control. The following list outlines the main HTML intrinsic controls:

See Chapter 5, "Interfacing VBScript with an HTML Form," for a full description of each HTML intrinsic control.

❏ Text box: A single-line text box for data input.

❏ Password: A single-line area to enter text; the screen output is replaced by asterisks.

❏ Submit button: A command button that instructs the browser to send the matched data field names and values to the server.

❏ Reset button: A command button that instructs the browser to reset all controls in the form to their default values.

❏ Button: Rarely used in normal HTML documents because it requires an attached script to give it functionality.

❏ Audio or radio button: A round option button used in sets when you're asking the user to make a choice of one from many.

❏ Checkbox: A square button used either singularly or in sets when you're asking the user to select fixed options.

❏ Select: A drop-down list of options; although it is not specified with the <INPUT> tag, it is still treated as an intrinsic control.

You can also treat HTML hyperlinks and anchors as intrinsic controls, although in the strict sense, they aren't controls. What I mean by this is that you must attach code to them manually because the ActiveX Control Pad doesn't recognize them as programmable controls.

HTML intrinsic controls have programmable events; that is, you can attach a subroutine or event handler to the control so that when the user clicks a button, for example, the program or script executes. Again, HTML intrinsic controls do not give you the depth of functionality that an ActiveX control does, but you will find them adequate for most situations.

Making HTML Controls Interactive with VBScript

To demonstrate how simply and quickly you can add ActiveX scripting to an HTML page, you're going to create a page that allows you to type a text or numerical value in one text box and then shows it in another text box when you press the button. You've got to start somewhere!

First, open the ActiveX Control Pad and, using the template it offers, create an HTML page with some HTML intrinsic controls on it. The following code shows the first part:

```
<HTML>
<HEAD>
<TITLE>The easy peasy VBScript page</TITLE>
</HEAD>
<BODY BGCOLOR="white">
<CENTER>
<H2>Wow...this is easy!!</H2><P>
```

Start the definition of an HTML form; as you can see, this is a form with a difference.

```
<FORM NAME="Form1">
```

The first thing that you notice about the preceding <FORM> tag is that it has a name, which you do not usually give to an HTML form. You provide the name here so that you can easily reference the form within the Script Wizard. The other thing to note is that the ACTION and METHOD elements of the form tag are missing; because the data in this form isn't submitted anywhere, these elements are irrelevant.

Enter the first of the HTML intrinsic controls, text1. The definition is exactly the same as you would enter for any HTML text box within an HTML form:

```
<INPUT TYPE=TEXT NAME="text1">
```

Include a paragraph break, the second text box, and another paragraph break:

```
<P>
<INPUT TYPE=TEXT NAME="text2">
<P>
```

Add an HTML button. Although you're probably accustomed to using SUBMIT or RESET buttons, you can use the straightforward BUTTON type rather than SUBMIT because you don't want the data to be sent anywhere. Call it cmdButton1. Set the caption on the face of the button to Click Me using the VALUE element:

```
<INPUT TYPE=BUTTON NAME="cmdButton1" VALUE="Click Me">
```

Finish the rest of the normal HTML as follows:

```
</FORM>
</CENTER>
</BODY>
</HTML>
```

Save the file as vbeasy.htm, and open it in your Microsoft Internet Explorer 3.0 browser. It should look like the file in Figure 2.1.

Figure 2.1.
Your vbeasy.htm *file as it should look in the browser.*

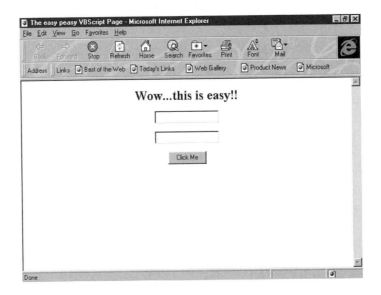

A section of program code or a subroutine that is linked to an object's event is called an *event handler*.

Create the VBScript subroutine that copies whatever you typed in the top text box into the bottom text box when you click the button. Attach the subroutine to the button, and because it should execute every time the button is clicked, link the subroutine to the button's OnClick event. Open the file you've just created (vbeasy.htm) in the ActiveX Control Pad.

Open the ActiveX Script Wizard either by clicking the Script button (which looks like an ancient scroll) or by selecting Script Wizard from the Tools menu.

In the left Events pane, you can see that the Script Wizard recognizes the Form1 HTML form as an object. You attach the script to the click event of the cmdButton1, which is contained within Form1, by performing the following steps:

1. Click the plus sign to the left of the Form1 object. The Script Wizard displays the contents of Form1, including the only form event, OnSubmit.

2. Click the plus sign to the left of the cmdButton1, which displays the events (or should I say, event) available for the cmdButton1 button.

3. Select the OnClick event by clicking it once.

Your Script Wizard should look like the one in Figure 2.2.

Figure 2.2.

The Script Wizard displaying the events and objects for your Form1 HTML object.

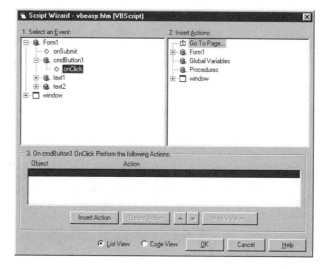

You want the button's click event to act upon the text2 text box, so specify the action that the event takes as follows:

1. In the right Action pane, click the plus sign to the left of Form1. The Script Wizard displays the objects within the form along with the properties and methods available for the form.

2. Click the plus sign to the left of the Text2 object. You can see the individual properties and methods for the Text2 object.

3. Double-click the Value property.

The dialog box that is now displayed, shown in Figure 2.3, invites you to enter a value to be displayed in the text box.

Figure 2.3.

Click on the Custom button to display the custom value dialog.

However, you don't want to enter an explicit text string here because you want to display whatever is held in the value of Text1, which is a variable value. To enter a variable, perform the following steps:

1. Click the Custom button. You see the dialog box shown in Figure 2.4, which allows you to enter the variable name.

2. Enter Form1.Text1.Value in the dialog box. This Value property holds the text string that has been entered into the Text1 textbox. When cmdButton1 is clicked, Text1's Value property is assigned to Text2's Value property, thereby displaying the contents of Text1 in Text2.

3. Click OK.

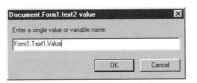

Figure 2.4.
The custom dialog lets you enter variable names rather than explicit values.

The property that holds the textual contents of a text box control is called Value in HTML, but it's called Text in ActiveX.

The Script Wizard generates the required <INPUT> tag for the button, which includes the language element that tells the browser which scripting engine to use, the event (in this case, OnClick), and the actual code itself (Document.Form1.text2.value = Form1.Text1.Value). Your vbeasy.htm HTML source, complete with VBScript code, should look like what you see in Figure 2.5. I've dropped down part of the line containing the button definition so that you can read it. (By default, ActiveX uses a much wider screen.)

Figure 2.5.   ·
vbeasy.htm *in the ActiveX Control Pad.*

```
ActiveX Control Pad - [vbeasy.htm]
File  Edit  View  Tools  Window  Help

<HTML>
<HEAD>
<TITLE>The easy peasy VBScript Page</TITLE>
</HEAD>
<BODY BGCOLOR="white">
<CENTER>
  <H2>Wow...this is easy!!</H2><P>
    <FORM NAME="Form1">
      <INPUT TYPE=TEXT NAME="text1">
<P>
      <INPUT TYPE=TEXT NAME="text2">
<P>
        <INPUT LANGUAGE="VBScript" TYPE=BUTTON VALUE="Click Me"
          ONCLICK="Document.Form1.text2.value = Form1.Text1.Value"
          NAME="cmdButton1">
    </FORM>
</CENTER>
</BODY>
</HTML>

For Help, press F1                                    CAP  NUM
```

All you need to do is save the file and run it with your Internet Explorer browser. Type some text in the top text box and click the button, and if all goes well, the string from the top text box is copied automatically into the bottom text box.

Spicing Up a Home Page with VBScript

Now, you'll make a currently flat (by which I mean normal, inactively HTML coded) HTML home page interactive using only VBScript and HTML—not an ActiveX control for miles around. For an example, you're going to use the fictitious home page shown in Figure 2.6. You can find the current home page on the CD-ROM at \SOURCE\ CHAPTER2\INDEX1.HTM. Although the page is adequate, it's hardly what you'd term interactive.

Figure 2.6.

The home page of the Apprentice Lumberjacks.

In this example, you add only a text box; the rest of the page remains as it is, with the addition, of course, of some simple VBScript. One of the main things this demonstrates to you is the use of scripts attached to HTML hyperlinks, which can add great value to any page.

Here's what you're going to do with this home page:

❏ Add a text box to display descriptions of the links.

❏ Add a custom procedure for each link to display the description whenever the mouse passes over the link.

❏ Add a custom procedure to display an Alert box when the user clicks a certain link.

First, load the file into the ActiveX Control Pad, as shown in Figure 2.7.

Figure 2.7.

The HTML source for the home page.

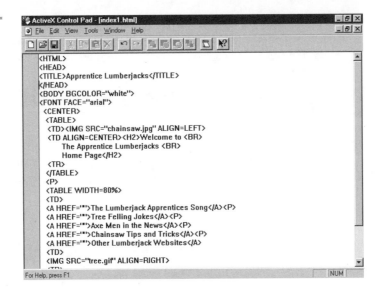

Directly above the first hyperlink, create a simple HTML form called Form1 and add an HTML text box with a width of 40 and the name Text1. This is the text box that is used to display the descriptions of the links. The form is necessary in HTML to let you reference the text box from a script.

```
<FORM NAME="Form1">
<INPUT TYPE="text" NAME="text1" SIZE=40><P>
</FORM>
```

Attaching VBScript to an HTML Hyperlink

To attach scripts to the hyperlinks, you must give them names by including ID elements within the <A HREF> tags. Call the first link Link1, the second Link2, and so on, like this:

Control and object names can contain numerical characters but not spaces.

```
<A HREF="" ID="Link1">The Lumberjack Apprentices Song</A><P>
<A HREF="" ID="Link2">Tree Felling Jokes</A><P>
<A HREF="" ID="Link3">Axe Men in the News</A><P>
<A HREF="" ID="Link4">Chainsaw Tips and Tricks</A><P>
<A HREF="" ID="Link5">Other Lumberjack Websites</A>
```

To attach code to HTML hyperlinks, perform the following steps:

1. Specify which scripting engine the browser must use.

2. Specify the event that triggers the execution of a procedure.

3. Specify the name of the procedure to execute.

After each ID reference, add the Language element and the OnMouseOver event—as though it too is an HTML element. Finally, reference the soon-to-be-created ShowDesc custom procedure:

```
LANGUAGE="vbscript" OnMouseOver="ShowDesc()"
```

The parentheses after ShowDesc contain a value that is passed to the procedure and used to determine which of five different descriptions should be displayed. Number these from 0 to 4. Your links section should now look like the following code:

```
<A HREF="" ID="Link1" LANGUAGE="VBScript" OnMouseOver="ShowDesc(0)" >
➥The Lumberjack Apprentices Song</A><P>
<A HREF="" ID="Link2" LANGUAGE="VBScript" OnMouseOver="ShowDesc(1)" >
➥Tree Felling Jokes</A><P>
<A HREF="" ID="Link3" LANGUAGE="VBScript" OnMouseOver="ShowDesc(2)" >
➥Axe Men in the News</A><P>
<A HREF="" ID="Link4" LANGUAGE="VBScript" OnMouseOver="ShowDesc(3)" >
➥Chainsaw Tips and Tricks</A><P>
<A HREF="" ID="Link5" LANGUAGE="VBScript" OnMouseOver="ShowDesc(4)" >
➥Other Lumberjack Websites</A>
```

As far as the HTML alterations go, that's really all you need to do. The next thing you need is a procedure that is executed every time the mouse passes over a link.

Launch the Script Wizard either by clicking the Script button or by selecting Script Wizard from the Tools menu. You'll notice that the left Events pane contains only the window object and the text box control because the hyperlinks are not treated as controls or objects.

Adding a Custom Procedure

Because hyperlinks are not treated as controls or objects, you must attach the code by hand as a custom procedure as follows:

1. Right-click anywhere in the right Actions pane to display the Actions pop-up menu.

2. Select New Procedure from the pop-up menu. The caption above the code window reads "Procedure1 performs the following Actions."

3. Select the Code View option button at the bottom of the Script Wizard dialog. The code window changes to allow you to type in code directly, as shown in Figure 2.8. It is in fact two separate sections if you look closely; the top section contains only the name of the procedure, known as the procedure prototype, and the lower section is where you type the script.

Figure 2.8.

The script section of the Script Wizard in Code View mode.

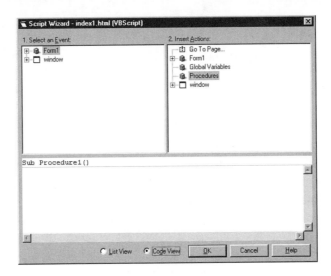

4. Change the procedure name from `Procedure1` to `ShowDesc`, and inside the parentheses, enter the word `LinkNo`.

```
Sub ShowDesc(LinkNo)
```

5. Move to the lower section of the code window and enter the following code:

```
Document.Form1.Text1.Value = LinkDesc(LinkNo)
```

I'll explain the right side of the preceding code. `LinkDesc` is the name you give to an array that holds the descriptions. `LinkNo` is the name that you give to a variable that stores the number, which enters the procedure from the link definition. Chapter 10, "Using the Power of Arrays," covers arrays in detail. An array is a series of data values that can be accessed individually by their ordinal numbers—that is, where they are in the array. One twist is that arrays in VBScript can only start at position 0. As a result, the first data element of an array must be accessed using the number 0. Look back at the definition you entered for the links:

```
<A HREF="" ID="Link1" LANGUAGE="VBScript" OnMouseOver="ShowDesc(0)" >
➥The Lumberjack Apprentices Song</A><P>
```

Because this is the first link, you need to pass the number 0 to the `ShowDesc` procedure, which then gets the first description string from the `LinkDesc` array and copies it into the `Text1` text box.

6. Add the following line of code, which effectively disables the status message at the bottom of the browser window when the mouse passes over one of the links.

```
Window.Status = ""
```

The procedure is now complete, and your window should look like the one in Figure 2.9.

Figure 2.9.
The completed custom procedure within the Script Wizard.

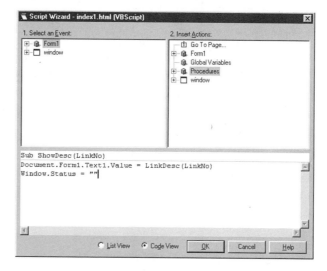

Adding a Global Variable

You need to add the definition for the array that holds the description strings for each link. You want the script engine to load the data into the array only once as the page downloads to the browser; therefore, you need to use a global variable for the array. A global variable is available to all procedures in all scripts within the same HTML document. Global variables are defined outside any subroutine or function but inside the <SCRIPT> tags. Variables in VBScript are covered at length in Chapter 4, "Using the VBScript Language." The ActiveX Script Wizard makes it easy to define global variables as follows:

1. Right-click in the right Actions pane of the Script Wizard to invoke the Action pop-up menu.

2. Select the New Global Variable option to display the New Global Variable dialog box, as shown in Figure 2.10.

Figure 2.10.
Enter a name for the new global variable.

3. Enter the name `LinkDesc(4)` into the New Global Variable dialog box. This instructs the script engine to create an array with five elements—which means 4 is the highest number. Click OK.

Before you leave the Script Wizard, click the plus signs to the left of the Global Variables and Procedures items in the right pane. You see that the items you entered are shown within the object hierarchy for this page. Click OK for the Script Wizard to generate the script, which should look like what you see in Figure 2.11.

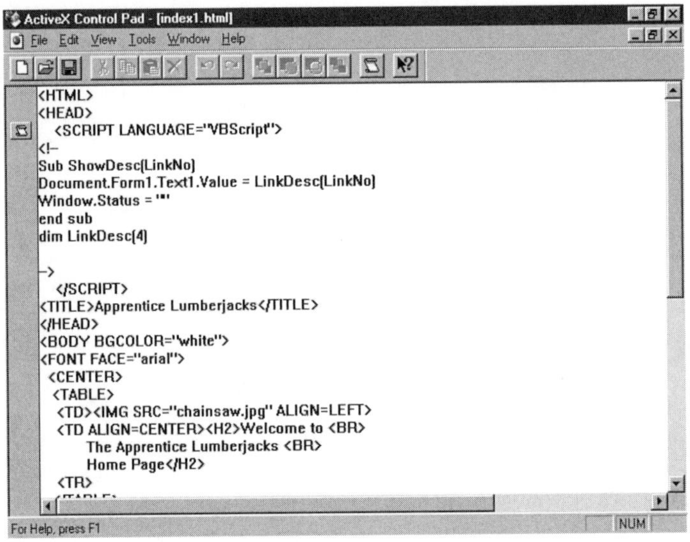

Figure 2.11.

The Script Wizard generates all the code for both the custom procedure and global variable.

```
<HTML>
<HEAD>
   <SCRIPT LANGUAGE="VBScript">
<!--
Sub ShowDesc(LinkNo)
Document.Form1.Text1.Value = LinkDesc(LinkNo)
Window.Status = ""
end sub
dim LinkDesc(4)

-->
   </SCRIPT>
<TITLE>Apprentice Lumberjacks</TITLE>
</HEAD>
<BODY BGCOLOR="white">
<FONT FACE="arial">
   <CENTER>
   <TABLE>
   <TD><IMG SRC="chainsaw.jpg" ALIGN=LEFT>
   <TD ALIGN=CENTER><H2>Welcome to <BR>
       The Apprentice Lumberjacks <BR>
       Home Page</H2>
   <TR>
```

Adding a Simple Array

The final stage of this makeover is adding the script that puts the descriptions of the links into the array `LinkDesc`. You have to do this manually because the Script Wizard doesn't have a facility for generating script code outside a subroutine or function. Directly under the definition of the array, `dim LinkDesc(4)`, enter the following code:

```
LinkDesc(0)="This is link One"
LinkDesc(1)="This is link Two"
LinkDesc(2)="This is link Three"
LinkDesc(3)="This is link Four"
LinkDesc(4)="This is link Five"
```

Because this section of code is outside a subroutine or function, it is executed once as the HTML page is downloaded to the browser. As the page is displayed, the array is full of data and ready to be used. You can enter somewhat more interesting descriptions than the ones I've shown here, which emphasize the care that you must take with arrays starting with the element 0.

Save the file and run it through your trusty Internet Explorer to instantly impress your friends and neighbors with your programming prowess.

Workshop Wrap-Up

Using VBScript with HTML controls is the easiest way to quickly build some active content into your Web pages without major disruption to your Web site. It's also a great way to start learning about what scripting and active content can do.

HTML intrinsic controls look and feel a little clunky after you've been playing with ActiveX controls, but the fact that HTML intrinsic controls load and run in the same time frame as the rest of the Web page is still a major advantage until everyone has fast direct or ISDN connections to the Web.

Next Steps

Now that you've seen how quickly and easily you can add VBScript to any HTML Web page, you can work on improving your VBScript skills to write more complex and meaningful scripts.

- ❏ Chapter 4, "Using the VBScript Language," discusses more about VBScript itself. Depending on what you need to achieve, consult any or all of the chapters in Part II, "Mastering the VBScript Language."

- ❏ To learn more about the ActiveX Control Pad, see Chapter 13, "Implementing an ActiveX Menu Control."

- ❏ Chapter 10, "Using the Power of Arrays," outlines more information about arrays.

- ❏ To take another, in-depth look at using VBScript with HTML objects, see Chapter 5, "Interfacing VBScript with an HTML Form."

- ❏ Using VBScript with image maps is covered in Chapter 17, "Using Client-Side Image Maps—the Easy Way."

Q&A

Q: I wanted to use ActiveX controls. Are you now saying I shouldn't?

A: Not at all. What I am saying is don't rush into tearing down your current Web site to replace it all with ActiveX. Use VBScript and HTML intrinsic controls as a sort of halfway house to fully active content. The Web has changed very rapidly over the past few months (my head is still spinning), but that doesn't mean you need to update your Web site at breakneck speed. Relax. Decide which of your pages are best suited to becoming all singing, all dancing, state-of-the-art ActiveX pages and which ones you can progressively update with a little scripting first. Then, you can add some more ActiveX later on. Don't forget that most users are still on 14.4kbps or 28.8kbps modem connections and will soon tire of sites that try to force a multitude of ActiveX controls on them.

THREE

Communicating with Your Users

The very essence of the Web is communication, and as a system of mass communication, it does the job admirably. Until now, most Web pages inadequately communicated on a one-to-one basis with the individual user, employing one of two methods for sending messages. First, you could hard-code the information into the HTML text of the Web page—the sort of "one size fits all" approach that is indicative of other mass media such as TV and print. Second, you could present the message in a completely new page that must be downloaded from the server for each particular visitor, taking time and wasting bandwidth.

As a computer-based media, the Web has a unique opportunity that is not available to other forms of mass media. You can instantly gear communication to the individual—or to be more precise, you can give the appearance of such. Active content, whether it's in the form of Java applets, ActiveX controls, or active scripting, gives you the opportunity to present Web pages that are flexible and fast and give the impression of a one-to-one dialog with the visitor.

This chapter introduces you to some very straightforward VBScript methods that help improve the way your Web page communicates with the user and increase the speed with which this is achieved. In these days of 200Mhz Pentium chips that process a full year's trading accounts five seconds before you've even pressed a button, Web users have expectations of processing speeds far beyond what the Web currently provides. Many users are frustrated by the length of time it takes just to complete a simple form to the satisfaction of the webmaster. Furthermore, the Web has as many different user interfaces as it has Web sites; you should not underestimate the advantage of providing a familiar interface when it comes to helping users get the most from your Web site as quickly as possible.

The methods and procedures you'll see in this chapter add a more Windows-type look and feel to your Web pages by presenting the user with familiar Windows dialog boxes and messages. VBScript and active content browsers such as Microsoft Internet Explorer 3.0 provide several built-in methods for displaying Windows-type dialog boxes, which include the following:

❏ The Alert box, shown in Figure 3.1, contains a variable message, an Exclamation mark icon, and a single OK button. The title is fixed.

Figure 3.1.
An Alert dialog box.

❏ The message box, shown in Figure 3.2, contains a variable message, a variable title, and a variable number and type of buttons. The default is a single OK button. You can get input from the message box in terms of which button the user clicked.

Figure 3.2.
A message dialog box.

❏ The Confirm box, shown in Figure 3.3, has to some extent superseded the traditional message box in that it contains a variable message, a question icon, and both OK and Cancel buttons. The title, however, is not variable and always displays Microsoft Internet Explorer. As with the message box, you can get input from the Confirm box in terms of which button the user clicked.

Figure 3.3.
A Confirm dialog box.

❑ The Prompt box, shown in Figure 3.4, allows the user to enter data from the keyboard. You can then process this input however you like. The Prompt box enables you to enter a variable message and also default text to speed up user entry. However, because Microsoft seems hell-bent on promoting the fact that you're using Internet Explorer at every opportunity, the Prompt title remains fixed.

Figure 3.4.
A Prompt dialog box.

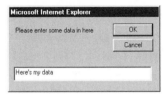

❑ The Input dialog box, shown in Figure 3.5, is a close relative to the message box, taken straight from the full version of VBA and Visual Basic. It performs the same task as the Prompt dialog box but lets you specify a title for the dialog box and also decide where on the screen the Input dialog box should appear.

Figure 3.5.
A Custom Input dialog box.

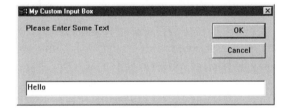

Now that you know about the dialog boxes, I want you to use them. The examples you will see are all based on a single HTML document, using an ActiveX button to generate the event that calls the particular dialog box. You can also use an HTML button, such as Submit. The document that you create can serve as a sort of help file of dialog boxes that you can refer to later to check out how each dialog works and experiment with its implementation.

Alerting Users with an Alert Box

The Alert box provides a simple, straightforward method of displaying information to the user. There is no decision-making process for the user. The Alert box contains one OK button; to clear the box, the user simply clicks the button. You can use the Alert box to tell the user quick and straightforward facts, such as, "Hey, you didn't fill in the ZIP code," or other friendly remarks. The Alert box is as easy to include in your script as it is for the visitor to use. One simple line of code is all it takes, and because the Alert box returns no value, there is no need for further processing when the Alert box is closed.

Open the ActiveX Control Pad containing the nice, fresh, default HTML template. Add an ActiveX button as follows:

1. Place your cursor after the `<BODY>` tag.
2. Select Insert ActiveX Control from the Edit menu.
3. Select Microsoft Forms 2.0 Command Button from the ActiveX Controls dialog, and click OK.
4. Change the `Caption` property of the Button to read `Show an Alert`. Click the Apply button at the top of the properties window.
5. Close the Object Editor window to generate the object definition code for the button.

Before you start the Script Wizard, change one of the default settings in the Control Pad, which will save you a lot of time and trouble later. Change the code window default to Code View rather than the standard default of List View. When the code window of the Script Wizard is in List View, you are not allowed to select certain methods and link them to events, which rather defeats the object of the exercise. To change the default, perform the following steps:

1. Select Options|Script from the Tools Menu, which invokes the Script Options dialog box as shown in Figure 3.6.

Figure 3.6.
The Script Options dialog box.

2. Click the Code View option and click OK.

For more information on the workings of the ActiveX Control Pad, see Chapter 13, "Implementing an ActiveX Menu Control."

Start the Script Wizard by either clicking the Script button or selecting Script Wizard from the Tools menu.

With the following procedure, you create an event handler for the click event of the button you just added to the page, which displays an Alert box to the user:

1. Click the plus sign to the left of `CommandButton1` in the left Events pane.

2. Select the click event. Notice that Script Wizard is now in Code View; the actual definition of the event handler appears in the code window.

3. Click the plus sign to the left of the window object in the right Actions pane. You see a list of methods for the window (browser) object. With these methods, you interface directly with the browser itself, controlling its actions from your script.

4. Double-click the Alert method. The following line is then automatically added to the script window:

   ```
   call window.alert(msg)
   ```

5. Replace the mnemonic `msg` with your own custom message—something cool and earth shattering such as "Hello World." (Is there no limit to this creative genius?)

6. Click OK, and the Script Wizard generates the required VBScript code. Because you are using an ActiveX button, the code is generated in a separate `<SCRIPT>` tag.

Just before you save the HTML file, give it a title of `VBScript Dialogs` and make the background of the page white. Save the file as `dialogs.htm`.

Unless otherwise stated, all examples in this book have a white background, using the `<BODY BGCOLOR="white">` tag.

Run the file with the browser, as shown in Figure 3.7. When the Alert box is showing, you cannot access the rest of the browser until you clear the Alert box by clicking OK. This obviously stops the user from simply ignoring the dialog box. Furthermore, any script that follows the Alert method does not execute until the user clicks OK and thereby passes control back to the browser or, in this case, the subroutine that originally called the Alert box.

Figure 3.7.

The first stage of your dialogs sample, the Alert box.

As you have seen, the Alert method is both easy and quick to use; however, you do have another way to generate an Alert box, and it's a method that allows you to specify your own title.

Creating a Simple Message Box

The message box is quite different from most of the other dialogs you will see in this chapter in that it is not a direct method of the window object. It is, in fact, a function built into VBScript and a direct descendant of its VBA and Visual Basic brethren. Because of this, the message box gives you the greatest flexibility, but at the same time, it requires slightly more thought when you create it.

For this part of the dialogs Web page, you need to add another command button. If `dialog.htm` isn't open in the ActiveX Control Panel, open it and follow these steps:

1. Add a paragraph (<P>) tag after the </OBJECT> tag.
2. Select Insert ActiveX Control from the Edit menu.
3. Select Microsoft Forms 2.0 Command Button from the ActiveX Controls dialog, and click OK.
4. Change the `Caption` property of the button to read `Show a Message Box`. Click the Apply button at the top of the properties window.
5. Change the `ID` property of the button to `CommandButton2` and click Apply.
6. Close the Object Editor window to generate the object definition code for the button.

The VBScript function you use to generate a message box on-screen is `MsgBox`. The `MsgBox` function has several elements within parentheses following the function name:

```
x = MsgBox(MessageText,Type,Title)
```

❑ `MessageText` is a string value that contains the actual message you want to display.

❑ `Type` is a numerical value that specifies the number and type of command buttons that appear on the dialog box and the icon used, if any. For a full description of the available types, see the section "Creating Custom Message Dialog Boxes," later in this chapter.

❑ `Title` is a string value containing the title to be displayed across the top of the dialog box.

❑ `x` is any variable to store the return value from the `MsgBox` function. If you do not specify a message box type, the function displays only an OK button and the return value is irrelevant. You can ignore the value of `x`, but you must still declare the function as shown previously.

To add the MsgBox function to the CommandButton2, start the Script Wizard (which you know how to do by now) and perform the following steps:

1. Click the plus sign to the left of CommandButton2 in the left Events pane.

2. Select the click event.

3. As you have already seen, the MsgBox function is not actually part of the browser's object hierarchy, so there's no point looking in the right pane; it isn't there! This is a situation for fingers on keys, so put the rodent to bed and enter the following line in the code window. In this first example of MsgBox, you only need an OK button, so the Type is 0:

```
x = MsgBox("This is my message to you",0,"My Message Box")
```

4. Click OK.

5. Save the file and run it with the browser, as shown in Figure 3.8.

Figure 3.8.
The second step, a simple message box.

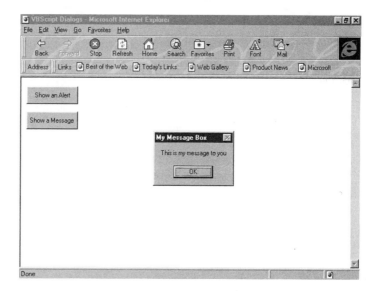

NOTE: For those of you with experience in either VBA or Visual Basic, please note that certain functions, such as MsgBox, appear on the surface to be direct replications. However, you'll usually find some minor differences; for example, the Type variable in MsgBox is not optional in VBScript, whereas it is optional in Visual Basic and VBA.

Apart from the capability to specify a title for your message box, you'll notice little difference between using a message box in this way and using the Alert method. The real power of MsgBox lies in its Type element, as you're about to see.

Creating Custom Message Dialog Boxes

Using `MsgBox` enables you to add fully functional Windows dialog boxes, the likes of which you have probably never seen in a Web page before. Furthermore, unlike the built-in `Alert` and `Confirm` methods, `MsgBox` lets you use a wide combination of buttons. The return value from `MsgBox` determines which button the user pressed. You can also specify which of the buttons is the default button when the dialog box appears—that is, which button has the focus. All this functionality is very easy to tap by simply setting the `Type` variable of the `MsgBox` function.

You choose the `Type` variable, which is numeric, by adding three numbers together: the Button type, the Icon type, and the Default Button type. Table 3.1 shows the values for each of the types.

Table 3.1. `MsgBox` definition values.

Type Value	Meaning
Button Types	
0	Display OK button only
1	Display OK and Cancel buttons
2	Display Abort, Retry, and Ignore buttons
3	Display Yes, No, and Cancel buttons
4	Display Yes and No buttons
5	Display Retry and Cancel buttons
Icon Types	
0	No icon
16	Display Stop icon
32	Display Question mark icon
48	Display Exclamation mark icon
64	Display Information icon
Default Button Types	
0	First button has focus
256	Second button has focus
512	Third button has focus

By adding one number from each of the three types, you can generate a wide range of different message boxes to suit almost every need.

To create a message box with Yes, No, and Cancel Buttons (3); a Question mark icon (32); and the No button (the second button, in this case) as the default (256), you set the MsgBox Type variable to 3 + 32 + 256 = 291.

To determine which button the user pressed, you examine the numeric variable of the return value, which is described in Table 3.2.

Table 3.2. MsgBox return values.

Return Value	Button Clicked
1	OK
2	Cancel
3	Abort
4	Retry
5	Ignore
6	Yes
7	No

Now, create an example that allows you to create any combination of types for the MsgBox dialog and determine which button was clicked. For this example, you continue working with the dialogs.htm file created earlier in the chapter. You add two text boxes to the page. The first text box is used for entering the value of the Type variable, and the second text box displays the return value of the message box.

You then amend the code for the CommandButton2 event handler to take the value from the first text box, convert it from a string to a number, and use it within the MsgBox function. Display the return value of the MsgBox function in the second text box—easy!

Open the file dialogs.htm in your ActiveX Control Pad, and to add the two new text boxes, execute the following steps:

1. Create a new line after the last </OBJECT> tag.
2. Add an HTML <P> tag.
3. Type Enter a Type Number and press return.
4. Select Insert ActiveX Control from the Edit menu.
5. Select Microsoft Forms 2.0 Text Box from the ActiveX Controls dialog and click OK. Make no changes to the default properties for this text box.
6. Close the Object Editor window to generate the object definition code for the text box.

For the second text box, follow these steps:

1. Create a new line after the last </OBJECT> tag.

2. Add an HTML <P> tag.

3. Type This is the result and press return.

4. Select Insert ActiveX Control from the Edit menu.

5. Select Microsoft Forms 2.0 Text Box from the ActiveX Controls dialog and click OK. Change the ID property of the control to TextBox2.

6. Close the Object Editor window to generate the object definition code for the second text box.

To edit the script you created earlier, find the event handler for CommandButton2. Two lines above this is a <SCRIPT LANGUAGE=VBScript> tag. To the left of this tag in the margin is a script icon; click the icon to launch the Script Wizard and load the script for CommandButton2. Make the following changes to the script:

1. Place your cursor to the left of the x variable and press return, which moves the code to the second line. On the first line, type the following:

```
y = CInt(TextBox1.Text)
```

What does this do? It takes the value entered into the first text box—the message box Type number you want to generate, which is always a string variable (even though you entered a number)—and converts this string into an integer using the CInt function. The resulting integer is placed into a variable called y.

2. Amend the MsgBox function by replacing the 0 with a y. Note that y is not surrounded by quotation marks:

```
x = MsgBox("This is my message to you",y,"My Message Box")
```

The number entered into the first text box is used by the MsgBox function to generate a particular style of message dialog.

3. Finally, add a new line of code under the MsgBox function:

```
TextBox2.Text = x
```

This line displays the return value of the MsgBox function in the second text box.

Your completed code section should now look like the one in Figure 3.9.

As always, click OK to generate the code, save the file, and run it with your browser, as shown in Figure 3.10. You can spend hours of fun generating any combination of message box types simply by entering a number in the first text box and clicking the button. The return value of the button you click on the message box is echoed in the second text box. Remember, Type numbers are generated by totalling the three numbers for each type section.

Figure 3.9.

The code to generate any combination of custom message box types.

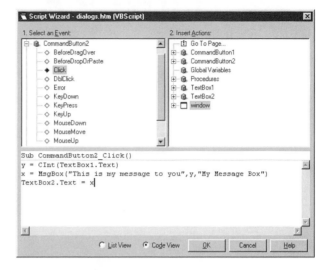

Figure 3.10.

dialogs.htm *in the browser.*

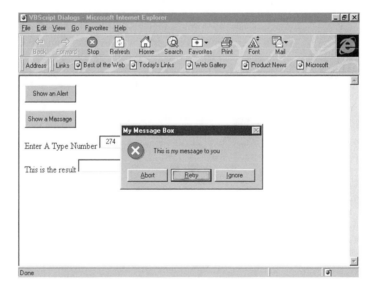

 # Adding User Confirmation

A simplified version of the message box, complete with Question mark icon and OK and Cancel buttons (analogous with MsgBox Type 33), is built into the browser's window object and accessed with the Confirm method. Whereas the MsgBox function returns a number based on the button type that was selected, the Confirm method returns True if the OK button was clicked and False if the Cancel button was clicked.

To test the `Confirm` method, add another button and text box to the `dialogs.htm` file. The button invokes the `Confirm` method, and the text box displays the result of the user's action. To add this functionality, perform the following steps:

1. Insert a paragraph tag after the last `</OBJECT>` tag.

2. Following the previous instructions, add a command button with a `Caption` property of `Confirm` and an `ID` property of `CommandButton3`.

3. Add another text box next to `CommandButton3` and set its `ID` property to `TextBox3`.

4. Open the Script Wizard.

5. Click the plus sign next to `CommandButton3` in the left Events window and select the click event.

6. Click the plus sign next to the window object in the right Actions pane.

7. Double-click the `Confirm` method, which automatically places the line `call window.confirm(msg)` in the code window.

8. Edit this line to read `x = window.confirm("Is this OK")`.

9. Add a new line in the code window under the current line and type `TextBox3.Text = x`.

Your Script Wizard window should look like the one in Figure 3.11.

Figure 3.11.
The code for the
`Confirm` *method in the*
Script Wizard.

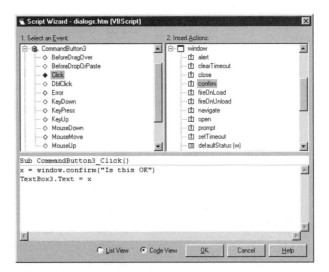

What you did is invoke the window object's `Confirm` method. When the user clicks `CommandButton3`, the Confirm dialog displays the message, `Is this OK`. The variable `x` stores the return value for the button that was clicked. The return value `x` then displays in `TextBox3`.

Click OK, save the file, and run it with the browser, as shown in Figure 3.12.

Figure 3.12.

The Confirm dialog box at work.

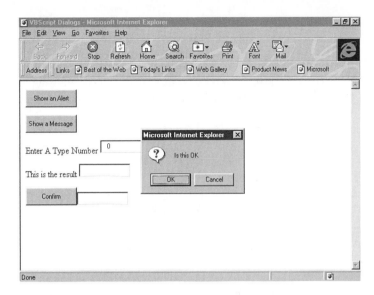

Dialog boxes can be useful for passing messages and information to the user, but what about information flow in the other direction? The next example shows you how to use the built-in Prompt method to take data input from the user of your Web page.

 # Creating an "Add Your Own" Links Page

What you construct in this section is actually not a full links page, nor is it a complete add-your-own system. The idea of this section is to show you how you can utilize the Prompt method to obtain input from the user. Completing an add-your-own links page requires some server-side scripting in which you must construct a device for storing the user input and then displaying all the links when they're required. Server-side scripts are also discussed in Chapter 6, "Checking Form Data."

The Prompt method is ideal for taking input from the user in situations where you have limited real estate on the particular Web page or you don't want to involve the user in loading a fresh page. Straight from the current page, you can take inputs without a text box in sight, so at the same time, the Prompt method improves the look of your page. As a result, you can build many different forms into a Web page using the Prompt method without cluttering the page.

The page you will create contains an HTML form. Wait a minute! I know I said the Prompt dialog was going to replace forms, but this example is a little different because all the fields are hidden. You have to use an HTML form at some stage to transfer the information from the Web page to the server. The data that comes from the Prompt dialog box is copied by the script into the relevant hidden field of the form; the user is never aware that a form exists on the page. When all the doing is done, you can programmatically submit the form to the server.

Get to work on creating the front end to your new interactive links page. Open the ActiveX Control Pad, and using the default page one template, create the top section of the HTML in this way:

```
<HTML>
<HEAD>
<TITLE>My Links Page</TITLE>
</HEAD>
<BODY BGColor="white">
<CENTER>
 <H2>Interactive Links to Cool Places</H2>
    <FORM ACTION="" METHOD="POST" NAME="form1">
        <INPUT TYPE=hidden NAME="lnkTitle">
        <INPUT TYPE=hidden NAME="lnkURL">
        <INPUT TYPE=hidden NAME="lnkDesc">
    </FORM>
```

This exercise leaves the Action element blank. I used a POST method, but you can use GET if it's required by your CGI script.

Following the instructions in the previous sections if necessary, add an ActiveX command button directly below the </FORM> tag. The only property you need to change is its caption; set it to something like Add your Link.

Launch the Script Wizard and perform the following steps:

1. Right-click anywhere in the right Actions frame.

2. Select New Global Variable from the pop-up Actions menu.

3. Enter CRLF into the New Global Variable dialog box and click OK.

   The global variable you created is used to hold two special characters that are interpreted by the program as a carriage return and a line feed (more about this later in this procedure).

4. Click the plus sign to the left of the CommandButton1 object in the Events (left) pane.

5. Select the click event.

6. Click the plus sign to the left of the window object in the Actions (right) pane.

7. Double-click the Prompt method.

8. Edit the Prompt definition to read

   ```
   UserTitle = window.prompt("Please enter the Title", "")
   ```

   This code invokes the window object's Prompt method, displaying a dialog box with the message "Please enter a Title." The second element, which in

For more information on constants and variables, see Chapter 4, "Using the VBScript Language."

this case is blank, is where you could enter a default value to display in the input box, as you'll see in the next code line. If the user clicks OK, the contents of the input box are copied to a variable called UserTitle.

9. Double-click the Prompt method again or copy and paste the first definition.

10. Edit the new Prompt definition to read

```
UserURL = window.prompt("Please enter the URL", "http://")
```

This code line displays the message "Please enter the URL," and this time, the input box is partially completed for the user with http://. The resulting input is copied to a variable called UserURL.

11. Double-click the Prompt method again or copy and paste the first definition under the second definition.

12. Edit the new Prompt definition to read

```
UserDesc = window.prompt("Please enter a short description", "")
```

13. Press Return to create a new line, and double-click the Confirm method under the window object in the right Actions pane.

14. Edit the Confirm definition as follows:

```
x = window.confirm("Thank you " & CRLF & "You entered: " & CRLF &
➥UserTitle & CRLF & UserURL & CRLF & UserDesc & CRLF & "Is this correct")
```

Note that this should be entered on one line.

I'll break this down to explain what you did. First, you know from the earlier parts of this chapter that you invoked a method of the window object called Confirm, which displays a dialog box containing a Question mark icon, Yes and No buttons, and a message. The message in the parentheses might look a tad confusing at first glance.

The ampersand (&) is used in VBScript to concatenate strings—meaning to join one string after the other:

```
"VB" & "Script" = "VBScript"
"Active" & "X" = "ActiveX"
```

You can actually use the + sign to concatenate strings, but it's considered good programming practice to use the & when dealing with strings. See Chapter 4, "Using the VBScript Language." As you can see, you created a complete message that consists of several individual segments: explicit text, variables containing data that were entered by the user, and the carriage return/line feed variable, which you'll define shortly.

15. Under the last line, enter the following lines of code, in which you assign the values entered by the user to the hidden fields in the HTML form. The values are then ready to be whisked away across the Net for processing by your server-side CGI script.

Make sure you don't use quotation marks around the variable names.

```
Document.form1.lnkTitle.Value = UserTitle
Document.form1.lnkURL.Value = UserURL
Document.form1.lnkDesc.Value = UserDesc
```

16. One final line of code is required:

```
rem call Document.form1.submit()
```

This line does not actually execute in this example; the rem statement turns this line of code into a remark or comment. To make this line of code operational, simply remove the rem statement, and it will perform exactly the same function from the script as occurs when a user clicks an HTML Submit button. Your script should now resemble Figure 3.13.

Figure 3.13.
The almost completed script in the Script Wizard.

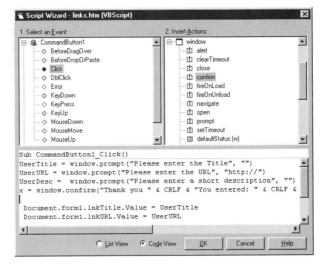

17. Click OK in the Script Wizard to generate the VBScript code.

18. Finally, edit the script from the text editor by including the following line of code under the dim CRLF line:

```
CRLF = Chr(10) & Chr(13)
```

This line of code inserts two ASCII characters that tell the program to execute a carriage return and a line feed.

TIP: Inserting ASCII or ANSI characters into strings using the chr(*n*) VBScript function is an easy way to include non-standard characters such as copyright or trademark logos into standard text strings. See the ASCII character set in Appendix F, "The ASCII Character Set."

Save the HTML file as `links.htm`. It should look something like what you see in Figure 3.14.

Figure 3.14.

`links.htm` *in the ActiveX Control Pad.*

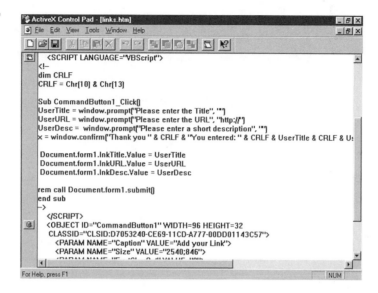

Run the page with your browser (see Figure 3.15) and click the Add your Link button. What follows is a series of Prompt input dialog boxes in which you enter information about the link you want to add to the page, as shown in Figures 3.15 through 3.18.

Figure 3.15.

`links.htm` *in Internet Explorer.*

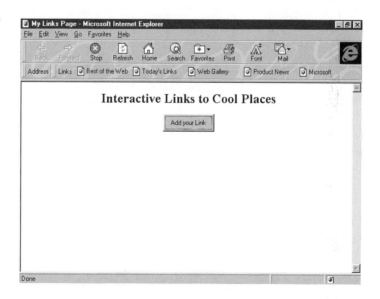

Figure 3.16 shows the first Prompt dialog asking for the title of the link. Enter a title and click OK.

Figure 3.16.

When the user clicks the button, a series of Prompt input dialogs is displayed.

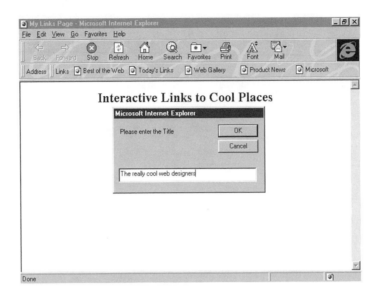

Now you are asked for the URL of the link, as shown in Figure 3.17. Again, enter the required details and click OK.

Figure 3.17.

Each time the user clicks OK, a new dialog appears.

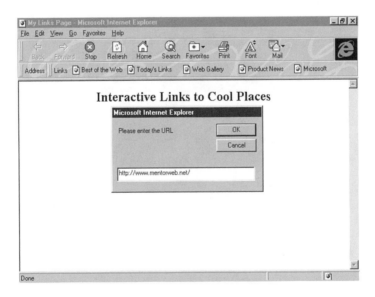

Finally, you are asked to input a short description for the site, as shown in Figure 3.18.

Figure 3.18.

The last input requested is a site description.

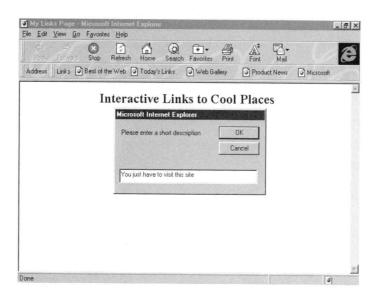

A Confirm dialog is used to display the details you have input (as shown in Figure 3.19), and it asks you to confirm whether the details are correct. What you don't have with this example is a decision-making process based on the user's response to the final confirmation, such as what to do if the user says "No."

Figure 3.19.

Finally, a Confirm dialog displays.

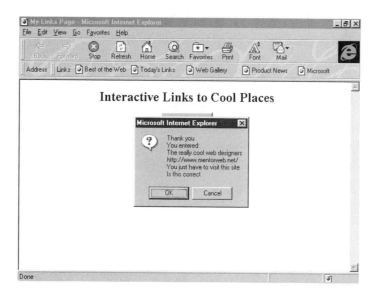

As you have seen, Prompt dialogs allow you to collect data from the user and then process that data. In certain situations, using the Prompt dialog provides a neat and tidy alternative to using the normal text box and Submit button. This method is especially useful if it is triggered from a text hyperlink to solicit a user's e-mail address for automatically sending information.

However, you should be aware of the limitations of the Prompt dialog box. First, it cannot accommodate checkboxes and options; it only displays a single-line text box. Second, it tends to contradict the now accepted nonlinear theory of Windows input. For example, in a normal form with four text boxes, the order in which you enter data is immaterial. It doesn't matter if you enter data in the fourth box first and then complete the first text box, and so on. Furthermore, if you want to edit data entered into a normal form, you can move directly to the data in the text box that needs editing; you don't have to go through all of the pop-up dialog boxes to get to the offending item. As you can see, when you use pop-up dialog boxes to enter information, you fix the order in which the user inputs the data. (First, show box one, then box two, and so on.) If the user wants to edit one of the data fields, either you provide a second level of choice (which one do you need to edit?) or the user must move through all the dialog boxes sequentially until he finds the one to edit. For these reasons, I recommend that you use Prompt input dialogs sparingly and only for inputs of a few data fields.

Earlier in the chapter, you saw the `MsgBox` function, which enables you to create a custom message box for the user. VBScript provides a comparable customizable function for collecting data called `InputBox`.

 ## Creating a Custom Input Dialog Box

The `Prompt` method provides you with a neat dialog box for gathering data, but the alternate VBScript function, `InputBox`, allows you to use your own title for the dialog and position the dialog anywhere on the page.

As you're about to see, the `InputBox` dialog is somewhat larger on the screen than the one provided by `Prompt`. Look at a quick example using the `InputBox` function.

This time, you're not going to use any ActiveX controls. You use only the normal HTML controls, and all the work is done within the text editor of the ActiveX Control Pad.

First, open the ActiveX Control Pad and work on the HTML template provided. Enter the following to set up the HTML code:

```
<HTML>
<HEAD>
<TITLE>Using the Input Function</TITLE>
<BODY BGCOLOR="white">
<CENTER>
<H2>Example of using the Input function</H2>
<P>
<FORM NAME="Form1">
 <INPUT TYPE="button" NAME="CommandButton1" VALUE="Click Me"><P>
 <INPUT TYPE="text" NAME="TextBox1">
</FORM>
```

```
</CENTER>
</BODY>
</HTML>
```

Directly under the <TITLE> line, clear a space and type the following VBScript code:

```
<SCRIPT LANGUAGE="vbscript">
<!--
 Sub CommandButton1_OnClick
   strUserInput = InputBox("Please enter some text","My Custom Input Box",
➥"",2000,4000)
   Document.Form1.TextBox1.Value = strUserInput
 End Sub
-->
</SCRIPT>
```

I opted to show you the VBScript code in this way, rather than use the Script Wizard, to demonstrate that you have several ways to add script to a page. Had you used the Script Wizard with an HTML control, as you saw in the previous chapter, all the code would have appeared in a single, almost illegible, line in the button's own HTML definition. The preceding method makes things much easier to read and debug.

The syntax for InputBox follows:

```
returnvalue = InputBox("Message","Title","Default Text",XPos,YPos)
```

This code line is fairly self explanatory except for XPos and YPos, and you might be wondering why I set these at 2000 and 4000, respectively. XPos is the position that the left edge of the dialog takes in relation to the left edge of the screen. YPos similarly measures the distance from the top of the dialog box to the top of the screen. The reason these values are so large is that InputBox, having joined the Web recently from a long-running engagement in Visual Basic, still works in twips. "Ah," I can hear you say, "That explains it…NOT." A standard 640×480 pixel setup has about 15 twips per pixel in both the x and y planes.

NOTE: Many Windows programming languages use twips as a measurement. The Microsoft Visual Basic help file topic says that a twip is "a unit of screen measurement equal to 1/20 of a printer's point. There are approximately 1440 twips to a logical inch or 567 twips to a logical centimeter, the length of a screen item measuring one inch or one centimeter when printed. A twip is a screen-independent unit used to ensure that placement and proportion of screen elements in your screen application are the same on all display systems." I couldn't have put it better myself! Unfortunately, because the twip is independent of the screen's pixel coordinate system, there is no set calculation of twips to pixels.

Save the file as `inputbox.htm` and run it with the browser, as shown in Figure 3.20.

Figure 3.20.

The InputBox *example.*

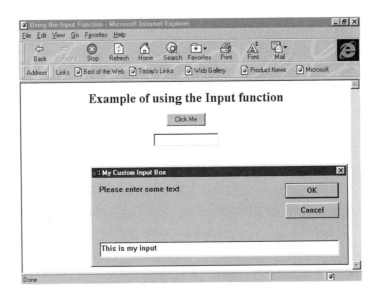

 ## Displaying Status Messages

The final part of this chapter on communicating with the user deals with that small, unobtrusive bar at the bottom of the browser called a status bar. The status bar is where the browser tells you that the filename of the link you passed over is "Shortcut to `http://...`" and where many sites display the moving JavaScript messages that you either love or hate (I'm saying nothing).

To create a simple message in the status window when the mouse passes over a hyperlink, all you do is build your hyperlink as follows:

```
<A HREF="" LANGUAGE="VBScript" OnMouseOver=
➥"Window.Status='This takes you anywhere'">Any Link</A>
```

This code uses the `OnMouseOver` event, which fires whenever the mouse passes over the link.

This event calls the `Status` method of the window object and passes the string `"This takes you anywhere"`. Note that the definition of the method must be surrounded by double quotes; if you need to use quotes inside the definition, you must use single quotes.

One limitation of changing the status bar is that there isn't a `OnMouseGoneAway` event to reset the status bar. Even when the mouse leaves the hyperlink, the text you placed in the status bar remains.

Workshop Wrap-Up

Finding new ways to communicate with others is what brought the Web into being. In this chapter, you saw how using a few simple built-in methods can improve the way your Web pages communicate with the users of your Web site.

Whether you use the built-in methods or the customizable VBScript functions, you can quickly and easily add dialog boxes that help visitors use your site in ways that are familiar to them. This familiarity speeds up the learning process that we all face when we visit a site for the first time.

Next Steps

You've just seen VBScript in action doing some real work. To see some other neat things that you can achieve with VBScript, take a look at the following chapters:

❏ Chapter 6, "Checking Form Data," contains details about submitting form data.

❏ To learn how to create some unique home pages using VBScript see Chapter 11, "Real-Life Examples I."

❏ For more information about VBScript's built-in functions, see Chapter 4, "Using the VBScript Language."

❏ Chapter 17, "Using Client-Side Image Maps—the Easy Way," describes how you can use VBScript to create effective and powerful image maps.

Q&A

Q: Is there a way to display a small browser window containing an HTML file with an input form, instead of an input or prompt dialog box?

A: Yes, you use the browser window's Open method to create a new window, and load an HTML file into that window. You can control the size of the window and its features such as menu bar, tool bar, and so on. You can see this in action in Chapter 18, "Interacting with the Browser."

Q: Why are there so many ways to achieve the same result—for example, two types of input dialog boxes and three types of output dialog boxes?

A: You'll find with most programming languages that have evolved over a long period of time that many functions and methods appear to (and in many cases do) replicate others within the language. One reason for this is that new functions and methods are added to the language to enhance the functionality of the old functions and methods, but because many programs (and programmers) rely on the old functions and methods, they can't be removed. However, this particular case is not an identical duplication because MsgBox and InputBox give greater flexiblity than Alert, Confirm, and Prompt. In this case, the duplication occurs because VBScript has built-in functions for MsgBox and InputBox, which have to be included in the language engine. Plus, VBScript must adhere to the Active Scripting Object Model, which specifies that the window object must have Alert, Confirm, and Prompt methods.

PART

II

Mastering the VBScript Language

FOUR

Using the VBScript Language

The Visual Basic Scripting Edition (VBScript) language is a subset of Microsoft Visual Basic for Applications (VBA) and Microsoft Visual Basic. You can use VBScript for interfacing both ActiveX controls and Java applets, as well as writing stand-alone scripts that act directly upon the browser object. The syntax (how you write the code) is clear and logical in the vast majority of cases; there are no cryptic symbols or constructs. In fact, much of the syntax predates even Visual Basic with its ancestral roots placed firmly in the early Basic languages. The vast majority of the algorithms and procedures used by the scripting language engine behind the scenes are tried and tested, giving you a robust basis and foundation to work from.

In the many hours I have spent working with VBScript, I have yet to encounter anything in the language that I would call a bug, which is probably due to the length of time that Visual Basic and its cousins have been around. Compare my VBScript experience with newer scripting languages that appear to be fraught with problems. I mention this not to advertise for those nice people at Microsoft, but to let you know that you can confidently program in VBScript. When an error does rear its ugly head, the error is probably yours and not the scripting engine's.

In this chapter, you'll see how you can create powerful scripts for your Web pages quickly and easily using the VBScript language. Even if you are experienced in Visual Basic or VBA, I still recommend that you read this chapter and the rest of the chapters in Part II regarding the VBScript language because there are a few differences in the implementation of the VBScript language that might take you by surprise.

Accessing VBScript Data and Data Subtypes

The most logical place to start with any programming language is the data types. Data types are crucial because they define how the computer stores data while the program is executing. The computer needs to know what type of data you are handling (for example, is *x* a string or a number?) so that it can allocate memory space. Different data types take up different amounts of memory, as you can see from the following list of fundamental data types:

- ❏ `Empty`: A value associated with a newly declared but as yet unassigned variable.
- ❏ `Null`: Similar to `Empty`, but `Null` must be assigned explicitly.
- ❏ `Boolean`: `True` or `False` (`0` or `-1`).
- ❏ `Byte`: One byte in length, it can hold whole numbers between 0 and 255.
- ❏ `Integer`: Uses two bytes and can hold whole numbers between -32768 and 32767.
- ❏ `Long`: Four bytes in length, the whole numbers it represents can range from -2,147,483,648 to 2,147,483,647.
- ❏ `Single`: Four bytes long, it can contain fractional numbers used in floating-point arithmetic, ranging from -3.402823E38 to -1.401298E-45 for negative numbers and 1.401298E-45 to 3.402823E38 for positive numbers.
- ❏ `Double`: Eight bytes long, it can contain very large fractional numbers.
- ❏ `Date`: Holds a representation of the date and time from January 1, 100 to December 31, 9999.
- ❏ `String`: A variable-length data type. The maximum string length you can use in VBScript is around two billion characters.
- ❏ `Object`: A special data type that can hold a reference to an ActiveX or intrinsic HTML object.
- ❏ `Error`: Used to store error numbers created by VBScript.

VBScript makes it easy for you to work with any of these data types without placing instructions in your program about which data type you need to use. VBScript uses what's known as a variant data type.

What Is a Variant Data Type?

A variant is a special data type that can contain any of the fundamental data types shown in the preceding list. It dynamically allocates memory space according to which data subtype is required. This means that you don't have to explicitly declare variables as a particular fundamental type (as you do with the majority of programming languages). A variant takes care of that for you.

As you can see from the following sample code, VBScript does not require you to tell it what type of data you want to place inside the variables `Qty` and `ProductName`. You simply assign your values to `Qty` and `ProductName` and let the variant data type do the rest.

```
<SCRIPT LANGUAGE = "vbscript">
<!--
Qty = 162
ProductName = "Paper Clip"
-->
</SCRIPT>
```

Finding Out What Data Type Is Held in a Variant

Although you do not need to assign the data type in VBScript, on many occasions you need to know what type of data the variant is holding. You can use the built-in `VarType` function to determine how the data in a variant is treated. Table 4.1 shows the return values of the `VarType` function and the corresponding contents of the variant.

Table 4.1. VarType return values.

Return Value	Data Type Held in Variant
0	Empty (uninitialized)
1	Null (no valid data)
2	Integer
3	Long (long integer)
4	Single (single-precision floating-point)
5	Double (double-precision floating-point)
7	Date
8	String
9	Object
10	Error

continues

Table 4.1. continued

Return Value	Data Type Held in Variant
11	Boolean
12	Array of variant
17	Byte
8192	Array

See Chapter 10, "Using the Power of Arrays," for a detailed explanation of the array data types.

Unlike VB and VBA, VBScript has no currency type.

To illustrate using the `VarType` function, I've expanded the short example used previously:

```
<HTML>
<HEAD>
<SCRIPT LANGUAGE = "vbscript">
<!--
Sub Button1_OnClick
Qty = 162
ProductName = "Paper Clip"
Alert "Qty is a type " & VarType(Qty) & " Variant"
Alert "ProductName is a type " & VarType(ProductName) & " Variant"
End Sub
-->
</SCRIPT>
</HEAD>
<BODY BGCOLOR="white">
<CENTER>
<INPUT TYPE=BUTTON NAME="Button1" VALUE="Click Me">
</CENTER>
</BODY>
</HTML>
```

When you run this HTML file with the browser and click the button, it shows two alert boxes, one after the other. The alert boxes report that `Qty` is a type 2 (see Table 4.1) integer and `ProductName` is a type 8 string data type variant.

Converting Data Types

If variant does all the work for you, you shouldn't need to worry about what data is held, and you shouldn't have to convert data types, right? Wrong! Look at the following example:

```
<HTML>
<HEAD>
<TITLE>Add two numbers</TITLE>
<SCRIPT LANGUAGE="vbscript">
<!--
Sub Button1_OnClick
FirstData = Document.Form1.Text1.Value
SecondData = Document.Form1.Text2.Value
Document.Form1.Text3.Value = FirstData + SecondData
End Sub
```

```
-->
</SCRIPT>
</HEAD>
<BODY BGCOLOR="white">
<CENTER>
<FORM NAME="Form1">
Enter a Number <INPUT TYPE="text" NAME="Text1"><P>
Enter a Number <INPUT TYPE="text" NAME="Text2"><P>
<INPUT TYPE="button" NAME="Button1" VALUE="Click Me to add"><P>
The Result is <INPUT TYPE="text" NAME="Text3">
</FORM>
</CENTER>
</BODY>
</HTML>
```

You are asked to enter a number in the top text box and a number in the middle text box. When you click the button, a simple addition is performed on the two numbers:

```
Sub Button1_OnClick
FirstData = Document.Form1.Text1.Value
SecondData = Document.Form1.Text2.Value
Document.Form1.Text3.Value = FirstData + SecondData
End Sub
```

If you don't have a browser handy, Figure 4.1 shows you what happens.

Figure 4.1.

Trying to add two numbers together from an HTML form.

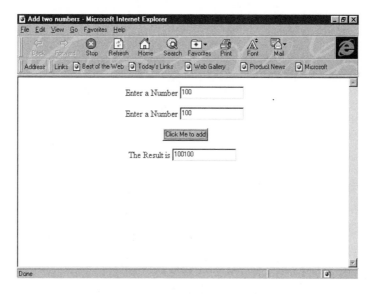

Surprised? Both numbers were added together—sort of—but the data types are strings, so 100 + 100 is not 200, but 100100. The reason for this is that HTML forms can return only string data; they never return numerical data. Variant treated the incoming data correctly. It's just that nobody told it you really wanted numbers!

Help is at hand: VBScript has a range of functions that allow you to convert data to all manner of types:

- ❏ `CBool` converts the current data type to a Boolean.
- ❏ `CByte` converts the current data type to a byte.
- ❏ `CDate` converts the current data type to a date.
- ❏ `CDbl` converts the current data type to a double precision.
- ❏ `CInt` converts the current data type to an integer.
- ❏ `CLng` converts the current data type to a long integer.
- ❏ `CSng` converts the current data type to a single precision.
- ❏ `CStr` converts the current data type to a string.

You use the conversion functions like this:

```
result = CInt(variable)
```

Here's the previous example, reworked slightly to convert the incoming data to double-precision numerical data types:

```
Sub Button1_OnClick
FirstData = CDbl(Document.Form1.Text1.Value)
SecondData = CDbl(Document.Form1.Text2.Value)
Document.Form1.Text3.Value = FirstData + SecondData
End Sub
```

The addition now works fine and dandy as long as the user remembers to make a numerical entry. 100 + 100 really does equal 200; however (there's always a however), if the user enters something such as `Fred` and `100`, an error is generated, and the program comes to a grinding halt—which is not good. In Chapter 6, "Checking Form Data," you'll see how the `IsNumeric` function traps errant data entry.

Declaring Variables and Constants

In this section, you'll see how to handle data within your script by declaring variables and constants. But before you get down to it, you should first get acquainted with what variables and constants are.

What's a Variable?

A variable is a name that you give to an area of memory—a memory location—which holds a value used in your program. It is a placeholder that is easily remembered and recognizable. For example, you wouldn't want to remember that the contents of the `Text1` text box are in memory location `00AC0744:002606C8`, but it's easy to remember `MyData`.

Another problem is that data moves around in memory, so you'd have to manually keep up with its new location, which might be virtually impossible. When you use a variable name, the language engine looks in a table of variable names and goes to the current memory location of the data. It is also good programming practice to denote what type of data you expect to use within the variable, which is done by using a three-letter lowercase prefix like this:

```
intMyIntegerData
lngMyLongData
strMyStringData
```

Variables can have their values changed during their lifetimes, as the name suggests. You can amend them at will, but sometimes you need to use a fixed value throughout your script, and this is where constants come in.

What's a Constant?

In strict terms, VBScript has no constants. A constant is a variable whose value is fixed throughout its lifetime. In other flavors of Visual Basic, you declare a constant explicitly with the CONST directive, and if any part of your program attempts to change the value, a runtime error is generated.

VBScript has no CONST directive. Any constants are "virtual," so the safest way to declare a constant is to use the code convention of uppercase characters for your constant's name, like this:

```
MY_CONSTANT
```

An addition to the normal convention is to always use more than one word for the constant name and separate them with an underscore. The underscore separates them visually from HTML elements that should be uppercase but are always only a single word.

The next concept you need to know about constants and variables is that where you define a variable or constant affects where you have access to that variable or constant and how long its lifetime is. This designation is called *scope*.

What's Scope?

The scope of a variable or constant determines whether all subroutines and procedures within the HTML document can use it or only one subroutine can use it. Look at this example:

```
1:<SCRIPT LANGUAGE="vbscript">
2:<!--
3:Sub MySubRoutine()
4:dim intMyInteger
5:intMyInteger = 5
```

```
6:Document.Form1.Text3.Value = CInt(Document.Form1.Text1.Value) + intMyInteger
7:End Sub
8:-->
9:</SCRIPT>
```

The line numbers in the preceding code segment let me refer to a particular part of the script; they don't appear in the real script.

Line 4 declares the variable `intMyInteger`, and line 5 assigns a value to it. This variable is only available to the `MySubRoutine` procedure; when the procedure is complete at line 7, the variable `intMyInteger` ceases to exist. Any calls to a variable called `intMyInteger` in other scripts on the page force the creation of a completely new variable. This is an example of *local* scope.

Now look at this example:

```
1:<SCRIPT LANGUAGE="vbscript">
2:<!--
3:dim strMyString
4:Sub MySubRoutine()
6:strMyString = Document.Form1.Text1.Value
7:Document.Form1.Text2.Value = UCase(strMyString)
8:End Sub
9:Sub AnotherSubRoutine()
10:Alert strMyString
11:End Sub
12:-->
13:</SCRIPT>
```

Notice this time that the variable `strMyString` is declared on line 3, outside of either of the two subroutines, but of course within the `<SCRIPT>` tag. On line 6, the contents of `Text1` are assigned to `strMyString`. In line 10, the value of `strMyString` is displayed to the user in an alert box. Assuming that `MySubRoutine` is executed before `AnotherSubRoutine`, the alert box shows the contents of `Text1` because `strMyString` is still active. It was not destroyed as you saw in the last example because it has *script-level* scope. It is available to all the subroutines and functions on the page.

To declare a variable with script-level scope, you simply declare it outside of a subroutine. Look at this next example:

```
<SCRIPT LANGUAGE="vbscript">
<!--
Sub MyButton_OnClick
Alert "Hello World"
End Sub
-->
</SCRIPT>
<SCRIPT LANGUAGE="vbscript">
<!--
dim intMyInteger
Sub AnotherButton_OnClick
Alert "Hello Again"
End Sub
-->
</SCRIPT>
```

This time, `intMyInteger` is declared outside of any subroutines or functions but appears within the second `<SCRIPT>` block. This change doesn't matter. The script engine still treats `intMyInteger` as a variable with script-level scope because the script engine gathers all the scripts on the page prior to creating the in-memory program.

What's a Global Variable?

You will often encounter the term *global variable*, which is exactly the same as a script-level scoped variable, but it's easier to say!

Later in this chapter, you'll see how to use the ActiveX Control Pad to declare a global variable, which in VBScript is the same as a global constant.

Declaring Variables

Earlier, you saw that you do not need to strictly declare variables because the variant data type takes care of the nitty gritty. However, you might write complex scripts with several different functions passing data around. If others will use and possibly maintain your script, it is good programming practice to declare variables explicitly.

NOTE: You can force the script to shout at you if you don't declare a variable by using the OPTION EXPLICIT directive under the first <SCRIPT> tag. This instructs the scripting engine to generate a runtime error if it encounters an undeclared variable.

As you saw from the short code snippets earlier in this chapter, the way to declare either a variable or a constant in VBScript is by using the `Dim` keyword. The following code shows a full working example to demonstrate the use of local and global (or script-level) constants and variables. The line numbers are included purely for reference, so don't type them into your HTML file.

```
1:<HTML>
2:<HEAD><TITLE>SCOPE</TITLE>
3:<SCRIPT LANGUAGE="vbscript">
4:<!--
5:Dim intGlobalVariable
6:Dim MY_GLOBAL_CONSTANT
7:MY_GLOBAL_CONSTANT = 3

8:Sub Button1_OnClick
9: Dim intLocalVariable
10:   intLocalVariable = CInt(Document.Form1.Text1.Value)
11:   intLocalVariable = intLocalVariable * MY_GLOBAL_CONSTANT
12:   Alert intLocalVariable
13:   intGlobalVariable = intLocalVariable
14:End Sub

15:Sub Button2_OnClick
16: Dim intLocalConstant
```

```
17: intLocalConstant = 6
18: intGlobalVariable  = intGlobalVariable / intLocalConstant
➥ + MY_GLOBAL_CONSTANT
19: Alert intGlobalVariable
20: End Sub

-->
</SCRIPT>
</HEAD>

<BODY BGCOLOR="white">
<CENTER>
<FORM NAME="Form1">
Please enter a number
<INPUT TYPE="text" NAME="Text1"><P>
<INPUT TYPE="button" NAME="Button1" VALUE="Click Me"><P>
<INPUT TYPE="button" NAME="Button2" VALUE="Then Click Me">
</FORM>
</CENTER>
</BODY>
</HTML>
```

As this page loads into the browser, the script engine automatically executes lines 5 through 7. This means that the global variable `intGlobalVariable` is available for any of the scripts on the page, as is the global constant `intGlobalConstant`, which had the number 3 assigned to it in line 7.

When you load this page (`scope.htm`) into the browser, you are asked to enter a number into the text box. When you click the first button, the `Button1_OnClick` event handler springs into action.

As the `Button1_OnClick` event handler begins execution in lines 8 and 9, a new `intLocalVariable` variable is created. The value that you entered into the text box is then converted to an integer and assigned to the local variable in line 10. Line 11 uses the global constant (which has a value of 3) to perform a simple calculation and returns the result to the same local variable. The value of the local variable is then shown to the world through the Alert box in line 12. The final line of this procedure copies the result to the global variable. As the subroutine ends, the local variable is destroyed in memory and no longer exists; however, you've ensured that its final value lives on in the global variable.

Click `Button2` to fire the `Button2_OnClick` event. Line 16 declares a global constant. You can see that there is no difference in the language between constants and variables; the only reason you know it's a constant (apart from its name, in this case) is the clue from the coding convention. A number is assigned to the local constant so that using the constant is the same as using that number—in this case, 6.

You can use constants for any of the other data types, too.

Line 18 performs a simple calculation using the local constant and both the global variable and constant. Line 19 then displays the result. As before, when the procedure ends in Line 20, the local constant is destroyed. Just to prove that the values of the global constant and variable are still there, click the second button again. This time, the result of the first calculation from Button 1 is held in the global variable and is still available for use.

When you understand global or local constants and variables, you have the basis to do some neat things, and it really isn't rocket science. The ActiveX Control Pad enables you to easily declare global variables.

Declaring Global Variables in the ActiveX Control Pad

The Script Wizard of the ActiveX Control Pad has a built-in object for global variables and constants, making it as easy as point and click to create global variables for your scripts. Follow the creation of a simple Web page that uses a global variable.

Open the ActiveX Control Pad, and in the default HTML page, amend the following lines—just to make the thing look a little better:

1. Change the title to `Global Variables in ActiveX`.

2. Change the `<BODY>` tag to read `<BODY BGCOLOR="white">`.

3. Add a `<CENTER>` tag under the `<BODY>` tag.

4. Under the `<CENTER>` tag, add an ActiveX command button (a Microsoft Forms 2.0 Command Button).

Chapter 1, "Getting to Grips with ActiveX," provides details on how to add ActiveX controls to the HTML page.

5. Change the command button's `Caption` property to read `Click to See My Global Variable`. If necessary, you can change the command button's `AutoSize` property to `True`, which increases the width of the button to accommodate the long caption.

6. Close the Object Editor to generate the object code for the command button.

7. Invoke the Script Wizard by any of the usual methods.

You can find details about the Script Wizard in Chapter 1.

8. Select the `CommandButton1` click event.

9. Right-click anywhere in the right Actions pane. The Actions pop-up menu displays.

10. Select New Global Variable from the pop-up menu. You see the New Global Variable dialog box, as shown in Figure 4.2.

11. Enter the name for the new global variable as `intMyGlobalVariable` and click OK.

12. You might have noticed that a plus sign appears to the left of the global variable object in the right Actions pane. Click it and your new global variable name displays under global variables. To use `intMyGlobalVariable` in

your script, simply double-click it. This places a reference to it in the script pane. Add = `567` after the variable name in the script pane, and press Return.

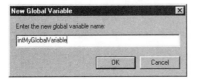

Figure 4.2.
The New Global Variable dialog box.

13. Double-click `intMyGlobalVariable` again to create another reference to it in the script. Add the word `Alert` and a space before this new reference. Your Script Wizard should now look like the one in Figure 4.3.

Figure 4.3.
The Script Wizard with your new global variable.

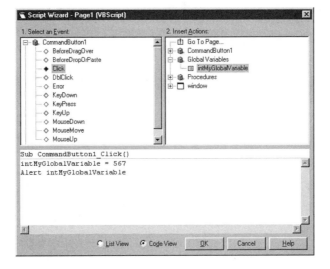

14. Click OK to automatically generate the script in your HTML file, as shown in Figure 4.4.

The Script Wizard creates two different script blocks, one in the head section that defines the global variable and a second just above the command button definition that contains the main script.

TIP: If you want to create this variable as a constant, you move the line that assigns its value to appear just below the `Dim` statement in the top script block.

Save the file as `variable.htm` and run it with your browser.

Figure 4.4.

The HTML with the global variable definition and script.

Using VBScript Operators to Calculate and Compare

One of the main uses of any programming language is comparing values and performing calculations based on those values and data. VBScript offers you a rich set of comparison and arithmetical operators to perform all types of operations from the very simple to the highly complex.

Comparison Operators

Comparison operators need very little introduction; they are the symbols used to compare one value with another value and return either `True` or `False`. The comparison operators available in VBScript are as follows:

- ❏ = compares the equality of two arguments.
- ❏ <> compares the inequality of two arguments.
- ❏ > determines whether the left argument is greater than the right argument (or whether the right argument is less than the left).
- ❏ < determines whether the left argument is less than the right argument.
- ❏ <= determines whether the left argument is less than or equal to the right argument.
- ❏ >= determines whether the left argument is greater than or equal to the right argument.

I used the word *argument* in the preceding definitions. An argument can be a single variable or value or a complete calculation in itself, as shown in the following examples:

```
If x = 10 Then
```

```
If y > ((10 * 2) - (30.333 / 76)) Then
```

The result of a comparison is always a Boolean `True` or `False`.

Arithmetical Operators

Arithmetical operators in VBScript act exactly as you would expect. The following list presents no surprises:

+	Addition
-	Subtraction
/	Division
*	Multiplication
^	Exponentiation
\	Integer division
Mod	Modulo arithmetic
&	String concatenation

The next application uses comparison and arithmetic operators. Because it's a long application, I won't discuss every last line and object, only the areas relevant to this chapter.

Figure 4.5 shows the application called the Mr Frosty Air Conditioner Web page. Visitors to the site can enter the dimensions of their rooms in meters; the script calculates the volume of the room and then compares the volume with the maximum capacities of the Mr Frosty Air Conditioner range.

Figure 4.5.

The Mr Frosty Air Conditioners Web page.

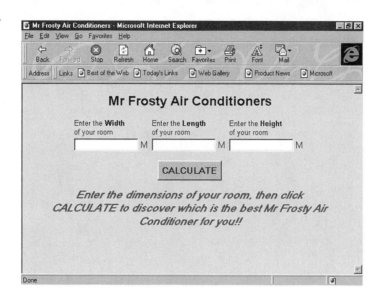

The following is the full source code for the page:

```
<HTML>
<HEAD>
<TITLE>Mr Frosty Air Conditioners</TITLE>
</HEAD>
<BODY BGCOLOR="aqua">
<FONT FACE="arial" SIZE=2>
<CENTER>
<H2>Mr Frosty Air Conditioners</H2>
<P>
    <FORM NAME="Form1">
<TABLE>
<TD><FONT SIZE=2>Enter the <B>Width</B><BR> of your room
<TD><FONT SIZE=2>Enter the <B>Length</B><BR> of your room
<TD><FONT SIZE=2>Enter the <B>Height</B><BR> of your room
<TR>
<TD><INPUT TYPE=text NAME="roomwidth">M
<TD><INPUT TYPE=text NAME="roomlength">M
<TD><INPUT TYPE=text NAME="roomheight">M
<TR>
</TABLE>
<P>
        <SCRIPT LANGUAGE="VBScript">
<!--
dim MODELA_MAX
dim MODELB_MAX
dim MODELC_MAX

MODELA_MAX = 130
MODELB_MAX = 500
MODELC_MAX = 1000

Function WhichModel(lngRoomVolume)
 If lngRoomVolume < MODELA_MAX then
```

```
  WhichModel = "Mini Syberia"
  Exit Function
 End If

 If lngRoomVolume < MODELB_MAX then
  WhichModel = "Midi Artic"
  Exit Function
 End If

 If lngRoomVolume < MODELC_MAX then
  WhichModel = "Maxi Antarctica"
  Exit Function
 End If

 WhichModel = "Golly Jeepers that's BIG!!"

End Function

Sub CommandButton1_Click()
 dim intW
 dim intL
 dim intH
 dim lngVol
 dim strMsg

intW = CInt(Document.Form1.roomwidth.value)
intL = CInt(Document.Form1.roomlength.value)
intH = CInt(Document.Form1.roomheight.value)
lngVol = intW * intL * intH

strMsg = "Your room is " & CStr(lngVol) & " cubic Metres"
strMsg = strMsg & Chr(10) & Chr(13)
strMsg = strMsg & "You need our " & WhichModel(lngVol) & " Model"
Label1.Caption = strMsg
end sub
-->
        </SCRIPT>

        <OBJECT ID="CommandButton1" WIDTH=120 HEIGHT=36
         CLASSID="CLSID:D7053240-CE69-11CD-A777-00DD01143C57">
            <PARAM NAME="ForeColor" VALUE="0">
            <PARAM NAME="VariousPropertyBits" VALUE="268435483">
            <PARAM NAME="Caption" VALUE="CALCULATE">
            <PARAM NAME="Size" VALUE="3175;952">
            <PARAM NAME="FontEffects" VALUE="1073741825">
            <PARAM NAME="FontHeight" VALUE="240">
            <PARAM NAME="FontCharSet" VALUE="0">
            <PARAM NAME="FontPitchAndFamily" VALUE="2">
            <PARAM NAME="ParagraphAlign" VALUE="3">
            <PARAM NAME="FontWeight" VALUE="700">
        </OBJECT>
    </FORM>
<P>
    <OBJECT ID="Label1" WIDTH=533 HEIGHT=80
     CLASSID="CLSID:978C9E23-D4B0-11CE-BF2D-00AA003F40D0">
        <PARAM NAME="ForeColor" VALUE="16711680">
        <PARAM NAME="BackColor" VALUE="16776960">
        <PARAM NAME="VariousPropertyBits" VALUE="276824083">
        <PARAM NAME="Caption" VALUE="Enter the dimensions of your room,
        ➥then click
```

```
CALCULATE to discover which is the best Mr Frosty Air Conditioner for you!!">
        <PARAM NAME="Size" VALUE="14111;2116">
        <PARAM NAME="FontEffects" VALUE="1073741827">
        <PARAM NAME="FontHeight" VALUE="280">
        <PARAM NAME="FontCharSet" VALUE="0">
        <PARAM NAME="FontPitchAndFamily" VALUE="2">
        <PARAM NAME="ParagraphAlign" VALUE="3">
        <PARAM NAME="FontWeight" VALUE="700">
    </OBJECT>
</BODY>
</HTML>
```

The application uses a combination of HTML controls and ActiveX controls. The first script you encounter is the definition of the constants used for holding the maximum values for the model range:

```
        <SCRIPT LANGUAGE="VBScript">
<!--
dim MODELA_MAX
dim MODELB_MAX
dim MODELC_MAX

MODELA_MAX = 130
MODELB_MAX = 500
MODELC_MAX = 1000
```

Follow the script not as it appears on the page, but in the logical sequence that starts with the user clicking the button. This application provides no check to ensure that the data entered is the correct type. For example, if someone types in Four instead of 4, you're in trouble.

The event handler for the click event starts with a declaration of several variables that are used within the procedure:

```
Sub CommandButton1_Click()
 dim intW
 dim intL
 dim intH
 dim lngVol
 dim strMsg
```

Remember that all data coming from an HTML form is string data, so the first job is to convert the incoming data to numerical data so that you can perform calculations on it:

```
intW = CInt(Document.Form1.roomwidth.value)
intL = CInt(Document.Form1.roomlength.value)
intH = CInt(Document.Form1.roomheight.value)
```

Now, you can calculate the room's volume by simply multiplying all the values together:

```
lngVol = intW * intL * intH
```

The next section starts to build the message that is displayed to the user. Note that the numerical room volume variable (lngVol) is converted to a string:

```
strMsg = "Your room is " & CStr(lngVol) & " cubic Metres"
strMsg = strMsg & Chr(10) & Chr(13)
```

The next line makes a call to the function WhichModel. WhichModel compares the volume to the maximum volumes of the product range. If the room volume is less than the product's maximum capacity, it is safe to recommend the product. Starting with the smallest unit, the comparisons continue until one of the If...Then statements returns True. At this point, the model name is returned to the line calling the function, effectively replacing the function call with the product name:

```
strMsg = strMsg & "You need our " & WhichModel(lngVol) & " Model"
Function WhichModel(lngRoomVolume)
 If lngRoomVolume < MODELA_MAX then
  WhichModel = "Mini Syberia"
  Exit Function
 End If

 If lngRoomVolume < MODELB_MAX then
  WhichModel = "Midi Artic"
  Exit Function
 End If

 If lngRoomVolume < MODELC_MAX then
  WhichModel = "Maxi Antarctica"
  Exit Function
 End If

 WhichModel = "Golly Jeepers that's BIG!!"

End Function
```

For more details on functions and If...Then statements, see Chapter 9, "Making Your Program Flow."

Finally, the message that has been created is copied to the label caption and displayed on-screen, as shown in Figure 4.6.

Figure 4.6.

Mr Frosty makes his recommendation.

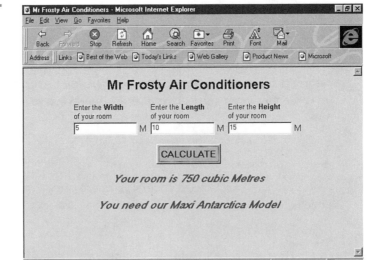

Workshop Wrap-Up

In this chapter, you started to build the foundations of VBScript programming by learning the data type variant and its subtypes, how to find out what data is held in variant using `VarType`, and also how to convert that data using the conversion functions.

You used variables and constants and learned the difference between global and local scope and how it is defined within the program. Finally, you looked at how you can use VBScript to compare values and perform calculations and other arithmetic.

Next Steps

Now you have seen the foundations of programming in VBScript. To start creating real applications, take at look at the following chapters:

- ❏ For more information about `If...Then` conditional statements, see Chapter 9, "Making Your Program Flow."
- ❏ Chapter 10, "Using the Power of Arrays," contains more information about arrays.
- ❏ To learn how to trap incoming data problems, see Chapter 6, "Checking Form Data."

Q&A

Q: You mentioned naming conventions earlier. What are they, and why do we have them?

A: Naming or coding conventions allow different people to read the same programming code and understand quickly what is happening within the script or program. It also helps you later, when you need to make amendments to a script that you wrote possibly many months previously. It's simply a common set of notations. When you see a name such as `MY_COLOR`, you know that it's a constant. Other conventions cover variables that can use an abbreviation of the data subtype in lowercase as the first three characters of the name. For example, an integer variable can be called `intMyVar`.

Q: I've used other programming languages before. With them, I have to specify what type of data I'm using in the variable and stick rigidly to that. Why is VBScript so different?

A: As you have seen, the variant data type almost eliminates the need to define the type of data you will hold within a particular variable. Microsoft wanted VBScript to be as easy as possible to use, so that first-time programmers who had arrived at VBScript from HTML could create scripts with the minimum amount of fuss and bother. With the variant data type, they have achieved just that.

FIVE

Interfacing VBScript with an HTML Form

A lot of the VBScript work you undertake is linked in some way to the form because VBScript is ideal for interfacing with user inputs. As you saw in Chapter 2, "Using VBScript with HTML Controls," you can easily and quickly add VBScript to current HTML pages without major renovation. In this chapter, you'll learn about three HTML form elements that probably cause the most confusion when it comes to adding script to a form. Text boxes are straightforward, but the three elements that afford choice to the user are not.

The three choice elements in HTML forms are as follows:

- ❏ SELECT isn't strictly a control because it isn't specified with the <INPUT> tag; however, it is used very frequently and is probably the easiest of the three to work with. Select lists are specified as follows:

```
<SELECT NAME="MySelect">
<OPTION>The First Option
<OPTION>The Second Option
</SELECT>
```

❑ RADIO is the small, round indented button that designates one of many choices when it's used together with other radio buttons of the same name. A radio button is specified within an INPUT tag as follows:

```
<INPUT TYPE="radio" NAME="myRadio" VALUE="OptionValue">
```

❑ CHECKBOX is the small, square indented box that is either on (checked) or off (unchecked). This gives the user a series of options to select—one, none, some, or all. A checkbox is specified within an INPUT tag as follows:

```
<INPUT TYPE="checkbox" NAME="myCheck" VALUE="CheckValue">
```

In this chapter, you create a form from which the user can select a range of options. Specifically, this is part of the order form for the fictitious "Mega Choice Mail Order" Web site, promoting its new product, the "LazeeGeek Computer Users Head Prop," as shown in Figure 5.1. I think I ate too much cheese last night!

Figure 5.1.
The multichoice order form.

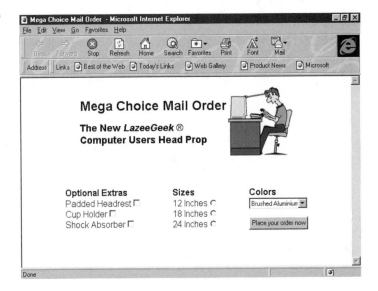

As you see, the users select from a range of optional extras using the checkboxes; they select one size using the radio buttons. Finally, they select the color of their choice from a drop-down list, courtesy of a <SELECT> tag.

Listing 5.1 shows the complete source code for the Web page (mega1.htm), and you can find it on the CD-ROM that accompanies this book. Each task in this chapter breaks down a specific section of the source code to show you how the code fits together. Note that I created this whole page with Notepad; however, you can use the ActiveX Control Pad's Text Editor or your own favorite HTML editor if you want. The line numbers shown in the following source code are for the purpose of explanation and should not form part of the final document.

Listing 5.1. `mega1.htm`.

```
<HTML>
<HEAD>
<!-- ***************************************
     *      LAZEEGEEK HEAD PROP EXAMPLE      *
     ***************************************
-->
<TITLE>
Mega Choice Mail Order
</TITLE>

1:<SCRIPT LANGUAGE="vbscript">
2:<!--
3:OPTION EXPLICIT

4:Sub Button1_OnClick
5:'====================DECLARE VARIABLES AND CONSTANTS==============
6:    Dim intColor
7:    Dim i
8:    Dim strOptExtras, strTheSize, strTheColor, strMainMessage
9:    Dim intOptQty, intResponse
10:    Dim blnSize

11:    Dim CRLF
12:    CRLF = Chr(10) & Chr(13)

13:'====================DETERMINE SIZE SELECTION====================

14:blnSize = False
15:For i = 0 to Document.OrderForm.Elements.Count -1
16:  If Document.OrderForm.Elements(i).Name = "choice1" Then
17:    If Document.OrderForm.Elements(i).Checked Then
18:       blnSize = True
19:       strTheSize =  "Size: " & Document.OrderForm.Elements(i).Value
20:       Exit For
21:    End if
22:  End if
23:Next

24:If Not blnSize Then
25:  Alert "You must select a size"
26:  Exit Sub
27:End If

28:'=====================DETERMINE COLOR SELECTION====================

29:intColor = Document.OrderForm.Colors.SelectedIndex
30:strTheColor = "Color: " & Document.OrderForm.Colors.Options(intColor).Text

31:'=====================DETERMINE OPTIONAL EXTRAS====================

32:strOptExtras = "Options: "
33:intOptQty = 0

34:If Document.OrderForm.option1.Checked Then
35:  strOptExtras = strOptExtras & Document.OrderForm.option1.Value & " "
36:  intOptQty = intOptQty + 1
37:End If
```

continues

Listing 5.1. continued

```
38:If Document.OrderForm.option2.Checked Then
39:If intOptQty > 0 Then
40:  strOptExtras = strOptExtras & "and "
41:End if
42:  strOptExtras = strOptExtras & Document.OrderForm.option2.Value & " "
43:  intOptQty = intOptQty + 1
44:End If

45:If Document.OrderForm.option3.Checked Then
46:If intOptQty > 0 Then
47: strOptExtras = strOptExtras & "and "
48:End If
49:  strOptExtras = strOptExtras & Document.OrderForm.option3.Value
50:  intOptQty = intOptQty + 1
51:End If

52:If intOptQty = 0 Then
53:  strOptExtras = "No Options Required"
54:End If

55:'=======================SHOW MESSAGE ===================================

56:strMainMessage = "Thanks for your order" & CRLF
57:strMainMessage = strMainMessage & strTheSize & CRLF
58:strMainMessage = strMainMessage & strTheColor & CRLF
59:strMainMessage = strMainMessage & strOptExtras & CRLF
60:strMainMessage = strMainMessage & "Is this correct?"

61:intResponse = MsgBox(strMainMessage,36,"Order Details")


62:End Sub
63:-->
64:</SCRIPT>

</HEAD>

<BODY BGCOLOR="white">
<FONT FACE="arial" SIZE=2>
<CENTER>
<TABLE>
<TD>
<H2>Mega Choice Mail Order</H2>
<H3>The New <I>LazeeGeek</I> &reg; <BR>Computer Users Head Prop</H3>
<TD>
<IMG SRC="headprop.gif">
<TR>
</TABLE>


<FORM NAME="OrderForm">
<TABLE CELLPADDING=20 CELLSPACING=20>
<!--COLUMN ONE ---- OPTIONAL EXTRAS -->
<TD VALIGN=TOP>
<B>Optional Extras</B><BR>
Padded Headrest<INPUT TYPE="checkbox" NAME="option1" Value="Padded
➥Headrest"><BR>
Cup Holder<INPUT TYPE="checkbox" NAME="option2" Value="Cup Holder"><BR>
Shock Absorber<INPUT TYPE="checkbox" NAME="option3" Value="Shock Absorber"><BR>
```

```
<!--COLUMN TWO ---- SIZE CHOICE -->
<TD VALIGN=TOP>
<B>Sizes</B><BR>
12 Inches<INPUT TYPE="radio" NAME="choice1" Value="12 Inches"><BR>
18 Inches<INPUT TYPE="radio" NAME="choice1" Value="18 Inches"><BR>
24 Inches<INPUT TYPE="radio" NAME="choice1" Value="24 Inches"><BR>

<!--COLUMN THREE ---- COLOR & BUTTON -->
<TD VALIGN=TOP>
<B>Colors</B><BR>
<SELECT NAME="Colors">
<OPTION>Brushed Aluminium
<OPTION>Black
<OPTION>Blue
<OPTION>Green
<OPTION>Red
</SELECT><P>
<INPUT TYPE="button" NAME="Button1" VALUE="Place your order now">
<TR>
</TABLE>


</FORM>
</BODY>
</HTML>
```

TASK | Building an HTML Form to Work with VBScript

To give you some understanding of how VBScript interacts with forms and form elements, I'll briefly discuss the hierarchy of HTML objects. A document is an object that belongs to the window object (that is, the window object is its parent). Because the window object is implicit, you usually do not need to specify it in the code line. You can have only one document per window; however, a frame is treated as a window.

NOTE: If the document is held within a frame, you must explicitly call the frame first. To learn about frames with VBScript, see Chapter 18, "Interacting with the Browser."

A form object belongs to the document, and a document can have any number of forms. The element objects—such as text boxes and other input controls—are objects that belong to the form, and again, a form can have any number of elements. To access the value of a form element from your script, you use the following syntax:

```
Document.FormName.ElementName.Value
```

When either building or amending an HTML form that you intend to interface using VBScript, the main thing to keep in mind is that you must give your form and its elements a name. Giving them names simplifies matters greatly, although it is not absolutely necessary as I now demonstrate with the following short example:

```
<HTML>
 <HEAD>
  <SCRIPT LANGUAGE="vbscript">
   Sub CommandButton1_OnClick
    strTheInput = Document.Forms(0).Elements(0).Value
    Alert strTheInput
   End Sub
  </SCRIPT>
 </HEAD>
 <BODY>
 <FORM>
  <INPUT TYPE="text">
  <INPUT TYPE="button" NAME="CommandButton1" VALUE="Click Me">
 </FORM>
 </BODY>
</HTML>
```

In this example, neither the form nor the text box has a name. VBScript places all forms into an array of forms, starting at number 0; it also places all form elements, such as buttons and text boxes, into an elements array, again starting at number 0.

For more details about arrays, see Chapter 10, "Using the Power of Arrays."

To access the contents of this text box, you must know within which form it resides and the text box's ordinal number within the form. In this particular example, knowing the number isn't much of a problem because you have only one form and two elements; the text box is the first, so it is element 0.

```
strTheInput = Document.Forms(0).Elements(0).Value
```

You can now see that it is much easier to name all your forms and elements and refer to them by name. In fact, to access values when you send the information to the server, you need names for your elements anyway.

Look at the form used in the main example in this chapter, which is shown in the following code segment. Notice that the three radio buttons have the same name so that you can check only one button at any one time, leaving the other two unchecked. When you give the buttons the same name, the browser adds this functionality for you. The form is constructed with everyday HTML objects and requires no further explanation:

```
<FORM NAME="OrderForm">
<TABLE CELLPADDING=20 CELLSPACING=20>
<!--COLUMN ONE ---- OPTIONAL EXTRAS -->
<TD VALIGN=TOP>
<B>Optional Extras</B><BR>
Padded Headrest<INPUT TYPE="checkbox" NAME="option1" Value="Padded
➡Headrest"><BR>
Cup Holder<INPUT TYPE="checkbox" NAME="option2" Value="Cup Holder"><BR>
Shock Absorber<INPUT TYPE="checkbox" NAME="option3" Value="Shock Absorber"><BR>
```

```
<!--COLUMN TWO ---- SIZE CHOICE -->
<TD VALIGN=TOP>
<B>Sizes</B><BR>
12 Inches<INPUT TYPE="radio" NAME="choice1" Value="12 Inches"><BR>
18 Inches<INPUT TYPE="radio" NAME="choice1" Value="18 Inches"><BR>
24 Inches<INPUT TYPE="radio" NAME="choice1" Value="24 Inches"><BR>

<!--COLUMN THREE ---- COLOR & BUTTON -->
<TD VALIGN=TOP>
<B>Colors</B><BR>
<SELECT NAME="Colors">
<OPTION>Brushed Aluminium
<OPTION>Black
<OPTION>Blue
<OPTION>Green
<OPTION>Red
</SELECT><P>
<INPUT TYPE="button" NAME="Button1" VALUE="Place your order now">
<TR>
</TABLE>
</FORM>
```

Take a look at the scripts required for you to interact with each of the three elements; as you are about to see, each element requires a very different approach.

Determining Which HTML Option (Radio Button) Is Clicked

To give the correct functionality to an HTML button, you must give all the radio buttons in a set the same name. This in itself causes a problem. As you saw previously, the best way to access an element is via its name, but now you have three controls with the same name, so what happens when you use the code?

```
Document.OrderForm.Choice1.Value
```

The answer is that an error occurs. How does the scripting engine know exactly which Choice1 you are referring to? In Visual Basic and Visual Basic for Applications and with the ActiveX radio control, this confusion isn't a problem because you can specify an index number to distinguish the control as unique. In fact, it is regular practice to create a group of the same controls with the same name distinguished only by an index number. The HTML radio button has no such indexing feature. What do you do? Take a look at the following code from the example:

```
13:'====================DETERMINE SIZE SELECTION====================

14:blnSize = False
15:For i = 0 to Document.OrderForm.Elements.Count -1
16:  If Document.OrderForm.Elements(i).Name = "choice1" Then
17:    If Document.OrderForm.Elements(i).Checked Then
18:       blnSize = True
19:       strTheSize =  "Size: " & Document.OrderForm.Elements(i).Value
20:       Exit For
```

```
21:    End if
22:  End if
23:Next

24:If Not blnSize Then
25:  Alert "You must select a size"
26:  Exit Sub
27:End If
```

To learn more about
`For...Next` loops and
`If...Then` conditional
statements, see Chapter
9, "Making Your
Program Flow."

Notice that the code reverts to using the elements array. Line 15 uses the element's `Count` property. The `Count` property holds the total number of elements within a particular form. Because the elements array begins with zero, you subtract one from the total and start the loop at `0`. If your form has 10 objects, for example, you reference them as `Elements(0)` to `Elements(9)`.

The name of the radio button is used in line 16 to check whether the current element object is the one you want. Don't forget that going through all the form elements in this way returns every element, such as checkboxes, buttons, and so on. If the program finds the name `choice1`, you know you have the right object. Notice that you can use `Elements(i)` as though it were the object's name and access all the element's properties in the same way. For example, the following two lines are the same:

```
Document.OrderForm.choice1.Name
Document.OrderForm.Elements(i).Name
```

`i` represents the ordinal number of the `choice1` element.

When the program locates one of the three radio buttons, you must find out whether it is checked, which line 17 evaluates. If the radio button is checked, line 17 evaluates to `True`, and lines 18 and 19 are executed. If the button is not checked, the loop continues.

Line 18 sets a flag to `True`, which is used in line 24 to determine whether the user selected any size. If he didn't choose a size, a warning message displays, and the script's execution halts. Line 19 copies the value of the checked radio button to a variable that is used later to get confirmation from the user.

After you find the checked radio button, you know there can be only one, so any further execution of the loop is a waste of time. Line 20 jumps out of the loop using the `Exit For` statement.

Determining Which HTML Checkbox Is Checked

The method for determining which checkbox is checked is different from the method for finding the checked radio button. First, you must consider that several permutations could be present. The user could have selected one, two, all, or none of the options. The following segment shows the code used for the checkbox inspection:

```
31:'=====================DETERMINE OPTIONAL EXTRAS=====================

32:strOptExtras = "Options: "
33:intOptQty = 0

34:If Document.OrderForm.option1.Checked Then
35:   strOptExtras = strOptExtras & Document.OrderForm.option1.Value & " "
36:   intOptQty = intOptQty + 1
37:End If

38:If Document.OrderForm.option2.Checked Then
39: If intOptQty > 0 Then
40:   strOptExtras = strOptExtras & "and "
41: End if
42:   strOptExtras = strOptExtras & Document.OrderForm.option2.Value & " "
43:   intOptQty = intOptQty + 1
44:End If

45:If Document.OrderForm.option3.Checked Then
46: If intOptQty > 0 Then
47:   strOptExtras = strOptExtras & "and "
48: End If
49:   strOptExtras = strOptExtras & Document.OrderForm.option3.Value
50:   intOptQty = intOptQty + 1
51:End If

52:If intOptQty = 0 Then
53:   strOptExtras = "No Options Required"
54:End If
```

The `Checked` property of the checkbox object returns `True` if the checkbox is checked and `False` otherwise. The first two lines of code, 32 and 33, initialize the variables used in this section. As you see, the parts of this section are similar to each other. A test is performed (lines 34, 38, and 45) to find out whether the checkbox is checked, and if it is, the value of that checkbox is concatenated to the string (lines 35, 42, and 49).

A counter (`intOptQty`) determines whether any checkboxes are checked. If none are checked, the value of the counter remains at zero. At various stages (lines 39 and 46), the counter is tested to determine whether the current checkbox is the first or a subsequent option. If it is a second or third option, the word `and` is concatenated to the string (lines 40 and 47). The counter is incremented every time a checked checkbox is encountered (lines 36, 43, and 50).

Determining the Selection from an HTML Select

The HTML select object is very straightforward to use and has several useful built-in properties. It also contains a kind of options sub-object, which has its own properties.

Here are the main properties of the select object:

❏ `Length` returns an integer value of the number of options declared using the `<OPTION>` tag within the `<SELECT>` block:

```
intNoofOptions = Document.Form1.MySelect.Length
```

❏ `SelectedIndex` returns an integer value of the index number (zero is the first list item) of the option the user has selected:

```
intColor = Document.OrderForm.Colors.SelectedIndex
```

The `Option` object is an array of strings that contains a list of options defined with the `<OPTION>` tag. The first one is always indexed at `0`. The `Option`'s `Text` property returns a string containing the text entered in the HTML file directly after the `<OPTION>` tag. You can only use it by specifying which option you want to reference:

```
30:strTheColor = "Color: " & Document.OrderForm.Colors.Options(intColor).Text
```

In the example, the selected item is determined using the `SelectedIndex` property of the select object. This value is then used to return the text of the option:

```
28:'=====================DETERMINE COLOR SELECTION=====================

29:intColor = Document.OrderForm.Colors.SelectedIndex
30:strTheColor = "Color: " & Document.OrderForm.Colors.Options(intColor).Text
```

NOTE: Unlike the ActiveX drop-down list (combo), the HTML version is read-only, which means you cannot add items or change the text in any way after the HTML file is rendered in the browser.

TASK # Confirming a User's Selection

The final part of the script builds the message string from the variables that had values assigned to them in the course of the selection-checking processes described previously.

When the message string is complete, it is used in a message box of type 36 (Yes and No buttons and a Question Mark icon), as shown in Figure 5.2. In a real form, you would make some further decisions and carry out further processes based on the return value of this message box, which you collect in the `intResponse` variable.

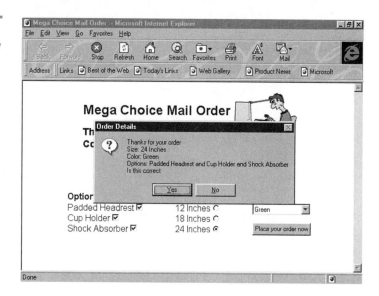

Figure 5.2.

The message box asking the user to confirm his order.

Workshop Wrap-Up

In this chapter, you learned several ways that you can write scripts to determine the values selected by the users prior to sending data to the server. You saw how to loop through the form's elements to find particular controls, and you used a control's properties to point to the selected option.

You worked entirely with HTML intrinsic objects and saw the hierarchy of window, document, form, and element. You saw several examples of the dot notation used to refer to properties of an object.

In the next chapter, you'll see how to programmatically submit data to the server using VBScript.

Next Steps

Now that you've seen how to use HTML form elements with VBScript, you can create interactive documents using your current HTML pages as a base. For further information, see these chapters:

❏ To learn more about form data and data verification, see Chapter 6, "Checking Form Data."

❏ Chapter 9, "Making Your Program Flow," describes `For...Next` loops and `If...Then` conditional statements.

❏ When you're working with strings, read Chapter 7, "Manipulating Strings."

❏ For more information about LazeeGeek Computer Users Head Props, fill in the form!

Q&A

Q: Can all the HTML Intrinsic Controls be interfaced with VBScript?

A: Yes. The Active Scripting Object Model (see Appendixes B, "HTML Intrinsic Controls: Properties, Events, and Methods," and D, "Active Scripting Object Model") defines the type and minimum functionality of HTML controls and objects used in an active scripting environment such as MSIE 3.x. It also specifies the properties, methods, and events that each should have. However, each HTML control is slightly different, so what you can do with one control, you might not be able to do with another.

Q: Why would I want to use HTML Intrinsic Controls when I have all these ActiveX controls that perform much better?

A: There are several reasons why you could choose HTML Intrinsic Controls. Suppose you have a complex form that you have been developing and maintaining for some time. Rather than scrap the whole form, you could enhance what you already have by adding some scripting to it. There's also the consideration of download time, which should be much quicker using HTML controls, although all the ActiveX form controls should be immediately available to users of Windows 95. Finally, by using ActiveX controls, you are completely blocking users of Netscape Navigator from your form, whereas if you had used HTML controls, those users would at least be able to use the form (albeit without the scripted functionality).

SIX

Checking Form Data

Almost every Web site, especially those run by commercial or semi-commercial organizations, solicits information from the user. Whether it's a simple request for further information or the user places a complex order, the information that you as webmaster receive is by and large unchecked, and you therefore rely upon the user to enter the details correctly.

The usual remedy to this is to write a server-side CGI script, which is not too onerous a task. However, the user must wait for the information to travel to the server, the script to run, and a new Web page to appear in the browser before he finds out whether his information is within the limits. If the information isn't valid, he re-enters the offending section and waits again. This current method of data verification obviously wastes time and bandwidth and assumes that you have access to the server's `CGI-BIN` or `CGI-LOCAL` directories and that you have the resources to create a server-side script in languages such as Perl or PHP/FI.

When you add client-side data verification, you can perform all this verification at the browser. The user is immediately aware—even as he is typing—of whether the data is acceptable. You cannot stop the mischievous netizens who insist on filling out forms using e-mail addresses such as `me@imnottelling.com`, but at least you can do something to reduce the amount of totally unusable information.

This chapter concentrates on the data-verification methods you can add to a current HTML form without using ActiveX controls. Part of Chapter 16, "Real-Life Examples II," shows you how to build an interactive form with ActiveX controls and the HTML layout control.

The main object of the exercise is to stop poorly formatted data or data that doesn't fit your criteria from reaching the server. This means that you have to perform some type of validation on the data before it is submitted. The form object has an OnSubmit event that is fired either when the user clicks the Submit button or when the script calls the form object's submit method—ideal for handling the validation process.

Alerting Users During the Data Entry

Prior to submission, while the user is entering data, you can use several methods to alert the user to a problem with his input. The HTML text box has an OnChange event that fires when the focus moves away from the text box only if the text is different from the last time the event fired. For example, you can enter, This is some text, into an empty HTML text box, and the OnChange event fires when you move to the next text box or control. Return to the text box, delete the word text, retype it, and move away. Because the text is unchanged, the OnChange event doesn't fire—quite logical really!

NOTE: The ActiveX text box Change() event does not work in this way. The Change() event is fired with every keystroke, and placing validation code in the Change() event handler can drive a user to distraction if it is not implemented thoughtfully.

Using the OnChange event, you can test for data acceptability and caution the user if the test fails. Of course, this method on its own doesn't really solve your problem because the user can simply choose to click OK on the Alert box and then ignore its warning—which means you still receive bad data at the server. There is no substitute for preventing poor data from being submitted. However, ongoing verification during the entry phase used in conjunction with a final verification helps both you and the users.

A Data Verification Example

Listing 6.1 shows the source code for the example you use in this chapter; Figure 6.1 shows the Web page when it's run in the browser. It contains five HTML text boxes. The first is an optional field that contains no verification. Two fields require a numerical entry, one requires a date, and one asks for the user's e-mail address. As the user enters data and moves to the next field, the data is verified, and if the script finds a problem, it alerts the user. The verification takes place in a series of functions that can be called from any of the fields, which allows for speedy maintenance should you need to add further verifiable fields to the form. Finally, the user clicks the submit button, which is a normal button. The data is reverified, and if it's found to be correct, the form data is submitted to the server.

The line numbers are included in the code for explanation purposes and do not appear in the finished HTML page.

Listing 6.1. The sample source code for `validate.htm`.

```
<HTML>
<HEAD>
<TITLE>Data Validation</TITLE>

1:<SCRIPT LANGUAGE="vbscript">

2:Function ValidateNumber(ByVal TheNumber, ByVal FieldName)
3: If Not IsNumeric(TheNumber) Then
4:   x = MsgBox("Invalid Numeric Entry",16,FieldName)
5:   ValidateNumber = False
6: Else
7:   ValidateNumber = True
8: End If
9:End Function

10:Function ValidateDate(ByVal TheDate, ByVal FieldName)
11: If Not IsDate(TheDate) Then
12:   x = MsgBox("Invalid Date",16,FieldName)
13:   ValidateDate = False
14: Else
15:   ValidateDate = True
16: End If
17:End Function

18:Function IsEMail(ByVal TheEMail, ByVal FieldName)

19: If InStr(TheEMail, "@") > 2 Then
20:     If Len(TheEMail) - InStr(TheEMail, "@") > 6 Then
21:         If InStr(InStr(TheEMail, "@"),TheEMail,".") > 0 Then
22:             If Len(TheEMail) - InStr(InStr(TheEMail, "@"),TheEMail,".") => 2
                ➥Then
23:                 ValidateEMail = True
24:             Else
25:                 ValidateEMail = False
26:             End If
27:         Else
28:             ValidateEMail = False
29:         End If
30:     Else
31:         ValidateEMail = False
32:     End If
33: Else
34:     ValidateEMail = False
35: End If

36: If ValidateEMail = True Then
37:     IsEMail = True
38: Else
```

continues

Listing 6.1. continued

```
39:    x = MsgBox("Invalid Entry",16,FieldName)
40:    IsEMail = False
41:End If

42:End Function


43:Sub txtQty_OnChange
44: x = ValidateNumber(Document.Form1.txtQty.Value, "Quantity")
45:End Sub

46:Sub txtSize_OnChange
47: x = ValidateNumber(Document.Form1.txtSize.Value, "Size")
48:End Sub

49:Sub txtDate_OnChange
50: x = ValidateDate(Document.Form1.txtDate.Value, "Date")
51:End Sub

52:Sub txtEmail_OnChange
53: x = IsEMail(Document.Form1.txtEmail.Value, "EMail")
54:End Sub

55:Sub cmdButton1_OnClick
56:  If ValidateNumber(Document.Form1.txtQty.Value, "Quantity") And _
57:    ValidateDate(Document.Form1.txtDate.Value, "Date") And _
58:    ValidateNumber(Document.Form1.txtSize.Value, "Size") And _
59:    IsEMail(Document.Form1.txtEmail.Value, "EMail") Then
60:      Document.Form1.Submit
61:  Else
62:      Exit Sub
63:  End If
64:End Sub

65:</SCRIPT>

</HEAD>

<BODY BGCOLOR="white">
<FORM NAME="Form1" ACTION="http://www.vbscripts.com/test/formtest.phtml"
➥METHOD=POST>
<PRE>
Your Name       <INPUT TYPE="text" NAME="txtUserName">
Quantity        <INPUT TYPE="text" NAME="txtQty">
Size in Metres  <INPUT TYPE="text" NAME="txtSize">
Date            <INPUT TYPE="text" NAME="txtDate">
Your EMail      <INPUT TYPE="text" NAME="txtEmail">
<INPUT TYPE="Button" NAME="cmdButton1" VALUE="Submit Now">
</PRE>
</FORM>
</BODY>
</HTML>
```

Figure 6.1.

The sample form in the browser.

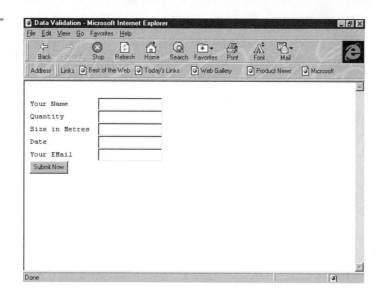

For more details on PHP/FI server-side scripting, see the address http://www.vex.net/php/. You can find the source code for formtest.phtml on the CD-ROM.

Creating the Form

The form itself is a straightforward HTML form; no surprises here. The form's action is set to a PHP/FI-scripted HTML page, which simply displays the data entered in the form. The HTML for the form is shown in the following code block:

```
<FORM NAME="Form1" ACTION="http://www.vbscripts.com/test/formtest.phtml"
➥METHOD=POST>
<PRE>
Your Name        <INPUT TYPE="text" NAME="txtUserName">
Quantity         <INPUT TYPE="text" NAME="txtQty">
Size in Metres   <INPUT TYPE="text" NAME="txtSize">
Date             <INPUT TYPE="text" NAME="txtDate">
Your EMail       <INPUT TYPE="text" NAME="txtEmail">
<INPUT TYPE="Button" NAME="cmdButton1" VALUE="Submit Now">
</PRE>
</FORM>
```

 ## Validating Numeric Data Entries

Each of the verifications is held in a separate function. Functions in VBScript are procedures that return a value to the code that called them. The following code is the function that validates the numerical data:

```
2:Function ValidateNumber(ByVal TheNumber, ByVal FieldName)
3: If Not IsNumeric(TheNumber) Then
4:   x = MsgBox("Invalid Numeric Entry",16,FieldName)
5:   ValidateNumber = False
6: Else
7:   ValidateNumber = True
8: End If
9:End Function
```

The function prototype in line 2 requires that two values are passed into the function: first, `TheNumber`, which is the value to be validated, and second, `FieldName`, which is the name of the field being validated.

The keyword `ByVal` instructs the scripting engine to pass only the value of these variables into the function. For more detail on functions and procedures, see Chapter 9, "Making Your Program Flow."

Line 3, where the actual verification takes place, introduces you to a new concept, negation.

Suppose x equals 10. The statement `If x = 10 Then` returns `True`, and the lines following the `If...` statement execute. However, reversing the condition is known as negation; if x is *not* equal to 10, the code lines between the `If` and `End If` execute if you write the statement as `If Not x = 10 Then`. To learn more about `If...Then` conditional statements, see Chapter 9.

Determining whether a series of characters is numeric isn't an easy task if you consider the logic that must be performed. However, VBScript's built-in checking functions include `IsNumeric`. If the entered string can be converted to a number, the function returns `True`; if it cannot be converted, the function returns `False`. Remember that all data coming from an HTML form is string data; for instance, the number 400 appears to the program as `"400"`.

For more details on the `MsgBox` function, see Chapter 3, "Communicating with Your Users."

Lines 4 and 5 execute only if the data entered into the field cannot be converted into a number (such as non-numeric characters). Line 4 displays a message box to the user informing him or her that the entry is invalid; the message box uses an OK button and a Stop icon. The user then has the option to return to the field and retype the entry. Line 5 sets the function's own return value to `False`.

Line 6 is part of the `If...Then...Else` conditional statement. Line 7, which executes only if the `IsNumeric` function returns `True`, sets the function's own return value to `True`.

Lines 8 and 9 finish the `If...Then` statement and end the function, passing execution back to the code that called the function and returning a value of either `True` or `False`.

 ## Validating Date Entries

The function for validating the date in this example is very similar to the numerical validation function:

```
10:Function ValidateDate(ByVal TheDate, ByVal FieldName)
11: If Not IsDate(TheDate) Then
12:   x = MsgBox("Invalid Date",16,FieldName)
13:   ValidateDate = False
14: Else
```

```
15:  ValidateDate = True
16: End If
17:End Function
```

The function prototype in line 10 requires that two values are passed into the function: first, `TheDate`, which is the date entered by the user to be validated, and second, `FieldName`.

Line 11 is where the date verification takes place. To learn more about `If...Then` conditional statements, see Chapter 9.

The `IsDate` function, which is built into the VBScript engine, saves you from writing a huge script to cover all possible combinations that are valid dates—12-Jun-96, 12-June-1996, 12-6-96, 12/06/96, 06/12/96, and so on. The `IsDate` function operates on the user's date setting in the International section of his Windows system. What is a valid date in one country might be invalid in another. Suppose a user in Sweden types the date `96.06.12`, which is a valid date format in Sweden, because his Windows system is set to Swedish date formats. `IsDate` correctly returns `True`. However, this presents a problem when you send the data to the server.

Instead of writing a mammoth server-side script to handle every possible date format in the world, you can restrict the date to a certain format and display it to the user—for example, *mm-dd-yy*. You can then create a script that checks for this rather rigid date format.

Chapter 8, "Adding Date and Time Functions," shows a more flexible alternative that breaks the user's date input into month, day, and year and rearranges it to your desired format.

Lines 12 and 13 execute only if the data entered into the field is not a valid date. Line 14 is part of the `If...Then...Else` conditional statement. Line 15, which executes only if the `IsDate` function returns `True`, sets the function's own return value to `True`.

Lines 16 and 17 finish the `If...Then` statement and end the function, passing execution back to the code that called the function and returning a value of either `True` or `False`.

 # Verifying String Data Entries

Verifying string data can become somewhat complicated because you must decide what the string pattern should look like and hard code that pattern into the script, as the following code shows:

```
18:Function IsEMail(ByVal TheEMail, ByVal FieldName)

19: If InStr(TheEMail, "@") > 2 Then
20:    If Len(TheEMail) - InStr(TheEMail, "@") > 6 Then
21:       If InStr(InStr(TheEMail, "@"),TheEMail,".") > 0 Then
22:          If Len(TheEMail) - InStr(InStr(TheEMail, "@"),TheEMail,".") => 2
```

```
            ➥Then
23:             ValidateEMail = True
24:         Else
25:             ValidateEMail = False
26:         End If
27:     Else
28:         ValidateEMail = False
29:     End If
30:     Else
31:         ValidateEMail = False
32:     End If
33: Else
34:     ValidateEMail = False
35: End If

36: If ValidateEMail = True Then
37:     IsEMail = True
38: Else
39:     x = MsgBox("Invalid Entry",16,FieldName)
40:     IsEMail = False
41:End If

42:End Function
```

The pattern of an e-mail address at minimum should be ***@***.***, where * is alphanumeric. Lines 19 to 22 check for this minimum pattern.

For more details about InStr, Len, and other character-manipulation functions, read Chapter 7, "Manipulating Strings."

Line 19 uses the InStr function to find the @ character somewhere in the string. InStr returns the position of the character if found or 0 if it is not found within the search string. The criteria you set for the first part of the pattern is that the @ character must appear at least three characters in from the left. As a result, the InStr function in line 19 must return at least 3 for the first part of the pattern to be true.

If you want to learn more about If and Then, read Chapter 9.

If the first part succeeds, the second part of the pattern dictates that there must be a minimum of seven characters after the @ symbol. Line 20 tests this condition by subtracting the position of the @ symbol from the length of the overall string, which is found with the Len function.

```
20:     If Len(TheEMail) - InStr(TheEMail, "@") > 6 Then
```

In the minimum pattern, the length of the string is 11 characters, and the @ symbol resides at position 4; therefore, the minimum number of characters to the right of the @ is 7. Line 20 tests for any amount greater than 6.

The next stage is a little more complex. Line 21 determines whether a . (period) appears somewhere after the @ symbol. Notice that the InStr function appears twice in line 21:

```
21:     If InStr(InStr(TheEMail, "@"),TheEMail,".") > 0 Then
```

The full syntax of InStr is

```
InStr(Start,String1,String2)
```

In Line 21, you use the position of the @ symbol to determine where InStr should start its search for the . symbol. If it does find a . symbol somewhere after the @ symbol, the function returns the position of the character, and you can proceed to the final part of the pattern, which is determining whether the . symbol appears at least two characters in from the right. As you know, the e-mail address could be a .com, .edu, .com.bh, .co.uk, and so on.

```
22:        If Len(TheEMail) - InStr(InStr(TheEMail, "@"),TheEMail,".") => 2
           ➥Then
```

Line 22 uses the position of the @, the position of the ., and the overall length of the string to determine how many characters appear after the . symbol. Two or more characters at the end makes the pattern complete and fits our definition of the minimum e-mail address. Of course, as I said earlier, this doesn't stop someone from entering aaa@aaa.aaa.

If the validation of the e-mail address fails at any stage, the variable ValidateEmail is set to False. Finally, the script makes a check of the variable, and if all is well, the function's own return value is set to True. If the data is invalid, the return value is set to False, and a warning message is displayed to the user.

Implementing an OnChange Event

Where were all these functions called? What set them going? When the user enters a new or changed value in one of the text boxes and then moves away from that text box, an OnChange event fires. The following segment shows the event handlers for each of the text boxes, not including the first text box, which is not validated:

```
43:Sub txtQty_OnChange
44: x = ValidateNumber(Document.Form1.txtQty.Value, "Quantity")
45:End Sub

46:Sub txtSize_OnChange
47: x = ValidateNumber(Document.Form1.txtSize.Value, "Size")
48:End Sub

49:Sub txtDate_OnChange
50: x = ValidateDate(Document.Form1.txtDate.Value, "Date")
51:End Sub

52:Sub txtEmail_OnChange
53: x = IsEMail(Document.Form1.txtEmail.Value, "EMail")
54:End Sub
```

I put these event handlers out on their own so that you can read them easily, but it is legal to write the event handler within the HTML definition of the text box in this way:

```
 <INPUT LANGUAGE="vbscript" TYPE=text ONCHANGE=" x = call
ValidateNumber(Document.Form1.txtSize.value,&quot;Size&quot;)"
         NAME="txtSize">
```

In fact, if you create these event handlers within the ActiveX Control Pad, that is exactly the automatic code that the Control Pad creates.

 # Implementing a Validate and Submit Routine

As mentioned in the introduction to the chapter, the main goal of data validation is to reduce the amount of poor data or to eliminate it altogether. What the example accomplishes so far is really a cosmetic exercise in informing the user of the invalidity of his data entry, hoping that this spurs him into action to change the entry. However, the script doesn't guarantee this. The ultimate precaution is to hide the data submission behind a wall of validation. Only after all the validation checks that you specify are completed successfully is the data submitted to the server, as you can see from the following code:

```
55:Sub cmdButton1_OnClick
56:  If ValidateNumber(Document.Form1.txtQty.Value, "Quantity") And _
57:    ValidateDate(Document.Form1.txtDate.Value, "Date") And _
58:    ValidateNumber(Document.Form1.txtSize.Value, "Size") And _
59:    IsEMail(Document.Form1.txtEmail.Value, "EMail") Then
60:      Document.Form1.Submit
61:  Else
62:      Exit Sub
63:  End If
64:End Sub
```

Lines 56 through 59 are actually the same line, joined together at runtime with the special underscore character. All checks must return True for the overall statement to be True. One of the nice things about this method of checking is that each check is carried out regardless of the result of the last. The user receives a prompt for all fields that fail the test.

NOTE: Because you use functions to perform the validation, you can call them from many different places within your script, rather than rewrite the same code over and over.

When the data is in order, line 60 calls the form's submit method and the data is on its way.

Using the `OnSubmit` Event

The ActiveX and VBScript documentation refers to using the `OnSubmit` event to perform data validation in such a way that prevents form submission if the validation fails. However, the documentation does not describe the very odd way in which the `OnSubmit` event must be implemented.

`OnSubmit` is an event and, as such, the code attached to that event should be within an event handler. But the `OnSubmit` event must be used as though it is a function. Here's how you declare the prototype for the `OnSubmit` "event."

```
Function myForm_OnSubmit()
```

This is done so that `OnSubmit` can return a value. `OnSubmit` returns `True` if the form data is validated, in which case the form data is submitted; it returns `False` if the form data fails validation, in which case the form data is not submitted.

Within the `OnSubmit` event handler/function, you can include calls to all your validation routines, as this amendment to the previous example shows:

```
55:Function Form1_OnSubmit
56:  If ValidateNumber(Document.Form1.txtQty.Value, "Quantity") And _
57:    ValidateDate(Document.Form1.txtDate.Value, "Date") And _
58:    ValidateNumber(Document.Form1.txtSize.Value, "Size") And _
59:    IsEMail(Document.Form1.txtEmail.Value, "EMail") Then
60:      Form1_OnSubmit = True
61:  Else
62:      Form1_OnSubmit = False
63:  End If
64:End Sub
```

To use this code with the previous example, you would also have to change the button control type to `Submit`.

Workshop Wrap-Up

In this chapter, you saw that client-side data verification is economical in terms of time and bandwidth. You can use several methods to ensure that data is formatted correctly and to alert users to any problems with their data along the way. Here's a brief summary:

❏ Use the `OnBlur` or `OnChange` events to determine when a user has finished working on one field and moved onto another field—your signal to check the data.

❏ Forcing the cursor back to the field can cause an infinite loop.

❏ Check for a valid numeric value using `IsNumeric`.

❏ Check for a valid date value using `IsDate`.

❏ If you have to check a string for a particular pattern, decide what the rules of that pattern are and how you are going to check for those rules before you start programming.

❏ Always make the submission of data to the server conditional upon successful data validation.

Next Steps

You have just learned how to interactively and programatically validate data and then submit that data to the server. To brush up on your skills to create even more complex validation routines, look at the following chapters:

❏ Chapter 7, "Manipulating Strings," discusses formatting and breaking down strings.

❏ For more information about date and time functions, see Chapter 8, "Adding Date and Time Functions."

❏ When you use `If...Then` conditional statements, consult Chapter 9, "Making Your Program Flow."

Q&A

Q: If I put my validation routines on the client side, isn't it possible for someone to see what could be sensitive information?

A: Yes, and for this reason, you should be careful what you place in a client-side validation routine. For example, don't write a script that says something like `if myform.password.value <> "letmein" then`.... If you do, you've just blown it!

SEVEN

Manipulating Strings

String manipulation is important for data verification and formatting strings to your specifications prior to submitting data to the server. For example, you can ensure that all text strings are uppercase to stay in line with your database design.

VBScript gives you a rich set of functions to help you manipulate strings and characters. All the string functions are very easy to use, which means that you can add complex string checking and formatting to your Web pages in just a few lines of code.

You can also use VBScript's string-manipulation functions to parse a complete string quickly and easily. For example, you can split a phrase such as "This is a string" into its individual words. Using a similar routine, you can search for a particular string within another string, as you saw in the last chapter where you validated an e-mail address by searching for the @ character.

This chapter looks deeper into the syntax of the most widely used string functions. A complete list of string functions is available in Appendix C.

In this chapter, you

- ❏ Learn how to make a string all uppercase or all lowercase
- ❏ Convert strings into ASCII numbers
- ❏ Convert ASCII numbers into strings
- ❏ Determine the length of a string
- ❏ Learn how to return sections of the string
- ❏ Find one string within another

Tasks in this chapter:

- ❏ Making a string all lowercase characters
- ❏ Making a string all uppercase characters
- ❏ Converting ASCII codes to string characters
- ❏ Converting string characters to ASCII codes
- ❏ Finding the length of a string
- ❏ Returning the leftmost characters of a string
- ❏ Returning the rightmost characters of a string
- ❏ Returning any part of a string
- ❏ Finding one string within another

NOTE: The sample in this chapter was designed so that you can add as much or as little of its functionality as you want. First, build the sampler template, and then you can add various sections. You can use each task in this chapter within the sampler template as a stand-alone page if you want. Add the form definitions inside the <TABLE> tags and the subprocedures inside the <SCRIPT> tags.

Constructing the Strings Sampler HTML Template

You can use your favorite HTML editor, Notepad, or even the text editor of the ActiveX Control Pad to write the HTML and script code. This sample doesn't use any ActiveX controls, so you don't need to use the ActiveX Control Pad to produce the script sections. The HTML code for the example document is shown here:

```
<HTML>
<HEAD>
<SCRIPT LANGUAGE="vbscript">

</SCRIPT>
</HEAD>

<BODY BGCOLOR="white">
<CENTER>
<H2>String Manipulation</H2>
<TABLE BORDER=1>

</TABLE>
</CENTER>
</BODY>
</HTML>
```

After you build your template, save it as `strings.htm`. You're ready to start adding some string-manipulation functions.

Making a String All Lowercase Characters

VBScript has two functions for converting a string to either all uppercase or all lowercase letters. Non-alphabetical characters within the string remain untouched. First, look at the function to change the string to lowercase.

Adding the Uppercase and Lowercase Sample Form Definition

The lowercase and uppercase data entry for the sample application is held within the same form. Enter a string in the text box `text1`, and click either the Make Uppercase or Make Lowercase button. The result appears in the Output text box. The HTML code for the sample form is as follows:

```
<FORM NAME="frmUprLwr">
<TR><TD>
Enter a string   <INPUT TYPE="text" NAME="Text1">
</TD><TD>
<INPUT TYPE="button" NAME="MakeLowerCase" VALUE="Lower Case">
<INPUT TYPE="button" NAME="MakeUpperCase" VALUE="Upper Case">
</TD><TD>
<INPUT TYPE="text" NAME="Output">
</TD></TR>
</FORM>
```

  is a non-breaking space that is used to force a space character into the HTML.

Adding the Lowercase Conversion Procedure

To convert a string to lowercase, you use the LCase function. LCase takes only one variable—the string that you want to convert. LCase returns a string of lowercase characters. Only the characters A to Z are converted; all other characters (such as @, !, <, and so on) remain in their normal state.

Line numbers are shown for the purpose of explanation and should not be included within the final code.

Enter the following event handler for the MakeLowerCase button's OnClick event in the <SCRIPT> tags of the sampler template:

```
2:  Sub MakeLowerCase_OnClick
3:     Document.frmUprLwr.Output.Value = LCase(Document.frmUprLwr.Text1.Value)
4:  End Sub
```

Making a String All Uppercase Characters

Conversion to uppercase or lowercase is useful if you have to check a particular alphabetical-character word or even a phrase that the user entered. Suppose you have a text box that enables the user to enter a word such as "Admin." You check to see whether the word was entered in order to invoke a further process, but here's your problem: Did the user type "Admin," "admin," or even "AdMiN"? Character strings are literal and "AdMiN" does not equal "admin." A solution is to convert the string entered by the user to an uppercase "ADMIN" and then check to see whether it matches "ADMIN."

This procedure takes its input from the form used in the lowercase example.

Adding the Uppercase Procedure

The VBScript function for converting a string to uppercase is UCase, and it takes just one variable, the string you want to convert. To add uppercase conversion functionality to the sampler, enter the following event handler for the MakeUpperCase button's OnClick event in the <SCRIPT> tags of the sampler template:

```
5:  Sub MakeUpperCase_OnClick
6:   Document.frmUprLwr.Output.Value = UCase(Document.frmUprLwr.Text1.Value)
7:  End Sub
```

Converting ASCII Codes to String Characters

The American Standard Code for Information Interchange (ASCII) seven-bit character set represents letters and symbols found on a standard U.S. keyboard. The ASCII character set is the same as the first 128 characters (0–127) in the ANSI character set.

The American National Standards Institute (ANSI) eight-bit character set, which is used by Microsoft Windows, enables you to represent up to 256 characters (0–255). The first 128 characters (0–127) correspond to the letters and symbols on a standard U.S. keyboard. The second 128 characters (128–255) represent special characters, such as letters in international alphabets, currency symbols, and fractions.

ASCII and ANSI codes are the means by which the computer stores alphabetical and other characters by converting the character to a number, as detailed previously. You can access these numbers to perform special string manipulations. For example, you can simulate the UCase and LCase functions by performing a simple calculation on the individual string characters. (Uppercase characters are always the lowercase character's ASCII code minus 32.) You also can create simple encryption methods by subjecting each character in the string to a calculation.

With the many built-in string-manipulation functions available to you in VBScript, the usefulness of having direct access to ASCII/ANSI codes is starting to diminish. To demonstrate the codes and their string representations, the following sample page automatically prints every character in the set from 32 to 255:

```
<HTML>
<SCRIPT LANGUAGE="vbscript">
Document.Write "<BODY BGCOLOR='white'>"
For x = 32 to 255
 Document.Write CStr(x) & " " & Chr(x) & "<BR>"
next
Document.Write "</BODY>"
</SCRIPT>
</HTML>
```

The ANSI/ASCII characters from 0 to 32 are either system calls, nondisplaying characters, or nonsupported characters. The most common use for the lower numbers are codes 10 and 13, which correspond to the line feed and carriage return. Note that several Windows controls, such as the message box, can display true carriage returns only by embedding a line feed followed by a carriage return, as in the following example:

```
<HTML>
<HEAD>
 <SCRIPT LANGUAGE="vbscript">
  Sub ShowMessage_OnClick
   Dim strMessage
   Dim CRLF
    CRLF = Chr(10) & Chr(13)
    strMessage = "This is the first line" & CRLF
    strMessage = strMessage & "This is the second line"
    x = MsgBox(strMessage,0,"My Message")
  End Sub
 </SCRIPT>
</HEAD>

<BODY BGCOLOR="white">
<CENTER>
<INPUT TYPE="button" NAME="ShowMessage" VALUE="Click Me">
</CENTER>
</BODY>
</HTML>
```

Adding the ASCII-to-String Form to the Sample

Enter the following HTML form to the sample template within the <TABLE> tags:

```
<FORM NAME="frmAscChr">
<TR><TD>
Enter a Number   <INPUT TYPE="text" NAME="Text1" SIZE=10>
</TD><TD>
<INPUT TYPE="button" NAME="MakeString" VALUE="Convert to a String">
</TD><TD>
<INPUT TYPE="text" NAME="Output">
</TD></TR>
</FORM>
```

The conversion function from ASCII code to string, Chr(), takes only one variable, the ASCII code, which must be a number.

First, the procedure checks to ensure that the value entered in the text1 text box can be converted to a number. If it cannot, a warning message displays to the user and the subroutine terminates. This verification is usually not necessary because, most of the time, you generate the ASCII code from within the script, rather than obtaining it from a form input.

For more details about verification and the IsNumeric function, see Chapter 6, "Checking Form Data."

If the verification is successful, a second check makes sure the number is within ASCII limits. Here, I've restricted the lower limit to 32 because some of the lower numbers are used for system functions such as beeping.

Finally, the conversion itself takes place. Because an HTML form can return only string data, the value contained in Text1 must be converted to an integer prior to being used as an ASCII code. Without this conversion, a Type Mismatch runtime error occurs. The following code shows how to validate the entry and convert the value within MakeString's OnClick event:

```
8:  Sub MakeString_OnClick
9:   If Not IsNumeric(Document.frmAscChr.Text1.Value) Then
10:    Alert "Only Numbers are allowed"
11:    Exit Sub
12:   End if

13:   If CInt(Document.frmAscChr.Text1.Value) > 255 OR _
14:    CInt(Document.frmAscChr.Text1.Value) < 32 Then
15:    Alert "Must be between 32 and 255"
16:    Exit Sub
17:   End If

18:   Document.frmAscChr.Output.Value =
         ➥Chr(CInt(Document.frmAscChr.Text1.Value))
19:  End Sub
```

Add the preceding subroutine to your sample HTML template between the `<SCRIPT>` tags.

Converting String Characters to ASCII Codes

For finding the numeric representation of a character in the ANSI/ASCII character set, VBScript provides the `Asc()` function, which is the reverse of the `Chr()` function.

Adding the String-to-ASCII Form to the Sample

Simply add the following lines of HTML between the `<TABLE>` tags to include the form that calls the sample event handler:

```
<FORM NAME="frmChrAsc">
<TR><TD>
Enter a Character   <INPUT TYPE="text" NAME="Text1" SIZE=10>
</TD><TD>
<INPUT TYPE="button" NAME="MakeNumber" VALUE="Convert to a Number">
</TD><TD>
<INPUT TYPE="text" NAME="Output">
</TD></TR>
</FORM>
```

Converting from string data to ASCII code couldn't be much simpler; the `Asc()` function accepts a string character and returns the ASCII code. You can give the function a full string such as `"What Is This"`; however, it converts only the first character of the string to an ASCII code.

The data retrieved from an HTML form is always string data (even if the user has typed in a number), and the function accepts string data, so there is not much point in verifying that which cannot be wrong! That's why the procedure is a simple one-liner.

When data is passed from an HTML form, it is always in the form of a string. Therefore, a numeric entry such as `100` appears to your script as the string `"100"`.

Type the following lines between the `<SCRIPT>` tags of the template, and you've got instant ASCII convertibility:

```
20:  Sub MakeNumber_OnClick
21:   Document.frmChrAsc.Output.Value = Asc(Document.frmChrAsc.Text1.Value)
22:  End Sub
```

 # Finding the Length of a String

Determining the length of a string is seldom very useful on its own. However, when you combine this function with the other string-manipulation functions, you can perform almost any string formatting and checking you might need and exercise real power over your character strings. (See Listing 7.1.) In fact, many string operations wouldn't even be possible without determining the length of the string or the length of part of a string.

Listing 7.1. Adding the form to the sample page.

```
<FORM NAME="frmLen">
<TR><TD>
Enter a String   <INPUT TYPE="text" NAME="Text1">
</TD><TD>
<INPUT TYPE="button" NAME="GetLength" VALUE="Find String Length">
</TD><TD>
<INPUT TYPE="text" NAME="Output">
</TD></TR>
</FORM>
```

Adding the Length Procedure to the Sample Page

You determine the length of a string using the VBScript Len() function, which receives one variable: the string to be sized. Len returns an integer that is the number of characters in the string.

No data-type checking is involved in this particular procedure, so you can add it as you use it within a script:

```
23:  Sub GetLength_OnClick
24:   Document.frmLen.Output.Value = Len(Document.frmLen.Text1.Value)
25:  End Sub
```

NOTE: The length of a string includes any leading or trailing spaces that the user entered. For example, if you enter "   string   " (four spaces, six characters, and four spaces without the quotation marks) into the text box, the Len() function returns 13. To clear leading spaces, use LTrim(*string*); to clear trailing spaces, use RTrim(*string*). To clear both leading and trailing spaces, use Trim(*string*) as follows:

```
newstring = LTrim(oldstring)
newstring = RTrim(oldstring)
newstring = Trim(oldstring)
```

Returning the Leftmost Characters of a String

Being able to access particular parts of a string is an important part of string manipulation. Take a look at the function that returns a given number of characters starting with the leftmost character.

Adding the Left Procedure Form to the Sample Page

The following code segment shows the HTML code that you can add between the <TABLE> tags on the sampler page to use the left function example:

```
<FORM NAME="frmLeft">
<TR><TD>
Enter a String   <INPUT TYPE="text" NAME="Text1">
</TD><TD>
x<INPUT TYPE="text" NAME="LeftChars" SIZE=10>
<INPUT TYPE="button" NAME="GetLeft" VALUE="Get Left x Chars">
</TD><TD>
<INPUT TYPE="text" NAME="Output">
</TD></TR>
</FORM>
```

To return the leftmost character or characters of a string, use the Left() function. The syntax for using the Left function is

```
strVariable = Left(SourceString, n)
```

n is the number of characters from the leftmost character you need to return. See the previous note regarding leading spaces in the string, because they can seriously affect the resulting string, giving you unpredictable results.

The number of left characters you specify cannot be a negative number. If the number specified is greater than the length of the string, the whole string is returned.

The following code shows the Left() function at work in the sample application. Add this code between the <SCRIPT> tags of your strings sampler:

```
26:  Sub GetLeft_OnClick
27:   If Not IsNumeric(Document.frmLeft.LeftChars.Value) Then
28:    Alert "Only Numbers are allowed in the x Box"
29:    Exit Sub
30:   Else
31:    intNoLeft = CInt(Document.frmLeft.LeftChars.Value)
32:   End if

33:   If intNoLeft < 0 Then
34:    Alert "You cannot use a negative value"
35:    Exit Sub
36:   End if
```

```
37:   Document.frmLeft.Output.Value = Left(Document.frmLeft.Text1.Value,
➥intNoLeft)
```

```
38:   End Sub
```

The procedure first validates that the entry is numeric; if it is, the entry is then converted to an integer. The integer is checked to ensure that it is positive or 0. The result of the Left function is displayed in the form's Output text box.

Returning the Rightmost Characters of a String

To complement the Left function, Microsoft also provides you with a Right() function, which returns the rightmost *n* characters of a string.

Adding the Right Procedure Form to the Sample Page

The following code segment shows the HTML code that you can add between the <TABLE> tags on the sampler page to use the Right function example:

```
<FORM NAME="frmRight">
<TR><TD>
Enter a String   <INPUT TYPE="text" NAME="Text1">
</TD><TD>
x<INPUT TYPE="text" NAME="RightChars" SIZE=10>
<INPUT TYPE="button" NAME="GetRight" VALUE="Get Right x Chars">
</TD><TD>
<INPUT TYPE="text" NAME="Output">
</TD></TR>
</FORM>
```

To return the rightmost character or characters of a string, use the Right() function. The syntax for using the Right function is

```
strVariable = Right(SourceString, n)
```

n is the number of characters up to the rightmost character you want to return. See the previous note regarding leading spaces in the string, because they can seriously affect the resulting string, giving you unpredictable results. *n* cannot be a negative number. If the number specified is greater than the length of the string, the whole string is returned.

The following code shows the Right() function in the sample application. Add this code between the <SCRIPT> tags of your strings sampler:

```
39:  Sub GetRight_OnClick
40:   If Not IsNumeric(Document.frmRight.RightChars.Value) Then
41:    Alert "Only Numbers are allowed in the x Box"
42:    Exit Sub
```

```
43:    Else
44:      intNoRight = CInt(Document.frmRight.RightChars.Value)
45:    End if

46:    If intNoRight < 0 Then
47:      Alert "You cannot use a negative value"
48:      Exit Sub
49:    End if

50:    Document.frmRight.Output.Value = Right(Document.frmRight.Text1.Value,
       ➥intNoRight)
51:  End Sub
```

TASK

Returning Any Part of a String

You saw how to return the right section of a string and how to return the left section of a string, but what about a section of the string that sits somewhere in the middle?

Microsoft thought about that one, too. The function is called `Mid()`, and you can have some serious fun with it. If you use `Mid()` in conjunction with the other string-manipulation functions such as `Len()` and `InStr()` (which you'll see later in this chapter), you can even build a mini parsing tool.

Adding the `Mid` Form to the Sampler Page

Parsing is the art of chopping up a string into useful bits. For another example of using `InStr()`, see Chapter 6, "Checking Form Data."

Add the following code between the `<TABLE>` tags in the sampler template:

```
<FORM NAME="frmMid">
<TR><TD>
Enter String   <INPUT TYPE="text" NAME="Text1"><BR>
Enter Mid String Length   <INPUT TYPE="text" NAME="Text2" SIZE=6>
</TD><TD>
Start at   <INPUT TYPE="text" NAME="MidChars" SIZE=6>
<INPUT TYPE="button" NAME="GetMid" VALUE="Get Mid String">
</TD><TD>
<INPUT TYPE="text" NAME="Output">
</TD></TR>
</FORM>
```

The `Mid()` function has two different syntaxes. The first is

```
strVariable = Mid(SourceString, intStart)
```

This first syntax returns a string starting with the character located at `intStart` and ending with the last character of the string. This method is similar to using `Right()`; the subtle difference is that you can use `Mid()` without knowing how many characters come after the start character position.

The second syntax is

```
strVariable = Mid(SourceString, intStart, intLength)
```

The second syntax returns a string of length `intLength` starting with the character located at `intStart`. Both `intStart` and `intLength` can be other scripted manipulation functions. In both syntax cases, `intStart` cannot be less than 1.

To demonstrate `Mid()`, type the following code (without the line numbers) between the `<SCRIPT>` tags in the strings sampler page:

```
52:    Sub GetMid_OnClick

53:      If Not IsNumeric(Document.frmMid.MidChars.Value) OR _
54:        Not IsNumeric(Document.frmMid.Text2.Value)Then
55:       Alert "Only Numbers are allowed"
56:       Exit Sub
57:      Else
58:       intStart = CInt(Document.frmMid.MidChars.Value)
59:       intMidStrLen = CInt(Document.frmMid.Text2.Value)
60:      End if

61:      If intStart > Len(Document.frmMid.Text1.Value) OR intStart < 1 Then
62:        Alert "Start Number must be less than the string length and greater
           ➥than 0"
63:        Exit Sub
64:      End if

65:      strSource = Document.frmMid.Text1.Value

66:      Document.frmMid.Output.Value = Mid(strSource, intStart, intMidStrLen)

67:    End Sub
```

Finding One String Within Another

Suppose that you need to know whether a string contains a given character or series of characters and, if it does, where in the string the character or string of characters begins. This is probably the most common string-manipulation problem on the face of the earth. "I know it's probably in there, but it might not be; if it isn't, it should be, and if it is, I want it on its own."

VBScript's `Instr()` function comes to the rescue. `Instr()` finds one string within another string and tells you where the string is located. You can also tell `Instr` where to start looking, which is a particularly important feature. Suppose that you have a fairly long string that might contain several instances of the string you're looking for. If you couldn't tell `Instr` where to start looking, you'd find only the first instance, but by giving `Instr` a starting point, you can find the first instance, jump past it to find the second, and so on.

Adding the String Search Form to the Sampler Page

Include the following HTML code in the sampler page table to try the string search function:

```
<FORM NAME="frmInStr">
<TR><TD>
Enter Source String   <INPUT TYPE="text" NAME="Text1"><BR>
Enter Search String   <INPUT TYPE="text" NAME="Text2" SIZE=10>
</TD><TD>
Start at   <INPUT TYPE="text" NAME="StartChars" SIZE=6>
<INPUT TYPE="button" NAME="GetInStr" VALUE="Find String">
</TD><TD>
<INPUT TYPE="text" NAME="Output">
</TD></TR>
</FORM>
```

InStr() takes three variables and returns a string. The syntax for InStr() follows:

```
strVariable = InStr(intStart, strSource, strSearch)
```

The starting position for the search (intStart) cannot be less than 1 or greater than the length of the string. If InStr finds the search string within the source string, it returns the starting position of the string. If it doesn't find the string, it returns zero.

To try InStr, add the following code to your sampler application. Enter a string, a search string, and the starting position for the search.

```
68:  Sub GetinStr_OnClick

69:    If Not IsNumeric(Document.frmInStr.StartChars.Value) Then
70:     Alert "Start must be numeric"
71:     Exit Sub
72:    Else
73:     intStart = CInt(Document.frmInStr.StartChars.Value)
74:    End if

75:    If intStart > Len(Document.frmInStr.Text1.Value) OR intStart < 1 Then
76:     Alert "Start Number must be less than the string length and greater
         ➥than 0"
77:     Exit Sub
78:    End if

79:    strSource = Document.frmInStr.Text1.Value
80:    strSearch = Document.frmInStr.Text2.Value

81:    Document.frmInStr.Output.Value = InStr(intStart, strSource, strSearch)

82:  End Sub
```

The Completed String-Manipulation Sampler

Figure 7.1 shows what the final string-manipulation sampler pages look like in the browser.

Figure 7.1.

The string-manipulation sampler.

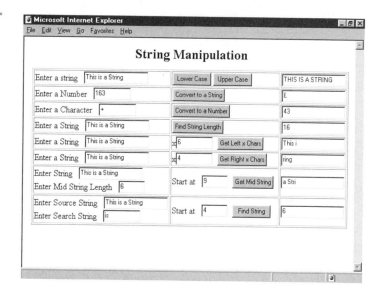

Listing 7.2 contains the complete source code for the page.

Listing 7.2. The `strings.htm` code.

```
<HTML>
<HEAD>
1:  <SCRIPT LANGUAGE="vbscript">
2:  Sub MakeLowerCase_OnClick
3:    Document.frmUprLwr.Output.Value = LCase(Document.frmUprLwr.Text1.Value)
4:  End Sub

5:  Sub MakeUpperCase_OnClick
6:    Document.frmUprLwr.Output.Value = UCase(Document.frmUprLwr.Text1.Value)
7:  End Sub

8:  Sub MakeString_OnClick
9:    If Not IsNumeric(Document.frmAscChr.Text1.Value) Then
10:     Alert "Only Numbers are allowed"
11:     Exit Sub
12:   End if

13:   If CInt(Document.frmAscChr.Text1.Value) > 255 OR _
14:   CInt(Document.frmAscChr.Text1.Value) < 20 Then
15:     Alert "Must be between 20 and 255"
16:     Exit Sub
17:   End If

18:   Document.frmAscChr.Output.Value =
      ➥Chr(CInt(Document.frmAscChr.Text1.Value))
19:   End Sub

20:  Sub MakeNumber_OnClick
21:    Document.frmChrAsc.Output.Value = Asc(Document.frmChrAsc.Text1.Value)
22:  End Sub
```

continues

Listing 7.2. continued

```
23:  Sub GetLength_OnClick
24:    Document.frmLen.Output.Value = Len(Document.frmLen.Text1.Value)
25:  End Sub

26:  Sub GetLeft_OnClick
27:   If Not IsNumeric(Document.frmLeft.LeftChars.Value) Then
28:     Alert "Only Numbers are allowed in the x Box"
29:     Exit Sub
30:   Else
31:     intNoLeft = Cint(Document.frmLeft.LeftChars.Value)
32:   End if

33:    If intNoLeft < 0 Then
34:      Alert "You cannot use a negative value"
35:      Exit Sub
36:    End if

37:    Document.frmLeft.Output.Value = Left(Document.frmLeft.Text1.Value,
    ➡intNoLeft)

38:  End Sub

39:  Sub GetRight_OnClick
40:   If Not IsNumeric(Document.frmRight.RightChars.Value) Then
41:     Alert "Only Numbers are allowed in the x Box"
42:     Exit Sub
43:   Else
44:     intNoRight = CInt(Document.frmRight.RightChars.Value)
45:   End if

46:    If intNoRight < 0 Then
47:      Alert "You cannot use a negative value"
48:      Exit Sub
49:    End if

50:    Document.frmRight.Output.Value = Right(Document.frmRight.Text1.Value,
➡intNoRight)
51:  End Sub

52:   Sub GetMid_OnClick

53:    If Not IsNumeric(Document.frmMid.MidChars.Value) OR _
54:       Not IsNumeric(Document.frmMid.Text2.Value)Then
55:     Alert "Only Numbers are allowed"
56:     Exit Sub
57:    Else
58:     intStart = CInt(Document.frmMid.MidChars.Value)
59:     intMidStrLen = CInt(Document.frmMid.Text2.Value)
60:    End if

61:    If intStart > Len(Document.frmMid.Text1.Value) OR intStart < 1 Then
62:      Alert "Start Number must be less than the string length and
         ➡greater than 0"
63:      Exit Sub
64:    End if

65:    strSource = Document.frmMid.Text1.Value
```

```
66:    Document.frmMid.Output.Value = Mid(strSource, intStart, intMidStrLen)

67:    End Sub

68:    Sub GetinStr_OnClick

69:    If Not IsNumeric(Document.frmInStr.StartChars.Value) Then
70:     Alert "Start must be numeric"
71:     Exit Sub
72:    Else
73:     intStart = CInt(Document.frmInStr.StartChars.Value)
74:    End if

75:    If intStart > Len(Document.frmInStr.Text1.Value) OR intStart < 1 Then
76:      Alert "Start Number must be less than the string length and
          ➥greater than 0"
77:      Exit Sub
78:    End if

79:    strSource = Document.frmInStr.Text1.Value
80:    strSearch = Document.frmInStr.Text2.Value

81:    Document.frmInStr.Output.Value = InStr(intStart, strSource, strSearch)

82:    End Sub

83: </SCRIPT>
</HEAD>

<BODY BGCOLOR="white">
<CENTER>
<H2>String Manipulation</H2>
<TABLE BORDER=1>

<FORM NAME="frmUprLwr">
<TR><TD>
Enter a string   <INPUT TYPE="text" NAME="Text1">
</TD><TD>
<INPUT TYPE="button" NAME="MakeLowerCase" VALUE="Lower Case">
<INPUT TYPE="button" NAME="MakeUpperCase" VALUE="Upper Case">
</TD><TD>
<INPUT TYPE="text" NAME="Output">
</TR>
</FORM>

<FORM NAME="frmAscChr">
<TR><TD>
Enter a Number   <INPUT TYPE="text" NAME="Text1" SIZE=10>
</TD><TD>
<INPUT TYPE="button" NAME="MakeString" VALUE="Convert to a String">
</TD><TD>
<INPUT TYPE="text" NAME="Output">
</TD></TR>
</FORM>

<FORM NAME="frmChrAsc">
<TR><TD>
Enter a Character   <INPUT TYPE="text" NAME="Text1" SIZE=10>
</TD><TD>
```

continues

Listing 7.2. continued

```
<INPUT TYPE="button" NAME="MakeNumber" VALUE="Convert to a Number">
</TD><TD>
<INPUT TYPE="text" NAME="Output">
</TD></TR>
</FORM>

<FORM NAME="frmLen">
<TR><TD>
Enter a String   <INPUT TYPE="text" NAME="Text1">
</TD><TD>
<INPUT TYPE="button" NAME="GetLength" VALUE="Find String Length">
</TD><TD>
<INPUT TYPE="text" NAME="Output">
</TD></TR>
</FORM>

<FORM NAME="frmLeft">
<TR><TD>
Enter a String   <INPUT TYPE="text" NAME="Text1">
</TD><TD>
x<INPUT TYPE="text" NAME="LeftChars" SIZE=10>
<INPUT TYPE="button" NAME="GetLeft" VALUE="Get Left x Chars">
</TD><TD>
<INPUT TYPE="text" NAME="Output">
</TD></TR>
</FORM>

<FORM NAME="frmRight">
<TR><TD>
Enter a String   <INPUT TYPE="text" NAME="Text1">
</TD><TD>
x<INPUT TYPE="text" NAME="RightChars" SIZE=10>
<INPUT TYPE="button" NAME="GetRight" VALUE="Get Right x Chars">
</TD><TD>
<INPUT TYPE="text" NAME="Output">
</TD></TR>
</FORM>

<FORM NAME="frmMid">
<TR><TD>
Enter String   <INPUT TYPE="text" NAME="Text1"><BR>
Enter Mid String Length   <INPUT TYPE="text" NAME="Text2" SIZE=6>
</TD><TD>
Start at   <INPUT TYPE="text" NAME="MidChars" SIZE=6>
<INPUT TYPE="button" NAME="GetMid" VALUE="Get Mid String">
</TD><TD>
<INPUT TYPE="text" NAME="Output">
</TD></TR>
</FORM>

<FORM NAME="frmInStr">
<TR><TD>
Enter Source String   <INPUT TYPE="text" NAME="Text1"><BR>
Enter Search String   <INPUT TYPE="text" NAME="Text2" SIZE=10>
</TD><TD>
Start at   <INPUT TYPE="text" NAME="StartChars" SIZE=6>
<INPUT TYPE="button" NAME="GetInStr" VALUE="Find String">
</TD><TD>
```

```
<INPUT TYPE="text" NAME="Output">
</TD></TR>
</FORM>

</TABLE>
</BODY>
</HTML>
```

Workshop Wrap-Up

In this chapter, you saw all the major string-manipulation functions at work and built a sampler page that will prove useful for experimenting with your own applications.

The following list outlines a summary of the string functions you saw in this chapter:

❑ To convert a string to all uppercase characters, use `UCase("String")`.

❑ To convert a string to all lowercase characters, use `LCase("String")`.

❑ To convert from ASCII codes to strings, use `Chr(x)`.

❑ To convert from strings to ASCII codes, use `Asc("String")`.

❑ To return the leftmost x characters, use `Left("String",x)`.

❑ To return the rightmost x characters, use `Right("String",x)`.

❑ To return any part of the string, use `Mid("String",Start,Length)`.

❑ To find one string within another, use `InStr(Start,"Source","Search")`.

❑ To remove leading spaces, use `LTrim("String")`.

❑ To remove trailing spaces, use `RTrim("String")`.

❑ To remove leading and trailing spaces at the same time, use `Trim("String")`.

Next Steps

Now that you've seen some fairly advanced and sophisticated techniques for manipulating string values, have a look at the following chapters:

❑ To learn more about using strings with arrays, see Chapter 10, "Using the Power of Arrays."

❑ Chapter 19, "Baking Cookies with VBScript," discusses using string manipulation within a cookie file.

Q&A

Q: Is there a built-in VBScript function that can be used to format strings in a certain way, like the Visual Basic Format() function?

A: Unfortunately, due to size constraints, Microsoft left the Format() function out of the first release of VBScript. However, using a combination of the techniques you have seen in this chapter, you can replicate the functionality of Format(). It is rumored that later releases of VBScript will include a scaled-down version of Format().

EIGHT
Adding Date and Time Functions

Times and dates were invented for client-side processing; the ancient scholars and monks must have had Web browsers in the back of their minds—forward-thinking guys!

Every client computer contains several variables that tell the computer what time it is and what the date is. In DOS, it's as easy as `c:>date`. (For those of you too young to remember DOS, it means disk operating system, something we used regularly in the old days.)

If it's so easy to learn the computer's time and date variables, why did I spend hours writing a program that acquires the domain of the client requesting a Web page (such as `.bh` for Bahrain), dips into a database to find out how many hours they are ahead or behind GMT, adds this to the time at the server, and then decides whether it is morning, afternoon, or evening where the client is? That kind of program was necessary because until the advent of client-side scripting, you had no way to access the date and time variables on the client computer. HTML just doesn't have a tag for time or date.

Dates and times are ideal for creating semi-personalized and variable Web pages, and they include some of the variables you can actually obtain from the client machine. (No doubt some lobby group will make a proposal to ban this because it impinges on privacy.) You could even take this concept further and make an almost completely different page based on the time of day. Get your imagination around that one!

In this chapter, you

- ❏ Find the time on the client's computer
- ❏ Perform calculations on dates and times
- ❏ Split up the date variable
- ❏ Learn about the built-in VBScript time and date functions
- ❏ Use the `LastModified` document property
- ❏ Build a Web page that automatically welcomes the user based on the time of day
- ❏ Build a Web page that automatically highlights new items

Tasks in this chapter:

- ❏ Accessing the client's date and time variables
- ❏ Welcoming users in their own time zones
- ❏ Rearranging the date
- ❏ Calculating with dates and times
- ❏ Using the date last modified variable
- ❏ Automating What's New

Accessing the Client's Date and Time Variables

First, take a look at how you access the time and date variables that are held in the client's computer. As with everything in VBScript, the function names are easy and logical. To grab the date and use it in your script, you write the following:

```
myDate = Date()
```

To access the client's time, use

```
myLawyer = Time()
```

To get both date and time in one variable, use

```
myVariable = Now()
```

The functions do not take any variables and therefore the parentheses, which must be there because these are functions, remain empty.

What do these three variables return? It depends upon your window settings. All three functions are formatted based upon the date, time, and international settings of your window system. The easiest way to see what they return and how to use them is to try them.

Listing 8.1 contains a quick HTML page that contains three buttons: one for displaying the time, one for the date, and one for both. You can find it on the CD-ROM.

Listing 8.1. The `datetime.htm` code.

```
<HTML>
 <HEAD>
  <SCRIPT LANGUAGE="vbscript">
   Sub DoTime_OnClick
    Document.Form1.Output.Value = Time()
   End Sub

   Sub DoDate_OnClick
    Document.Form1.Output.Value = Date()
   End Sub

   Sub DoNow_OnClick
    Document.Form1.Output.Value = Now()
   End Sub
  </SCRIPT>
 </HEAD>

<BODY BGCOLOR="white">
<CENTER>
<FORM NAME="Form1">
<INPUT TYPE="button" NAME="DoTime" Value="Show the current Time"><P>
<INPUT TYPE="button" NAME="DoDate" Value="Show the current Date"><P>
```

```
<INPUT TYPE="button" NAME="DoNow" Value="Show both Date and Time"><P>
<INPUT TYPE="text" NAME="Output">
</FORM>
</CENTER>
</BODY>
</HTML>
```

Figure 8.1 shows what Listing 8.1 looks like with the browser.

Figure 8.1.

The date and time example.

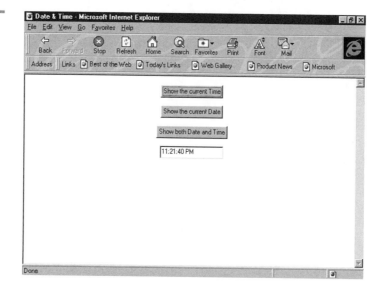

NOTE: The computer stores the complete date and time as a double-precision number. The whole number part represents the date from 1/1/100 to 31/12/9999. 1/1/1900 is represented by the number 2. The fractional part of the number represents the time. 12:00 noon is .5.

 # Welcoming Users in Their Own Time Zones

How do you usually welcome someone to a Web site? "Hello" and "Welcome to my Web site" are very general greetings. They have to be general if you don't know what part of the day the user is in. This is the age of the interactive personalized Web page, right? Shouldn't you say, "Good morning," "Good afternoon," and "Good evening"?

As I said at the beginning of this chapter, it is possible to write a server-side script that roughly determines the time where the user is, but it is not recommended. VBScript gives you more time and date functionality than a Rolex watch, so put away your sundial and look at the sample welcome page in Figure 8.2.

Figure 8.2.
Welcoming your Web page visitor.

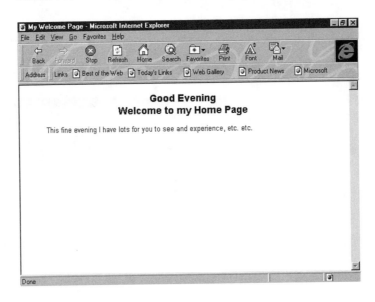

How is it done? This welcome page uses the `Hour()` function within VBScript. Unlike the `Now()` and `Time()` functions in Windows 95 that return a 12-hour clock format, `Hour()` always returns the hour in 24-hour format. You need only to check whether the hour is before 12 (morning), between 12 and 18 (afternoon), or after 18 (evening). The result is printed on the Web page using the document's `write` method.

Creating the Welcome Page HTML Template

Using your favorite HTML editor or Notepad, create the following HTML Web page template and save it as `timeofday.htm`:

```
<HTML>
<HEAD>
 <TITLE>My Welcome Page</TITLE>
 <SCRIPT LANGUAGE="vbscript">
  <!--TIME OF DAY FUNCTION GOES HERE -->
 </SCRIPT>
</HEAD>
<BODY BGCOLOR="White">
<FONT FACE="arial" SIZE=2>
<CENTER>
<H3>

<!-- CUSTOM HEADING GOES HERE -->

<BR>
Welcome to my Home Page
```

```
</H3>
</CENTER>
<P>
<BLOCKQUOTE>
This fine
<!--CUSTOM TIME OF DAY GOES HERE-->
I have lots for you to see and experience, etc. etc.
</BODY>
</HTML>
```

Creating the Time of Day Function

Now edit the file, adding the following function to the <SCRIPT> tags within the <HEAD> section:

```
Function TimeOfDay()
    If Hour(Now()) < 12 Then
       TimeOfDay = "Morning"
    End if

    If Hour(Now()) =>12 AND Hour(Now()) < 18 Then
       TimeOfDay = "Afternoon"
    End if

    If Hour(Now()) => 18 Then
       TimeOfDay = "Evening"
    End if
End Function
```

The TimeOfDay custom function uses the Now() function to pass the current time to the Hour() function. As a result, the Hour() function returns the hour at the time the script runs.

Comparisons on the hour value determine whether it is morning, afternoon, or evening, according to the definitions mentioned earlier. You could optimize the previous code by copying the hour value into a variable first and then using that variable within the If.....Then comparisons.

Now you need some code within the body of the HTML file that calls the TimeOfDay function when necessary.

Adding the Function Calls to the HTML Page

In the comment section marked Custom heading goes here, type the following short script:

```
<SCRIPT LANGUAGE="vbscript">
Document.Write "Good " & TimeOfDay()
</SCRIPT>
```

This script contains no function or subdefinition, which means that the script executes as the file is loaded into the browser. In other words, as the browser reaches this section, it executes the script code.

This code calls the `Write` method, passing to it the word `"Good"` and the result of the `TimeOfDay()` function—either `Morning`, `Afternoon`, or `Evening`. The `Write` method prints onto the HTML page at the next available position.

Having taken care of the heading, you need to add the function call to place the time of day into the paragraph below the headings. Type the following code into the HTML page at the point that says `Custom Time of Day Goes Here`:

```
<SCRIPT LANGUAGE="vbscript">
Document.Write LCase(TimeOfDay())
</SCRIPT>
```

For more information about `LCase` and other string-manipulation functions, see Chapter 7, "Manipulating Strings."

Again, this code executes as the file loads. Notice that this time, to make the word fit in with the rest of the paragraph, the script calls the `LCase` function to convert the result of `TimeOfDay` to all lowercase characters.

Take a look at some other related functions that you can use to dissect the date.

Rearranging the Date

In Chapter 6, "Checking Form Data," you saw how to use the `IsDate()` function to verify that an entry could be translated to a real date. You also saw that this function checks only that the entry is within the limitations of the date format used by the client machine and could be meaningless to you after the date is received at the server. For example, `96.3.1` is a valid date in some countries but could give your database palpitations.

The solution is to first check that the entry is a valid date and then reformat the date to your liking. VBScript has three built-in functions to help you do this:

```
Day()
Month()
Year()
```

The full syntax is

```
variable = Day(datevariable)
variable = Month(datevariable)
variable = Year(datevariable)
```

Regardless of where the user's window format placed the year, month, and day, these three functions return the correct digit. It's a simple task for you to rearrange these digits within a string in the order of your choosing, whether it's the British style of `dd/mm/yy`, the American style of `mm/dd/yy`, or any other combination, for that matter.

Creating the HTML Template for the Date Rearranger

First, create the HTML template with the following code:

```
<HTML>
<HEAD>
<TITLE>Date Re-Arrangement</TITLE>
<SCRIPT LANGUAGE="vbscript">
<!-- Date rearrangement script goes here -->
</SCRIPT>
</HEAD>
<BODY BGCOLOR="white">
<CENTER>

<FORM NAME="Form1">
Enter a date  
<INPUT TYPE="text" NAME="InputDate">
<P>
<INPUT TYPE="button" NAME="ChangeDate" VALUE="Change Date Format">
<P>
<INPUT TYPE="text" NAME="OutputDate">
</FORM>

</CENTER>
</BODY>
</HTML>
```

When it's entered, save the file as `mixdate.htm`.

Adding the Date Rearrangement Function

Unfortunately, unlike Visual Basic and Visual Basic for Applications, the VBScript language does not have a `Format` function.

In the following code that does all the work, I added line numbers to make it easier to follow the description; however, don't add these line numbers to your script:

```
1:Function MixDate(StartDate)
2:  Dim strSeparator
3:  Dim strTheMonth
4:  Dim strTheYear
5:  Dim strTheDay
6:  Dim strFinalDate

7:    strSeparator = "/"

8:    strTheMonth = Month(StartDate)
9:    strTheYear = Year(StartDate)
10:   strTheDay = Day(StartDate)

11:   strFinalDate = strTheDay & strSeparator & _
12:                  strTheMonth & strSeparator & _
13:                  strTheYear

14:   MixDate = strFinalDate

15: End Function
```

Line 1 is the function definition that specifies the name of this custom function and also specifies that it expects to receive a variable when it is called. In this case, the variable is the date value entered by the user.

Lines 2 through 6 define several variables that are used locally during the execution of the function.

Line 7 assigns a forward slash (/) character to the `strSeparator` variable, which separates the day, month, and year in the final format. If you want to receive dates with other types of separators (for example, dashes -), simply edit this line.

The next three lines—8, 9, and 10—are where the work really starts. The variables you created at the beginning of the function are assigned their respective values by calling the built-in `Day()`, `Month()`, and `Year()` functions, which operate on the date value passed in at the start.

NOTE: VBScript has similar functions for splitting the time variables—`Hour()`, `Minute()`, and `Second()`—which can be used in exactly the same way as `Day()`, `Month()`, and `Year()`.

You've now split the date into its three main constituents and defined your own separator for the date. All that remains is sticking the date back together in the order of your choice, using sticky tape, staples, or whatever comes to hand. In this case, lines 11, 12, and 13 concatenate the string into a *day, month, year* format. You could just as easily edit this to be *year, month, day*.

Finally, line 14 copies the reformed date to the return value of the function itself. When the function completes in line 15 and execution is passed back to the code that called it, the reformed date is returned.

You need to add some code that calls the custom function when it is needed.

Adding the Function Call to the Date Rearrangement Page

For this example, the function call comes from the event handler for the `ChangeDate` button. Type the following code into the `<SCRIPT>` tags just above the custom function:

```
Sub ChangeDate_OnClick
  If IsDate(Document.Form1.InputDate.Value) Then
    Document.Form1.OutputDate.Value = MixDate(Document.Form1.InputDate.Value)
  Else
    Alert "Not a valid date format"
  End If
End Sub
```

The first job is to check that the value entered into the text box can in fact be treated as a date. If it can't, a warning message displays and nothing happens.

If the user entered a valid date in the text box, the value is passed to the `MixDate` function. The value that is returned from the `MixDate` function is copied into the `OutputDate` text box.

Remember *not* to re-validate the rearranged date because it could fail on some client machines!

You can now validate date values and also return them to the server in whatever format you need for further processing. All of this processing is done quickly and efficiently at the client, as shown in Figure 8.3.

As you can see from this sample page, `December 12 96` is a valid date, but I doubt it would fit into anyone's date formatting system.

Figure 8.3.

The date rearrangement function at work.

 # Calculating with Dates and Times

What's `1st July 1996` plus 231 days? Or 47 days prior to the `23rd February 1997`? Unless you're a mathematical genius, you probably need to count days on a calendar. Actually, that's what computers are for—and also what the next example is for.

In this example, you build a date calculator, a fairly straightforward application in which you enter a date and then choose whether you want to add or subtract *x* number of days, months, or years to or from the original date. Have fun entering your birth date and finding out when you'll turn 10,000 days old.

Creating the Date Calculator HTML Template

The form contains a text box in which you enter a date. Under the form is a drop-down selection list containing a choice of the operator to use—either plus or minus. Next to this list is a text box in which you enter the date difference and another selection list containing the time period—days, years, or months.

The button starts the whole thing and a text box shows the result—simple! Use the following code for your HTML page:

```
<HTML>
<HEAD>
<TITLE>Date Calculator</TITLE>
<SCRIPT LANGUAGE="vbscript">

</SCRIPT>
</HEAD>

<BODY BGCOLOR="white">
<FONT FACE="arial" SIZE=2>
<CENTER>

<H2>Date Calculator</H2>
<FORM NAME="Form1">
Enter a Date  
<INPUT TYPE="text" NAME="InputDate">
<P>

<SELECT NAME="operation">
<OPTION>Add
<OPTION>Take Away
</SELECT>

<INPUT TYPE="text" NAME="Number" SIZE=6>

<SELECT NAME="period">
<OPTION>Days
<OPTION>Months
<OPTION>Years
</SELECT>

<P>
<INPUT TYPE="button" Name="Calculate" VALUE="Calculate Now">
<P>
Result  
<INPUT TYPE="text" NAME="Result">
</FORM>
</CENTER>

</BODY>
<HTML>
```

After you build your template, save it as `datecalc.htm` and test it in the browser. Yes, I know that it didn't do anything. It's time to add the calculation script.

Adding the Date Calculation Script

Take this one step at a time. First, add the following code under the `<SCRIPT>` tag:

```
Sub Calculate_OnClick

  If Not IsDate(Document.Form1.InputDate.Value) Then
   Alert "This is not a valid date"
   Exit Sub
  End If
```

As you know by now, this subroutine is an event handler for the Calculate command button. This first part of the script ensures that the date you entered is a valid date format. Now, add the second stage:

```
StartDate = Document.Form1.InputDate.Value
StartMonth = Month(StartDate)
StartDay = Day(StartDate)
StartYear = Year(StartDate)
```

You might recognize this section from the date rearrangement example you saw earlier in this chapter; it's pretty much identical. You split the date into its constituent parts. Continue your work by adding the following code:

```
If Document.Form1.operation.SelectedIndex = 1 Then
 Difference = 0 - CInt(Document.Form1.Number.Value)
Else
 Difference = CInt(Document.Form1.Number.Value)
End if
```

You might remember this section (or one like it) from an earlier chapter. Here, you learn which of the options the user (or you) chose from the list. Remember, the first item on the list is always index 0. You know that you placed "Take Away" in the second slot on the list, which is index number 1. If the selectedIndex property is 1, you perform a subtraction. The easiest way to write this section is to always perform an addition. If you really want an addition, use a positive number; if you want to subtract, use a negative number. You change the difference to negative if the user selected Take Away. Now enter the next section:

```
Select Case Document.Form1.period.SelectedIndex
 Case 0
  EndDate = DateSerial(StartYear, StartMonth, StartDay + Difference)
 Case 1
  EndDate = DateSerial(StartYear, StartMonth + Difference, StartDay)
 Case 2
  EndDate = DateSerial(StartYear + Difference, StartMonth, StartDay)
End Select
```

This section performs the actual mathematics and also sticks back together the constituent parts of the date. The Select block saves you from typing umpteen different If...Thens. You can learn more about Select...Case in Chapter 9, "Making Your Program Flow."

This section uses the second selection list—day, month, or year—as its condition. As you saw in the last section, if the user wants to take a number of days away from the starting date, the difference is negative. DateSerial puts the date back together in its correct form, adjusting months and years accordingly so that you don't end up with the 125th of March. Add the following section to the end of your code:

```
 Document.Form1.Result.Value = EndDate

End Sub
```

Copy the result into the result text box and end the subroutine. As your final task, check back through your code. Listing 8.2 shows the complete source code.

Listing 8.2. The `datecalc.htm` code.

```
<HTML>
<HEAD>
<TITLE>Date Calculator</TITLE>
<SCRIPT LANGUAGE="vbscript">
 Sub Calculate_OnClick

 If Not IsDate(Document.Form1.InputDate.Value) Then
  Alert "This is not a valid date"
  Exit Sub
 End if

  StartDate = Document.Form1.InputDate.Value
  StartMonth = Month(StartDate)
  StartDay = Day(StartDate)
  StartYear = Year(StartDate)

  If Document.Form1.operation.SelectedIndex = 1 Then
   Difference = 0 - CInt(Document.Form1.Number.Value)
  Else
   Difference = CInt(Document.Form1.Number.Value)
  End if

  Select Case Document.Form1.period.SelectedIndex
   Case 0
    EndDate = DateSerial(StartYear, StartMonth, StartDay + Difference)
   Case 1
    EndDate = DateSerial(StartYear, StartMonth + Difference, StartDay)
   Case 2
    EndDate = DateSerial(StartYear + Difference, StartMonth, StartDay)
  End Select

  Document.Form1.Result.Value = EndDate

 End Sub

</SCRIPT>
</HEAD>

<BODY BGCOLOR="white">
<FONT FACE="arial" SIZE=2>
<CENTER>

<H2>Date Calculator</H2>
<FORM NAME="Form1">
Enter a Date  
<INPUT TYPE="text" NAME="InputDate">
<P>
<SELECT NAME="operation">
<OPTION>Add
<OPTION>Take Away
</SELECT>
<INPUT TYPE="text" NAME="Number" SIZE=6>
<SELECT NAME="period">
```

```
<OPTION>Days
<OPTION>Months
<OPTION>Years
</SELECT>
<P>
<INPUT TYPE="button" Name="Calculate" VALUE="Calculate Now">
<P>
Result  
<INPUT TYPE="text" NAME="Result">
</FORM>
</CENTER>

</BODY>
<HTML>
```

Save your file and run it with the browser. It should perform as shown in Figure 8.4.

Figure 8.4.

The date calculator sample.

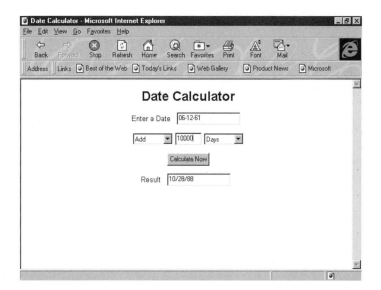

 Using the Date Last Modified Variable

As you surf around the Net, you often see pages that tell you when the page you are looking at was last modified. You might even have some of these yourself. A last modified date is as useful for you, the webmaster, as it is for the site visitor. But you have to hard code the last modified date into your HTML page, and therefore you have to remember to manually update this HTML coded date when you update the page. If you forget to change the date, its usefulness is lost. So, wouldn't it be nice to have a last modified date that updates itself automatically when you amend the page? Well, now you can do this by simply adding this short piece of VBScript to any HTML page and even adding it to your HTML page template. It requires almost no thought and certainly no maintenance on your part.

The document object carries with it the date you last modified the document. It's easy to acquire the document's LastModified property and display it to the world:

```
Document.Write Document.LastModified
```

Listing 8.3 shows a sample page that uses the LastModified property.

Listing 8.3. The `lastmod.htm` code.

```
<HTML>
<HEAD>
<TITLE>Last Updated</TITLE>
</HEAD>
<BODY BGCOLOR="white">
<!--

YOUR PAGE GOES HERE

-->

<FONT FACE="arial" SIZE=1>
<B>
<CENTER>
<SCRIPT LANGUAGE="vbscript">
<!--
  Document.Write "This page was last modified on "
  Document.Write Document.LastModified
-->
</SCRIPT>
</CENTER>
</B>

</BODY>
</HTML>
```

Figure 8.5 shows what Listing 8.3 looks like in the browser.

Place the script at the bottom of your HTML page, and without any further work on your part, this code always shows the day, date, and time that the document was last saved, which is useful for both you and the visitor.

Figure 8.5.

A maintenance-free "last modified" message.

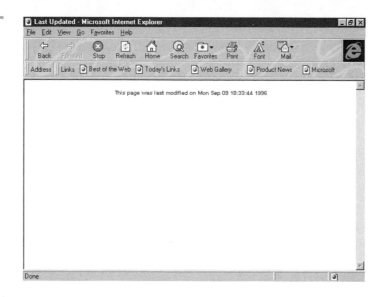

 # Automating What's New

The next example is a really neat way of using client-side processing and VBScript. It saves you time and automatically maintains your page. When you add some feature or modify part of your site, you often stick in a "new" graphic to alert users to the fact that something has changed. Unless you regularly maintain the page, this new graphic can remain there long after its "sell-by" date. We've all seen pages that denote something as new when in fact we saw the same thing several months previously. We'd never do that on our own Web sites—would we?

The following sample application displays the new graphic based on the date at the client machine. All you have to do is supply a sell-by date. After this date is reached, the graphic no longer appears.

Creating the What's New Template

First, create the following HTML template document:

```
<HTML>
<HEAD>
 <TITLE>My NEW Welcome Page</TITLE>
```

```
<SCRIPT LANGUAGE="vbscript">

</SCRIPT>
</HEAD>

<BODY BGCOLOR="White">
<FONT FACE="arial" SIZE=3>

<CENTER>
<H3>
Welcome to my Home Page
</H3>
<P>

<A HREF="">My Links Page</A><P>

<A HREF="">Photos from my last vacation</A><P>

<A HREF="">My Resum&eacute;</A>

</CENTER>
</BODY>
</HTML>
```

Save the template as `whatsnew.htm`, and you're ready to attack the scripting.

Adding the Subroutine to Automatically Insert a "New" Graphic

Place the following subroutine inside the `<SCRIPT>` tags in the `<HEAD>` section:

```
Sub Sellby(LastDate)
   If DateValue(Now()) < DateValue(LastDate) Then
     Document.Write "<IMG SRC=" & Chr(34) & "new.gif" & Chr(34) &
     ➥" ALIGN=MIDDLE>"
   End If
End Sub
```

The `Sellby` subroutine takes one variable, a sell-by date—which is basically the date at which you decide the item is no longer new. The `DateValue` function, which you saw in the previous section, is used here to convert whatever is brought into the subroutine to a date and to place both the value returned by `Now()` and the `LastDate` on a level playing field so that you can compare one with the other.

If the date at the browser is less than (earlier than) the `LastDate` variable, you are still within the new period, so you want to show the `new.gif` graphic.

The `Document.Write` method writes a line of code to the document defining an image tag. Because the string passed to `Document.Write` must be enclosed in quotation marks, you cannot use quotes for the image filename. This line builds in the quotes (ASCII code 34) programmatically using the `Chr()` function. The program actually sees this line as `<IMG SRC="new.gif" ALIGN=MIDDLE>`.

Adding the Calls to the Subroutine

Now you can display a new graphic based upon the date at the browser, but you need a way to call this routine into action. Before each hyperlink, insert the following code:

```
<SCRIPT LANGUAGE="vbscript">
  SellBy ("12 Sept 96")
</SCRIPT>
```

You don't have to stick to a certain date format; just remember that the format you use must be capable of conversion to a date by `DateValue()`. Here's the completed hyperlink section, showing several variations of the date format:

```
<SCRIPT LANGUAGE="vbscript">
  SellBy ("12 Sept 96")
</SCRIPT>
<A HREF="">My Links Page</A><P>

<SCRIPT LANGUAGE="vbscript">
  SellBy ("August 14")
</SCRIPT>
<A HREF="">Photos from my last vacation</A><P>

<SCRIPT LANGUAGE="vbscript">
  SellBy ("10/12/96")
</SCRIPT>
<A HREF="">My Resum&eacute;</A>
```

Figure 8.6 shows what your file looks like when you fire it up in the browser.

Figure 8.6.

The "New!" graphics added automatically—or not.

Workshop Wrap-Up

In this chapter, you saw how to use the built-in date and time functionality of VBScript and the browser with the document's `LastModified` property.

You discovered how easy it is to grab the client's date and time variables and manipulate them. You also saw how quickly you can include the VBScript built-in functions to perform calculations on the time and date variables and reformat any date or time.

Next Steps

Now that you've seen how to use the built-in date and time functionality of VBScript, you can produce all sorts of neat client-side applications. See the following chapters to add further client-side time and date power:

❏ To learn how to check for valid dates, see Chapter 6, "Checking Form Data."

❏ To see another neat way of using date and time functions, read Chapter 19, "Baking Cookies with VBScript."

❏ To learn how to implement a continuous clock on your Web page, see Chapter 23, "Real-Life Examples IV."

Q&A

Q: Visual Basic has many date and time functions and features that save a lot of time and trouble. Are they going to be included in VBScript at some point?

A: Keep a look out for the next release of VBScript, which could be out by the time you read this. It is rumored that additional date and time functions will be included in the next release, although most of the Visual Basic date and time functions can be replicated using the methods shown in this chapter.

Q: How do I save the date when a user last visited my site?

A: The only way that you can store data on the client machine is via the cookie file. For more information on cookies, see Chapter 19.

NINE

Making Your Program Flow

To achieve more than the simplest "Hello World" task in any programming language, you need to get into some real programming. Just as trying to hold a conversation in French knowing only *Bonjour* can be somewhat limiting, programming in VBScript can be difficult knowing only Alert "Hello World".

To write scripts or programs that achieve a goal or provide a solution, you first need to clearly define the task at hand. Because VBScript is a logical and easy-to-use language, you will soon see that the definition you have come up with for your problem can be translated directly into a program.

But writing modern event-driven programs with VBScript is not a straightforward, start-to-finish affair. Many times, you need the program to make decisions and, based on that decision, maybe jump to another part of the program. Or, perhaps, a calculation is required to produce a value you use regularly in the program, so your program jumps off in another direction to get that value and then comes back to continue. This is where managing program flow becomes vital.

In this chapter, you'll see the main constituents of program flow. Program flow is dictated by calls to functions and procedures, loops, and decisions—parts of the program that force execution to be either diverted somewhere else in the program or held in a certain part for a given period. Before this gets too cryptic, let's move on and see this in action.

Subroutines

Subroutines are small, almost self-contained programs that are called by another part of the program as they are required. The term *subroutine* can be thought of as a general term for the individually defined sections of the overall script.

Subroutines in VBScript include the following:

❏ Event handlers: The code within an event handler is executed as the result of an action acting upon the object or control to which the event is attached, as in the following example:

```
Sub myButton_OnClick
Alert "Hello World"
End Sub
```

❏ Functions: A function returns a value to the part of the script that called it, as in the following example:

```
Function ConvertToInches(Feet)
ConvertToInches = Feet * 12
End Function
```

❏ Procedures: A procedure does not return a value. It is usually a self-contained program that can be called from anywhere within the overall script.

```
Sub myCustomSub()
Window.Status = "Hello World"
End Sub
```

Declaring Custom Functions

Functions are separate subroutines that return a value—simple as that. Declaring a function is very straightforward:

```
Function myFunctionName()
.....
End Function
```

You use the keyword `Function`, followed by the name you've given to the function. The parentheses are used to hold the variable names for any values being passed into the function from outside, which is covered later in this section. To complete the function definition, use the words `End Function`. The following is a quick example, with the result shown in Figure 9.1.

```
<HTML>
<HEAD>
<TITLE>My Function</TITLE>
<SCRIPT LANGUAGE="vbscript">
 Sub myButton_OnClick
  myVar = Document.Form1.Input.Value
  Document.Form1.Output.Value = myFunction(myVar)
```

```
End Sub

Function myFunction(ByVal AnyValue)
  myFunction = AnyValue & " added by my function"
End Function

</SCRIPT>
</HEAD>
<BODY BGCOLOR="white">
<CENTER>
<FORM NAME="Form1">
Input   <INPUT TYPE="text" NAME="Input"><P>
<INPUT TYPE="button" NAME="myButton" VALUE="Click Me"><P>
Output  <INPUT TYPE="text" NAME="Output" SIZE=40></FORM>
</CENTER>
</BODY>
</HTML>
```

Figure 9.1.

The custom function (myfunction.htm) in the browser.

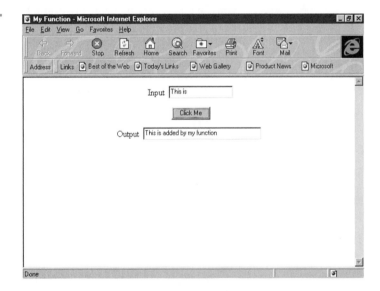

In this example, execution of the script commences when you click the button. This fires an OnClick event, which is handled by the myButton_OnClick event handler, shown here:

```
Sub myButton_OnClick
 myVar = Document.Form1.Input.Value
 Document.Form1.Output.Value = myFunction(myVar)
End Sub
```

The value in the Input text box is copied into the myVar variable. The next line basically says to the program, "Go and do myFunction, take myVar with you and bring back the result; then show that result in the Output text box." So, off it goes to myFunction, taking myVar with it. Here's the myFunction function:

```
Function myFunction(ByVal AnyValue)
  myFunction = AnyValue & " added by my function"
End Function
```

This function has been defined to receive one variable, which can be any variable. The ByVal keyword tells the scripting engine that it wants to receive just the value of the passed variable. If you try to call this function without any variables (or arguments), like

```
x = myFunction()
```

or if you call it with more than one argument, like

```
x = myFunction(y, a, I, strMyString)
```

you generate a runtime error. The number of arguments (or variables) must be the same. The names you use for the argument are irrelevant, but the order in which they appear is the same. Here is an example:

```
a = 10
b = 20
c = 30
d = 40
x = anyFunction(a,b,c,d)

Function anyFunction(e,f,g,h)
```

Within the anyFunction function, the values are e = 10, f = 20, g = 30, and h = 40.

To return the result of the function to the code that called it, you use the function name as the left side of an assignment, like this:

```
myFunction = AnyValue & " added by my function"
```

When the execution reaches the End Function, the value that has been assigned to the function is passed back to the calling script as the result.

But why not just put the code in line with the rest of the program? Well, it really depends on what you are trying to achieve. Let's say you use a particular calculation in many different parts of the program. Each time you use the calculation, you have to enter the same lines of code. It would be much easier to enter the code once in a function, and then call the function each time you need to use the calculation. Another benefit of a function is that it makes the code easier to read. Separating the code that performs a calculation makes for a tidier, less cluttered appearance. Look at the following "before and after" example:

```
<SCRIPT LANGUAGE="vbscript">
Sub cmdButton1_OnClick
  x = CDbl(Document.Form1.Text1.Value)
  y = CDbl(Document.Form1.Text2.Value)
```

```
  z = x * 34 + y
  b = z / (35 * 9) + 1
  i = b ^ 789 - 93
  Document.Form1.Text3.Value = CStr(i)
End Sub

Sub cmdButton2_OnClick
  x = CDbl(Document.Form1.Text4.Value)
  y = CDbl(Document.Form1.Text5.Value)
  z = x * 80 + y
  b = z / (35 * 9) + 1
  i = b ^ 789 - 93
  Document.Form1.Text6.Value = CStr(i)
End Sub


Sub cmdButton3_OnClick
  x = CDbl(Document.Form1.Text7.Value)
  y = 989
  z = x * 20 + y
  b = z / (35 * 9) + 1
  i = b ^ 789 - 93
  Document.Form1.Text9.Value = CStr(i)
End Sub

</SCRIPT>
```

In this totally imaginary script, each of three buttons has a similar event handler. But notice the subtle differences in each one. The following is how it could be rescripted using a single function:

```
<SCRIPT LANGUAGE="vbscript">

Function myFunction(ByVal x, ByVal y, ByVal v)
  x = CDbl(x)
  y = CDbl(y)
  z = x * v + y
  b = z / (35 * 9) + 1
  i = b ^ 789 - 93
  myFunction = CStr(i)
End Function

Sub cmdButton1_OnClick
  Document.Form1.Text3.Value = myFunction(Document.Form1.Text1.Value,
➥Document.Form1.Text2.Value, 34)
End Sub

Sub cmdButton2_OnClick
  Document.Form1.Text6.Value = myFunction(Document.Form1.Text4.Value,
➥Document.Form1.Text5.Value, 80)
End Sub

Sub cmdButton3_OnClick
  Document.Form1.Text9.Value = myFunction(Document.Form1.Text7.Value, 989, 20)
End Sub

</SCRIPT>
```

Not only does it look tidier, but it is also easier to maintain. Any modification to the formula needs to be made in only one place rather than three, which reduces the chance of error.

TASK Declaring Custom Procedures

A custom procedure is a subroutine that doesn't return a value. Like functions, procedures can accept variables from other parts of the program. To declare a custom procedure, you use the Sub keyword, followed by the name of the procedure.

```
Sub myProcedure()
....
End Sub
```

You can use two types of syntax to call a custom procedure. The first method is to use the keyword Call, like this:

```
Call myProcedure()
```

If you use the keyword Call, you must use parentheses around the argument list or use empty parentheses. The other method is to simply use the procedure name without the word Call, like this:

```
myProcedure
```

If you omit the keyword Call, you cannot use parentheses around your argument list.

The following example uses both methods. The result is shown in Figure 9.2.

```
<HTML>
<HEAD>
<TITLE>My Custom Procedure</TITLE>
<SCRIPT LANGUAGE="vbscript">
Sub Button1_OnClick
 Call DoComplexMessage("First Message")
End Sub

Sub Button2_OnClick
 DoComplexMessage "Second Message"
End Sub

Sub DoComplexMessage(ByVal Message)
 Dim CRLF
 Dim strTitle
 Dim strMainMessage
 CRLF = Chr(10) & Chr(13)
 strTitle = "My Custom Procedure"

 strMainMessage = "Hello this is the " & Message & CRLF
 strMainMessage = strMainMessage & "This is my procedure to show " & CRLF
 strMainMessage = strMainMessage & "a message box which is similar " & CRLF
 strMainMessage = strMainMessage & "from both buttons"
```

```
    x = MsgBox(strMainMessage,0,strTitle)

End Sub

</SCRIPT>
</HEAD>
<BODY BGCOLOR="white">
<CENTER>
<INPUT TYPE="button" NAME="Button1" VALUE="Button 1">
<INPUT TYPE="button" NAME="Button2" VALUE="Button 2">
</CENTER>
</BODY>
</HTML>
```

Figure 9.2.
The custom procedure,
`proc.htm`, *in the*
browser.

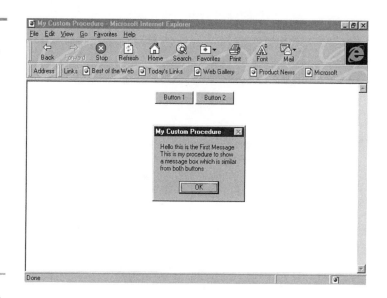

You can improve the
readability of your code
by using verbs in your
custom procedure
names—for example,
`ShowTheTime()` or
`OpenNewWindow()`.

Both event handlers for the buttons call the `DoComplexMessage` procedure. One uses
`Call` and parentheses, and the other simply uses the procedure name. As you can
clearly see, the use of a custom procedure in this example removes the need for you
to write the same code more than once.

 ## Using the ActiveX Control Pad to Create Subroutines

The ActiveX Control Pad enables you to quickly create custom procedures and
functions, and it also makes it easy to add the calls to your custom procedures and
functions.

To see how this works, let's re-create the example used in the last section using the
ActiveX Control Pad.

1. Open the ActiveX Control Pad and, using the HTML template provided, create the HTML part of the page, which should now look like what you see in Figure 9.3.

Figure 9.3.

The custom procedure example's HTML.

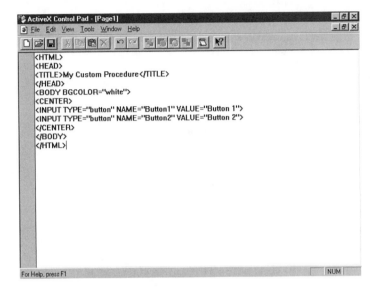

2. Now open the Script Wizard by clicking the script button on the toolbar or selecting Script Wizard from the Tools menu.

3. To create a custom procedure, right-click anywhere in the right actions pane, and select New Procedure from the pop-up menu. The Script Wizard then opens a new custom procedure in the script pane and gives it a default name of `Procedure1()`. (See Figure 9.4.)

4. Rename the procedure by changing `Procedure1` to `DoComplexMessage`, and add `ByVal Message` between the parentheses.

5. Enter the following code into the script pane:

```
Dim CRLF
Dim strTitle
Dim strMainMessage
CRLF = Chr(10) & Chr(13)
strTitle = "My Custom Procedure"

strMainMessage = "Hello this is the " & Message & CRLF
strMainMessage = strMainMessage & "This is my procedure to show " & CRLF
strMainMessage = strMainMessage & "a message box which is similar " &
➡CRLF
strMainMessage = strMainMessage & "from both buttons"

x = MsgBox(strMainMessage,0,strTitle)
```

Figure 9.4.

The new custom procedure.

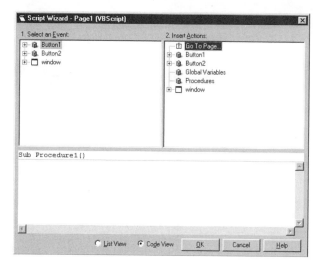

The Script Wizard automatically adds the `End Sub` statement.

6. Click the plus sign that appears next to the word `Procedures` in the right actions pane, and you can see that your new custom procedure is available to be used by any of the events. Your Script Wizard should now resemble the one in Figure 9.5.

Figure 9.5.

The completed custom procedure.

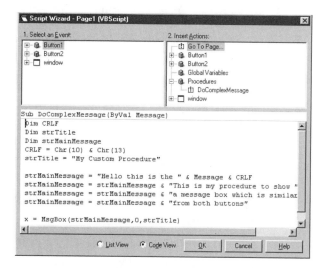

7. To call the custom procedure from the buttons events, click the plus sign to the left of `Button1` in the left events frame, and select the `OnClick` event.

8. Double-click the `DoComplexMessage` procedure in the right actions pane. Automatically, the Script Wizard adds the words `Call DoComplexMessage()` to the script pane.

9. Edit the statement by adding "`First Message`" between the parentheses. Your Script Wizard now looks like the one in Figure 9.6.

Figure 9.6.

Calling the procedure from the `OnClick` *event.*

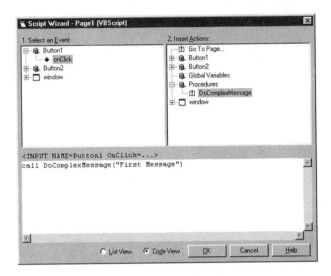

10. Repeat this for `Button2`, using "`Second Message`" between the parentheses.

11. To finish, click OK and the Script Wizard automatically generates the code, which looks like this:

```
<HTML>
<HEAD>
    <SCRIPT LANGUAGE="VBScript">
<!--
Sub DoComplexMessage(ByVal Message)
 Dim CRLF
 Dim strTitle
 Dim strMainMessage
 CRLF = Chr(10) & Chr(13)
 strTitle = "My Custom Procedure"

 strMainMessage = "Hello this is the " & Message & CRLF
 strMainMessage = strMainMessage & "This is my procedure to show "
➥ & CRLF
 strMainMessage = strMainMessage & "a message box which is similar "
➥ & CRLF
 strMainMessage = strMainMessage & "from both buttons"

 x = MsgBox(strMainMessage,0,strTitle)
end sub
-->
    </SCRIPT>
<TITLE>My Custom Procedure</TITLE>
</HEAD>
<BODY BGCOLOR="white">
<CENTER>
```

```
<INPUT LANGUAGE="VBScript" TYPE=button VALUE="Button 1"
➥ONCLICK="call DoComplexMessage(&quot;First Message&quot;)"
 NAME="Button1">
<INPUT LANGUAGE="VBScript" TYPE=button VALUE="Button 2"
➥ONCLICK="call DoComplexMessage(&quot;Second Message&quot;)"
 NAME="Button2">
</CENTER>
</BODY>
</HTML>
```

Note that the custom procedure code is identical to the one you created manually earlier. However, the Script Wizard places event handlers for HTML Intrinsic controls within the HTML definition of the control. Save the file and test it in the browser.

NOTE:
You can also create custom functions using the ActiveX Script Wizard. Follow the previous instructions, and simply replace the word Sub with Function. When the Script Wizard generates the code, it will automatically place End Function rather than End Sub at the end of the script.

Making Decisions with If and Select

Adding some pseudo-intelligence to your script is possible only if you can enable your script to make decisions. You can add decision-making capabilities in two ways.

If...Then Else and ElseIf

The If...Then conditional statement is the most widely used construct in any programming language. It is easy and quick to use and enables you to branch the program based on the result of the condition, like this:

```
If myVariable = yourVariable Then
    Alert "got a match"
End
```

If...Then statements can also be nested, which means you can have a condition that is tested only if the condition of the first statement is true. Here is an example:

```
If myVariable = yourVariable Then
    If aVariable = bVariable Then
        Alert "Both sets match"
    End If
End If
```

For the code within the conditional statement to execute, the condition must evaluate True.

```
if x = 10 then
    Alert "yes, x does equal 10"
end if
```

But what happens if it evaluates to False? Well, normally execution continues with the code directly after the End If statement. However, you can add an Else statement within the condition, which makes the code execute only if the condition is False. Here is an example:

```
If x = 10 then
    Alert "Yes, x does equal 10"
Else
    Alert "No, x does not equal 10"
End If
```

You can even add a further condition within the Else section. Just use the ElseIf keyword, like this:

```
If x = 10 then
    Alert "Yes, x does equal 10"
ElseIf x = 20 Then
    Alert "x does not equal 10 but it equals 20"
Else
    Alert "x does not equal 10 or 20"
End If
```

You can turn the condition on its head and have the code execute only if the condition evaluates to False. This is done by including the negation operator Not.

```
If Not x = 10 Then
 Alert "Sorry but x does not equal 10"
End If
```

Note that, in truth, the overall statement still evaluates to True. Essentially, the statement says, "Does x not equal 10? Yes, it doesn't."

Select Case

The other type of conditional statement you have at your disposal is the Select Case block. With Select Case, you start with a known value and then use the Case statement to compare whether the case variable matches the selection variable. If the comparison evaluates to true, the line following Case is executed. After execution, the program continues with the line following End Select.

```
Select Case x
Case 5
    Alert "x equals 5"
Case 10
    Alert "x equals 10"
Case 15
    Alert "x equals 15"
End Select
```

Again, let's look at how you can have at least one line of the block execute no matter what the result. You use Case Else, like this:

```
Select Case x
Case 5
    Alert "x equals 5"
Case 10
    Alert "x equals 10"
Case 15
    Alert "x equals 15"
Case Else
    Alert "I dont care what value x is but its not 5, 10 or 15"
End Select
```

NOTE: Unlike `Select Case` in Visual Basic, the VBScript version does not allow statements like `Case Is < 8` or `Case Is 10 To 100`. All values for the `Case` statements must be explicit, which restricts its usage drastically.

TASK   Looping with For and Do

What do you do if you need to execute the same section of code many times over, possibly with a slight change to the code? You could write the code over and over again, like this:

```
x = 0
Document.Write x
Document.Write x + 1
Document.Write x + 2
Document.Write x + 3
Document.Write x + 4
Document.Write x + 5
```

This could continue on, and copying and pasting it wouldn't take too long to reach 100! But there's a much easier method to achieve the same result. It's known as a *loop*.

VBScript gives you two ways in which you can repeat the same code as many times as you want:

❑ `For...Next`

❑ `Do...Loop`

For...Next Loops

A `For...Next` loop enables you to repeat execution of the code held within the loop a given number of times. You specify the upper and lower parameters of the loop counter, and the scripting engine increments the loop counter automatically as the loop is executed.

```
For x = 1 to 100
  do some code 100 times
Next
```

NOTE: VB programmers should keep in mind that in VBScript, you can use only `Next`. You do not have the option to use the old `Next x` as you do in VB4.

By default, the loop counter is incremented by one every time the program reaches the `Next` statement, until the upper limit is reached, at which point the program continues execution with the line following `Next`.

Let's have a look at a few variations on the `For...Next` theme. First, what if you want the counter to increment in reverse, or maybe increment by more than one each time? There's a special keyword called `Step`. `Step` is used to change the behavior of the increment. If `Step` is negative, the loop goes backward, like so:

```
For x = 100 to 0 Step -1
    Do something 100 times
Next
```

In this example, x starts at `100` and is reduced by `1` with every loop until it reaches `0`, at which point the loop is terminated. `Step` can be any number, and that number then becomes the increment.

```
For x = 0 to 100 Step 2
    Do something 50 times
Next
```

Second, what if you want to initially loop a certain number of times, but jump out of the loop if a particular condition is met? For this, you use `Exit For`. `Exit For` takes the execution out of the loop and resumes the program at the line immediately following the `Next` statement.

```
For x = 0 to 50
 y = y + 1
  If y = z then
   Exit For
  End If
Next
```

Do...Loop

Another way you can repeat the same code over and over is to use a `Do...Loop` statement, like this:

```
Do
code to execute for ever
Loop
```

But, actually, it's not like this at all. If you wrote that into your script, your script would never finish. You need to give the loop a condition so that it knows when to stop repeating. The two conditions are `While` and `Until`.

A Do While loop repeats while a condition is True, as in the following example:

```
x = 2
Do While x < 10
 x = x + 1
Loop
```

A Do Until loop repeats until a condition is True, as in the following example:

```
Do Until x = 10
 x = x + 1
Loop
```

As with the For...Next loop, you have several options that you can use with the Do...Loop statement. The first is Exit Do. Again, this is to allow an exit route for your program in case the need arises.

```
Do While x < 100
 x = x + 1
 z = z - 1
  If z = 50
   Exit Do
  End if
Loop
```

The next option is to place the While or Until on the same line as Loop, rather than on the same line as Do, like this:

```
Do
 x = x + 1
Loop Until x = 100
```

The difference is that placing While or Until next to Loop forces the statement block to be executed at least once. If the condition is placed next to Do, and the condition is True as the program arrives at the statement block, then the loop is not executed. Here is an example:

```
x = 200
Do While x < 100
 This code never executes
Loop
```

However, if the code was rewritten like the following, the code executes once:

```
x = 200
Do
 This Code executes only once
Loop While x < 100
```

Workshop Wrap-Up

In this chapter, you've been through the main language components that enable you to control the flow within your script. From defining subroutines and functions, to decision-making statements, and finally how to execute code over and over. Here's a brief summary:

❏ Functions are subroutines that return a value.

❏ Procedures are subroutines that do not return a value.

❏ Event handlers are subroutines that are called in response to an action acting upon an object or control.

❏ Use `If...Then` or `If...Else...Then` to execute code based on the result of a condition.

❏ Use `Select Case` to specify which code should execute.

❏ Loop a given number of times with `For...Next`. Use `Step` to change the default increment.

❏ `Do While Loop` repeats while a condition is `True`.

❏ `Do Until Loop` repeats until a condition is `True`.

❏ `Do Loop While` and `Do Loop Until` repeat at least once.

Next Steps

Now you know how to create scripts that can make decisions, branch to other parts of the script, repeat sections of code, and generally perform like they know what they're doing. You can add even more functionality to your scripts by looking at the following chapters:

❏ To complete your knowledge of the VBScript language elements, see Chapter 10, "Using the Power of Arrays."

❏ For a further example of using `If...Then` and loops, see Chapter 5, "Interfacing VBScript with an HTML Form."

❏ For an example of using `Select Case`, see Chapter 8, "Adding Date and Time Functions."

Q&A

Q: How do you decide when to subdivide a program into smaller sections?

A: Many of the reasons for creating separate subroutines and functions will give you an idea about when it is right to create a separate subroutine. Subroutines save coding. If you find yourself coding the same lines over and over, you probably need a subroutine. If you have a routine that returns a value, and that value might (now or in future) be needed by several parts of the program, or if the routine to produce the value is more than a few lines of code, I would suggest that it be placed in its own function.

TEN

Using the Power of Arrays

What is an array? An array is a series of memory locations that holds data sequentially in elements. You can access the data by referencing an element within the array.

In this chapter, you'll see three types of arrays:

- ❏ A static array has a predefined size; the number of elements in a static array cannot vary.
- ❏ A dynamic array can have its size (number of elements) increased and decreased while the program is running.
- ❏ A multidimension array stores data in two, three, or even more dimensions. The best way to imagine a multidimension array is to think of the first dimension elements each having their own arrays attached to them.

Defining a Static Array

To include an array in your script, you must first instruct VBScript to create an array and also tell it how many elements you want the array to have by providing the highest element index:

```
Dim myArray(9)
```

In this chapter, you

- ❏ Use arrays in your scripts
- ❏ Learn about static and dynamic arrays
- ❏ Learn about multidimension arrays
- ❏ Build a sample Web that uses a static array
- ❏ Build a sample Web that uses a dynamic array
- ❏ Check the data subtype of an array
- ❏ Build a sample Web that uses a multidimension array

Tasks in this chapter:

- ❏ Displaying the day
- ❏ Adding a dynamic array to a Web page
- ❏ Adding a multidimension array to a Web page

This code creates an array called `myArray` with 10 elements. Remember that VBScript arrays always start with position 0, so when you reference this array, the maximum element or index number you can use is 9.

To access data from or assign data to the array, you simply refer to the array name and the element number:

```
myArray(3) = "Tuesday"
```

This code places the word `"Tuesday"` in the fourth element of the array (fourth not third). You can use a loop to access the data in an array like this:

```
For I = 0 to 9
 Alert myArray(i)
Next
```

Displaying the Day

Here's a quick example that lets you display the day of the week on your page. First, you must build an array of days, and then you use the built-in `Weekday()` function to access the correct day:

```
<HTML>
<HEAD>
<TITLE>My Weekday Page</TITLE>
<SCRIPT LANGUAGE="vbscript">
Dim myDays(6)
myDays(0) = "Saturday"
myDays(1) = "Sunday"
myDays(2) = "Monday"
myDays(3) = "Tuesday"
myDays(4) = "Wednesday"
myDays(5) = "Thursday"
myDays(6) = "Friday"
</SCRIPT>
</HEAD>

<BODY BGCOLOR="white">
<FONT FACE="arial">
<CENTER>
<H2>Guess What!!... Today is
<SCRIPT LANGUAGE="vbscript">

 myNow = Now()
 myWeekDay = WeekDay(myNow)
 strDay = myDays(myWeekDay)

 Document.Write strDay

</SCRIPT>
</H2>
</CENTER>
</BODY>
```

The first script block sets up the array with seven elements. Then, the script assigns strings to each element. Note that the VBScript Weekday() function is programmed to return 0 when it's Saturday:

```
Dim myDays(6)
myDays(0) = "Saturday"
myDays(1) = "Sunday"
myDays(2) = "Monday"
myDays(3) = "Tuesday"
myDays(4) = "Wednesday"
myDays(5) = "Thursday"
myDays(6) = "Friday"
```

Because this first script is outside any subroutine, it executes immediately upon loading and also creates the array with global scope, which means that any other script on the page can access it. The next script block, which appears in the headline tag, is also outside of any subroutine, so it also executes upon loading:

```
myNow = Now()
myWeekDay = WeekDay(myNow)
strDay = myDays(myWeekDay)

Document.Write strDay
```

I split the procedure into four lines so that you can see how it works. First, the date is retrieved using Now() and assigned to the myNow variable. Next, the number of the day of the week (from 0 to 6, starting at Saturday) is returned using WeekDay(), and the value is assigned to the myWeekDay variable. The next line dips into the array at the element number corresponding to the day of the week. The value retrieved from the array is assigned to strDay, which is then printed on the Web page using the Write method. I showed this in four lines of code, but in reality, you need only one line:

```
Document.Write myDays(WeekDay(Now()))
```

Now that you've typed all that code and tried it with the browser, as shown in Figure 10.1, you might be interested to know that the file days.htm is on the CD-ROM at \SOURCE\CHAPTER10.

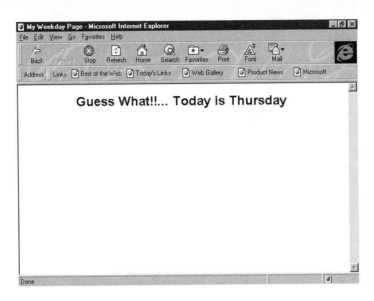

Defining a Dynamic Array

Dynamic arrays are ideal when you aren't sure at the outset how many elements you need for the array and you want to define or redefine the array during the program's execution. Defining a dynamic array is similar to defining a static array, except you simply leave out the number of elements:

```
Dim myDynamicArray()
```

This instructs VBScript to create a dynamic array that you will dimension at a later stage in the program. To dimension the dynamic array, you use the `Redim` keyword and specify a number of elements:

```
ReDim myDynamicArray(9)
```

You can dimension an array at any time within the script. However, when it comes to resizing (or redimensioning) a dynamic array, you must be careful. Resizing a dynamic array creates a brand new array with the newly requested number of elements. Any data you had stored in the old array is lost. Help comes in the form of the `Preserve` keyword. When you use `Preserve` after the `Redim`, the contents of the old array are copied into the new array automatically. However, if you specify a lower number of elements, the data in the upper elements is lost. The following examples illustrate the use of dynamic arrays:

❑ `Dim myDynamicArray()` defines a dynamic array.

❑ `ReDim myDynamicArray(9)` specifies 10 (0 through 9) elements.

❑ `ReDim Preserve myDynamicArray(19)` increases the number to 20 elements and preserves any data already stored in the array.

❑ `ReDim Preserve myDynamicArray(14)` reduces the number to 15 elements. Only the data in elements 0 to 14 is preserved; the data in elements 15 to 19 is lost forever.

You can add new data to the dynamic array whenever you need to, increasing the size of the array as you go, but what happens when you want to access that data again? You are obviously storing it for a purpose! How do you find out how many elements you now have in your ever-expanding dynamic array? The answer is a function called `UBound()`.

`UBound()` returns the largest element number. In an array of 20 elements, `UBound` returns the number 19. You use the `UBound` function like this:

```
i = UBound(myDynamicArray)
```

To show how a dynamic array works in practice, construct a sample Web page in the next section.

Adding a Dynamic Array to a Web Page

This example uses a very simple array to store the information given by the user. The Web page is a basic travel survey in which the user enters the names of cities visited in the past year. Of course, you don't know how many cities a user might have visited, so this is an ideal job for a dynamic array. Perform the following steps to build this example:

1. First, here's the HTML part of things, which you need to build, save, and test:

```
<HTML>
<HEAD>
<TITLE>Travel Survey</TITLE>
<SCRIPT LANGUAGE="vbscript">

</SCRIPT>
</HEAD>

<BODY BGCOLOR="white">
<FONT FACE="arial" SIZE=3>
<CENTER>
<H2>Travel Survey</H2>
<P>
<BLOCKQUOTE>
Enter all the cities you have traveled to in the
past year, enter as many or as few as you like.
</BLOCKQUOTE>
<P>
 <FORM NAME="Form1">
    <INPUT TYPE="Text" NAME="Input">
    <INPUT TYPE="Button" NAME="cmdAddOne" VALUE="Add to List">
    <INPUT TYPE="Button" NAME="cmdFinish" VALUE="Finish">
 </FORM>
```

```
</CENTER>
</BODY>
</HTML>
```

2. After you build the HTML page, you can add the scripted sections within the
   <SCRIPT> tags. First, add the global variable declarations, constants, and
   assignments:

```
Dim strCities()
Dim CRLF

ReDim strCities(0)
CRLF = Chr(10) & Chr(13)
```

   The first line defines a dynamic array called strCities. The next line defines
   a global constant called CRLF. The dynamic array has to have a starting point,
   so it is immediately redimensioned to one element (index 0). Finally, this
   section includes the carriage return and line feed variable for use later in a
   message box.

3. Now, enter the event handler for the Add to List button:

```
Sub cmdAddOne_OnClick
  If Len(Document.Form1.Input.Value) > 0 Then
      ReDim Preserve strCities(UBound(strCities)+1)
      strCities(UBound(strCities)) = Document.Form1.Input.Value
      Document.Form1.Input.Value = ""
  End If
End Sub
```

   The first line of the event handler is a verification to check whether the user
   actually entered some data prior to clicking the button. If he didn't, the
   program simply jumps to End Sub, and nothing is done.

   Next comes the important code to increase the size of the array by one
   element. You'll recall that I said all arrays in VBScript start with element 0.
   Because of the way this script is constructed, element 0 is never used; this is
   a result of simplifying the code so that it is the same for each click of the
   button. The element number is obtained by finding the current highest
   element number using UBound (a mnemonic for upper boundary) and then
   adding one to it. Therefore, the first time this button is clicked, UBound
   returns 0; the first element is 1. If you desperately want to use element 0,
   you have to check to see whether this is the first time around and not
   add one.

   The next line assigns whatever the user entered in the input text box to the
   highest element, which you find by using UBound. On the first button click,
   the highest element is number 1. The next line empties the text box ready
   for the user to enter the next city, and after the final tidying up, it is the
   user's turn.

4. Now you need to add the event handler for the Finish button, which
   retrieves the data from the array and displays it to the user:

```
Sub cmdFinish_OnClick
   Dim i
   Dim strMsg

   strMsg = "You have visited " &  UBound(strCities)
   strMsg = strMsg & " cities in the past year" & CRLF

   For i = 1 to UBound(strCities)
       strMsg = strMsg & strCities(i) & CRLF
   Next

   MsgBox strMsg,0,"Cities"
End Sub
```

The first two lines of the event handler create two local variables, one for the loop counter and the other to hold the message.

The first part of the message includes the number of cities visited by the user. You quickly obtain this by returning the highest index number in the array.

Now, you have to return the values held in each element of the array (apart from the first element 0, which in this case is not used). The loop assigns the values of 1 through the maximum number of cities entered to the loop counter i, which can then access the array element. The value of each element is then concatenated to the message string followed by the carriage-return character.

When all the elements have been accessed, the message is displayed to the user in a message box, and that is that, as they say. Just for fun, Listing 10.1 shows the complete HTML and script.

Listing 10.1. The `travel.htm` code.

```
<HTML>
<HEAD>
<TITLE>Travel Survey</TITLE>
<SCRIPT LANGUAGE="vbscript">
Dim strCities()
Dim CRLF

ReDim strCities(0)
CRLF = Chr(10) & Chr(13)

Sub cmdAddOne_OnClick
  If Len(Document.Form1.Input.Value) > 0 Then
     ReDim Preserve strCities(UBound(strCities)+1)
     strCities(UBound(strCities)) = Document.Form1.Input.Value
     Document.Form1.Input.Value = ""
  End If
End Sub

Sub cmdFinish_OnClick
  Dim i
  Dim strMsg
```

continues

Listing 10.1. continued

```
strMsg = "You have visited " &  UBound(strCities)
strMsg = strMsg & " cities in the past year" & CRLF

For i = 1 to UBound(strCities)
    strMsg = strMsg & strCities(i) & CRLF
Next

MsgBox strMsg,0,"Cities"
End Sub

</SCRIPT>
</HEAD>

<BODY BGCOLOR="white">
<FONT FACE="arial" SIZE=3>
<CENTER>
<H2>Travel Survey</H2>
<P>
<BLOCKQUOTE>
Enter all the cities you have traveled to in the
past year, enter as many or as few as you like.
</BLOCKQUOTE>
<P>
 <FORM NAME="Form1">
    <INPUT TYPE="Text" NAME="Input">
    <INPUT TYPE="Button" NAME="cmdAddOne" VALUE="Add to List">
    <INPUT TYPE="Button" NAME="cmdFinish" VALUE="Finish">
 </FORM>
</CENTER>
</BODY>
</HTML>
```

Figure 10.2 shows what happens when you run Listing 10.1 with the browser.

Figure 10.2.

The contents of the dynamic array.

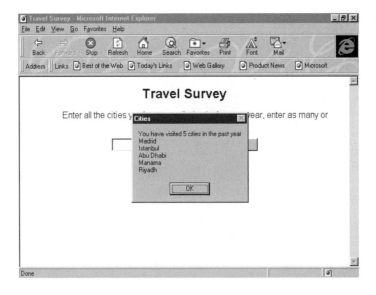

Multidimension Arrays

A multidimension array allows you to build a temporary mini-database in memory. Consider a single-dimension array as simply a row of elements (as shown in Figure 10.3), starting at 0 and containing a given number of elements, each holding a self-contained piece of information or data.

Figure 10.3.
A single-dimension array.

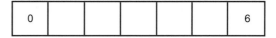

If you add a second dimension, the array takes on the appearance of a spreadsheet with rows and columns. You declare a two-dimension array by specifying the number of rows and number of columns:

```
Dim MyMultiArray(6,3)
```

This code creates a multidimension array in memory consisting of seven rows and four columns. You can access each element within this two-dimension array by referencing its coordinates, `arrayname(row,column)`, as shown in Figure 10.4. It is as though each element of the single-dimension array had its own unique array.

Figure 10.4.
A two-dimension array.

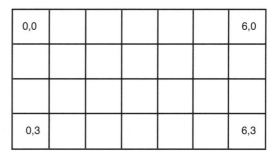

Now, you add a third dimension to the array. Think of each element of the two-dimension array having its own unique array, as shown in Figure 10.5. A three-dimension array is declared like this:

```
Dim MyMultiArray(6,3,2)
```

Figure 10.5.

A three-dimension array.

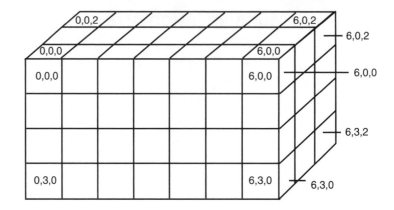

You can create a multidimension array with up to 64 dimensions, although more than three or four dimensions makes it difficult to visualize the array.

CAUTION: Multidimension arrays can eat memory very quickly. Consider the following:

```
Dim myArray(9,9,9)
myArray(0,0,0) = "This is a string thankyou"
```

These two lines of code actually zap 25KB of memory in the blink of an eye because memory is reserved for all elements of the array, whether they contain data or not. The string added to the array is 25 bytes long, so every element of the array is set to hold 25 bytes. Therefore, *10 elements × 10 elements × 10 elements × 25 bytes = 25,000 bytes.*

Add another similar dimension and you eat up a quarter of a megabyte of memory!

Adding a Multidimension Array to a Web Page

A multidimension array can act very much like a database. To demonstrate this, continue with the travel theme from earlier in the chapter. This time, you add an ActiveX control to help display the data dynamically, too.

1. Open the ActiveX Control Pad. Using the text editor and the default template provided, create the following HTML page:

```
<HTML>
<HEAD>
    <SCRIPT LANGUAGE="vbscript">
<!-- SCRIPT TO GO HERE  -->
    </SCRIPT>
</HEAD>
<BODY BGCOLOR="white">
<CENTER>
```

```
<H2>Improved Travel Survey</H2>
    <FORM NAME="Form1">
Enter City   <INPUT TYPE=text NAME="City"><BR>
Enter Airline Used   <INPUT TYPE=text NAME="Airline"><BR>
Enter Duration of Stay   <INPUT TYPE=text NAME="Duration"><BR>
Enter Purpose of Visit   <INPUT TYPE=text NAME="Purpose"><BR>
Enter Comments   <INPUT TYPE=text NAME="Comments"> <BR>
        <INPUT TYPE=button VALUE="Add To Survey" NAME="cmdAddOne">
<HR>

<!-- ACTIVEX COMBO TO GO HERE -->

 
<SELECT NAME="DataField">
<OPTION> Choose a Data Field
<OPTION>Airline
<OPTION>Duration
<OPTION>Purpose
<OPTION>Comment
</SELECT>
<BR>
<INPUT TYPE=button VALUE="Show Data" NAME="cmdShowData">
<BR>
</FORM>
</CENTER>
</BODY>
</HTML>
```

2. After you create the page, save it as `multi.htm` and test it with the browser. The interface should look like the one in Figure 10.6.

Figure 10.6.

The `multi.htm` *file— with only HTML code.*

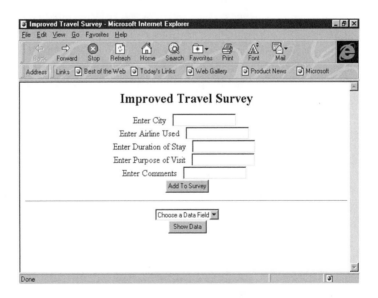

3. Now you need to add an ActiveX Combo box. Place your cursor below the line marked `<!-- ACTIVEX COMBO TO GO HERE -->`.

4. Select Insert ActiveX Control from the Edit menu.

A combo control is a combination of a text box and a drop-down list.

5. Select Microsoft Forms 2.0 Combo.

6. Change the ID property of the control to Cities.

7. Change the Text property of the control to Select A City. This appears in the text box section of the control but is not an item of the list.

8. Close the Object Editor and the code to create the control is added to your HTML at the cursor position.

9. Save the page and check it with the browser.

10. Now add the script code. First, code the following global variables, constants, and array definition:

```
Dim myMultiArray(4,4)
Dim CITY
Dim AIRLINE
Dim DURATION
Dim PURPOSE
Dim COMMENTS
Dim CurrentElement
CurrentElement = 0

CITY = 0
AIRLINE = 1
DURATION = 2
PURPOSE = 3
COMMENTS = 4
```

The first direction creates the two-dimension array with five elements in each dimension, providing a total of 25 elements. All of the first dimension, elements (0,0) to (4,0) (which is also the first element of the second dimension), holds the city names. You can imagine these as column headers. The second element of the second dimension, (0,1) to (4,1), stores the airline name; this is analogous to a row in a spreadsheet or matrix. The third element of the second dimension, (0,2) to (4,2), stores the duration of the visit. The fourth element of the second dimension, (0,3) to (4,3), stores the purpose of the visit, and the fifth element of the second dimension, (0,4) to (4,4), stores the comments of the user.

Because this is a fixed array, there is a maximum number of entries you can accept (five). You also need to know which element to add the data to by using the CurrentElement global variable, which is initialized at 0.

11. Now you can add the code for the cmdAddOne event handler, which adds data to the array:

```
Sub cmdAddOne_OnClick
  If CurrentElement = 4 Then
   Alert "Sorry, no more"
   Exit Sub
  End If
```

This first section checks to make sure you haven't reached the limit of the array. If you have, it displays a warning and terminates the event. Add the next section:

```
myMultiArray(CurrentElement,CITY) = Document.Form1.City.Value
myMultiArray(CurrentElement,AIRLINE) = Document.Form1.Airline.Value
myMultiArray(CurrentElement,DURATION) = Document.Form1.Duration.Value
myMultiArray(CurrentElement,PURPOSE) = Document.Form1.Purpose.Value
myMultiArray(CurrentElement,COMMENTS) = Document.Form1.Comments.Value
```

This section copies the values entered by the user into the relevant array elements. Notice how the use of constants makes the code much easier to read and understand.

```
CurrentElement = CurrentElement + 1
```

Increment the `CurrentElement` counter by one.

```
call Document.Form1.Cities.AddItem(Document.Form1.City.Value)
```

This line adds the city name entered by the user to the list of cities in the `Cities` ActiveX combo box using the control's `AddItem` method.

```
Document.Form1.City.Value = ""
Document.Form1.Airline.Value = ""
Document.Form1.Duration.Value = ""
Document.Form1.Purpose.Value = ""
Document.Form1.Comments.Value = ""

End Sub
```

Finally, clear the text boxes to be ready for the next entry and end the event handler.

12. All that remains now is handling the click event for the show data button. Clicking the button displays a selected field for a selected city. Here's the code:

```
Sub cmdShowData_OnClick

 If CurrentElement = 0 Then
  Exit Sub
 End If
```

This first section ensures that the button wasn't clicked before any data was present in the array.

```
intDataField = Document.Form1.DataField.SelectedIndex
intCity = Document.Form1.Cities.ListIndex
```

Using the `DataField`'s `SelectedIndex` property, determine which field the user selected. The `ListIndex` property is the equivalent property for an ActiveX control.

```
If intCity < 0 Or intDataField = 0 Then
 Exit Sub
End If
```

If no selection was made from the Cities combo, the `ListIndex` property returns -1. The HTML `Select` has no such functionality, but you might have

noticed when you created this HTML `Select` that the first `<OPTION>` was
"`Select a Field`". This is in effect the header and occupies position `0` in the
select box. If `SelectedIndex` returns `0`, you know again that no selection was
made.

```
strMsg = "City:   " & myMultiArray(intCity,CITY) & "   "
strMsg = strMsg &  Document.Form1.DataField.Options(intDataField).Text
➥& ": "
strMsg = strMsg &  myMultiArray(intCity,intDataField)
Alert strMsg

End Sub
```

Finally, construct the message that consists of the city name, the field name,
and the field value.

Listing 10.2 shows the complete source code.

Listing 10.2. The completed `multi.htm`.

```
<HTML>
<HEAD>
    <SCRIPT LANGUAGE="vbscript">
Dim myMultiArray(4,4)
Dim CITY
Dim AIRLINE
Dim DURATION
Dim PURPOSE
Dim COMMENTS
Dim CurrentElement
CurrentElement = 0

CITY = 0
AIRLINE = 1
DURATION = 2
PURPOSE = 3
COMMENTS = 4

Sub cmdAddOne_OnClick
  If CurrentElement = 4 Then
   Alert "Sorry, no more"
   Exit Sub
  End If

  myMultiArray(CurrentElement,CITY) = Document.Form1.City.Value
  myMultiArray(CurrentElement,AIRLINE) = Document.Form1.Airline.Value
  myMultiArray(CurrentElement,DURATION) = Document.Form1.Duration.Value
  myMultiArray(CurrentElement,PURPOSE) = Document.Form1.Purpose.Value
  myMultiArray(CurrentElement,COMMENTS) = Document.Form1.Comments.Value

  CurrentElement = CurrentElement + 1

  call Document.Form1.Cities.AddItem(Document.Form1.City.Value)

Document.Form1.City.Value = ""
Document.Form1.Airline.Value = ""
Document.Form1.Duration.Value = ""
Document.Form1.Purpose.Value = ""
Document.Form1.Comments.Value = ""
```

```
End Sub

Sub cmdShowData_OnClick

  If CurrentElement = 0 Then
   Exit Sub
  End If

  intDataField = Document.Form1.DataField.SelectedIndex
  intCity = Document.Form1.Cities.ListIndex

  If intCity < 0 Or intDataField = 0 Then
   Exit Sub
  End If

strMsg = "City:   " & myMultiArray(intCity,CITY) & "  "
strMsg = strMsg &  Document.Form1.DataField.Options(intDataField).Text  &   ": "
strMsg = strMsg &  myMultiArray(intCity,intDataField)
Alert strMsg

End Sub
    </SCRIPT>
</HEAD>
<BODY BGCOLOR="white">
<CENTER>
<H2>Improved Travel Survey</H2>
    <FORM NAME="Form1">
Enter City   <INPUT TYPE=text NAME="City"><BR>
Enter Airline Used   <INPUT TYPE=text NAME="Airline"><BR>
Enter Duration of Stay   <INPUT TYPE=text NAME="Duration"><BR>
Enter Purpose of Visit   <INPUT TYPE=text NAME="Purpose"><BR>
Enter Comments   <INPUT TYPE=text NAME="Comments"> <BR>
        <INPUT TYPE=button VALUE="Add To Survey" NAME="cmdAddOne">
<HR>
        <OBJECT ID="Cities" WIDTH=139 HEIGHT=24
 CLASSID="CLSID:8BD21D30-EC42-11CE-9E0D-00AA006002F3">
    <PARAM NAME="VariousPropertyBits" VALUE="746604571">
    <PARAM NAME="DisplayStyle" VALUE="3">
    <PARAM NAME="Size" VALUE="3669;635">
    <PARAM NAME="MatchEntry" VALUE="1">
    <PARAM NAME="ShowDropButtonWhen" VALUE="2">
    <PARAM NAME="Value" VALUE="Select A City">
    <PARAM NAME="FontCharSet" VALUE="0">
    <PARAM NAME="FontPitchAndFamily" VALUE="2">
    <PARAM NAME="FontWeight" VALUE="0">
</OBJECT>
 
<SELECT NAME="DataField">
<OPTION> Choose a Data Field
<OPTION>Airline
<OPTION>Duration
<OPTION>Purpose
<OPTION>Comment
</SELECT>
<BR>
        <INPUT TYPE=button VALUE="Show Data" NAME="cmdShowData">
<BR>
    </FORM>
</CENTER>
</BODY>
</HTML>
```

Save the page and try it out in the browser, as shown in Figures 10.7 and 10.8.

Figure 10.7.

The completed travel survey version 2.

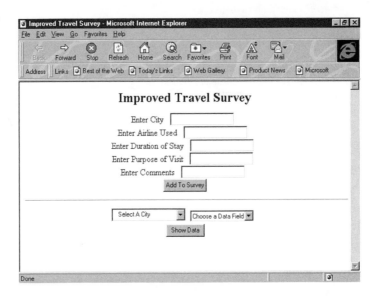

Figure 10.7.

The completed travel survey version 2.

Figure 10.8.

Travel survey version 2, completed with result.

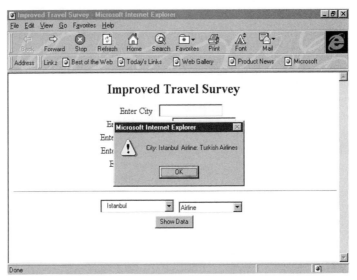

Figure 10.8.

Travel survey version 2, completed with result.

> **NOTE:** You can add further functionality to this page. Because you created constants to represent the field names, you can use them to access all the data of the same field, such as airlines, like this:
>
> ```
> for i = 0 to 4
>  strMsg = strMsg &  myMultiArray(i,AIRLINE)
> next i
> ```
>
> To access all the fields for a particular city, you use something like this:
>
> ```
> cityNumber = 3
> For i = CITY to COMMENTS
>    strMsg = strMsg &  myMultiArray(cityNumber,i)
> Next i
> ```

Data Types with Arrays in VBScript

As you know, VBScript uses only one data type, the variant. Variant holds whatever data subtype is necessary for the data it is currently storing. In Chapter 4, "Using the VBScript Language," you learned how to use VarType() to determine what data subtype is held within a variant.

If a variant is holding an array, VarType() returns 8192 plus the normal VarType return value for the data within the array.

For example, if you have an array that consists of integer data, which has a normal VarType return value of 2, VarType returns 8194, as this short example shows:

```
intMyArray(10)
intMyArray(0) = CInt(Document.Form1.Input.Value)
x = VarType(intMyArray)
```

For more details on data subtypes, see Chapter 4, "Using the VBScript Language."

Remember that in normal circumstances, if you transfer any data from the HTML form directly into an array or any other variable, the variable is cast automatically as a data subtype of string. Other data subtypes must be invoked explicitly as shown in the previous example.

Workshop Wrap-Up

In this chapter, you saw how to use arrays to add much more programmatic functionality to your Web pages. Here are some main points to remember about arrays:

- ❑ Declare a static array using Dim myArray(8).
- ❑ The number of elements you define in an array is always one more than the highest element number because the first element is always 0.
- ❑ To declare a dynamic array, use Dim myDynamicArray().

❏ Dimension and redimension a dynamic array using `ReDim`.

❏ To prevent losing data when you redimension a dynamic array, use the `Preserve` keyword.

Next Steps

Now you've seen how to use arrays in your scripts to create database-like functionality in your Web pages, giving your applications power and purpose. But you can't neglect the user interface. To improve the look and feel of your applications, look at these chapters:

❏ To learn more about using the ActiveX Control Pad with forms, see Chapter 13, "Implementing an ActiveX Menu Control."

❏ Chapter 14, "Using the HTML Layout Control," shows you how to build Windows-like forms.

Q&A

Q: How do I vary the contents of an array? All you've shown here is a hard-coded list of values.

A: At the moment, the only way you can change the values list for a client-side array is to use a CGI server-side script to build the Web page as the client requests the page. You basically replace the value lists with a server-side script, but a lot depends upon the database system and Web server platform you are using, and that really goes well beyond the scope of this book. Whichever system you use, the page downloaded to the client will look identical to the ones used in this chapter, and the way you handle arrays at the client is the same.

ELEVEN

Real-Life Examples I

This chapter describes three sample Web pages created using VBScript with techniques introduced in Part II, "Mastering the VBScript Language" (Chapters 4 through 10). The examples include

Example 1: A credit-card number validation program for an online mail-order company

Example 2: A home page that's different every time you load it

Example 3: A links page that caters to both daytime and nighttime audiences

Example 1: Mega Mail Order Credit Card Payments

Document title: Credit Card Verification Form

Files:

Page file: cardver.html (see Figure 11.1)

Images:

❏ visa.gif

❏ master.gif

❏ amex.gif

Figure 11.1.

cardver.html.

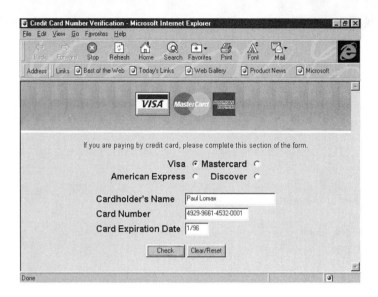

Description: Mega Mail Order, the company you first met in Chapter 5, "Interfacing VBScript with an HTML Form," accepts credit-card payments over the Internet for its new wonder product—the LazeeGeek Computer Users Head Prop. However, like all companies that accept credit-card numbers, it gets its share of mischievous visitors who complete the form with fictitious credit-card details, knowing very well that the order cannot be processed and that they'll never receive the goods. It must be said that very few people set out to defraud; in fact, the vast majority of credit-card failures are due to simple mistakes by the users. However, it does waste time. Mega Mail Order's sales clerks call the authorization center only to be told that the transactions cannot be authorized.

The usual answer is to create or obtain a CGI script that validates the credit-card number. Using a simple algorithm, it is possible to determine whether a credit-card number is false or genuine. However, it is much quicker and more efficient to process the validation at the client machine rather than at the server.

The validation routines check the expiration date of the card and then perform a check on the card number to see whether it passes through the algorithm. There are actually three algorithms for 13-, 15-, and 16-digit cards.

NOTE:
The use of credit cards for payment on the Internet has been a controversial subject for many months. I have my own opinions, but I'm not writing a book on that! If you do plan to accept credit cards at your Web site, you should note a few important points.

Only accept credit-card details through the Secure Sockets Layer (SSL). For this, you need a digital certificate from VeriSign, which can be obtained at `http://www.verisign.com/`.

When you receive the credit-card details via SSL from the client, do not use a CGI script to e-mail the form details to your home or office location (assuming you use a remote server), unless you use an equally safe encryption method for transmitting the e-mail. You might be wondering how to obtain your order details. The safest method is to store the details on the server and send an e-mail to yourself alerting you that an order is ready to be collected from the server. Set up a password-secure form that you and you alone can log into (again, through SSL), and collect the details online. This type of server-side processing is beyond the scope of this book.

If you plan to use this script on your Web site, remember that client-side scripts are currently visible via the View Source menu option. It wouldn't take long for an experienced programmer to learn how to change the script in order to get around your validation. Suppose the hacker saves a copy of the form to a local drive, amends it, gets back online, loads the hacked page from his hard drive, enters garbage in the form, and submits it. If you run a credit-card form like this on a normal server, there is nothing you can do; the now unvalidated data hits your server and causes all the same problems you had before. However, if you run the form from a secure server, the hacker gets stuck completely. The form must come from the secure server to establish the SSL connection. The hacker simply cannot create the SSL link without down-loading the credit-card form from your server. The form's action parameter is set to an `https://` location. Therefore, if data is sent to the server "in the clear," it will not be understood. This obviously is another good reason to accept credit cards only via an SSL connection.

Finally, this script can only validate the fact that the number is a real credit-card number. You still need to obtain an authorization number from the credit-card company.

Techniques Applied

Dates: (See Chapter 8, "Adding Date and Time Functions.") The script obtains the current month and year from the user's machine and compares this against the expiration date given by the card holder. The expiration date is first checked to ensure that it is a valid date (as far as the computer is concerned). The user can enter any valid combination of month and year, including Aug-97, 8/97, and August 97. The fact that this sort of validation using a server-side CGI script is a very complex program is another good reason to use client-side scripting and VBScript in particular.

Subroutines and functions: (See Chapter 9, "Making Your Program Flow.") The program consists of several functions and related subroutines, as well as event handlers.

String manipulation: (See Chapter 7, "Manipulating Strings.") The program has to remove any spaces, commas, dashes, or whatever the client used to delimit the series of numbers. You achieve this by looking at the problem in reverse; that is, you look for the numbers rather than the delimiters, so that it does not matter which delimiting character the user included within the card number. You use more string manipulation in the actual algorithm itself, which must split the overall credit-card number into individual numbers.

String conversion: (See Chapter 7.) After the numbers (which are actually string representations of numbers) are dissected, a calculation is performed on them, so they must be converted to integers.

Operators: (See Chapter 4, "Using the VBScript Language.") On several occasions, the script uses a range of comparison, logical, and arithmetic operators.

Loops and decisions: (See Chapter 9.) The program contains several `If...Then` and `Select Case` statements, as well as a nested `Select Case` block.

Arrays: (See Chapter 10, "Using the Power of Arrays.") One of the three algorithms uses a static, single-dimension array as temporary storage for the individual numbers of the credit-card number.

HTML intrinsic controls: (See Chapter 5.) The form uses only HTML controls; no ActiveX controls are used.

Figure 11.2 shows what happens when a user tries to enter the details of a credit card that has expired. Keep in mind, though, that this part of the validation works with the client machine's date variable, which is under the control of the user.

Figure 11.3 shows that the algorithm has either sucessfully foiled a potential fraud or has alerted the user to a typing error.

Until I stumbled across the algorithm that forms the basis of this credit-card verification program, it had never struck me that credit-card numbers are constructed in a particular way. They just seemed like a bunch of random numbers!

Figure 11.2.

cardver.html
*detecting an expired
card.*

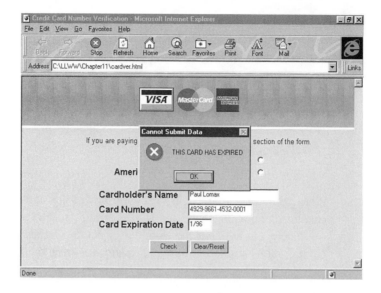

Figure 11.3.

cardver.html
*detecting a credit-card
fraudster—me!*

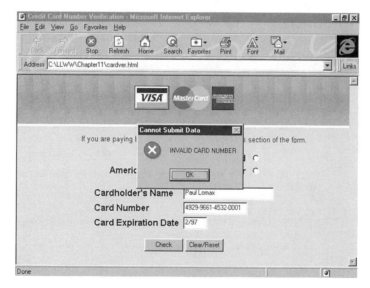

However, credit-card numbers are all put together in such a way that by applying an algorithm to them, you can very quickly identify a bogus number. No matter what type of card is being used, the numbering systems all work in a similar way, so here's how they work. First, multiply every other digit by two—that is (depending on the card type), digits 1, 3, 5, and so on, or 2, 4, 6, and so on. If the result of the multiplication is greater than 10, add the two digits. For example, let's say the second digit of a credit-card number is 6. If you multiply it by 2, that equals 12; if you add 1 and 2, that equals

3. When you've done this for every other number, add all the digits of the credit-card number. If the result is divisible by 10 (such as 50, 60, or 70), the number is genuine. If it does not divide by 10, the number is false. Here is an example:

Credit-card number: 4578-7895-1232-0051

With a 16-digit number, you multiply digits 1 through 15 by 2, and reduce them to single-digit results, as described in the preceding paragraph.

New number: 8558-5895-2262-0011

Now add all these digits together. The result is 67—a bogus number.

While porting this example to VBScript from Perl, I tested the algorithm on over 60 credit-card numbers that had been received on one of my clients' Web sites. Amazingly, the two that the algorithm rejected were also the two that had failed authorization—probably not that amazing when you think about it!

The complete listing for the credit-card verification example is shown in Listing 11.1.

Listing 11.1. The `cardver.html` code.

```
<HTML>
<HEAD>
<TITLE>Credit Card Number Verification</TITLE>
<SCRIPT LANGUAGE="vbscript">
'
'Create two variables with global scope
'
     Dim paymethod
     Dim TheCardType


'
'This is the main subroutine and is called by the button's
'onclick event handler
'
Sub VerifyCard
    dim strCleanNo
    dim verified
    dim currdate

 'check the date if bad then quit
 If Not GoodDate() Then
  Exit Sub
 End If

 'take all spaces etc out of the string
 strCleanNo = CleanString()

 'determine the type of card and send execution off in the right direction
 Select Case TheCardType
 Case "amex"
     verified = verifyAmex(strCleanNo)
 Case "visa"

     'this is a nested select
```

```
     Select Case Len(strCleanNo)
     Case 13
          verified = verifyV(strCleanNo)
     Case 16
          verified = verifyMC(strCleanNo)
     Case Else
          verified = False
     End Select

  Case "mastercard"
     verified = verifyMC(strCleanNo)
  Case "discovery"
     verified = verifyMC(strCleanNo)
  Case Else
     Alert  "Please select a Card Type"
     Exit Sub
End Select

  'is it ok or not?
  If Not verified Then
     i = MsgBox("INVALID CARD NUMBER",16,"Cannot Submit Data")
  Else
     i = MsgBox("The Card No. is OK",64,"Submitting Data....")
  End If
End Sub

'
'This is the function that checks the date
'
Function GoodDate()
 GoodDate = True
 If Not IsDate(Document.Form1.CardExp.Value) Then
     i = MsgBox("Invalid Expiry Date",16,"Cannot Submit Data")
     GoodDate = False
 Else
     currdate = Month(Now()) & " " & Year(Now())
     If DateValue(Document.Form1.CardExp.Value) < DateValue(currdate) Then
          i = MsgBox("THIS CARD HAS EXPIRED",16,"Cannot Submit Data")
          GoodDate = False
     End If
 End If
End Function

'
'This function validates an amex card
'
Function VerifyAmex(ByVal CardNo)
    Dim amexarray(14)
    Dim tot
    tot=0
'
'The first check - Amex Cards must be 15 digits
 If Len(CardNo) <> 15 Then
     VerifyAmex = False
     Exit Function
 End If
'
'Separate all digits in even numbered positions into
'an array - this will make the final addition easier For x = 2 to 10 step 2
```

continues

Listing 11.1. continued

```
        amexarray(x-1) = Mid(CardNo,x,1)
 Next
 '
 'Now put the last four digits into the array too
 For x = 12 to 15
        amexarray(x-1) = Mid(CardNo,x,1)
 Next
 '
 'Multiply all the numbers in odd numbered positions
 'by two and reduce them to single digit answers
 For x = 1 to 11 Step 2
     y = Mid(CardNo,x,1) * 2
     If y >= 10 Then
 '
 'The Mod Function returns only the remainder of a division
 'when the result is calculated put it too into the array
        amexarray(x-1) =  (y Mod 10) + 1
     Else
        amexarray(x-1) = y
     End If
 Next
 '
 'Finally add up all the numbers you've got stored in the array
 For x = 0 to 14
        tot = tot + CInt(amexarray(x))
 Next
 '
 'If the tot variable is divisible by 10 then Mod will return
 '0, that is no remainder
 If tot Mod 10 = 0 Then
     VerifyAmex = True
 Else
     VerifyAmex = False
 End If

End Function

 '
 'This function checks visa 13 digit cards
 '
 Function VerifyV(ByVal CardNo)
     Dim vArray(12)
     Dim tot
     tot=0
 '
 'Move all the numbers in the even numbered positions
 'into an array
 For x = 2 to 12 step 2
     vArray(x-1) = Mid(CardNo,x,1)
 Next
 '..and the thirteenth number
     vArray(12) = Mid(CardNo,13,1)
 '
 'mulitply all the numbers in the odd numbered positions by 2
 'and reduce to a single digit result
 For x = 1 to 11 Step 2
     y = Mid(CardNo,x,1) * 2
     If y >= 10 Then
```

```
'
'Mod returns the remainder of a division
'when you have a single digit result add that
'to the array also.
        vArray(x-1) =  (y Mod 10) + 1
    Else
        vArray(x-1) = y
    End If
Next
'
'run through the whole array adding up the numbers
'as you go
For x = 0 to 12
    tot = tot + CInt(vArray(x))
Next
'
'check to see if the result is divisible by 10
If tot Mod 10 = 0 Then
    VerifyV = True
Else
    VerifyV = False
End If

End Function


'Although it says MC it's actually a multi purpose 16 digit checker
'
Function VerifyMC(ByVal CardNo)
    Dim tot
    tot=0

'first check, must be 16 digits
If Len(CardNo) <> 16 Then
    VerifyMC = False
    Exit Function
End If
'
'this one's slightly different, without using an array
'firstly add up all the numbers occupying even numbered
'positions
For x = 2 to 16 step 2
    tot = tot + CInt(Mid(CardNo,x,1))
Next
'
'all the numbers in odd numbered locations are multiplied
'by 2 and reduced to single digit results, then added to
'the running total
For x = 1 to 15 Step 2
    y = Mid(CardNo,x,1) * 2
    If y >= 10 Then
        tot = tot + CInt((y Mod 10) + 1)
    Else
        tot = tot + CInt(y)
    End If
Next
'
'again check that the result is divisible by 10
If tot Mod 10 = 0 Then
```

continues

Listing 11.1. continued

```
     VerifyMC = True
Else
     VerifyMC = False
End If

End Function

'
'This function looks for numbers in the card number string, thereby
'removing all non numeric characters
'
Function CleanString()
    dim strLen
    dim strCounter
    dim strClean
    dim strDirty
'
'copy the complete number as entered by the user in
'the srtDirty variable
 strDirty = Trim(Document.Form1.cardnumber.value)
'
'find its total length
 strLen = Len(strDirty)
'
'initalize the variable which will hold the final
'cleaned credit card number
 strClean = ""
'
'it's easier to check for numbers and reject everything else
 For strCounter = 1 to strLen
    If Asc(Mid(strDirty,strCounter,1)) < 58 AND
    ➥Asc(Mid(strDirty,strCounter,1)) > 47 Then
'
'if this character is a number, concatenate it to the clean
number thereby removing all dashes, spaces or whatever
delimiter the user has included.
        strClean = strClean  & Mid(strDirty,strCounter,1)
    End If
 Next
'
'return the final credit card number minus delimiters
 CleanString = strClean
End Function

'et voila
</SCRIPT>

</HEAD>
<BODY BACKGROUND="bground.jpg">
<FONT FACE="arial" SIZE=2>
<CENTER>
<TABLE>
<TD><IMG SRC="visa.gif">
<TD><IMG SRC="master.gif">
<TD><IMG SRC="amex.gif">
```

```
</TABLE>
<P>
<BR><BR>
<BLOCKQUOTE>
If you are paying by credit card, please complete this section
of the form.
</BLOCKQUOTE>
    <FORM NAME="Form1">

<TABLE>
<TD ALIGN=RIGHT><B>Visa</B>
<TD>
<!--
    The event handlers attached to the following controls
    were added using the ActiveX Control Pad
>
<INPUT LANGUAGE="vbscript" TYPE=RADIO VALUE="visa"
➥ONCLICK="TheCardType= &quot;visa&quot;"
        NAME="cardtype">

<TD ALIGN=RIGHT><B>Mastercard</B>
<TD><INPUT LANGUAGE="vbscript" TYPE=RADIO VALUE="mastercard"
➥ONCLICK="TheCardType= &quot;mastercard&quot;"
        NAME="cardtype">
<TR>
<TD ALIGN=RIGHT><B>American Express</B>
<TD><INPUT LANGUAGE="vbscript" TYPE=RADIO VALUE="amex"
➥ONCLICK="TheCardType= &quot;amex&quot;"
        NAME="cardtype">

<TD ALIGN=RIGHT><B>Discover</B>
<TD><INPUT LANGUAGE="vbscript" TYPE=RADIO VALUE="discovery"
➥ONCLICK="TheCardType= &quot;discovery&quot;"
➥NAME="cardtype">
<TR>
</TABLE>
<P>
<TABLE>
<TD><B>Cardholder's Name</B>
<TD><INPUT TYPE=TEXT SIZE=30 NAME="cardholder">
<TR>
<TD><B>Card Number</B>
<TD><INPUT TYPE=TEXT SIZE=20 NAME="cardnumber">
<TR>
<TD><B>Card Expiration Date</B>
<TD><INPUT TYPE=TEXT SIZE=5 NAME="cardexp">
<TR>
</TABLE>
<P>
        <INPUT LANGUAGE="vbscript" TYPE=button VALUE="Check"
        ➥ONCLICK=" call VerifyCard()">
        <INPUT TYPE=RESET VALUE="Clear/Reset">
    </FORM>
</BODY>
</HTML>
```

Example 2: Randolph Randal's Random Home Page

Document title: Randolph Randal's Random Home Page

Files:

Page file: `random.html` (see Figures 11.4, 11.5, and 11.6)

Images:

- ❏ `0.jpg`
- ❏ `1.jpg`
- ❏ `2.jpg`
- ❏ `3.jpg`
- ❏ `4.jpg`

Figure 11.4.

`random.html`.

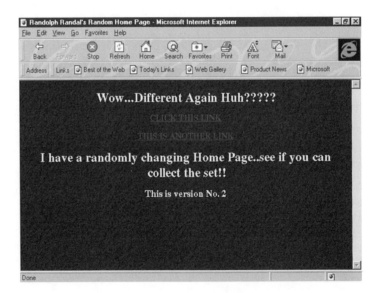

Description: To keep visitors interested, Randolph Randal randomized his home page. The page uses the simple random function built into VBScript to return a number between 0 and 4. Randolph then uses this number to select the background graphic for the page and also extract data from a prebuilt array of link colors, font colors, and so on.

Figure 11.5.

random.html—*same page, same code, different look.*

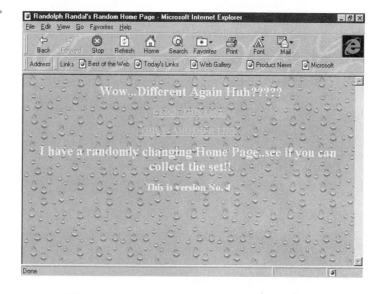

Figure 11.6.

random.html *again. You get the picture? You can have some fun with this concept.*

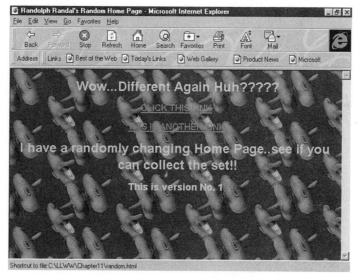

Techniques Applied

Subroutines and functions: (See Chapter 9.) The program consists of two script blocks with no subroutines, so the scripts execute upon loading in the browser.

Arrays: (See Chapter 10.) The page uses a number of single-dimension static arrays to store the page style data.

Language elements: The page uses the `Rnd()` function and several other basic language elements. It also uses the `Document.Write` method, which was used in several examples in this Part. Chapter 18, "Interacting with the Browser," discusses `Document.Write` in more detail.

The complete listing for Randolph Randal's Random Home Page (`random.html`) is shown in Listing 11.2.

Listing 11.2. The `random.html` code.

```
<HTML>
<TITLE>Randolph Randal's Random Home Page</TITLE>
</HEAD>
<SCRIPT LANGUAGE="vbscript">
 'create arrays for the body tag variables
 Dim Lnk(4)
 Dim VLnk(4)
 Dim FColor(4)
 Dim Fnt(4)
 'create a global variable
 Dim x

 'Variables for Version No. 1
 Lnk(0) = "Fuchsia"
 Vlnk(0) = "Silver"
 FColor(0) = "Lime"
 Fnt(0) = "arial"

 'Variables for Version No. 2
 Lnk(1) = "blue"
 Vlnk(1) = "fushia"
 FColor(1) = "white"
 Fnt(1) = "times roman"

 'Variables for Version No. 3
 Lnk(2) = "green"
 Vlnk(2) = "maroon"
 FColor(2) = "blue"
 Fnt(2) = "arial"

 'Variables for Version No. 4
 Lnk(3) = "lime"
 Vlnk(3) = "teal"
 FColor(3) = "yellow"
 Fnt(3) = "ms sans serif"

 'Variables for Version No. 5
 Lnk(4) = "navy"
 Vlnk(4) = "gray"
 FColor(4) = "black"
 Fnt(4) = "arial"

 'initialize the generator
 RANDOMIZE

 'generate a random number twixt none and four
 x = Int((5 - 1 + 1) * Rnd)
```

```
'turn said number into a string making sure there are no spaces
strX = Trim(CStr(x))

'add the jpg file extension and you've got a file name
randomimage = strX & ".jpg"

'write the randomly generated body tag into the document
Document.Write "<BODY BACKGROUND=" & Chr(34) & randomimage & Chr(34)
Document.Write " TEXT=" & FColor(x)
Document.Write " LINK=" & Lnk(x)
Document.Write " VLINK=" & Vlnk(x)
Document.Write ">"
Document.Write "<FONT FACE=" & Fnt(x) & " SIZE=3>"
</SCRIPT>

<CENTER>
<H2>Wow...Different Again Huh?????</H2>
<B>
<A HREF="">CLICK THIS LINK</A>
<P>
<A HREF="">THIS IS ANOTHER LINK</A>
<P>
</B>
<H2>I have a randomly changing Home Page..
➥see if you can collect the set!!</H2>
<H3>This is version No.

<!--
This writes the Version Number using the x global variable
-->
<SCRIPT LANGUAGE="vbscript">
Document.Write CStr(x+1)
</SCRIPT>

</H3>
</CENTER>
</FONT>
</BODY>
</HTML>
```

Example 3: Tim Day's Link Page

Document title: Tim Day's Link Page

Files: The page file is `links.html` (see Figures 11.7 and 11.8), and the images are `day.jpg` and `stars.gif`.

Description: Tim Day's link page uses the client machine's time variable to create a different look and different links for day and night users of the site.

Figure 11.7.
`links.html` *by day.*

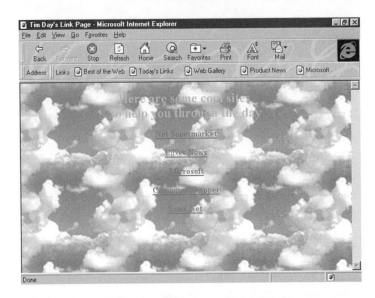

Figure 11.8.
`links.html` *by night.*

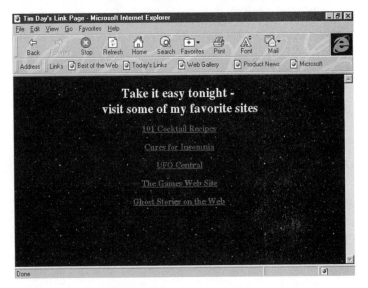

Techniques Applied

Dates: (See Chapter 8.) The script obtains the hour from the user's machine and calculates whether it is day or night.

Subroutines and functions: (See Chapter 9.) The program consists of two script blocks with no subroutines, so the scripts execute upon loading in the browser.

Operators: (See Chapter 4.) On several occasions, the script uses a range of comparison, logical, and arithmetic operators.

Decisions: (See Chapter 9.) The program uses the `If...Then` conditional operator to determine day or night.

Arrays: (See Chapter 10.) The body tag variables use several single-dimensional static arrays. In addition, the link descriptions and link URLs use a pair of two-dimensional arrays.

The complete code for `links.html` is shown in Listing 11.3.

Listing 11.3. The `links.html` code.

```
<HTML>
<TITLE>Tim Day's Link Page</TITLE>
</HEAD>
<SCRIPT LANGUAGE="vbscript">
 'create arrays for the body tag variables
 Dim Lnk(1)
 Dim VLnk(1)
 Dim FColor(1)
 Dim Fnt(1)
 Dim Greet(1)

 'declare two dimensional arrays for the links
 Dim LinkDesc(1,4)
 Dim LinkURL(1,4)

 'declare two constants
 Dim DAYTIME
 Dim NIGHTTIME
 DAYTIME = 1
 NIGHTTIME = 0
 'create a global variable
 Dim x

 'Variables for Nighttime Version
 Lnk(NIGHTTIME) = "blue"
 Vlnk(NIGHTTIME) = "fushia"
 FColor(NIGHTTIME) = "yellow"
 Fnt(NIGHTTIME) = "times roman"
 Greet(NIGHTTIME) = "Take it easy tonight - <BR> visit some of my favorite
sites"

 'Variables for Daytime Version
 Lnk(DAYTIME) = "red"
 Vlnk(DAYTIME) = "teal"
 FColor(DAYTIME) = "orange"
 Fnt(DAYTIME) = "ms sans serif"
 Greet(DAYTIME) = "Here are some cool sites <BR>to help you through the day"

 'Descriptions for the Links
 LinkDesc(NIGHTTIME,0) = "101 Cocktail Recipes"
 LinkDesc(NIGHTTIME,1) = "Cures for Insomnia"
 LinkDesc(NIGHTTIME,2) = "UFO Central"
```

continues

Listing 11.3. continued

```
LinkDesc(NIGHTTIME,3) = "The Games Web Site"
LinkDesc(NIGHTTIME,4) = "Ghost Stories on the Web"
LinkDesc(DAYTIME,0) = "Net Supermarket"
LinkDesc(DAYTIME,1) = "C¦Net News"
LinkDesc(DAYTIME,2) = "Microsoft"
LinkDesc(DAYTIME,3) = "Computer Shopper"
LinkDesc(DAYTIME,4) = "Sams.Net"

'URLs for the Links - these aren't real links ;-)
LinkURL(NIGHTTIME,0) = "http://1"
LinkURL(NIGHTTIME,1) = "http://2"
LinkURL(NIGHTTIME,2) = "http://3"
LinkURL(NIGHTTIME,3) = "http://4"
LinkURL(NIGHTTIME,4) = "http://5"
LinkURL(DAYTIME,0) = "http://1"
LinkURL(DAYTIME,1) = "http://2"
LinkURL(DAYTIME,2) = "http://3"
LinkURL(DAYTIME,3) = "http://4"
LinkURL(DAYTIME,4) = "http://5"

'Determine whether it's day or night
TheHour = Hour(Now())
If TheHour >= 5 and TheHour < 20 Then
    x = DAYTIME
    theimage = "day.jpg"
Else
    x = NIGHTTIME
    theimage = "stars.gif"
End If



'write the body tag etc into the document
Document.Write "<BODY BACKGROUND=" & Chr(34) & theimage & Chr(34)
Document.Write " TEXT=" & FColor(x)
Document.Write " LINK=" & Lnk(x)
Document.Write " VLINK=" & Vlnk(x)
Document.Write ">"
Document.Write "<FONT FACE=" & Fnt(x) & " SIZE=3>"
Document.Write "<CENTER>"
Document.Write "<H2>" & Greet(x) & "</H2><P><B>"

'write the links
For i = 0 to 4
 Document.Write "<A HREF=" & Chr(34) & LinkURL(x,i) & Chr(34) & "><P>"
 Document.Write LinkDesc(x,i)
 Document.Write "</A>"
Next

</SCRIPT>
</CENTER>
</FONT>
</BODY>
</HTML>
```

PART

III

Building an ActiveX Web Site

by Rogers Cadenhead

TWELVE

Using VBScript with ActiveX Controls

The VBScript programming language is only half of Microsoft's current Internet programming strategy. The other half is ActiveX, a way to develop programmable objects that can be added to Web pages alongside images, text, Java applets, and other media.

VBScript provides access to the intrinsic HTML controls—buttons, text fields, radio buttons, and other things that are common to Web-based forms. You encounter these controls any time you register to join a Web site, order a product through the Web, or use a feedback page to tell Shaquille O'Neal how much you enjoy `http://www.shaq.com`.

If you want to create sophisticated programs to run on a Web page, you might want to extend the possibilities beyond intrinsic controls by using ActiveX controls.

Overview of ActiveX Components

ActiveX controls are components that extend the capabilities of Web pages. They were previously known as OCX or OLE controls, a type of software-development component that might be familiar to some readers.

An ActiveX control is developed using a language such as Visual C++, Visual Basic, or Delphi. Like an OCX, an ActiveX component is designed to be used by some other software—a Web browser, in this case.

More than 1,000 ActiveX controls are available for use, according to Microsoft. In addition to being usable on Web pages, these controls can be used with other types of software developed with programming languages such as Java, Borland C++ and Delphi, Visual Basic, and Visual C++.

These controls are developed in other languages, but their operation can be modified and customized with the use of HTML code and VBScript programs. ActiveX controls are placed on a Web page using a special extended HTML tag called <OBJECT> and a supporting tag called <PARAM>.

The <OBJECT> Tag

The <OBJECT> tag, proposed by the World Wide Web Consortium as a future standard, is used to place an object on a Web page. The primary type of object discussed in this chapter is an ActiveX control, but the tag considers an object to be any type of media that can be put on a page. <OBJECT> was proposed by the Consortium as a way to replace several current HTML tags and attributes—the <IMG> tag, the Java <APPLET> tag, the DYNSRC attribute used for audio and video by Microsoft, and other proprietary extensions to HTML. <OBJECT> also is flexible enough in design to handle new forms of media not yet invented for the Web.

Attributes are used with the <OBJECT> tag to specify the following information:

- ❏ The object's name
- ❏ The type of object
- ❏ The URL address where the object can be found
- ❏ Layout information such as height, width, spacing, border width, alignment, and so on
- ❏ An ID code to verify the object's identity

If the object has parameters, they can be set with the <PARAM> tag. This tag has two attributes: NAME and VALUE. The NAME attribute gives the parameter a name, and VALUE sets up a value for that parameter.

Although <OBJECT> is intended to be used with a broad range of media, the only example of it in current use is the ActiveX control.

Generating <OBJECT> HTML Code

As you'll see later in this chapter, when you use the ActiveX Control Pad to add an ActiveX object to a Web page, an <OBJECT> tag is added automatically to the page. Here's an example of an ActiveX control's <OBJECT> tag:

```
<OBJECT ID="SpinButton1" WIDTH=16 HEIGHT=32
 CLASSID="CLSID:79176FB0-B7F2-11CE-97EF-00AA006D2776">
    <PARAM NAME="Size" VALUE="423;846">
</OBJECT>
```

This <OBJECT> tag creates an ActiveX spin button control with up and down arrows to change a value. Java programmers will recognize the <PARAM> tag, because it has the same attributes (NAME and VALUE) and the same usage as it does with the Java <APPLET> tag. Eventually, Microsoft Internet Explorer and other browsers plan to enable the <OBJECT> tag to handle Java applets in addition to ActiveX controls.

Because this HTML code is added automatically by the ActiveX Control Pad, you do not need to enter it yourself into a Web page's HTML file. However, an understanding of the elements of an <OBJECT> tag will help you understand ActiveX controls.

The ID attribute of the <OBJECT> tag gives the object a name. One of the biggest advantages of VBScript and ActiveX is the capability of one object to communicate with another object. A VBScript program can be used for one element on a page— for example, a <FORM> button—to modify another program, such as an ActiveX control. ID is needed for one object to know how to contact another.

The CLSID attribute identifies the type of object and provides some identifying characteristics of the object. In the preceding example, the CLSID was set to a complicated string of numbers and letters:

```
CLSID:79176FB0-B7F2-11CE-97EF-00AA006D2776
```

This has two parts. The section before the colon, CLSID, identifies this object as an ActiveX control. Another example of an identifier would be java:, representing an applet programmed in that language.

The section after the colon indicates some registration information that reveals where the ActiveX control can be found on the user's Windows system. ActiveX controls are downloaded to the user's system and run locally. The CLSID gives the browser enough information to find, identify, and run the control. It also creates a unique identifier for the ActiveX control. No matter how many ActiveX controls are implemented across the Internet, each will use part of the CLSID to establish its identity.

ActiveX controls, previously known as OCX or OLE controls, offer added functionality to Web page developers. In addition to being usable on the World Wide Web, ActiveX controls have an advantage over other Internet programming solutions such as Java applets and Netscape plug-ins.

These controls can be used immediately in other applications. For example, a control that performs an image editing task on the Web can be plugged into a software program as easily as it was placed on a page.

Downloading Objects from the Web

ActiveX controls are downloaded from the Web and executed locally on the user's computer. An ActiveX-enabled Web browser will behave differently if it encounters a new control than if it has seen the control previously.

If you are using a browser that can handle ActiveX controls and you come to a page containing a control, a check will be made to determine whether you have downloaded the control previously. This check will use the CLSID attribute of the <OBJECT> tag to determine whether the ActiveX control is present on your system.

If you haven't downloaded the control previously, a special certificate window will be opened that is similar to the one shown in Figure 12.1.

Figure 12.1.

An ActiveX control verification certificate.

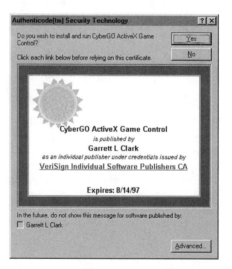

This certificate is part of ActiveX's security plan. Because ActiveX controls are executed on the user's system, there is obvious potential for a programmer to run malicious code. In order to run an ActiveX control, you need some means of identifying the author as a trustworthy source.

The VeriSign company is handling ActiveX developer certification for a large number of the existing controls. The certificate window that opens when you encounter a new control on a Web page has a link to a control verification source such as VeriSign and probably a link to the developer's Web site.

As the certification window states, you should click the links on the certificate before accepting its validity. If you're satisfied that everything looks legitimate, you can click Yes to download and install the control.

CAUTION: In the certification window, checkboxes enable you to reduce the number of security checks that you require for future checks. You can accept every future control from a company, or even every future control that comes from the verification company such as VeriSign.

Although ActiveX is still in relative infancy as a technology, it seems prudent to leave these checkboxes blank. You must go through more security checks before loading a control, but the loss in time should be regained by the more secure environment. When ActiveX and control verification systems such as VeriSign have become more established, you can elect to accept all of their certifications without question.

If you elect to download a control, it downloads and begins running automatically. Figure 12.2 shows the CyberGO ActiveX control, which can be used with Internet Explorer 3.0 after a security certificate is accepted. To try CyberGO, visit the following Web page:

`http://www.brlabs.com/cybergo/cybergostart.html`

Figure 12.2.
An ActiveX control, the CyberGO game from Brilliance Labs.

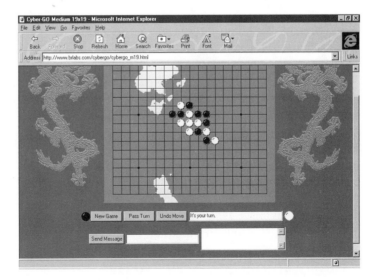

After the control has been downloaded and executed, it remains on the user's computer so that it does not have to be reloaded each time the control is found on a Web page. The only time that an ActiveX control will be downloaded more than once is when a new version is offered that the user does not yet have.

This enables much quicker access to an ActiveX control than is presently possible with Java applets, which download again each time they are encountered. However, the disadvantage is that ActiveX controls take up space on a user's hard drive. In the present version of Internet Explorer, ActiveX controls are stored in a subdirectory called `Windows/Occache`.

To see a sampling of the ActiveX controls that have been made available, the Internet information service CNET has introduced an ActiveX file directory and news site at the following URL:

`http://www.activex.com`

When a control is on your system, you can use it as a component in your own Web pages and software projects. CNET's ActiveX site has many controls available that cater to programmers in need of useful components.

Empowering Netscape Navigator with ActiveX and VBScript

At the time of this writing, Microsoft Internet Explorer 3.0 is the only popular browser that implements VBScript and ActiveX controls as part of its "out-of-the-box" functionality. (Given that most people acquire Internet Explorer through an Internet download, however, that box metaphor might be outdated—perhaps "out-of-the-executable-archive"?)

Netscape Navigator, the browser used by more than 70 percent of the Web's audience at present, can handle ActiveX and VBScript through special software called a plug-in. If you're unfamiliar with the term, a plug-in is software that has an established link to existing software. This link enables the plug-in to add functionality to the core program. Many Internet users listen to audio programming over the Net by using a RealAudio plug-in. When Netscape or Internet Explorer encounters a RealAudio file, the software knows to run a RealAudio player program to read in the file and crank up the PC's audio.

NCompass Labs has developed an ActiveX plug-in called ScriptActive for users of some versions of Netscape Navigator. It currently works on Windows 95, NT, and 3.5.1 systems running Navigator 3.0 or Navigator Gold 3.0. You must be running a 486 or better PC with 8MB of RAM.

Downloading ScriptActive

The ScriptActive plug-in is offered for a free 30-day trial period, after which it must be purchased from NCompass. Send e-mail to `ncompass@ncompasslabs.com` for current pricing information.

If you have the right software and system, you can download the NCompass ScriptActive plug-in from the following URL:

`http://www.ncompasslabs.com/binaries/index.htm`

The file is about 3.5MB in size, so it can take 30 minutes or more to download depending on the speed of your Internet connection. When it's done, you have a single executable file. Run it to start the ScriptActive setup program, which takes you through the steps required to add the plug-in to your version of Navigator.

During the installation, the setup program attempts to find where Navigator is located on your system. If it locates Navigator, you can confirm that it's the right version of the software, or choose a different location manually. If no version of Navigator is found, you'll have to find it yourself to continue installing ScriptActive.

One question you might be asked during the installation process is whether to replace an existing file with an older one that came with ScriptActive. ScriptActive, like most Windows software, uses dynamic link libraries (DLLs) that take care of some tasks. These libraries are often shared between programs, so you might have a better, newer version of a DLL than the one ScriptActive wants to install.

If you're asked whether to replace an existing file with an older version of it, you should keep the existing file in almost all circumstances. If you don't, it might alter the performance of some other software on your system.

After the installation is complete, you have to restart your system in order for the plug-in to work correctly.

Trying the Plug-In

After you have downloaded and finished installing ScriptActive, you're ready to try it out. Load Netscape Navigator if it isn't already loaded, and visit the following URL:

`http://www.ncompasslabs.com/products/scriptactive_link.htm`

This page has a link to a showcase of ScriptActive techniques. The plug-in enables VBScript and ActiveX, and it also works with JavaScript, the scripting language developed by Netscape that is similar in scope and function to VBScript. Figure 12.3 shows an example of one of these showcase ActiveX controls running on Netscape Navigator.

This is one of the advantages of the present competitiveness in the browser market. Because companies are after the widest possible segment of the Web audience, a "kitchen sink" approach is being taken toward new technology. If Netscape comes up with a new idea that gains popularity, Microsoft won't be far behind in adopting it or adopting a compatible solution.

Figure 12.3.
An ActiveX control running on Netscape Navigator 3.0.

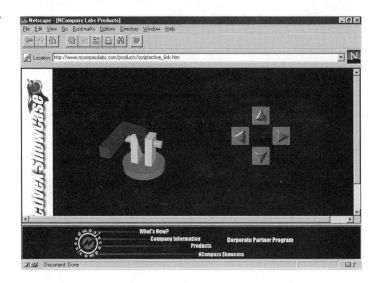

The time you spend learning something such as ActiveX and VBScript can help you reach an audience beyond the users of Microsoft Internet Explorer. As more evidence of this, NCompass Labs offers as part of its ScriptActive package a tool to read <OBJECT> tags in HTML files and add <EMBED> tags to accompany them. The <EMBED> tag is Netscape's current implementation of an <OBJECT> tag, and the ScriptActive tool makes an ActiveX page work for both Internet Explorer 3.0 and Netscape Navigator 3.0.

An HTML Page Using a Sample ActiveX Control

As you saw earlier, ActiveX controls are added to an HTML page by using the <OBJECT> tag. This is normally placed in a document automatically by a tool such as the ActiveX Control Pad. You get a chance to use that software in the next chapter.

Here, you will create an HTML page and add an <OBJECT> to the page manually.

Enter the full text of Listing 12.1 into any text editor, and save the file as object.html. If your editor has a special file format, as Microsoft Word does, make sure to choose the ASCII text or plain text option when saving the HTML file.

Listing 12.1. The full HTML source code of object.html.

```
1: <HTML>
2: <HEAD>
3: </HEAD>
4: <BODY>
5: <FORM NAME="Form">
```

```
 6: <OBJECT ID="TextBox1" WIDTH=96 HEIGHT=24
 7:  CLASSID="CLSID:8BD21D10-EC42-11CE-9E0D-00AA006002F3">
 8:     <PARAM NAME="VariousPropertyBits" VALUE="746604571">
 9:     <PARAM NAME="Size" VALUE="2540;635">
10:     <PARAM NAME="FontCharSet" VALUE="0">
11:     <PARAM NAME="FontPitchAndFamily" VALUE="2">
12:     <PARAM NAME="FontWeight" VALUE="0">
13: </OBJECT>
14: </FORM>
15: </BODY>
16: </HTML>
```

When you're done, load the `object.html` page into Internet Explorer 3.0, or Netscape Navigator 3.0 if you have installed the ScriptActive plug-in. The page should resemble the one in Figure 12.4.

Figure 12.4.

The output of `object.html` *in Internet Explorer 3.0.*

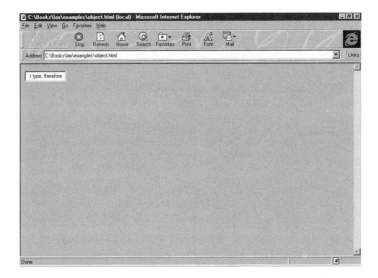

ActiveX controls have several properties that can be set up using the `<PARAM>` tag. The properties vary based on the kind of control: The one in the example is a plain text box like those used with the HTML `<FORM>` tag.

Controls typically are highly customizable through the use of properties. The five `<PARAM>` tags set here are only a small portion of the total number of properties associated with these text box controls.

The `CLASSID` attribute to the `<OBJECT>` tag identifies the type of object. At present, when `<OBJECT>` is used solely to place ActiveX controls on a page, this identifier is not as important as it will be later if the tag becomes a Web standard. In this case, the `clsid:` portion of `CLASSID` indicates that the object is an ActiveX control, and the remainder of `CLASSID` is an unwieldy alphanumeric string. This string identifies the type of control and its location on the user's system.

The ID attribute is set up so that an object can communicate with other objects—VBScript programs, other controls, Java applets, or anything else that is compatible with ActiveX controls.

Adding a Label Object

The Web page you have created has a text field, but it's a little obtuse without a label indicating what is supposed to be entered in the field. The most basic ActiveX controls are intrinsic HTML form objects—buttons, text fields, radio buttons, and the other elements of a Web page form.

When these are created as ActiveX controls, you don't use HTML code such as the following:

```
<INPUT NAME="permit" TYPE=Radio VALUE="Yes">
```

Instead, you add the form element to a Web page using the <OBJECT> tag, because it gives you much more control over the element's appearance and behavior. To add a label in front of the text field that you have created in object.html, open the file and insert a blank line right after the <BODY> tag. In the space you just opened up, add the following <OBJECT> HTML code:

```
<OBJECT ID="Label1" WIDTH=96 HEIGHT=24
 CLASSID="CLSID:978C9E23-D4B0-11CE-BF2D-00AA003F40D0">
    <PARAM NAME="Caption" VALUE="The meaning of life (5 words or less): ">
    <PARAM NAME="Size" VALUE="2540;635">
    <PARAM NAME="FontCharSet" VALUE="0">
    <PARAM NAME="FontPitchAndFamily" VALUE="2">
    <PARAM NAME="FontWeight" VALUE="0">
</OBJECT>
```

This puts a label in front of the text field. The Caption parameter sets the value of the label's caption, and the WIDTH and HEIGHT attributes set the size of the element. This is one immediate benefit of using a control form object instead of standard HTML: You can change the size. As the other parameters indicate, you can change the appearance as well.

Adding a Button Object

Because these elements have been created as controls, you can access and modify their properties from VBScript. To see this in action, add a button that checks whether the correct answer has been entered in the text field.

Return to object.html and add a blank line above the </BODY> tag at the bottom of the document. At the spot of that blank line, add the following HTML code:

```
<P>
<OBJECT ID="cmdGuess" WIDTH=96 HEIGHT=32
 CLASSID="CLSID:D7053240-CE69-11CD-A777-00DD01143C57">
    <PARAM NAME="Caption" VALUE="Am I Right?">
    <PARAM NAME="Size" VALUE="2540;846">
    <PARAM NAME="FontCharSet" VALUE="0">
    <PARAM NAME="FontPitchAndFamily" VALUE="2">
    <PARAM NAME="ParagraphAlign" VALUE="3">
    <PARAM NAME="FontWeight" VALUE="0">
</OBJECT>
```

The Web page that you have created has an Am I Right? button, but if you load the page and try it out, nothing happens. In order for something to happen in response to the click of the cmdGuess object, you need to add a short VBScript program to object.html.

Adding a VBScript Program

VBScript programs can be put in a Web page by placing the programming commands in between an opening <SCRIPT> tag and a closing </SCRIPT> tag. The program is not displayed on-screen to Web users, but it can be seen by anyone who views the source code of the page.

This is one of the disadvantages of using a scripting language on a Web page. If some of the code needs to be hidden from users, a different programming solution such as Java or ActiveX must be used for the hidden parts.

The VBScript program inside a <SCRIPT> tag can be put anywhere in an HTML document. By convention, the code is put in the top part of a Web page between the opening <HEAD> tag and the closing </HEAD> tag.

Add the following HTML code to object.html one line below the starting <HEAD> tag:

```
<SCRIPT LANGUAGE="VBScript">
<!--

Sub cmdGuess_Click
    If Form.TextBox1.Value = "pizza" Then
        Form.cmdGuess.caption = "You're Right!"
        Form.cmdGuess.enabled = 0
    Else
        Form.cmdGuess.caption = "Guess Again"
    End If
End Sub

-->
</SCRIPT>
```

When you're done, the HTML source code file should resemble Listing 12.2.

Listing 12.2. The full HTML source code of the new `object.html`.

```
 1: <HTML>
 2: <HEAD>
 3: <SCRIPT LANGUAGE="VBScript">
 4: <!--
 5:
 6: Sub cmdGuess_Click
 7:     If Form.TextBox1.Value = "pizza" Then
 8:         Form.cmdGuess.caption = "You're Right!"
 9:         Form.cmdGuess.enabled = 0
10:     Else
11:         Form.cmdGuess.caption = "Guess Again"
12:     End If
13: End Sub
14:
15: -->
16: </SCRIPT>
17: </HEAD>
18: <BODY>
19: <FORM NAME="Form">
20: <OBJECT ID="Label1" WIDTH=96 HEIGHT=24
21:  CLASSID="CLSID:978C9E23-D4B0-11CE-BF2D-00AA003F40D0">
22:     <PARAM NAME="Caption" VALUE="The meaning of life (5 words or less): ">
23:     <PARAM NAME="Size" VALUE="2540;635">
24:     <PARAM NAME="FontCharSet" VALUE="0">
25:     <PARAM NAME="FontPitchAndFamily" VALUE="2">
26:     <PARAM NAME="FontWeight" VALUE="0">
27: </OBJECT>
28: <OBJECT ID="TextBox1" WIDTH=96 HEIGHT=24
29:  CLASSID="CLSID:8BD21D10-EC42-11CE-9E0D-00AA006002F3">
30:     <PARAM NAME="VariousPropertyBits" VALUE="746604571">
31:     <PARAM NAME="Size" VALUE="2540;635">
32:     <PARAM NAME="FontCharSet" VALUE="0">
33:     <PARAM NAME="FontPitchAndFamily" VALUE="2">
34:     <PARAM NAME="FontWeight" VALUE="0">
35: </OBJECT>
36: <P>
37: <OBJECT ID="cmdGuess" WIDTH=96 HEIGHT=32
38:  CLASSID="CLSID:D7053240-CE69-11CD-A777-00DD01143C57">
39:     <PARAM NAME="Caption" VALUE="Am I Right?">
40:     <PARAM NAME="Size" VALUE="2540;846">
41:     <PARAM NAME="FontCharSet" VALUE="0">
42:     <PARAM NAME="FontPitchAndFamily" VALUE="2">
43:     <PARAM NAME="ParagraphAlign" VALUE="3">
44:     <PARAM NAME="FontWeight" VALUE="0">
45: </OBJECT>
46: </FORM>
47: </BODY>
48: </HTML>
```

Load the Web page into an ActiveX-enabled browser and you can attempt to guess the meaning of life in five words or less. When you click the button labeled Am I Right?, it changes to Guess Again if you are incorrect. The button remains Guess Again until you answer the question by entering pizza in the text field. When that occurs, the button changes to You're Right! and becomes light gray in color. Nothing happens when the button is clicked after this point, because the button's Enabled property has been set to 0, which in VBScript is used to represent a boolean value of `false`. This is another advantage of using ActiveX controls as opposed to standard HTML forms. The developer can control which form elements can be accessed and can set `Enabled` to 0 for any buttons or input fields that should not be used at a given time.

Figure 12.5 shows a screen capture from the final version of `object.html`.

Figure 12.5.
The output of the final `object.html`.

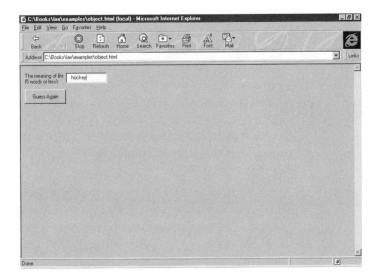

Workshop Wrap-Up

After typing in all of these <OBJECT> tags and painstakingly entering the numbers of the CLASSID attribute, you might be getting the idea that it's difficult to add objects to a Web page. That's not really the case. You've been made to suffer a little bit in order to learn the HTML foundation of ActiveX controls.

In the next chapter, you can learn an easier way to add objects that will let you forget most of the things you just learned about CLASSID. The ActiveX Control Pad, a development tool made available by Microsoft, makes it possible to add controls to a page without typing any <OBJECT> tags.

The objects that you created for the meaning of life example used several different parameters to set their property values. Each control comes with its own set of properties that can be modified, with guidelines for how to change them. There are often 20 properties or more that can be used to configure a control, even for a relatively simple object such as those used in `object.html`.

Using a tool such as the ActiveX Control Pad, you can see every property and modify them by changing values on a dialog box.

Next Steps

Now that you are more familiar with the use of ActiveX controls on a page, the following chapters are good places to continue:

- ❑ To learn more about using other objects such as Java applets with VBScript, see Chapter 15, "Using Java Applets with VBScript."
- ❑ To learn more about building using Form elements with VBScript, see Chapter 6, "Checking Form Data."
- ❑ To learn more about using the ActiveX Control Pad, see Chapter 13, "Implementing an ActiveX Menu Control."

Q&A

Q: I have used an `onClick` event in VBScript with an HTML intrinsic control, but the ActiveX control in the Workshop uses a `Click` event. Are these different?

A: Yes. VBScript uses the Click event with an ActiveX control and the `onClick` event with the intrinsic HTML form elements. It's easy to mistake the two and use the wrong one when developing a VBScript program. If you try to use an `onClick()` subroutine with an ActiveX control, the program will be loaded without any errors, but the subroutine will never be called.

Q: Is there a way to set the initial values of a control from VBScript?

A: You can create a main body of a VBScript by including code after the `<SCRIPT>` tag that is not included in a `Sub` statement. The VBScript interpreter assumes that this code should be executed immediately after the page is loaded.

For example, the following VBScript program sets the initial value of the caption for an ActiveX control button called `cmdClickMe`:

```
<SCRIPT>
<!--

cmdClickMe.Caption = "Click If You Dare"

-->
</SCRIPT>
```

Q: I've written a complicated VBScript in which a text field changes more than once between user input. However, the only change that shows up on-screen is the last change. Why is this?

A: An aspect of VBScript development that can frustrate programmers is the way it updates the Web page in response to VBScript. Screen updates do not take place each time a screen element is changed. Instead, all of the VBScript code is executed before the display changes. If you change a button's label to `Click Me` in line 22 of a subroutine, and change it again in line 706 to `Don't Click Me`, only `Don't Click Me` will be seen.

THIRTEEN

Implementing an ActiveX Menu Control

As often happens with a new technology, the imagination begins to run ahead of developments. After you start using VBScript and ActiveX on your Web pages, the likelihood is that you will not be content with the forms-type controls supplied with the ActiveX Control Pad, and you'll want to do more.

So where do you find a source of extra controls to satisfy your needs? Well, unlike Java applets, which are relatively new, ActiveX controls (formerly OCX controls) have been in development and use for quite some time. Consequently, hundreds or even thousands of ActiveX controls are available on the Web. The best place to start looking is the Microsoft ActiveX Gallery.

In this chapter, you

- ❏ See how to obtain new custom controls from the Microsoft ActiveX Gallery
- ❏ Learn how to use new controls in the ActiveX Control Pad
- ❏ Learn how to download a new control to the users of your page

Tasks in this chapter:

- ❏ Downloading new controls from the Web
- ❏ Implementing the ActiveX Menu control
- ❏ Downloading new controls to your users

Downloading New Controls from the Web

The Microsoft ActiveX Gallery is part of the Microsoft Site Builder Workshop site at `http://www.microsoft.com/workshop/`. There you'll find a large range of controls for a wide range of applications and solutions.

The address of the gallery at the time of this writing is `http://www.microsoft.com/activex/gallery/`. The site shown in Figure 13.1 lists controls available from Microsoft and also controls available from third-party vendors. The Microsoft controls are free to download and use, but before you use any control within your own Web pages, it is wise to check the copyright, usage, and other conditions of its use.

Figure 13.1.
The ActiveX Control Gallery.

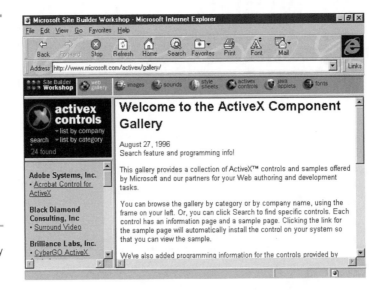

Check the Microsoft ActiveX Gallery regularly for new and updated controls.

To obtain a particular control from the Microsoft site, simply click the control name in the left lower frame. A page is then loaded to display a graphical snapshot of the control and a hyperlink to download the control, as shown in Figure 13.2.

For the example used in this chapter, you need to obtain the Microsoft Button menu control. When you click the hyperlink, a new page that contains the control is loaded. If you don't have the control loaded on your machine already, a control is downloaded to you from the Microsoft control repository. Just prior to the completion of the download, you are asked to confirm that you want to receive this control into your machine (as shown in Figure 13.3). This unique security feature ensures that users know what the source of a control is before they accept it onto the hard drive.

Figure 13.2.

Ready to download the menu control.

If the control loads on the new page immediately when you click "Download and run a working sample," you already had the control loaded onto your machine.

Figure 13.3.

The safety certificate for the menu control.

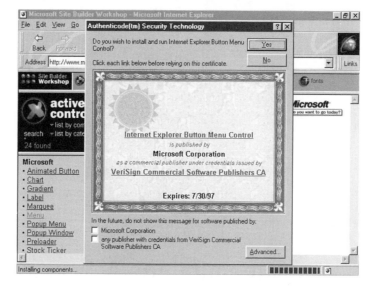

ActiveX controls are usually stored in your `windows\occache\` subdirectory.

NOTE: A major concern regarding ActiveX controls and Java applets is the potential security risk. As you will see later in this chapter, this security certificate follows the control around so that it also displays on the machine of a user visiting your site when that user downloads the control from you.

You can request that certificates not be shown again for Microsoft or for any VeriSign verified software company by checking the boxes at the bottom of the window, in which case controls will be automatically registered onto your machine on download.

After you accept the credentials of the control's author (in this case, Microsoft), the control is registered onto your machine and is ready to use.

The page to which you hyperlinked to download the control uses the new control (shown in Figure 13.4) so that you can see it in action. Before you leave the site, do two things:

1. Look at the source of the page that downloaded and demonstrated the control. Save the source to a text file for later reference.

2. Click the "View Programming Information" hyperlink to obtain a list of properties and methods for the control.

Figure 13.4.
The Menu control installed and working.

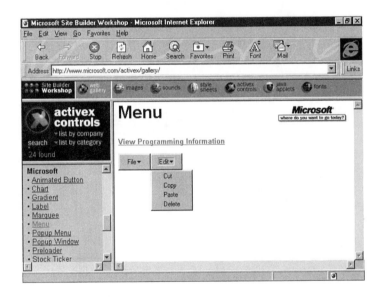

The source of the page also gives you the actual filename of the control—in this case, `btnmenu.ocx`.

Now that you've acquired your shiny new Menu Button control, you can access it from the ActiveX Control Pad and use it on your own Web pages.

Implementing the ActiveX Menu Control

This example uses the Microsoft ActiveX Menu control, sometimes known as the Button Menu. You will create a simple user interface on a Web page, using two Menu controls and adding some straightforward VBScript to implement the menu's functionality. This section shows you how to use a newly downloaded control through the ActiveX Control Pad. For details on how to do the same using the HTML Layout control, see Chapter 14, "Using the HTML Layout Control." Furthermore, in the first part of the example, you run both the HTML page and the control locally. In the next section, you learn how to place the control on your Web site for the use of your site visitors.

1. First, open the ActiveX Control Pad.

2. Place your cursor between the <BODY> tags, and select Insert ActiveX Control from the Edit menu.

3. The Insert ActiveX Control dialog is displayed. Select the BtnMenu object, as shown in Figure 13.5.

Figure 13.5.

Select the Menu control from the ActiveX Controls List.

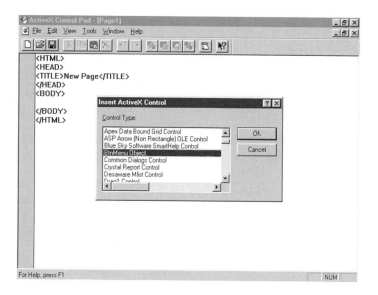

When the Button Menu object loads in the object editor, it does not have a default size. It looks rather odd, all crunched up in the corner as shown in Figure 13.6.

Figure 13.6.

The Menu control when it first loads.

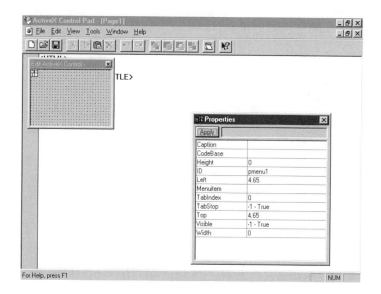

4. Place your cursor on one of the handles, and drag the control to a respectable size, as shown in Figure 13.7. The exact size is not really important for this exercise.

Figure 13.7.

The Menu control resized.

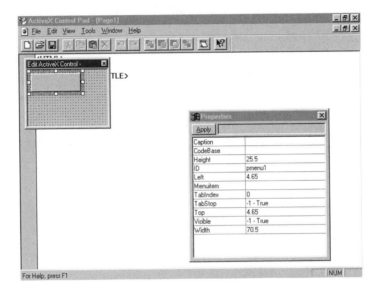

5. You don't need to set any properties other than the size at this stage. The caption and menu items will be set by VBScript code as the object loads. Therefore, all you need to do is close the object editor, and the Control Pad automatically generates the code for the menu object in the HTML page (see Figure 13.8).

Figure 13.8.

The definition code for the first Menu control.

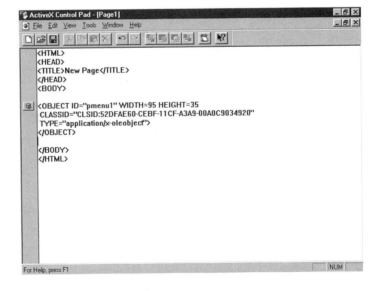

Some versions of the object produce spurious code. If this happens with your control, edit the object definition manually to match the one shown in Figure 13.8.

6. Your sample menu page will contain two Menu controls; the easiest way to generate a second object is to copy the code for the first object and paste it directly under the first. Then simply change the object ID to pMenu2, as shown in Figure 13.9.

Figure 13.9.

The definition code for both Menu controls.

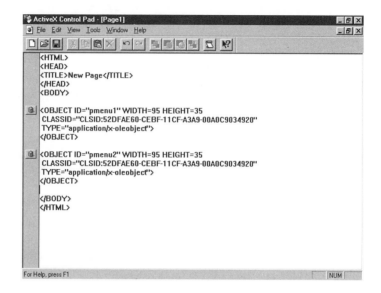

The menu captions and menu items are added using VBScript code in the Window object's OnLoad event. This means that as the page loads, it loads the controls within the page and then executes the code to fill in the menu options and caption. If you place this code in an event that occurs prior to the loading of the objects, you will generate a runtime error. Follow these steps to add the onLoad event handler code:

1. Open the ActiveX Script Wizard and click the plus sign to the left of the Window Object in the left events pane.

2. Select the onLoad event.

3. Click the plus sign to the left of the pmenu1 object in the right actions pane.

4. A full list of the menu object's properties and methods is now displayed. The method used to add menu items is called AddItem. Double-click this method name, and a line of code is automatically generated in the OnLoad event handler in the lower Script Window. (See Figure 13.10.)

5. You now need to manually edit the code you have been given and replace the variable placeholders with your own literal values. First, replace item with First Menu Option. Then replace index with 1.

Figure 13.10.
Starting the onLoad *event in the Script Wizard.*

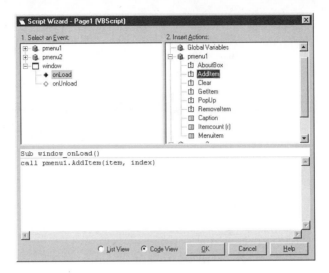

6. Repeat steps 4 and 5 to generate lines of code for a total of four menu options, as shown in Figure 13.11.

Figure 13.11.
The menu options for Menu One.

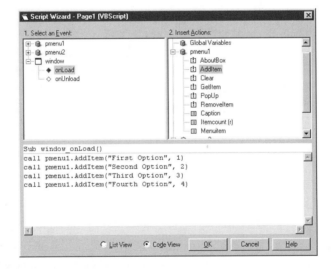

Unlike other VBScript arrays, the array of menu options in this control begins with the number 1.

7. Now you need to specify a caption that will appear on the face of the button menu. To do this, double-click the Caption property, and edit the automatic code (as shown in Figure 13.12) to read as follows:

```
pmenu1.Caption = "Menu One"
```

Figure 13.12.

The caption for Menu One.

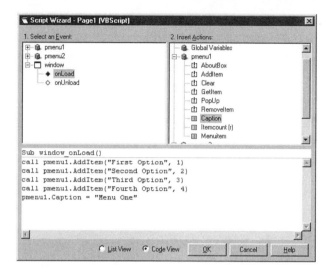

8. To add menu options for Menu Two (pmenu2), click the plus sign to the left of the pmenu2 object in the right actions pane, and then repeat steps from step 4 through 6. Your event handler should then resemble the one in Figure 13.13. Again, you might find it easier and quicker to simply cut and paste the code for the first menu and manually amend the variables.

Figure 13.13.

The complete onLoad *event.*

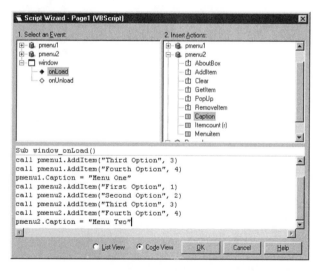

Now you have two menus on the page, both with captions and four options. But what happens when you click one of these options? The answer is that the menu object's select event is fired. Your next task, therefore, is to write code that will execute within the select event handler. The select event handler has one argument: the index number of the menu option that the user selected. Therefore, you have only one `select` event handler for the whole menu, but it executes differently for each menu option. The best way to achieve this is to use a `Select Case` control block.

For more details on **Select Case**, see Chapter 9, "Making Your Program Flow."

1. Click the plus sign to the left of the `pMenu1` object in the left events pane.

2. Choose the `Select` event.

3. Enter the following code into the event handler for Menu One's `Select` event:

```
Select Case item
 Case 1
  Alert "You selected Option One from Menu One"
 Case 2
  Alert "You selected Option Two from Menu One"
 Case 3
  Alert "You selected Option Three from Menu One"
 Case 4
  Alert "You selected Option Four from Menu One"
End Select
```

Now repeat this for `pMenu2`, amending the Alert captions to read `...from Menu Two`. The completed event handler for Menu Two's select event is shown in Figure 13.14.

Figure 13.14.

The complete event handler for Menu Two's Select event.

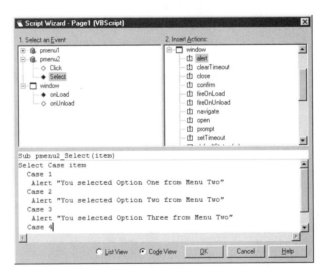

For this example, the coding is completed. Now click OK at the bottom of the Script Wizard window to make the Script Wizard generate the code into the HTML page, as shown in Figure 13.15.

Save the file as `menudemo.htm`, and test it through your MSIE3.0 browser. You should have two menus with four options each (see Figure 13.16). When clicked, the menus display an alert box informing you of which option was clicked (see Figure 13.17).

Figure 13.15.

The completed script is automatically generated and placed in the text editor.

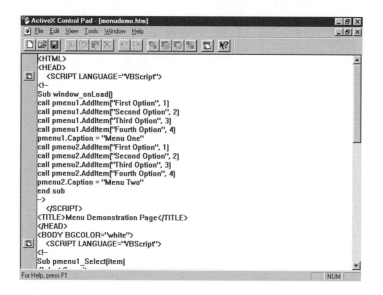

Figure 13.16.

Select a menu option.

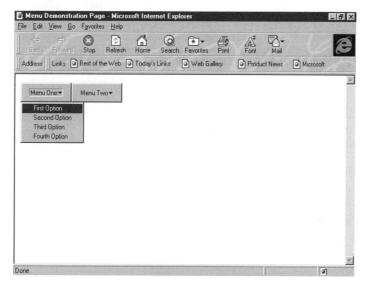

You can now run this page from your local hard drive, but what happens if you place it on your Web site? On your machine it will run OK. Internet Explorer first checks your hard drive for the `btnmenu.ocx` file and, if found, loads it and away you go. This is fine for you and the other users with the button menu control, but what about users who don't have the button menu control when they reach your page?

Figure 13.17.

The Select *event fires.*

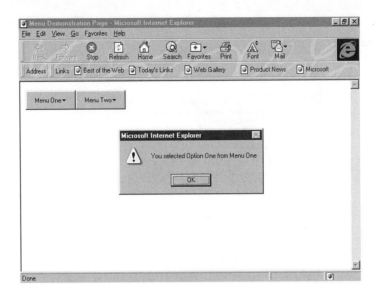

Downloading New Controls to Your Users

Every ActiveX control has a parameter property called CodeBase, which tells Internet Explorer (and any other ActiveX-enabled browser) where it can find a copy of the control if it cannot find one locally (on the client machine).

CodeBase has one major restriction. It must point at the same domain from which the page was loaded. The following list shows you how to set the CodeBase and test downloading the page from your Web site as though you are the user. For this example, I've used one of my domains, which happens to be called vbscripts.com (cheap promo!).

1. To change the CodeBase property, load the menudemo.htm file into the ActiveX Control Pad, and click the object icon next to the pmenu1 object definition.

2. Select the CodeBase property in the property editor and enter the full URL of the domain, the directory where you plan to store the control, and also the btnmenu.ocx filename. (See Figure 13.18.)

3. Don't forget to click the Apply button.

4. Close the object editor in order to generate the new Object definition, including the CodeBase, as shown in Figure 13.19.

If the CodeBase property is not set, MSIE3.0 knows to look only on the local drive for the control.

Figure 13.18.
Amending the
CodeBase *property.*

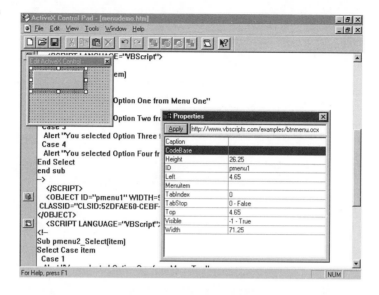

Figure 13.19.
The new control
definition.

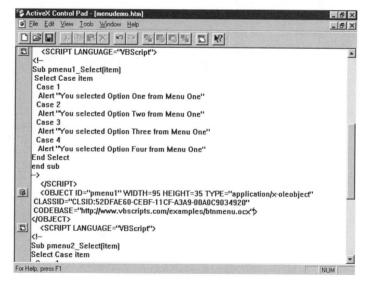

Repeat the amendment on the second menu object (pmenu2), and save the file.

Now transfer the HTML file (menudemo.htm) and the btnmenu.ocx file to your server, remembering to locate the OCX file in the place you specified in the CodeBase property. You can find the btnmenu.ocx file in your windows\occache\ subdirectory.

Before you do anything else, you must remove the btnmenu.ocx file from your machine; otherwise, the browser simply runs your local copy, and you haven't performed the test properly. Furthermore, if you still have MSIE3.0 open with the menu control in it, you must close the browser to free the control from memory. Just to be on the safe side, rather than simply deleting the file, copy it to another subdirectory and rename it.

You are now ready to test your first online ActiveX Web page (drum roll…). Fire up the browser, and enter the URL of the menudemo.htm file. As the file is loading, the status bar should tell you that it is installing a component. Then the security certificate is displayed as shown in Figure 13.20.

Figure 13.20.
The controls security certificate.

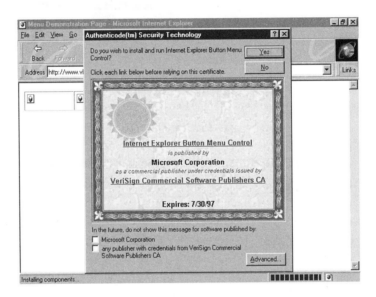

NOTE: One consideration when using ActiveX controls is the time that is taken to download from the Web site. As you know, this is unquantifiable because it depends upon the Internet connections for you, the client, and the server; the time of day; the wind direction; and a million other variables. However, don't forget that only those users who don't currently have this control will need to download it. And users who visit your site regularly or who visited another site with the same control will have almost instant access to the control because the browser loads their local copy.

I tend to think that it's all right to accept this control. Click OK, and the control completes its download and registers its presence on your machine. The Menu controls then appear on the page, ready to be used (as shown in Figure 13.21). Congratulations!

Figure 13.21.

The completed Web page working online.

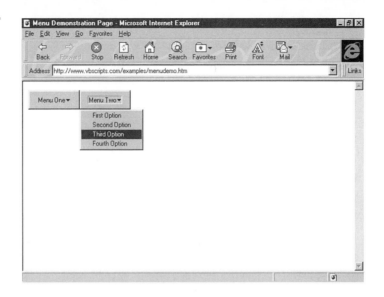

Here's the complete source code for the sample project `menudemo.htm`:

```
<HTML>
<HEAD>
    <SCRIPT LANGUAGE="VBScript">
<!--
Sub window_onLoad()
call pmenu1.AddItem("First Option", 1)
call pmenu1.AddItem("Second Option", 2)
call pmenu1.AddItem("Third Option", 3)
call pmenu1.AddItem("Fourth Option", 4)
pmenu1.Caption = "Menu One"
call pmenu2.AddItem("First Option", 1)
call pmenu2.AddItem("Second Option", 2)
call pmenu2.AddItem("Third Option", 3)
call pmenu2.AddItem("Fourth Option", 4)
pmenu2.Caption = "Menu Two"
end sub
-->
    </SCRIPT>
<TITLE>Menu Demonstration Page</TITLE>
</HEAD>
<BODY BGCOLOR="white">
    <SCRIPT LANGUAGE="VBScript">
<!--
Sub pmenu1_Select(item)
 Select Case item
  Case 1
   Alert "You selected Option One from Menu One"
  Case 2
   Alert "You selected Option Two from Menu One"
  Case 3
   Alert "You selected Option Three from Menu One"
  Case 4
   Alert "You selected Option Four from Menu One"
```

```
End Select
end sub
-->
    </SCRIPT>
    <OBJECT ID="pmenu1" WIDTH=95 HEIGHT=35 TYPE="application/x-oleobject"
 CLASSID="CLSID:52DFAE60-CEBF-11CF-A3A9-00A0C9034920"
 CODEBASE="http://www.vbscripts.com/examples/btnmenu.ocx">
</OBJECT>
    <SCRIPT LANGUAGE="VBScript">
<!--
Sub pmenu2_Select(item)
Select Case item
  Case 1
   Alert "You selected Option One from Menu Two"
  Case 2
   Alert "You selected Option Two from Menu Two"
  Case 3
   Alert "You selected Option Three from Menu Two"
  Case 4
   Alert "You selected Option Four from Menu Two"
End Select
end sub
-->
    </SCRIPT>
    <OBJECT ID="pmenu2" WIDTH=95 HEIGHT=35 TYPE="application/x-oleobject"
 CLASSID="CLSID:52DFAE60-CEBF-11CF-A3A9-00A0C9034920"
 CODEBASE="http://www.vbscripts.com/examples/btnmenu.ocx">
</OBJECT>
</BODY>
</HTML>
```

Workshop Wrap-Up

ActiveX controls open up a whole new world of possibilities for your Web pages. Controls that used to be available only in Windows applications now can be used in your Web pages—and, as you have seen, you can add them quickly and easily. As you travel the Net, keep your eyes open for new and interesting controls, many of which are available for free.

Next Steps

Now that you've had a taste of what ActiveX can really do for your Web site, you can find out more in these chapters:

❑ To see how to build incredibly cool Web pages using nothing but ActiveX controls, read the next chapter, "Using the HTML Layout Control."

❑ To learn more about using other controls, see Chapter 16, "Real-Life Examples II."

❑ To learn more about the internal working of ActiveX, see Chapter 21, "Advanced ActiveX Techniques."

Q&A

Q: What happens if a user has a version of the control that is different from the one on my server?

A: To ensure compatibility you can add the version number of the control with the CodeBase parameter, like this:

```
http://www.youdomain.com/subdir/btnmenu.ocx#Version=4,70,0,1161
```

Q: Great, but how do I know what version number my control is?

A: You can obtain the version number from the source of the page from which you obtained the control at the Site Builder workshop. Simply select View Source when you've downloaded a new control, and copy and paste the version number from their `CodeBase` parameter.

FOURTEEN

Using the HTML Layout Control

As you have seen so far in this book, the combination of ActiveX Controls and VBScript enables you to build Web pages and Web applications that have the look, feel, and functionality of Windows applications. However, one final piece needs to be fitted into the puzzle to make this picture complete: on-screen positioning.

Using HTML, paragraphs, text, graphics, and controls are positioned on-screen basically in the order that the browser finds them within the HTML source code. Recent developments such as tables have improved the situation somewhat, but it is still not possible within HTML to position a control at an exact location on the screen, nor is it possible to position controls independent of other controls.

The HTML Layout Control gives you the ability to position controls on-screen to the nearest pixel. The HTML Layout Control is a true Windows form that is included or embedded into your HTML document as a single ActiveX Control. The Layout Control handles all the individual controls you place within it, and using controls within a Layout affords a wider range of events, properties, and methods, enhancing the functionality of the ActiveX Controls even further.

In this chapter, you

- ❑ Learn how to use the HTML Layout Control
- ❑ See how to add new and additional controls to the HTML Layout Control tool box
- ❑ Learn how to manage overlapping controls
- ❑ Learn how to quickly and easily align controls
- ❑ Learn how to change the properties of many controls at once
- ❑ Create a Form using the HTML Layout Control
- ❑ See how to add a Layout to a Web page
- ❑ See how to add VBScript to an HTML Layout

Tasks in this chapter:

- ❑ Adding new toolbox controls to the HTML Layout Control
- ❑ Adding controls to a Layout
- ❑ Aligning controls on a Layout
- ❑ Creating a form using the HTML Layout Control
- ❑ Adding the HTML Layout form to a Web page
- ❑ Adding VBScript to an HTML Layout

An Overview of the HTML Layout Control

The HTML Layout Control is another ActiveX Control, with one difference: It contains and handles other ActiveX Controls. You can build a Layout quickly and easily using the drag and drop metaphor. It is a true visual development environment. If you have experience using other visual programming environments such as Visual Basic, Visual C++, or Delphi, you will almost instantly be familiar with the HTML Layout Control.

The definitions and declarations of the ActiveX Controls contained within a particular HTML Layout Control and the associated scripts are all held within one file, which is easily added to the HTML document. Another advantage of the Layout Control is that the object definition in the HTML document doesn't change. Therefore, you can make modifications to your Layout Control without changing the HTML document. Furthermore, the same Layout can be used in multiple documents—for example, as a shared tool bar or menu.

From the user's perspective, the HTML Layout Control is very similar to other ActiveX Controls, and a runtime version is loaded with the full installation of MSIE 3.0.

To create a Layout, you use the HTML Layout Control development area, which is accessed via the ActiveX Control Pad. Open the ActiveX Control Pad and select New HTML Layout from the File menu.

A blank Layout and the HTML Layout tool box are then displayed, as shown in Figure 14.1.

Figure 14.1.
A new Layout.

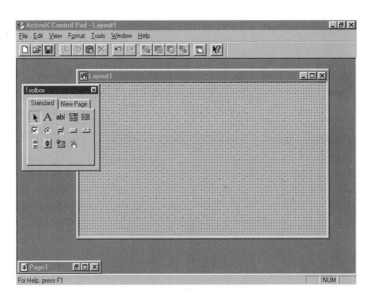

Now let's have a look at the features of the Layout development environment and how they work together.

The HTML Layout Control Tool Box

The HTML Layout Control tool box, shown in Figure 14.2, contains the ActiveX Controls that you have available to use in your new Layout.

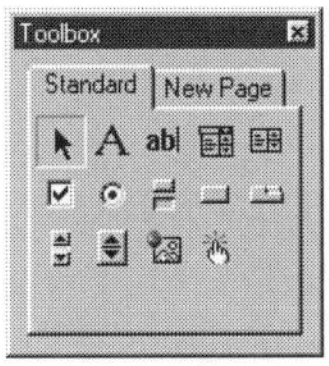

Figure 14.2.

The HTML Layout Control tool box.

When you first load the Layout Control, the tool box consists of two pages. However, you can add further pages to the tool box as required later.

The first page, named Standard, holds the controls that will always work with MSIE3.0. These are the Microsoft Forms 2.0 controls that you have used so far in the ActiveX Control Pad, plus a couple of MSIE-specific controls—the Image and the Hot Spot Controls.

The standard ActiveX Controls are as follows:

❑ Label

❑ Text Box

❑ Drop Down List (Combo Box)

❑ List

❑ Check Box

❑ Radio Button

❑ Toggle Button

❑ Command Button

❑ Tab Strip

❑ Scroll Bar

❑ Spin Button

❑ Image Control

❑ Hot Spot

The item at the top left of the tool box showing the arrow icon is not a control. It denotes that you are in selection mode.

The second page, and any subsequent pages, of the tool box that you create are for you to add further ActiveX Controls. Note that new controls that you download from the Web are not automatically available in the tool box. (See Chapter 13, "Implementing an ActiveX Menu Control.") Let's look at how you add further controls to the tool box.

Adding New Controls to the HTML Layout Control Tool Box

It's best not to add new controls to the Standard page of the tool box, because these are controls that will always work with MSIE 3.0.

To add a new control that you have downloaded from the Web, follow these steps:

1. Select the New Page tab on the tool box.

2. Right-click anywhere on the page, and a pop-up menu is displayed, as shown in Figure 14.3.

Figure 14.3.
The HTML Layout Control tool box menu.

3. Select Additional Controls from the pop-up menu. A list of all available ActiveX controls is then displayed in the Additional Controls dialog box, as shown in Figure 14.4.

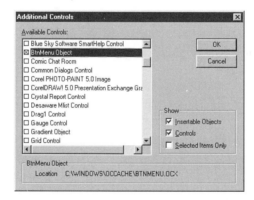

Figure 14.4.
The Additional Controls dialog box.

4. To add the BtnMenu Control that you downloaded from the Microsoft Site Builder Web site in the last chapter, simply check the box to the left of the control's name.

5. Click OK. The control's icon is added to the tool box (as shown in Figure 14.5), and the control is now ready for you to use in a new Layout.

Figure 14.5.

The new control added to the tool box.

NOTE: If you run out of room on a tool box page, you can either resize the tool box by dragging the sides and bottom, or you can add more pages. Simply right-click the tab at the top of a page to display the page management pop-up menu. Development teams can also share complete pages of controls using the import and export page facility.

The HTML Layout Control Tool Bar

The HTML Layout Control tool bar is the same tool bar you have used in the Control Pad (refer to Figure 14.1). However, when you have more than one control on the layout, the four *layering* buttons are enabled (see Figure 14.6).

Figure 14.6.

The HTML Layout Control tool bar.

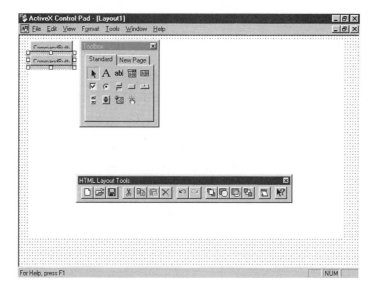

The layering buttons enable you to position overlapping controls in a second dimension—depth. The four buttons allow you to move a control forward, backward, to the front, and to the back. Later in the chapter, you'll see how this works in practice.

The tool bar itself is dockable, which means that it can be dragged from its usual place under the menu and can be free-floating or docked to the left, the right, or even the bottom of the screen.

Before you begin to create a real example, you need to know the following main functions of the HTML Layout Control:

❏ Adding controls to a Layout

❏ Accessing a control's properties

❏ Aligning controls on a Layout

❏ Managing overlapping controls

Adding Controls to a Layout

As you pass your mouse pointer over the tool box, the control icons become clickable buttons. Adding a control to the Layout is as simple as clicking the control's icon in the tool box and then clicking on the Layout in the approximate position where you need the control. Follow these steps to add a Command Button to your new Layout:

1. Pass your mouse over the Command Button icon in the tool box, and click the icon.

2. Now move your mouse onto the Layout background and click. A new Command Button will be placed in the approximate area where you clicked, as shown in Figure 14.7.

Figure 14.7.
A Command Button added to the Layout.

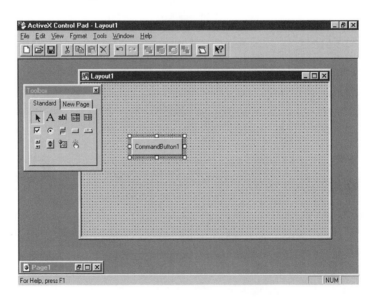

You can move and resize the button by dragging it using the mouse.

Accessing a Control's Properties

The majority of a control's properties are available and can be amended at design time. To launch the Properties window, either right-click the control and select Properties from the pop-up menu, or select Properties from the View menu.

The Properties window for the Command Button that you just added to the Layout is shown in Figure 14.8.

Figure 14.8.

The Properties window for the Command Button.

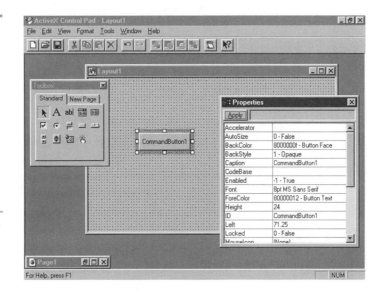

To access the properties for the Layout itself, right-click the Layout background, not a control.

Aligning Controls on a Layout

Let's look at how you can very quickly size and align multiple controls on a Layout. For this demonstration, you need to add two more Command Buttons to the Layout.

NOTE: Unlike adding ActiveX controls to an HTML file in the ActiveX Control Pad, when you add new controls of the same type to a Layout, the IDs are automatically numbered sequentially. For example, if you add a series of command buttons, their IDs are numbered CommandButton1, CommandButton2, and so on.

The Layout Control has a wide variety of menu options for sizing, spacing, and aligning controls, making the job of form building very quick and easy. To align the three buttons, follow these steps:

1. Select the first button. Then hold down the Shift key and select the other two buttons in turn.

2. From the Format menu, select Align, as shown in Figure 14.9.

Figure 14.9.

The Format and Align menus.

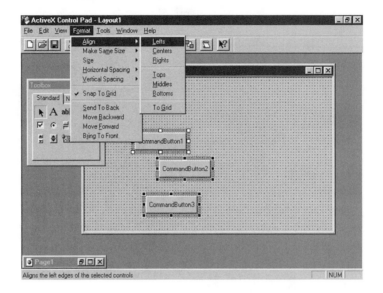

A quick method of selecting more than one control is to drag the mouse around the outside of the controls that you want to select so that the marquee encloses the controls.

NOTE: The Layout Control uses the alignment or size properties of one of the controls to align or size the others. This control is called the *dominant control*, and it is differentiated from the other controls by its white sizing handles.

3. Select Lefts from the Alignment menu. All the buttons now align to the same left position on the Layout.

4. With all three Command Buttons still selected, choose Vertical Spacing from the Format menu.

5. Select Make Equal from the Vertical Spacing menu. The buttons should now be perfectly aligned and positioned on the Layout, as shown in Figure 14.10.

Figure 14.10.

The buttons aligned and spaced.

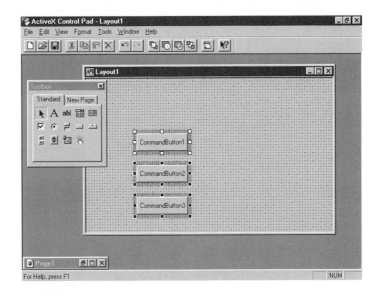

 TASK

Managing Overlapping Controls

One of the unique benefits of the Layout Control is its capability to layer controls (place one control on top of another), which is impossible in standard HTML.

To see how this works, drag the buttons so that CommandButton2 sits on top of CommandButton1 and CommandButton3 sits on top of CommandButton2. Then select CommandButton2, as shown in Figure 14.11.

Figure 14.11.

The buttons placed on top of each other.

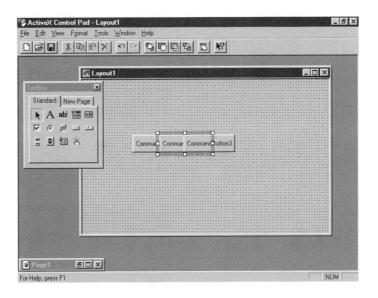

Note that the layering buttons on the tool bar are enabled when more than one control is present on the Layout.

To change the layer in which `CommandButton2` resides, use one of the following methods:

❑ Use the layering buttons on the tool bar.

❑ Use one of the layer options from the Format menu.

❑ Right-click the control and select one of the layer options from the Controls pop-up menu.

Using any of the preceding methods, you can move the button in these directions: to the front, forward one layer, back one layer, to the back.

Take a moment to play around with the different commands. The button is shown moved to the front layer in Figure 14.12.

Figure 14.12.
CommandButton2
brought to the front.

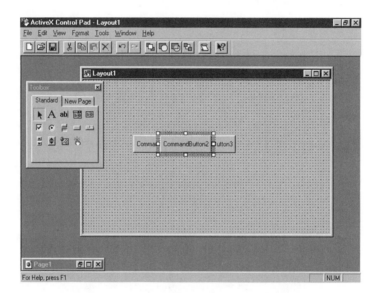

Layering buttons in this way doesn't have many practical uses—at least none that I can think of. But how often would you have liked to overlay one .gif or .jpg image on top of another? Combine this with the fact that you can change a control's position at runtime, and you're into the realm of very easy animation with relatively small graphics files. For an example of this, see Chapter 16, "Real-Life Examples II."

Creating a Form Using the HTML Layout Control

Now that you've experienced the main functionality of the Layout Control, it's time to create a real Layout. You will create a form, which you will then add to an HTML page. Then you add some scripting to the form to do some rudimentary validation.

1. To begin, open a new HTML Layout and resize the Layout to approximately 300 pixels wide and 200 pixels high. Note that the size of the Layout when you save it is the size that will be included in the HTML page.

2. Now change the `BackColor` property of the Layout to white by right-clicking on the Layout and selecting the Properties option from the control pop-up menu. Select `BackColor` and click the ellipsis button at the top of the Properties box to launch the color palette. Then simply click the white color box and click OK.

3. Add a label control to the Layout and drag it so that it is at the top of the Layout and about three quarters of the width across the Layout.

4. Change the `Caption` property of the label to `A HTML Layout Control Form`.

5. Change the `ForeColor` property of the label to a gray color. (Which one you choose is not important.)

6. Change the `Font` property to `14 point MS Sans Serif Bold`. The Layout should now resemble the one shown in Figure 14.13.

Figure 14.13.

The example form with the first label in place.

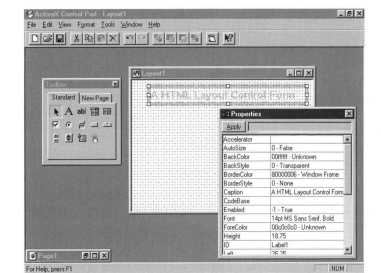

7. Change the `BackStyle` property of the label to `Transparent`.

   You will have a label with a shadow on this form. The label that you just created is actually the shadow.

8. Select the label and copy it to the clipboard by pressing Ctrl+C, clicking the copy tool bar button, or selecting Copy from the Edit menu. You could even use the edit options on the control's own pop-up menu by right-clicking the control.

9. Now click anywhere on the Layout and paste the copied label onto the Layout. Again you can use the hot key (Ctrl+V), the Edit menu, or the paste tool bar button.

10. You now have two identical labels. Change the `ForeColor` property of the second label to a shade of blue. (Again, it's not important which blue for this exercise.)

Note that the Layout Control has automatically incremented the ID of the copied label to `Label2`.

11. To give the appearance of a drop shadow, drag the blue label over the gray label so that they are slightly offset to each other, as shown in Figure 14.14. Because the `BackStyle` of the labels has been set to `transparent`, the gray label shows through.

Figure 14.14.
The "zero bandwidth" drop shadow.

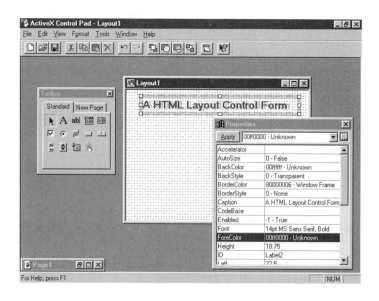

To find out how you can create similar effects in a normal HTML page, see "Cascading Style Sheets" on the Microsoft Site Builder Workshop site.

12. Now add three text boxes. Follow the earlier instructions to align them, space them vertically, and size them equally. See Figure 14.15.

13. You now need to add three labels—one to the left of each text box. As you can probably guess, these labels will denote what data is to be entered in the text box. Apart from their positions within the form and the caption properties, all the other properties of these labels will be the same (font face, color, and so on). Therefore, you can set these properties for all three labels at the same time.

14. Select all three labels and, on any one of the three, right-click and select Properties from the pop-up menu. Notice that in the Properties window, some properties—those that are the same for all the selected controls—are shown as their actual values. Other properties—those that are different for each selected control—say `mixed`, as shown in Figure 14.16.

Using this single property window, you can amend the properties for all three labels at the same time.

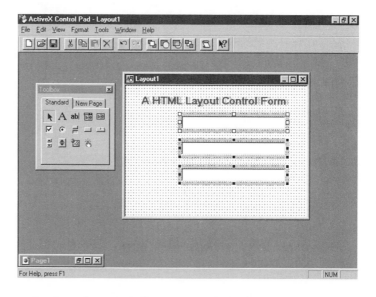

Figure 14.15.

Three equally sized, spaced, and aligned text boxes.

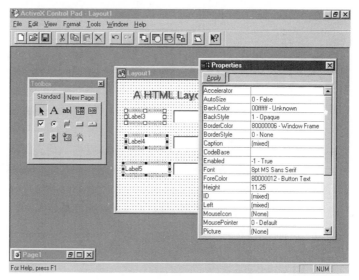

Figure 14.16.

Labels with shared properties.

15. Change the Font property to 10pt MS Sans Serif.

16. Change the ForeColor property to the same shade of blue used for the main label.

17. Change the BackStyle property to Transparent.

18. You can also give each control the same Left property (10 pixels), which aligns all of them to the left.

Your form should now resemble the one shown in Figure 14.17.

Figure 14.17.
The properties for all three labels are changed at the same time.

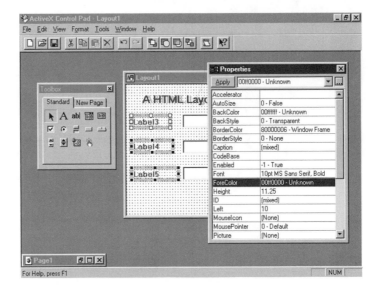

19. Change the Caption properties for each label individually: Name, EMail, and URL.

20. Add a Command Button toward the bottom of the form, and change its Caption property to Submit. Your completed form should now look like the one in Figure 14.18.

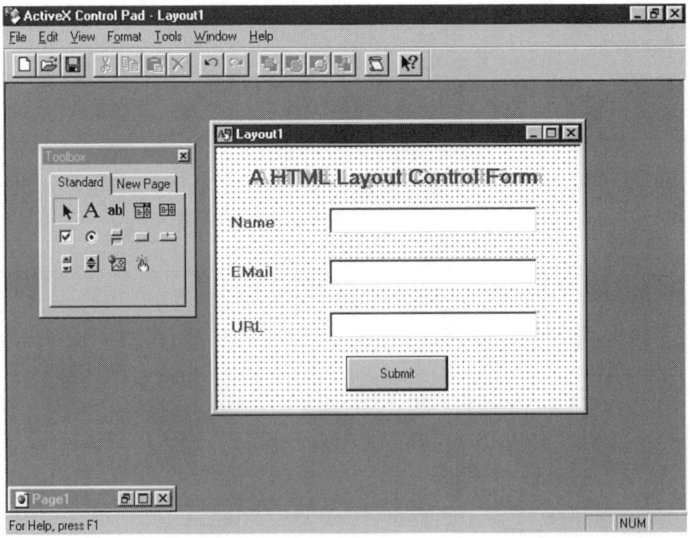

Figure 14.18.
The completed Layout.

21. Save the Layout as `myform.alx` by selecting Save from the File menu. Note that all Layouts have the extension `.alx`. You are now ready to use the Layout in an HTML page.

Adding the HTML Layout Form to a Web Page

Adding a prebuilt Layout Control to an HTML page is as easy, if not easier, than adding an ActiveX control.

1. Move to the HTML template, and change the background color to White.

2. Add a <CENTER> tag between the body tags.

3. Place the cursor between the center tags, and select Insert HTML Layout from the Edit menu. The file dialog for `.alx` files is then displayed, as shown in Figure 14.19.

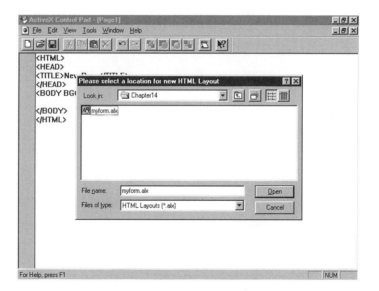

4. Select `myform.alx`, and click OK. The ActiveX Control Pad generates the required code to place the Layout on the HTML page, as shown in Figure 14.20.

5. Now simply save the HTML page as `myform.htm`, and load it into the browser. It should appear as shown in Figure 14.21.

Figure 14.20.

The HTML code to call the Layout Control.

Figure 14.21.

The Web page, complete with Layout form.

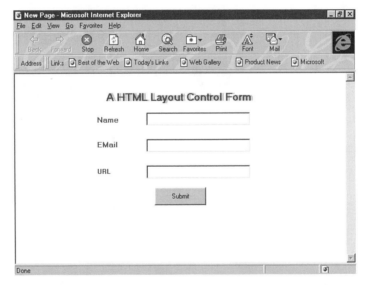

TASK ## Adding VBScript to an HTML Layout

Adding VBScript to an HTML Layout using the Script Wizard is as easy as using the ActiveX Control Pad. In this part of the example, you add two further labels, which will act as a warning to the user that his input is invalid. The labels are only made visible if a conditional test on the input fails.

1. Open the Layout created earlier: `myform.alx`.

2. Add two further labels. One label should be placed to the right of the EMail text box, and the other should be placed to the left of the URL text box.

3. Change the ID property of the first label to `InvalidEMail`.

4. Change the ID property of the second label to `InvalidURL`.

5. Amend these properties for both labels to the following values:

   ❏ `ForeColor = Red`

   ❏ `Caption = Invalid Input`

   ❏ `Visible = False`

   ❏ `Font = 10pt MS Sans Serif Bold`

Your Layout form should now look like the one in Figure 14.22.

Figure 14.22.
The form with the warning label added.

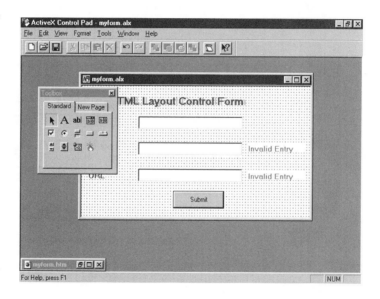

Note that even if a control's **Visible** property is set to **False**, the control is still visible at design time.

With the Layout Control still open, start the Script Wizard.

Locate the `TextBox2` Control in the left actions pane, and select the control's `Change` event. Enter the following code in the `Change` event handler.

```
If InStr(TextBox2.Text,"@")=0 Then
 EMailInvalid.Visible = True
Else
 EMailInvalid.Visible = False
End If
```

The code searches for the @ symbol somewhere within the user's entry. If it is found, the entry is considered valid; if it is not found, Instr() returns 0, the entry is considered invalid, and the warning label is shown (visible=True).

The code within the event handler is shown in Figure 14.23.

Figure 14.23.

The event handler for the TextBox2_Change event.

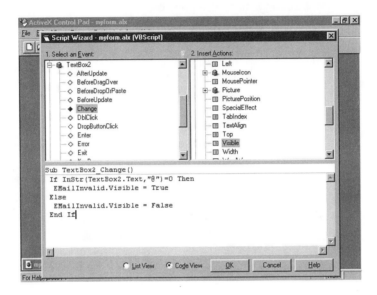

Now select the Change event for TextBox3, and enter the following code:

```
If Left(TextBox3.Text,4) <> "http" Then
 URLInvalid.Visible = True
Else
 URLInvalid.Visible = False
End If
```

This code simply makes sure that the first four characters are http. The rest of the event handler is similar to the first one. The completed event handler is shown in Figure 14.24.

Click OK and the Script Wizard adds the required code to the Layout Control's source. Save the Layout.

There is no need to make any changes to the HTML page that uses the Layout Control. Run the page though the browser. If you still have the browser open, you can simply click Refresh.

Figure 14.25 shows the page with the scripted Layout Control working.

Figure 14.24.

*The completed event
handler for the
TextBox3_Change
event.*

Figure 14.25.

*The Web page,
complete with scripted
Layout form.*

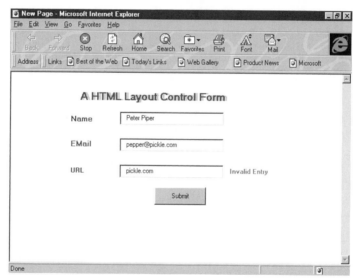

NOTE: To run this control and Web page from a Web server, simply change
the ALXPATH parameter in the HTML object definition, like this:

```
<PARAM NAME="ALXPATH" REF VALUE="http://www.mydomain.com/subdir/
➥myform.alx">
```

You might wonder where the VBScript code and all the definitions for the Layout
Control you just created went. You can open myform.alx in Notepad or a similar text

editor; or within the Layout Control, right-click any of the controls on the Layout (or click the Layout itself), and select View Source Code from the pop-up menu. The full source code held within `myform.alx` looks like this:

```
<SCRIPT LANGUAGE="VBScript">
<!--
Sub TextBox3_Change()
 If Left(TextBox3.Text,4) <> "http" Then
  URLInvalid.Visible = True
 Else
  URLInvalid.Visible = False
 End If
end sub
-->
</SCRIPT>
<SCRIPT LANGUAGE="VBScript">
<!--
Sub TextBox2_Change()
 If InStr(TextBox2.Text,"@")=0 Then
  EMailInvalid.Visible = True
 Else
  EMailInvalid.Visible = False
 End If
end sub
-->
</SCRIPT>
<DIV BACKGROUND="#ffffff" ID="Layout1" STYLE="LAYOUT:FIXED;
➥WIDTH:320pt;HEIGHT:178pt;">
    <OBJECT ID="Label1"
     CLASSID="CLSID:978C9E23-D4B0-11CE-BF2D-00AA003F40D0"
➥STYLE="TOP:11pt;LEFT:26pt;WIDTH:218pt;HEIGHT:19pt;ZINDEX:0;">
        <PARAM NAME="ForeColor" VALUE="12632256">
        <PARAM NAME="BackColor" VALUE="16777215">
        <PARAM NAME="VariousPropertyBits" VALUE="8388627">
        <PARAM NAME="Caption" VALUE="A HTML Layout Control Form">
        <PARAM NAME="Size" VALUE="7673;661">
        <PARAM NAME="FontEffects" VALUE="1073741825">
        <PARAM NAME="FontHeight" VALUE="280">
        <PARAM NAME="FontCharSet" VALUE="0">
        <PARAM NAME="FontPitchAndFamily" VALUE="2">
        <PARAM NAME="FontWeight" VALUE="700">
    </OBJECT>
    <OBJECT ID="Label2"
     CLASSID="CLSID:978C9E23-D4B0-11CE-BF2D-00AA003F40D0"
➥STYLE="TOP:11pt;LEFT:23pt;WIDTH:218pt;HEIGHT:19pt;ZINDEX:1;">
        <PARAM NAME="ForeColor" VALUE="16711680">
        <PARAM NAME="BackColor" VALUE="16777215">
        <PARAM NAME="VariousPropertyBits" VALUE="8388627">
        <PARAM NAME="Caption" VALUE="A HTML Layout Control Form">
        <PARAM NAME="Size" VALUE="7673;661">
        <PARAM NAME="FontEffects" VALUE="1073741825">
        <PARAM NAME="FontHeight" VALUE="280">
        <PARAM NAME="FontCharSet" VALUE="0">
        <PARAM NAME="FontPitchAndFamily" VALUE="2">
        <PARAM NAME="FontWeight" VALUE="700">
    </OBJECT>
    <OBJECT ID="TextBox1"
     CLASSID="CLSID:8BD21D10-EC42-11CE-9E0D-00AA006002F3"
➥STYLE="TOP:41pt;LEFT:79pt;WIDTH:146pt;HEIGHT:18pt;TABINDEX:2;ZINDEX:2;">
```

```
            <PARAM NAME="VariousPropertyBits" VALUE="746604571">
            <PARAM NAME="Size" VALUE="5159;635">
            <PARAM NAME="FontCharSet" VALUE="0">
            <PARAM NAME="FontPitchAndFamily" VALUE="2">
            <PARAM NAME="FontWeight" VALUE="0">
        </OBJECT>
        <OBJECT ID="TextBox2"
         CLASSID="CLSID:8BD21D10-EC42-11CE-9E0D-00AA006002F3"
➥STYLE="TOP:77pt;LEFT:79pt;WIDTH:146pt;HEIGHT:18pt;TABINDEX:3;ZINDEX:3;">
            <PARAM NAME="VariousPropertyBits" VALUE="746604571">
            <PARAM NAME="Size" VALUE="5159;635">
            <PARAM NAME="FontCharSet" VALUE="0">
            <PARAM NAME="FontPitchAndFamily" VALUE="2">
            <PARAM NAME="FontWeight" VALUE="0">
        </OBJECT>
        <OBJECT ID="TextBox3"
         CLASSID="CLSID:8BD21D10-EC42-11CE-9E0D-00AA006002F3"
➥STYLE="TOP:113pt;LEFT:79pt;WIDTH:146pt;HEIGHT:18pt;TABINDEX:4;ZINDEX:4;">
            <PARAM NAME="VariousPropertyBits" VALUE="746604571">
            <PARAM NAME="Size" VALUE="5159;635">
            <PARAM NAME="FontCharSet" VALUE="0">
            <PARAM NAME="FontPitchAndFamily" VALUE="2">
            <PARAM NAME="FontWeight" VALUE="0">
        </OBJECT>
        <OBJECT ID="Label3"
         CLASSID="CLSID:978C9E23-D4B0-11CE-BF2D-00AA003F40D0"
➥STYLE="TOP:45pt;LEFT:10pt;WIDTH:49pt;HEIGHT:11pt;ZINDEX:5;">
            <PARAM NAME="ForeColor" VALUE="16711680">
            <PARAM NAME="BackColor" VALUE="16777215">
            <PARAM NAME="VariousPropertyBits" VALUE="8388627">
            <PARAM NAME="Caption" VALUE="Name">
            <PARAM NAME="Size" VALUE="1720;397">
            <PARAM NAME="FontEffects" VALUE="1073741825">
            <PARAM NAME="FontHeight" VALUE="200">
            <PARAM NAME="FontCharSet" VALUE="0">
            <PARAM NAME="FontPitchAndFamily" VALUE="2">
            <PARAM NAME="FontWeight" VALUE="700">
        </OBJECT>
        <OBJECT ID="Label4"
         CLASSID="CLSID:978C9E23-D4B0-11CE-BF2D-00AA003F40D0"
➥STYLE="TOP:79pt;LEFT:10pt;WIDTH:53pt;HEIGHT:11pt;ZINDEX:6;">
            <PARAM NAME="ForeColor" VALUE="16711680">
            <PARAM NAME="BackColor" VALUE="16777215">
            <PARAM NAME="VariousPropertyBits" VALUE="8388627">
            <PARAM NAME="Caption" VALUE="EMail">
            <PARAM NAME="Size" VALUE="1852;397">
            <PARAM NAME="FontEffects" VALUE="1073741825">
            <PARAM NAME="FontHeight" VALUE="200">
            <PARAM NAME="FontCharSet" VALUE="0">
            <PARAM NAME="FontPitchAndFamily" VALUE="2">
            <PARAM NAME="FontWeight" VALUE="700">
        </OBJECT>
        <OBJECT ID="Label5"
         CLASSID="CLSID:978C9E23-D4B0-11CE-BF2D-00AA003F40D0"
➥STYLE="TOP:116pt;LEFT:10pt;WIDTH:60pt;HEIGHT:11pt;ZINDEX:7;">
            <PARAM NAME="ForeColor" VALUE="16711680">
            <PARAM NAME="BackColor" VALUE="16777215">
            <PARAM NAME="VariousPropertyBits" VALUE="8388627">
            <PARAM NAME="Caption" VALUE="URL">
            <PARAM NAME="Size" VALUE="2117;397">
```

```
            <PARAM NAME="FontEffects" VALUE="1073741825">
            <PARAM NAME="FontHeight" VALUE="200">
            <PARAM NAME="FontCharSet" VALUE="0">
            <PARAM NAME="FontPitchAndFamily" VALUE="2">
            <PARAM NAME="FontWeight" VALUE="700">
        </OBJECT>
        <OBJECT ID="CommandButton1"
         CLASSID="CLSID:D7053240-CE69-11CD-A777-00DD01143C57"
➥STYLE="TOP:143pt;LEFT:128pt;WIDTH:72pt;HEIGHT:24pt;TABINDEX:8;ZINDEX:8;">
            <PARAM NAME="Caption" VALUE="Submit">
            <PARAM NAME="Size" VALUE="2540;846">
            <PARAM NAME="FontCharSet" VALUE="0">
            <PARAM NAME="FontPitchAndFamily" VALUE="2">
            <PARAM NAME="ParagraphAlign" VALUE="3">
            <PARAM NAME="FontWeight" VALUE="0">
        </OBJECT>
        <OBJECT ID="EMailInvalid"
         CLASSID="CLSID:978C9E23-D4B0-11CE-BF2D-00AA003F40D0"
➥STYLE="TOP:79pt;LEFT:233pt;WIDTH:83pt;HEIGHT:11pt;DISPLAY:NONE;ZINDEX:9;">
            <PARAM NAME="ForeColor" VALUE="255">
            <PARAM NAME="BackColor" VALUE="16777215">
            <PARAM NAME="Caption" VALUE="Invalid Entry">
            <PARAM NAME="Size" VALUE="2911;397">
            <PARAM NAME="FontEffects" VALUE="1073741825">
            <PARAM NAME="FontHeight" VALUE="200">
            <PARAM NAME="FontCharSet" VALUE="0">
            <PARAM NAME="FontPitchAndFamily" VALUE="2">
            <PARAM NAME="FontWeight" VALUE="700">
        </OBJECT>
        <OBJECT ID="URLInvalid"
         CLASSID="CLSID:978C9E23-D4B0-11CE-BF2D-00AA003F40D0"
➥STYLE="TOP:116pt;LEFT:233pt;WIDTH:83pt;HEIGHT:11pt;DISPLAY:NONE;ZINDEX:10;">
            <PARAM NAME="ForeColor" VALUE="255">
            <PARAM NAME="BackColor" VALUE="16777215">
            <PARAM NAME="Caption" VALUE="Invalid Entry">
            <PARAM NAME="Size" VALUE="2910;397">
            <PARAM NAME="FontEffects" VALUE="1073741825">
            <PARAM NAME="FontHeight" VALUE="200">
            <PARAM NAME="FontCharSet" VALUE="0">
            <PARAM NAME="FontPitchAndFamily" VALUE="2">
            <PARAM NAME="FontWeight" VALUE="700">
        </OBJECT>
</DIV>
```

Workshop Wrap-Up

In this chapter, you've seen the HTML Layout Control, an excellent way to create reusable forms, menus, and in fact, any sort of ActiveX Web page. It's quick and easy, and above all, it can reduce the maintenance time on the overall Web site. The HTML Layout Control is a truly visual development environment for your Web pages, giving results that rival or exceed those produced using professional Windows development tools.

Next Steps

See the following chapters for more information and examples of using the HTML Layout Control:

❏ To see the HTML Layout Control in action again, this time using graphic animation in a young children's learning game, see Chapter 16, "Real-Life Examples II."

❏ A good example of a commercial application produced using the Layout Control is shown in Chapter 23, "Real-Life Examples IV."

Q&A

Q: What if I use nonstandard controls in my HTML Layout?

A: Using nonstandard controls in an HTML Layout is the same as using them directly on a Web page. You need to put a copy of a control on your server, and then set the CodeBase property of the control to point to your server.

by Rogers Cadenhead

Using Java Applets with VBScript

FIFTEEN

Everything consists of objects. This statement is true in the physical world where things are put together by combining other things. A bicycle consists of handlebars, two spoked wheels, a frame, a chain, a seat, pedals, safety reflectors, and brakes. Oops—there also should be an old baseball card tucked into the spokes.

Everything in the computer world also consists of objects, according to one way of thinking. *Object-oriented programming* is a term you might have encountered before. Also known as OOP, it is a way to organize computer software as a collection of objects. For instance, a word processing program could include a dictionary object that is used by a spell-checking object to correct errors in a document object.

A World Wide Web page can also be considered a collection of objects. Each resource on the page—images, video, and programs such as ActiveX controls and Java programs—is an object. One of these resource objects that can add a great deal of functionality to a Web page is a Java applet.

Applets are Java programs designed to run on the World Wide Web. Like ActiveX and VBScript, Java is an attempt to provide safe executable content on the Internet. Of the thousands of applets created to run on the Web, many are publicly available at sites such as Gamelan (`http://www.gamelan.com`) and Java Boutique (`http://www.j-g.com/java/`).

You can place Java applets on a Web page with the use of an HTML tag called `<APPLET>`, as you will discover in this chapter. Another way that will soon become available to offer Java programs is the `<OBJECT>` tag.

The `<OBJECT>` Tag

The `<OBJECT>` HTML tag places an object on a Web page. The object can be any media that someone would want to put on a page, whether it's an image, movie, program, or other offering. `<OBJECT>` was proposed by the World Wide Web Consortium, the group that establishes many standards for the Web, as a way to replace a bunch of different things—the `<IMG>` tag, the `<APPLET>` tag used by Java programs, the DYNSRC attribute used by Microsoft for audio and video, and other proprietary extensions to HTML. `<OBJECT>` was also proposed to handle future forms of Web media not yet devised. If a startup company in Rancho Cucamonga concocts a way to offer scratch-and-sniff on the Web, the `<OBJECT>` tag is designed to be broad enough to handle it.

Attributes are used with the `<OBJECT>` tag to specify the following information:

- ❏ The object's name
- ❏ The type of object
- ❏ The location where it can be found (its URL)
- ❏ Layout information such as height, width, spacing, border width, and alignment
- ❏ An ID code to verify its identity

If the object has parameters to establish configurable values, you can set them with the `<PARAM>` tag. This tag has two attributes: NAME and VALUE. The NAME attribute sets the name of the parameter, and VALUE gives that parameter a value. Using the `<PARAM>` tag is comparable to using the form in the ActiveX Control Pad to set up a property in an ActiveX control.

If you used the ActiveX Control Pad to add an ActiveX object to a Web page, an `<OBJECT>` tag was added automatically to the page. The following is an example of an ActiveX control's `<OBJECT>` tag:

```
<OBJECT ID="CommandButton1" WIDTH=96 HEIGHT=32
    CLASSID="CLSID:D7053240-CE69-11CD-A777-00DD01143C57">
      <PARAM NAME="Caption" VALUE="Click Me">
      <PARAM NAME="Size" VALUE="2540;846">
```

```
        <PARAM NAME="FontCharSet" VALUE="0">
        <PARAM NAME="FontPitchAndFamily" VALUE="2">
        <PARAM NAME="ParagraphAlign" VALUE="3">
        <PARAM NAME="FontWeight" VALUE="0">
</OBJECT>
```

This <OBJECT> tag creates an ActiveX command button control with the label Click Me. You can place Java applets on a Web page with HTML code similar to this. Although the <OBJECT> tag is not yet supported in Microsoft Explorer for Java applets, the <APPLET> tag is very similar to <OBJECT>.

Although you can put ActiveX controls on a Web page automatically by using the ActiveX Control Pad, you must place Java applets by hand by typing the HTML code into a Web page using a text editor. There's no facility within the ActiveX Control Pad—or any other authoring tool catering to Internet Explorer 3.0's new features— that enables automated placement of Java applets using the new <OBJECT> tag.

Don't complain. When your great-grandchildren are using their cerebral brainboards to telepathically design their home pages, you'll have something to brag about. To offer active Web content back in the 20th century, you had to tap out ASCII characters on a keyboard—40 miles in the snow, uphill both ways, in a patchwork coat made from discarded soup labels.

In the next section, you'll learn how to use the <APPLET> tag to add an object—a Java applet—to a Web page. If you're an experienced Java programmer, this first task will be review material for you.

 # Including Java Applets in Your HTML Pages

Java is a programming language developed by Sun Microsystems that was first released to the public in late 1994. It has several selling points that have made it a popular choice for software development in the past few years, especially for software that has Internet-oriented capabilities.

The language is object-oriented, a programming strategy that was developed to make it easier to reuse elements of a program in other programs. It also was devised to make software more reliable and easier to debug.

Another aspect of Java's design is that it enables programs to be platform indepen- dent. Like a World Wide Web page, the ideal circumstance for a Java program is that it be usable on any computer platform without a single modification.

The biggest attention-getter for Java is that you can run it on the World Wide Web. Java programs called *applets*, which are typically smaller than other types of programs, are offered on Web pages just like text, images, ActiveX controls, and other things.

A Java applet is created with any text editor and compiled into a pre-executable form called *bytecode*. You cannot run a bytecode program in the manner of other executable programs (such as .EXE and .COM files, two extensions that are familiar to DOS users). You must load the bytecode into a Java interpreter that runs it.

The reason for this two-step process is the platform-independence advantage mentioned previously. The compiled Java bytecode is not machine-specific. It needs to remain non-specific so that it can run without change on all platforms. Each Java-capable platform—such as Windows 95, Apple Macintosh, and SPARC Solaris systems at present—has its own Java interpreter that can run bytecode programs.

Java bytecode files have the .CLASS extension. A Java applet consists of a main class file and any other class files that are not part of the standard Java class library. To put a Java applet on a Web page, you put the applet's class files on the Web with .HTML files.

The original way to offer an applet on a Web page was to use the <APPLET> HTML tag. When this tag is encountered by a Java-capable Web browser such as Netscape Navigator 2.02 for Windows 95 or Internet Explorer 3.0, the browser loads the applet's class files and executes the program as part of the page. If you managed to use the World Wide Web without seeing a Java applet at this point, you've accomplished something, because the Web today has hundreds of Java applets. A recent check of the AltaVista search engine found more than 4,200 pages that include a byte or two of Java.

Creating a Java Applet

Sun Microsystems makes Java programming tools freely available on the World Wide Web. It offers the Java Developer's Kit (JDK)—a set of command-line tools to compile, debug, and run Java programs—on the Web at the following URL:

```
http://java.sun.com/java.sun.com/products/JDK/index.html
```

If you do not already have the JDK, you don't need to download and install it right now. It is more important to focus on how to incorporate existing Java applets into Web pages. The class file of a sample applet, Mercutio.class, is located on this book's CD-ROM in the \SOURCE\CHAP15 subdirectory. You can use Mercutio.class for this task.

In case you want to develop the Java applet or see what a simple applet looks like, the steps are covered here.

Writing the Program

Using any text editor, enter the text of Listing 15.1. The blank lines and indentation used in this listing are not important; the Java compiler ignores them. However, you should include them anyway because they make the program much easier for all non-computers to understand.

When you're done, save the file as Mercutio.java. If you're using a word processor that saves in a special format, such as Microsoft Word, make sure to save it as a plain ASCII or text file. The line numbers in the listings are included for reference in this chapter; they are not part of the Java source code and should not be typed in.

Listing 15.1. The complete listing of the Java source code file Mercutio.java.

```
 1: import java.awt.*;
 2:
 3: public class Mercutio extends java.applet.Applet {
 4:     Button b = new Button("Speak!");
 5:     TextField t = new TextField(45);
 6:     int phrase = 0;
 7:
 8:     public void init() {
 9:         String bt = getParameter("ButtonTitle");
10:         if (bt != null)
11:             b.setLabel(bt);
12:         add(b);
13:         add(t);
14:     }
15:
16:     public boolean action(Event evt, Object obj) {
17:         if (++phrase > 5) phrase = 0;
18:         switch (phrase) {
19:             case 0:
20:                 t.setText("If love be rough with you, be rough with
                        ➦love.");
21:                 break;
22:             case 1:
23:                 t.setText("Dost thou make us minstrels?");
24:                 break;
25:             case 2:
26:                 t.setText("Speak but one rhyme, and I am satisfied.");
27:                 break;
28:             case 3:
29:                 t.setText("Any man that can write may answer a letter.");
30:                 break;
31:             case 4:
32:                 t.setText("Go, villain, fetch a surgeon.");
33:                 break;
34:             default:
35:                 t.setText("They have made worms' meat of me.");
36:         }
37:         repaint();
38:         return false;
39:     }
40: }
```

Before you test the applet you just created, I want to explain the main parts of the Java program. The applet displays a phrase spoken by Mercutio, one of Romeo's more quotable friends in *Romeo and Juliet*. Two user-interface elements—a Speak! button and an empty text field—are created in lines 4 and 5. Lines 12 and 13 place these elements on the applet window.

Java programs are organized into sections called *methods*, which are analogous to subroutines or functions in other languages. Lines 16 through 39 contain the `action()` method, which executes every time a user clicks the button.

The `phrase` variable, created and initialized in line 6, keeps track of which Mercutio quote to display. Line 17 increments the value of `phrase` by 1, and if it is greater than 5, `phrase` is reset to 0.

Lines 18 through 36 use a big `switch...case` statement to display the right Mercutio phrase, and line 37 causes the applet window to be redrawn so that the new quote displays in the text field.

Now that you know what the Mercutio applet does, it's time to test it.

Compiling the Program

If you entered the source code of `Mercutio.java`, you need to compile it into a bytecode file. You can do this using the Java Developer's Kit compiler by entering the following line at a command prompt:

```
javac Mercutio.java
```

Compile the program using the JDK compiler or any other Java development tool that can create bytecode files. A bytecode file called `Mercutio.class` is created.

Those of you who are following along without writing the program should find `Mercutio.class` on the book's CD-ROM at `\SOURCE\CHAPTER15` if you haven't already. Put a copy of this file somewhere on your system's hard disk.

The Mercutio applet's class file is ready to be placed on a Web page. To do this, create a simple `.HTML` file and put the applet on it with a special HTML tag, `<APPLET>`.

Putting the Program on a Page

Using any text editor, enter Listing 15.2 and save the file as `Mercutio.html` (or `Mercutio.htm` if your platform does not support four-character file extensions such as `.HTML`). This HTML file should be placed in the same directory as the file `Mercutio.class`.

Listing 15.2. The full HTML source code of `Mercutio.html`.

```
1: <html>
2: <body>
3: <applet code="Mercutio.class" height=150 width=400>
4: </applet>
5: </body>
6: </html>
```

Now that you have a compiled applet and an HTML page to put it on, you can use any Web-capable browser to try it out. Load the file `Mercutio.html` into Internet Explorer 3.0, most versions of Netscape Navigator 2.0 or higher, or the AppletViewer tool that comes with the JDK.

Figure 15.1 shows the output of the Mercutio applet using Internet Explorer 3.0.

Figure 15.1.

The output of the Mercutio applet on a Web page.

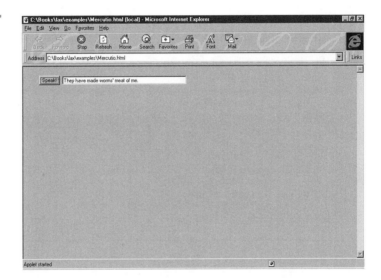

In its simplest form, an APPLET tag contains the following elements:

❑ The opening <APPLET> tag and closing </APPLET> tag.

❑ The CODE attribute, which identifies the name of the applet class file to load:
   `Mercutio.class`.

❑ The HEIGHT and WIDTH attributes, which define the size of the applet.

In the next section, you'll create a more complicated <APPLET> tag for the Mercutio applet in order to see what else you can set up.

Expanding the <APPLET> Tag

Return to the directory on your system that contains the files `Mercutio.class` and `Mercutio.html`. From that same directory, create a subdirectory called `java`, and move the file `Mercutio.class` into the new subdirectory.

If you examine the Web page `Mercutio.html` at this point, you get an error message stating that the Mercutio class file could not be found. The browser (or AppletViewer) expects to find the applet's class file in the same directory as the `.HTML` file that contains the applet.

You need to add a new attribute, `CODEBASE`, to Mercutio's `<APPLET>` tag. `CODEBASE` identifies the directory that contains the applet's class file. Load the file `Mercutio.html` into a text editor, and change it so that the `<APPLET>` tag appears as the following:

```
<applet code="Mercutio.class" codebase="java" height=150 width=400>
```

After making this change, you can run the Mercutio applet correctly because the browser knows to look in the `java` subdirectory. The `CODEBASE` attribute does not have to be a relative path to a subdirectory. It could also be a URL reference, such as `http://www.mcp.com/sams`.

Before saving `Mercutio.html`, add the following lines under the `APPLET` line you just modified:

```
<param name="ButtonTitle" value="Next!">
This applet requires a Java-enabled browser.
```

When you're done, `Mercutio.html` should look like the code in Listing 15.3.

Listing 15.3. The modified HTML source code of `Mercutio.html`.

```
1: <html>
2: <body>
3: <applet code="Mercutio.class" codebase="java" height=150 width=400>
4: <param name="ButtonTitle" value="Next!">
5: This applet requires a Java-enabled browser.
6: </applet>
7: </body>
8: </html>
```

After saving your changes, load the Web page into a browser or AppletViewer. You see that the button now has the label Next instead of Speak!. The `PARAM` tag sends parameters to a Java applet. The `NAME` attribute gives the parameter a name, and the `VALUE` attribute sets the value for that parameter. You can use as many `PARAM` tags as you need; if you can configure a Java applet with 413 different parameters, you can use 413 different `PARAM` tags.

You must place all `PARAM` tags between the opening `<APPLET>` tag and the closing `</APPLET>` tag.

The parameters are sent to a Java applet, but the applet program must do something with them, or they are ignored. In the source code of Mercutio.java, the following are lines 9 through 11:

```
String bt = getParameter("ButtonTitle");
       if (bt != null)
            b.setLabel(bt);
```

These statements retrieve the ButtonTitle parameter, if one was provided by the Web page, and use it to set the label of the button. If this parameter is not provided, the variable bt has the value null, and the default text is used for the button's label: Speak!

The other change you made to Mercutio.html was adding line 5, which states that a Java-enabled browser is required. This text is located between the opening and closing <APPLET> tags, and it displays only on Web browsers that are not Java capable. You can replace it with any text or HTML tags that you want to provide as an alternative. For example, a Java applet that displays an animated company logo could provide a non-animated logo for the Java impaired, as in the following:

```
<applet code="ExplodingTortugaMintsLogo.class" height=200 width=300>
<param name="BackGroundColor" value="#00FF00">
<img src="TortugaMintsLogo.gif" height=200 width=300 alt="Tortuga Mints">
</applet>
```

The GIF image file TortugaMintsLogo.gif displays only on browsers that do not handle Java applets.

Microsoft Internet Explorer, and perhaps other browsers by the time you read this, plan to offer the functionality of the <APPLET> tag with a new <OBJECT> tag. As you learn about the use of <OBJECT> in the next section, you will recognize a lot of familiar elements.

Incorporating the <OBJECT> Tag

Now that you understand how to add a Java applet to a Web page with the <APPLET> tag, it's time to see how the new <OBJECT> tag accomplishes the same thing.

NOTE: Microsoft Internet Explorer 3.0 documentation includes discussion of how Java applets are implemented with the <OBJECT> tag, but the use of the <OBJECT> tag is not fully implemented at the time of this writing. The description here is based on Microsoft's announced plans and the documentation from the World Wide Web Consortium about the tag.

Even after the <OBJECT> tag is fully implemented for Java use, the <APPLET> tag will be supported to maintain compatibility with existing Web pages. You can continue to use

<APPLET>, a tag that is supported by most current versions of Netscape Navigator and Internet Explorer 3.0. However, if you're using this book to integrate ActiveX and VBScript into your Web sites, the <OBJECT> tag should be part of your strategy as well.

At present, the only browser that supports the <OBJECT> tag in any form is Internet Explorer 3.0. However, because representatives from Netscape and Spyglass participated in the efforts to create this HTML extension, it is expected for their browsers to offer it at some point.

The following is an example of an <OBJECT> tag in use to place an ActiveX Forms 2.0 command button:

```
<OBJECT ID="CommandButton1" WIDTH=96 HEIGHT=32 CLASSID="CLSID:D7053240-CE69-
➡11CD-A777-00DD01143C57">
    <PARAM NAME="Size" VALUE="2540;846">
    <PARAM NAME="FontCharSet" VALUE="0">
    <PARAM NAME="FontPitchAndFamily" VALUE="2">
    <PARAM NAME="ParagraphAlign" VALUE="3">
    <PARAM NAME="FontWeight" VALUE="0">
</OBJECT>
```

This HTML code is created automatically by using the Insert ActiveX Control command in the ActiveX Control Pad. Some aspects of this code should be familiar to you. The WIDTH and HEIGHT attributes set the size of the control, and the <PARAM> tag is used in the same way it was used for Java applets in the last section. The NAME attribute gives the parameter a name, such as Size, and the VALUE attribute gives the named parameter a value, such as 2540;846.

The ID attribute of the <OBJECT> tag gives the object a name. The name is needed so that VBScript or other scripting languages can communicate with the object, as you'll see later in this chapter.

The last new aspect of the <OBJECT> tag from the preceding example is the CLASSID attribute. The first part, preceding the colon, indicates what the object is. In this case, CLSID represents an ActiveX control. The part after the colon is used to identify the object.

Based on the World Wide Web Consortium's proposal for the <OBJECT> tag, the following is an example of how you could declare a Java applet:

```
<object
  id="jvaMercutio"
  codebase="java\"
  codetype="application/java-vm"
  classid="java:Mercutio"
  width=400
  height=150>
<param name="ButtonTitle" value="Next!">
</object>
```

Because the support for <OBJECT> remains incomplete in Internet Explorer and unsupported in any form elsewhere, you need to use the <APPLET> tag for now to add Java programs to a Web page.

Integrating Java Applets and VBScript

In almost all cases, a Java applet is an island unto itself. It runs in the space allotted to it by a Web browser, and it cannot communicate with other programs or the Web page that called it. The other elements of the Web page also cannot communicate with the applet after it is loaded.

VBScript provides a way to make a Java applet a more communicative part of a Web page. VBScript programs have access to any public methods or public variables inside the Java program and can use them to change the performance of the applet.

One example of how you can use this is to change a Java applet's parameters as the applet is running. You use the <PARAM> tag with applets to establish settings that affect how a Java applet operates, but you use this tag only to establish an initial setting. After the applet begins running, the <PARAM> tag's work is done.

Take a look at the following HTML code to load an applet:

```
<applet code="DancingHeadline.class" width=400 height=125>
<param name="Headline" value="Disco lives forever!">
<param name="Blinking" value="Yes">
</applet>
```

This use of the <APPLET> and <PARAM> tags loads a Java applet called DancingHeadline.class and sends it a headline parameter with the value Disco lives forever!. Another parameter, called blinking, is set to the value Yes.

The blinking parameter controls whether or not the headline blinks on and off, a feature in the tradition of the often-loathed HTML <BLINK> tag. The following is the Java statement that loads the blinking parameter into its own variable:

```
String blinkStatus = getParameter("blinking");
```

If the blinkStatus variable was declared as a public variable, you can change it using VBScript.

To see how this is done, you will create an HTML page that uses VBScript to communicate with a Java applet.

Using the Light Applet

The VBScript and Java demonstration you will create is a Java traffic-light animation that changes in response to the click of intrinsic HTML <INPUT> buttons.

The compiled class file for this applet, Light.class, is on this book's CD-ROM in the \SOURCE\CHAP15 subdirectory. However, Listing 15.4 provides the full source code for Light.java to show how the applet was designed.

You can use this source code to create and compile the applet, or if you prefer, you can rely on the copy of Light.class from the CD-ROM.

Listing 15.4. The full source code of Light.java.

```
 1: import java.awt.*;
 2:
 3: public class Light extends java.applet.Applet {
 4:
 5:     Image light;
 6:     boolean red = false;
 7:     boolean yellow = false;
 8:     boolean green = false;
 9:
10:     public void init() {
11:         light = getImage(getCodeBase(), "traffic.gif");
12:     }
13:
14:     public void paint(Graphics g) {
15:         g.drawImage(light, 10, 10, this);
16:         if (red) {
17:             g.setColor(Color.red);
18:             g.fillOval(35,13,80,80);
19:         }
20:         if (yellow) {
21:             g.setColor(Color.yellow);
22:             g.fillOval(35,110,82,82);
23:         }
24:         if (green) {
25:             g.setColor(Color.green);
26:             g.fillOval(33,211,87,87);
27:         }
28:     }
29:
30:     public void turnOn(String color) {
31:         red = false;
32:         yellow = false;
33:         green = false;
34:         if (color.equals("red")) red = true;
35:         if (color.equals("yellow")) yellow = true;
36:         if (color.equals("green")) green = true;
37:         repaint();
38:     }
39: }
```

Going Over the Java Code

The following things are happening in this applet:

❑ Lines 5 through 8 declare four variables that are used in this applet. One variable, Image, stores a graphics file that is loaded elsewhere. The other three variables—`red`, `yellow`, and `green`—hold boolean values. They are equal to `true` if their specific lights are lit, or `false` otherwise. All three begin with a value of `false`, so none of the lights are lit.

❏ Line 11 loads the image file `traffic.gif` into the variable `light`. It is part of the `init()` method, which runs automatically when the applet is first loaded.

❏ Lines 14 through 28 are the `paint()` method. This is called any time the applet window needs to be repainted.

❏ Line 15 displays the image stored in `light` on the applet window.

❏ Lines 16 through 18 check to see whether the `red` variable has the boolean value of `true`. If it does, a red oval is drawn at the x,y position of `(35,13)` with a width of 80 and a height of 80.

❏ Lines 20 through 22 draw a yellow oval if the `yellow` variable equals `true`.

❏ Lines 24 through 26 draw a green oval if the `green` variable equals `true`.

❏ Lines 30 through 37 are the `turnOn()` method of the applet, which turns on a light based on the `color` parameter sent to the method. If `color` is equal to `red`, the value of the `red` boolean variable is set to `true`.

❏ Line 37 tells the applet that it needs to be repainted, and the `paint()` method is called.

The `turnOn()` Method

To understand how VBScript can interact with Java, you need to concentrate on the `turnOn()` method of the `Light` applet. You could call this method inside the Java applet with the following statement:

```
turnOn("yellow");
```

This statement results in the `yellow` boolean variable being set to `true`. Nothing is displayed right away because the `paint()` method handles all screen updating. However, when `repaint()` is called in line 37, the `paint()` method displays the traffic light with the yellow light illuminated.

This isn't the only way to change the light on display. The `turnOn()` method has a `public` declaration in front of it, and VBScript can call it.

Communicating with the Applet from VBScript

Create a new HTML page that will contain the Java applet and some other elements. Using any text editor, open a file and enter the text of Listing 15.5. Save the file as `traffic.html`. Make sure that the files `Light.class` and `traffic.gif` are in the same directory as `traffic.html`.

Listing 15.5. The full HTML source code of `traffic.html`.

```
 1: <html>
 2: <head>
 3: <title>Traffic Light demo</title>
 4: <SCRIPT language = "VBScript">
 5: <!--
 6: Sub RedButton_OnClick
 7:     document.jvaLight.turnOn("red")
 8: End Sub
 9:
10: Sub YellowButton_OnClick
11:     document.jvaLight.turnOn("yellow")
12: End Sub
13:
14: Sub GreenButton_OnClick
15:     document.jvaLight.turnOn("green")
16: End Sub
17:
18: -->
19: </SCRIPT>
20: </head>
21: <body>
22: <center>
23: <applet code="Light.class" id="jvaLight" height=325 width=148 align="left">
24: </applet>
25: <table cellpadding=30 border=0 align="left">
26: <tr>
27: <td>
28: <input type=button value="Red" name="RedButton">
29: </td>
30: <tr>
31: <td>
32: <input type=button value="Yellow" name="YellowButton">
33: </td>
34: </tr>
35: <tr>
36: <td>
37: <input type=button value="Green" name="GreenButton">
38: </td>
39: </tr>
40: </table>
41: </center>
42: </body>
43: </html>
```

Most of the syntax of this HTML file should be familiar to you. The <TABLE> tags arrange the Web page; you do not need them for any other reason in this example.

Lines 28, 32, and 37 place three intrinsic HTML form buttons on the page and give them the names `RedButton`, `YellowButton`, and `GreenButton`.

Lines 23 and 24 place the applet `Light.class` on the page. The new attribute to the <APPLET> tag is `id="jvaLight"`. This attribute gives the Java applet a name that a VBScript command can use to communicate with the applet.

A short VBScript program in lines 4 through 16 consists of three `OnClick` subroutines: `RedButton_OnClick`, `YellowButton_OnClick`, and `GreenButton_OnClick`. Each of these subroutines calls the `turnOn()` method of the Java applet. The following is an example:

```
document.jvaLight.turnOn("red")
```

`document.jvaLight` identifies the object that VBScript is communicating with—the Java applet with the `ID` value of `jvaLight`. The last part of the statement, `turnOn("red")`, is a call to the `turnOn()` method inside the applet.

When you load the Web page `traffic.html` into a browser, it should resemble the one in Figure 15.2.

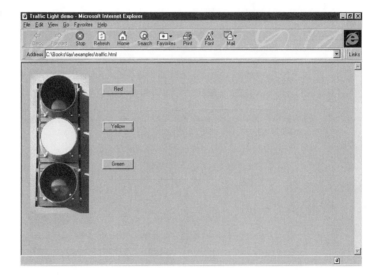

The traffic-light demonstration shows how VBScript can access a Java applet's `public` methods. It is also possible to set any `public` variables of an applet. The following statement shows a VBScript subroutine that sets a Java variable:

```
Sub SpeedUpButton_OnClick
    document.jvaRace.speed = document.jvaRace.speed + 1
End Sub
```

This example refers to a `speed` variable in a Java applet with an `ID` of `jvaRace`. `speed` is increased by 1 whenever the `SpeedUpButton` object's `OnClick` subroutine is called.

Using `public` variables from outside a Java applet can wreak havoc on the program if it has not been designed to handle the changes. As a part of object-oriented programming, the style embodied by the Java language, the use of a `public` variable means that it should be modifiable at any time by external objects—other Java programs, VBScript, and the like. If a variable cannot be changed without causing unexpected side effects or errors, it should not be declared `public`.

Workshop Wrap-Up

By working through the parts of this chapter, you have seen Java in action on a Web page, and you've seen how VBScript can be used to make it more responsive to other parts of a page.

You have also learned the present and future HTML tags that will be used for Java applets in Internet Explorer—APPLET and OBJECT. Java can be offered in conjunction with ActiveX and VBScript as a way to offer a more compelling and interactive experience on a Web site.

Next Steps

Now that you have learned about Java and VBScript, the following chapters are good places to continue:

- ❏ To learn more about using intrinsic HTML controls such as buttons with VBScript, see Chapter 2, "Using VBScript with HTML Controls."
- ❏ Chapter 6, "Checking Form Data," contains more details about building OnClick procedures in VBScript.
- ❏ For more information about using the ActiveX Control Pad, see Chapter 13, "Implementing an ActiveX Menu Control."

Q&A

Q: The <OBJECT> tag has been described as a proposal. Is there a way to track its progress toward official approval?

A: The World Wide Web Consortium maintains a Web site at http://www.w3.org. The current page for the <OBJECT> proposal, which is titled "Inserting Objects into HTML," is at the following URL:

http://www.w3.org/pub/WWW/TR/WD-object

Note, however, that the leading developers of Web browsers, Netscape and Microsoft, adopt most new HTML tags at their own initiative before the World Wide Web Consortium agrees on a standard.

Q: I noticed that ActiveX objects have a long numeric string in their CLASSID attribute such as CLSID:D7053240-CE69-11CD-A777-00DD01143C57. Java applets do not have this in the CLASSID. Why is the <OBJECT> tag implemented differently between ActiveX and Java in regard to CLASSID?

A: The difference comes about because of the way ActiveX and Java implement security. As methods to execute programs over the Web, both ActiveX and Java must provide a reliable way to prevent malicious or unintentionally damaging code from being run. Otherwise, viruses, Trojan horses, and other nasty things could occur on a user's computer when these Web-based programs run.

Java's security model relies on a secure language that does not allow programmers to write malicious code. Applets are restricted in the kinds of things they can do—no reading or writing files on the user's computer, no network connections to other Internet sites, and so on.

The ActiveX security model, on the other hand, generally relies on establishing a way to authenticate that a program comes from a trusted source. A user must approve an ActiveX control before downloading it, and a security certificate is presented to give users the ability to double-check the identity of the ActiveX program.

The different approach to the `CLASSID` attribute comes about because ActiveX uses that long alphanumeric string as part of its way to identify a control. Java does not implement that kind of security check, so a `CLASSID` such as `java:com.spiderbyte.Light` is all that is needed.

Q: My Java applet uses a second class file as part of its function. How can I access the `public` variables and methods of this second class file if there's no way to name it with an `ID` attribute?

A: Only classes that derive from `Java.applet.Applet` can be called or accessed from VBScript. If you want to call a method in another class, you have to create a method in your applet that calls the other class's method.

To reach the `public` variables in the other class, you have to create a method in the applet class. Think of the applet's class file as the gateway between VBScript and the other class files that compose your Java program.

SIXTEEN

Real-Life Examples II

This chapter describes two sample Web pages created using VBScript, with techniques introduced in Part III (Chapters 12 through 15). The following examples are included:

Example 1. A game designed for young children learning shape and color recognition.

Example 2. A multipage commercial Web site, navigated via an ActiveX Tab Strip control.

Example 1

Document title: Chesney Mouse

Files:

Page file: mouse.htm (Figures 16.1, 16.2, and 16.4)

Layout file: mouse.alx (Figure 16.3)

Images:

❏ bluesquare.gif

❏ bluecircle.gif

❏ bluetriangle.gif

❏ redsquare.gif

❏ redcircle.gif

❏ redtriangle.gif

❏ yellowsquare.gif

❏ yellowcircle.gif

❏ yellowtriangle.gif

❏ greensquare.gif

❏ greencircle.gif

❏ greentriangle.gif

❏ orangesquare.gif

❏ orangecircle.gif

❏ orangetriangle.gif

❏ mouse.gif

❏ cheese.gif

❏ hole1.gif

❏ hole2.gif

ActiveX controls:

❏ Label

❏ CommandButton

❏ IeImage

❏ IeTimer

NOTE: The IeImage and IeTimer controls are part of the full installation of Microsoft Internet Explorer 3.x (MSIE 3.x) final version. If you have a beta version of MSIE 3.0 or you did not carry out a full installation, you can also find the preceding controls on the CD-ROM in the \SOURCE\CHAPTER16 directory.

Description: The Chesney Mouse example is a simple game, designed with young preschool children in mind. The program randomly selects a color and a shape from a predefined range. The child has to click on the correct colored shape. If the correct object is selected, the mouse graphic (which follows the cursor around most of the time), collects the cheese from "behind" the object and takes it off to the mouse hole.

The example demonstrates several important concepts (as well as helping as refresher on color and shape recognition!). First, the 2D HTML elements, the colored objects, the mouse, and the cheese are on different layers of the display. Therefore, Chesney Mouse appears to go behind the colored objects. Furthermore, the mouse hole is built from two images—a front and a back. So as Chesney scuttles off into the mouse hole,

Example 1   281

he appears to be going inside a real hole; his image passes behind the front image but is on top of the back image.

The example also introduces the `IeTimer` ActiveX control. The timer event is fired at preset intervals while the timer is activated. Code can be written within the timer event handler—in this case, to move our friendly rodent and his favorite Emmantal cheese by two pixels either up or across.

Even though the screen is filled with graphic images, the total graphic content of the page is just over 11KB.

The simple animation is achieved by changing the image's top and left properties at runtime. The Layout control itself doesn't receive mouse events. Therefore, to control the movement of Chesney Mouse around the screen, a single blank image has been used across the entire background of the image, thereby giving you mouse move events.

Techniques Applied

ActiveX controls: (See Chapters 1, 12, 13, and 14.) The example uses a range of ActiveX controls. The example also demonstrates changing properties at runtime—in this case, to produce a simple animation.

HTML Layout control: (See Chapter 14, "Using the HTML Layout Control.") The entire example is built within a Layout control.

Layering: (See Chapter 14.) The mouse and cheese images are on one layer, the colored objects are on another layer, and the mouse hole is on two different layers.

Arrays: (See Chapter 10, "Using the Power of Arrays.") The ranges of colors and shapes are held within single-dimension static arrays.

Programming Elements: (See Chapter 9, "Making Your Program Flow.") A range of VBScript language elements is used, including conditional statements such as `If...Then`, `Select Case`, and `For...Next`. The VBScript random number generator is also used as shown in Figure 16.1.

When the start button is clicked, a random number is generated, which is then used to select a color and a shape. The color and shape are then displayed in a message that gives a clue about where the child can find the cheese.

The whole of the background is in fact an ActiveX image control, which means that wherever the mouse pointer moves on the screen, an event is fired. This event is used to position Chesney Mouse next to the mouse pointer.

If the child clicks on the correct colored shape, a short animation sequence takes control, allowing Chesney Mouse to run off to his mouse hole with the cheese, as shown in Figure 16.2.

Figure 16.1.
The program randomly selects a color and a shape.

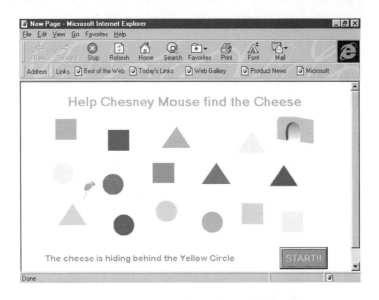

Figure 16.1.
The program randomly selects a color and a shape.

Figure 16.2.
The child's "reward."

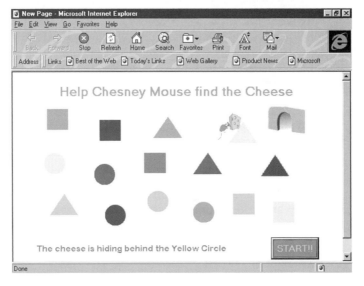

Because the Layout control has been used (see Figure 16.3), the various images are stacked in layers, which adds to the realism of the animation. As Chesney Mouse enters his mouse hole, he appears in front of the back of the hole and behind the front of the hole.

Positioning images in this way is an everyday event in normal Windows programming, but it would be impossible in normal HTML. As you can see, the Layout control enables you to produce applications that are usually the domain of Windows programmers. You can now accurately position objects on the Layout canvas to create a reusable file, which is quickly and easily added to your HTML page, as shown in Figure 16.4.

Example 1   283

Figure 16.3.

mouse.alx.

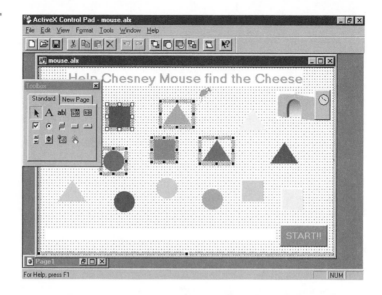

Figure 16.4.

The object declaration for the Layout control in the HTML page.

The Layout control file (shown in Listing 16.1) contains much more than purely graphical and visual references. The file is in fact the complete application for this example, containing all the objects and the script that enables the objects to interoperate.

The script commences by defining and populating the arrays that are used to hold the data for the colors and shapes. The user begins the game by clicking the start button, which activates the CommandButton1 click event handler. This event handler generates random numbers for both the object color and object shape, and it displays the clue message on the screen.

As the mouse is moved around the screen, the `Image1_MouseMove` event handler is executed. This event moves the Chesney Mouse image (`Mousey`) to the same location as the mouse pointer.

Each shape on the screen has its own event handler that is executed when the mouse button is pressed over the shape. A special reference name and the position of the shape are passed to the custom procedure `CheckForWin`.

The `CheckForWin` procedure compares the reference name of the stored shape with the reference name of the selected shape. If they are the same, the procedure moves the cheese image under the shape and activates the animation sequence by enabling the timer control.

The `IeTimer1_Timer` event is fired at regular intervals while the timer control is enabled. It moves the images of both the mouse and the cheese upward to a predetermined position and then across the screen until the mouse appears to enter his mouse hole, at which point the timer is disabled. All the controls and events are programmatically disabled during the animation sequence by the use of a flag called `Animating`.

Listing 16.1. The `mouse.alx` code.

```
<SCRIPT LANGUAGE="VBScript">
<!--
Dim Colors(4)
Dim Shapes(2)

Colors(0) = "Red"
Colors(1) = "Blue"
Colors(2) = "Green"
Colors(3) = "Yellow"
Colors(4) = "Orange"

Shapes(0) = "Square"
Shapes(1) = "Triangle"
Shapes(2) = "Circle"

Dim CurrentObject
-->
</SCRIPT>
<SCRIPT LANGUAGE="VBScript">
<!--
Sub CheckForWin(WhichObject, L, T, W, H)
 If Animating = True Then
  Exit Sub
 End If

 If CurrentObject = WhichObject Then
  Cheese.Top = (T + (H/2) - (Cheese.Height/2))
  Cheese.Left = (L + (W/2) - (Cheese.Width/2))
  Mousey.Top = Cheese.Top + 11
  Mousey.Left = Cheese.Left - 18
  IeTimer1.Enabled = True
```

Example 1   285

```
   Animating = True
  Else
   Alert "OOPS!"
  End If
 end sub

 -->
 </SCRIPT>
 <SCRIPT LANGUAGE="VBScript">
 <!--
 Sub shapes0_MouseDown(Button, Shift, X, Y)
  L = shapes0.Left
  T = shapes0.Top
  W = shapes0.Width
  H = shapes0.Height
  call CheckForWin("YellowTriangle",L,T,W,H)
 end sub

 -->
 </SCRIPT>
 <SCRIPT LANGUAGE="VBScript">
 <!--
 Sub CommandButton1_Click()
  If Animating = True Then
   Exit Sub
  End If

 RANDOMIZE
 CurrentColor = Int((4 - 0 + 1) * Rnd + 0)
 CurrentShape = Int((2 - 0 + 1) * Rnd + 0)

 Clue = "The cheese is hiding behind the "
 Clue = Clue & Colors(CurrentColor) & " "
 Clue = Clue & Shapes(CurrentShape)

 Label1.Caption = Clue
 CurrentObject = Colors(CurrentColor) & Shapes(CurrentShape)

 end sub
 -->
 </SCRIPT>
 <SCRIPT LANGUAGE="VBScript">
 <!--
 Sub Image1_MouseMove(Button, Shift, X, Y)
  If Animating = True Then
   Exit Sub
  End If

  Mousey.Left = X
  Mousey.Top = Y
 end sub
 -->
 </SCRIPT>
 <SCRIPT LANGUAGE="VBScript">
 <!--
 Sub shapes10_MouseDown(Button, Shift, X, Y)
  L = shapes10.Left
  T = shapes10.Top
  W = shapes10.Width
```

continues

Listing 16.1. continued

```
 H = shapes10.Height
call CheckForWin("OrangeCircle", L, T, W, H)
end sub
-->
</SCRIPT>
<SCRIPT LANGUAGE="VBScript">
<!--
Sub shapes1_MouseDown(Button, Shift, X, Y)
 L = shapes1.Left
 T = shapes1.Top
 W = shapes1.Width
 H = shapes1.Height
call CheckForWin("OrangeSquare",L,T,W,H)
end sub
-->
</SCRIPT>
<SCRIPT LANGUAGE="VBScript">
<!--
Sub shapes9_MouseDown(Button, Shift, X, Y)
 L = shapes9.Left
 T = shapes9.Top
 W = shapes9.Width
 H = shapes9.Height
call CheckForWin("OrangeTriangle",L,T,W,H)
end sub
-->
</SCRIPT>
<SCRIPT LANGUAGE="VBScript">
<!--
Sub shapes8_MouseDown(Button, Shift, X, Y)
 L = shapes8.Left
 T = shapes8.Top
 W = shapes8.Width
 H = shapes8.Height
call CheckForWin("GreenSquare",L,T,W,H)
end sub
-->
</SCRIPT>
<SCRIPT LANGUAGE="VBScript">
<!--
Sub shapes7_MouseDown(Button, Shift, X, Y)
 L = shapes7.Left
 T = shapes7.Top
 W = shapes7.Width
 H = shapes7.Height
call CheckForWin("YellowCircle",L,T,W,H)
end sub
-->
</SCRIPT>
<SCRIPT LANGUAGE="VBScript">
<!--
Sub shapes6_MouseDown(Button, Shift, X, Y)
 L = shapes6.Left
 T = shapes6.Top
 W = shapes6.Width
 H = shapes6.Height
call CheckForWin("RedTriangle",L,T,W,H)
end sub
```

Example 1   287

```
-->
</SCRIPT>
<SCRIPT LANGUAGE="VBScript">
<!--
Sub shapes5_MouseDown(Button, Shift, X, Y)
 L = shapes5.Left
 T = shapes5.Top
 W = shapes5.Width
 H = shapes5.Height
call CheckForWin("RedCircle",L,T,W,H)
end sub
-->
</SCRIPT>
<SCRIPT LANGUAGE="VBScript">
<!--
Sub shapes4_MouseDown(Button, Shift, X, Y)
 L = shapes4.Left
 T = shapes4.Top
 W = shapes4.Width
 H = shapes4.Height
call CheckForWin("RedSquare",L,T,W,H)
end sub
-->
</SCRIPT>
<SCRIPT LANGUAGE="VBScript">
<!--
Sub shapes3_MouseDown(Button, Shift, X, Y)
 L = shapes3.Left
 T = shapes3.Top
 W = shapes3.Width
 H = shapes3.Height
call CheckForWin("BlueSquare",L,T,W,H)
end sub
-->
</SCRIPT>
<SCRIPT LANGUAGE="VBScript">
<!--
Sub shapes2_MouseDown(Button, Shift, X, Y)
 L = shapes2.Left
 T = shapes2.Top
 W = shapes2.Width
 H = shapes2.Height
call CheckForWin("BlueCircle",L,T,W,H)
end sub
-->
</SCRIPT>
<SCRIPT LANGUAGE="VBScript">
<!--
Sub shapes14_MouseDown(Button, Shift, X, Y)
 L = shapes14.Left
 T = shapes14.Top
 W = shapes14.Width
 H = shapes14.Height
call CheckForWin("YellowSquare",L,T,W,H)
end sub
-->
</SCRIPT>
<SCRIPT LANGUAGE="VBScript">
<!--
```

continues

Listing 16.1. continued

```
Sub shapes13_MouseDown(Button, Shift, X, Y)
 L = shapes13.Left
 T = shapes13.Top
 W = shapes13.Width
 H = shapes13.Height
call CheckForWin("GreenTriangle",L,T,W,H)
end sub
-->
</SCRIPT>
<SCRIPT LANGUAGE="VBScript">
<!--
Sub shapes12_MouseDown(Button, Shift, X, Y)
 L = shapes12.Left
 T = shapes12.Top
 W = shapes12.Width
 H = shapes12.Height
call CheckForWin("GreenCircle",L,T,W,H)
end sub
-->
</SCRIPT>
<SCRIPT LANGUAGE="VBScript">
<!--
Sub shapes11_MouseDown(Button, Shift, X, Y)
 L = shapes11.Left
 T = shapes11.Top
 W = shapes11.Width
 H = shapes11.Height
 call CheckForWin("BlueTriangle",L,T,W,H)
end sub
-->
</SCRIPT>
<SCRIPT LANGUAGE="VBScript">
<!--
dim Animating

Sub IeTimer1_Timer()
 If Mousey.Top > 57 Then
  Mousey.Top = Mousey.Top - 2
  Cheese.Top = Cheese.Top - 2
 Else
  Mousey.Left = Mousey.Left + 2
  Cheese.Left = Cheese.Left + 2
   If Mousey.Left > 360 Then
     IeTimer1.Enabled = False
     Animating = False
   End If
 End If
end sub
-->
</SCRIPT>
<DIV BACKGROUND="#ffffff" ID="Layout3" STYLE="LAYOUT:FIXED;WIDTH:415pt;
➥HEIGHT:256pt;">
    <OBJECT ID="IeTimer1"
     CLASSID="CLSID:59CCB4A0-727D-11CF-AC36-00AA00A47DD2"
➥STYLE="TOP:30pt;LEFT:386pt;WIDTH:23pt;HEIGHT:41pt;ZINDEX:0;">
        <PARAM NAME="_ExtentX" VALUE="820">
        <PARAM NAME="_ExtentY" VALUE="1455">
        <PARAM NAME="Interval" VALUE="5">
```

Example 1   289

```
            <PARAM NAME="Enabled" VALUE="False">
        </OBJECT>
        <OBJECT ID="Image1"
         CLASSID="CLSID:D4A97620-8E8F-11CF-93CD-00AA00C08FDF" STYLE="TOP:0pt;
➥LEFT:4pt;WIDTH:409pt;HEIGHT:251pt;ZINDEX:1;">
            <PARAM NAME="BorderStyle" VALUE="0">
            <PARAM NAME="SizeMode" VALUE="3">
            <PARAM NAME="Size" VALUE="14429;8855">
            <PARAM NAME="PictureAlignment" VALUE="0">
            <PARAM NAME="VariousPropertyBits" VALUE="19">
        </OBJECT>
        <OBJECT ID="Label1"
         CLASSID="CLSID:978C9E23-D4B0-11CE-BF2D-00AA003F40D0"
➥STYLE="TOP:221pt;LEFT:8pt;WIDTH:323pt;HEIGHT:15pt;ZINDEX:2;">
            <PARAM NAME="ForeColor" VALUE="16744448">
            <PARAM NAME="BackColor" VALUE="16777215">
            <PARAM NAME="Size" VALUE="11395;529">
            <PARAM NAME="FontName" VALUE="Arial Rounded MT Bold">
            <PARAM NAME="FontEffects" VALUE="1073741825">
            <PARAM NAME="FontHeight" VALUE="240">
            <PARAM NAME="FontCharSet" VALUE="0">
            <PARAM NAME="FontPitchAndFamily" VALUE="2">
            <PARAM NAME="FontWeight" VALUE="700">
        </OBJECT>
        <OBJECT ID="Image2"
         CLASSID="CLSID:D4A97620-8E8F-11CF-93CD-00AA00C08FDF"
➥STYLE="TOP:34pt;LEFT:334pt;WIDTH:38pt;HEIGHT:35pt;ZINDEX:3;">
            <PARAM NAME="PicturePath" VALUE="hole1.gif">
            <PARAM NAME="AutoSize" VALUE="-1">
            <PARAM NAME="BorderStyle" VALUE="0">
            <PARAM NAME="SizeMode" VALUE="3">
            <PARAM NAME="Size" VALUE="1323;1217">
            <PARAM NAME="PictureAlignment" VALUE="0">
            <PARAM NAME="VariousPropertyBits" VALUE="19">
        </OBJECT>
        <OBJECT ID="Label2"
         CLASSID="CLSID:978C9E23-D4B0-11CE-BF2D-00AA003F40D0" STYLE="TOP:4pt;
➥LEFT:41pt;WIDTH:329pt;HEIGHT:22pt;ZINDEX:4;">
            <PARAM NAME="ForeColor" VALUE="12615935">
            <PARAM NAME="BackColor" VALUE="16777215">
            <PARAM NAME="VariousPropertyBits" VALUE="268435483">
            <PARAM NAME="Caption" VALUE="Help Chesney Mouse find the Cheese">
            <PARAM NAME="Size" VALUE="11606;776">
            <PARAM NAME="FontEffects" VALUE="1073741825">
            <PARAM NAME="FontHeight" VALUE="360">
            <PARAM NAME="FontCharSet" VALUE="0">
            <PARAM NAME="FontPitchAndFamily" VALUE="2">
            <PARAM NAME="FontWeight" VALUE="700">
        </OBJECT>
        <OBJECT ID="Cheese"
         CLASSID="CLSID:D4A97620-8E8F-11CF-93CD-00AA00C08FDF"
➥STYLE="TOP:49pt;LEFT:379pt;WIDTH:17pt;HEIGHT:23pt;ZINDEX:5;">
            <PARAM NAME="PicturePath" VALUE="cheese.gif">
            <PARAM NAME="AutoSize" VALUE="-1">
            <PARAM NAME="BorderStyle" VALUE="0">
            <PARAM NAME="SizeMode" VALUE="3">
            <PARAM NAME="Size" VALUE="582;794">
            <PARAM NAME="PictureAlignment" VALUE="0">
            <PARAM NAME="VariousPropertyBits" VALUE="19">
```

continues

Listing 16.1. continued

```
    </OBJECT>
    <OBJECT ID="Mousey"
     CLSID="CLSID:D4A97620-8E8F-11CF-93CD-00AA00C08FDF"
➡STYLE="TOP:26pt;LEFT:221pt;WIDTH:23pt;HEIGHT:26pt;ZINDEX:6;">
        <PARAM NAME="PicturePath" VALUE="mouse.gif">
        <PARAM NAME="AutoSize" VALUE="-1">
        <PARAM NAME="BorderStyle" VALUE="0">
        <PARAM NAME="SizeMode" VALUE="3">
        <PARAM NAME="Size" VALUE="794;926">
        <PARAM NAME="PictureAlignment" VALUE="0">
        <PARAM NAME="VariousPropertyBits" VALUE="19">
    </OBJECT>
    <OBJECT ID="shapes2"
     CLSID="CLSID:D4A97620-8E8F-11CF-93CD-00AA00C08FDF"
➡STYLE="TOP:169pt;LEFT:105pt;WIDTH:30pt;HEIGHT:29pt;ZINDEX:7;">
        <PARAM NAME="PicturePath" VALUE="bluecircle.gif">
        <PARAM NAME="AutoSize" VALUE="-1">
        <PARAM NAME="BorderStyle" VALUE="0">
        <PARAM NAME="SizeMode" VALUE="3">
        <PARAM NAME="Size" VALUE="1058;1032">
        <PARAM NAME="PictureAlignment" VALUE="0">
        <PARAM NAME="VariousPropertyBits" VALUE="19">
    </OBJECT>
    <OBJECT ID="shapes4"
     CLSID="CLSID:D4A97620-8E8F-11CF-93CD-00AA00C08FDF"
➡STYLE="TOP:98pt;LEFT:161pt;WIDTH:30pt;HEIGHT:28pt;ZINDEX:8;">
        <PARAM NAME="PicturePath" VALUE="redsquare.gif">
        <PARAM NAME="AutoSize" VALUE="-1">
        <PARAM NAME="BorderStyle" VALUE="0">
        <PARAM NAME="SizeMode" VALUE="3">
        <PARAM NAME="Size" VALUE="1058;979">
        <PARAM NAME="PictureAlignment" VALUE="0">
        <PARAM NAME="VariousPropertyBits" VALUE="19">
    </OBJECT>
    <OBJECT ID="shapes0"
     CLSID="CLSID:D4A97620-8E8F-11CF-93CD-00AA00C08FDF"
➡STYLE="TOP:56pt;LEFT:278pt;WIDTH:41pt;HEIGHT:30pt;ZINDEX:9;">
        <PARAM NAME="PicturePath" VALUE="yellowtriangle.gif">
        <PARAM NAME="AutoSize" VALUE="-1">
        <PARAM NAME="BorderStyle" VALUE="0">
        <PARAM NAME="SizeMode" VALUE="3">
        <PARAM NAME="Size" VALUE="1455;1058">
        <PARAM NAME="PictureAlignment" VALUE="0">
        <PARAM NAME="VariousPropertyBits" VALUE="19">
    </OBJECT>
    <OBJECT ID="shapes1"
     CLSID="CLSID:D4A97620-8E8F-11CF-93CD-00AA00C08FDF"
➡STYLE="TOP:38pt;LEFT:23pt;WIDTH:30pt;HEIGHT:29pt;ZINDEX:10;">
        <PARAM NAME="PicturePath" VALUE="orangesquare.gif">
        <PARAM NAME="AutoSize" VALUE="-1">
        <PARAM NAME="BorderStyle" VALUE="0">
        <PARAM NAME="SizeMode" VALUE="3">
        <PARAM NAME="Size" VALUE="1058;1005">
        <PARAM NAME="PictureAlignment" VALUE="0">
        <PARAM NAME="VariousPropertyBits" VALUE="19">
    </OBJECT>
    <OBJECT ID="shapes3"
     CLSID="CLSID:D4A97620-8E8F-11CF-93CD-00AA00C08FDF"
```

Example 1   291

```
➡STYLE="TOP:53pt;LEFT:98pt;WIDTH:30pt;HEIGHT:29pt;ZINDEX:11;">
        <PARAM NAME="PicturePath" VALUE="bluesquare.gif">
        <PARAM NAME="AutoSize" VALUE="-1">
        <PARAM NAME="BorderStyle" VALUE="0">
        <PARAM NAME="SizeMode" VALUE="3">
        <PARAM NAME="Size" VALUE="1058;1005">
        <PARAM NAME="PictureAlignment" VALUE="0">
        <PARAM NAME="VariousPropertyBits" VALUE="19">
    </OBJECT>
    <OBJECT ID="shapes5"
      CLASSID="CLSID:D4A97620-8E8F-11CF-93CD-00AA00C08FDF"
➡STYLE="TOP:113pt;LEFT:90pt;WIDTH:30pt;HEIGHT:29pt;ZINDEX:12;">
        <PARAM NAME="PicturePath" VALUE="redcircle.gif">
        <PARAM NAME="AutoSize" VALUE="-1">
        <PARAM NAME="BorderStyle" VALUE="0">
        <PARAM NAME="SizeMode" VALUE="3">
        <PARAM NAME="Size" VALUE="1058;1032">
        <PARAM NAME="PictureAlignment" VALUE="0">
        <PARAM NAME="VariousPropertyBits" VALUE="19">
    </OBJECT>
    <OBJECT ID="shapes6"
      CLASSID="CLSID:D4A97620-8E8F-11CF-93CD-00AA00C08FDF"
➡STYLE="TOP:98pt;LEFT:229pt;WIDTH:41pt;HEIGHT:30pt;ZINDEX:13;">
        <PARAM NAME="PicturePath" VALUE="redtriangle.gif">
        <PARAM NAME="AutoSize" VALUE="-1">
        <PARAM NAME="BorderStyle" VALUE="0">
        <PARAM NAME="SizeMode" VALUE="3">
        <PARAM NAME="Size" VALUE="1455;1058">
        <PARAM NAME="PictureAlignment" VALUE="0">
        <PARAM NAME="VariousPropertyBits" VALUE="19">
    </OBJECT>
    <OBJECT ID="shapes7"
      CLASSID="CLSID:D4A97620-8E8F-11CF-93CD-00AA00C08FDF"
➡STYLE="TOP:98pt;LEFT:19pt;WIDTH:30pt;HEIGHT:29pt;ZINDEX:14;">
        <PARAM NAME="PicturePath" VALUE="yellowcircle.gif">
        <PARAM NAME="AutoSize" VALUE="-1">
        <PARAM NAME="BorderStyle" VALUE="0">
        <PARAM NAME="SizeMode" VALUE="3">
        <PARAM NAME="Size" VALUE="1058;1032">
        <PARAM NAME="PictureAlignment" VALUE="0">
        <PARAM NAME="VariousPropertyBits" VALUE="19">
    </OBJECT>
    <OBJECT ID="shapes8"
      CLASSID="CLSID:D4A97620-8E8F-11CF-93CD-00AA00C08FDF"
➡STYLE="TOP:154pt;LEFT:285pt;WIDTH:30pt;HEIGHT:29pt;ZINDEX:15;">
        <PARAM NAME="PicturePath" VALUE="greensquare.gif">
        <PARAM NAME="AutoSize" VALUE="-1">
        <PARAM NAME="BorderStyle" VALUE="0">
        <PARAM NAME="SizeMode" VALUE="3">
        <PARAM NAME="Size" VALUE="1058;1005">
        <PARAM NAME="PictureAlignment" VALUE="0">
        <PARAM NAME="VariousPropertyBits" VALUE="19">
    </OBJECT>
    <OBJECT ID="shapes13"
      CLASSID="CLSID:D4A97620-8E8F-11CF-93CD-00AA00C08FDF"
➡STYLE="TOP:154pt;LEFT:26pt;WIDTH:41pt;HEIGHT:30pt;ZINDEX:16;">
        <PARAM NAME="PicturePath" VALUE="greentriangle.gif">
        <PARAM NAME="AutoSize" VALUE="-1">
        <PARAM NAME="BorderStyle" VALUE="0">
```

continues

Listing 16.1. continued

```
        <PARAM NAME="SizeMode" VALUE="3">
        <PARAM NAME="Size" VALUE="1455;1058">
        <PARAM NAME="PictureAlignment" VALUE="0">
        <PARAM NAME="VariousPropertyBits" VALUE="19">
    </OBJECT>
    <OBJECT ID="shapes11"
     CLASSID="CLSID:D4A97620-8E8F-11CF-93CD-00AA00C08FDF"
➡STYLE="TOP:101pt;LEFT:323;WIDTH:41pt;HEIGHT:30pt;ZINDEX:17;">
        <PARAM NAME="PicturePath" VALUE="bluetriangle.gif">
        <PARAM NAME="AutoSize" VALUE="-1">
        <PARAM NAME="BorderStyle" VALUE="0">
        <PARAM NAME="SizeMode" VALUE="3">
        <PARAM NAME="Size" VALUE="1455;1058">
        <PARAM NAME="PictureAlignment" VALUE="0">
        <PARAM NAME="VariousPropertyBits" VALUE="19">
    </OBJECT>
    <OBJECT ID="shapes12"
     CLASSID="CLSID:D4A97620-8E8F-11CF-93CD-00AA00C08FDF"
➡STYLE="TOP:150pt;LEFT:165pt;WIDTH:30pt;HEIGHT:29pt;ZINDEX:18;">
        <PARAM NAME="PicturePath" VALUE="greencircle.gif">
        <PARAM NAME="AutoSize" VALUE="-1">
        <PARAM NAME="BorderStyle" VALUE="0">
        <PARAM NAME="SizeMode" VALUE="3">
        <PARAM NAME="Size" VALUE="1058;1032">
        <PARAM NAME="PictureAlignment" VALUE="0">
        <PARAM NAME="VariousPropertyBits" VALUE="19">
    </OBJECT>
    <OBJECT ID="shapes14"
     CLASSID="CLSID:D4A97620-8E8F-11CF-93CD-00AA00C08FDF"
➡STYLE="TOP:165pt;LEFT:341pt;WIDTH:30pt;HEIGHT:29pt;ZINDEX:19;">
        <PARAM NAME="PicturePath" VALUE="yellowsquare.gif">
        <PARAM NAME="AutoSize" VALUE="-1">
        <PARAM NAME="BorderStyle" VALUE="0">
        <PARAM NAME="SizeMode" VALUE="3">
        <PARAM NAME="Size" VALUE="1058;1005">
        <PARAM NAME="PictureAlignment" VALUE="0">
        <PARAM NAME="VariousPropertyBits" VALUE="19">
    </OBJECT>
    <OBJECT ID="shapes9"
     CLASSID="CLSID:D4A97620-8E8F-11CF-93CD-00AA00C08FDF"
➡STYLE="TOP:49pt;LEFT:173pt;WIDTH:41pt;HEIGHT:30pt;ZINDEX:20;">
        <PARAM NAME="PicturePath" VALUE="orangetriangle.gif">
        <PARAM NAME="AutoSize" VALUE="-1">
        <PARAM NAME="BorderStyle" VALUE="0">
        <PARAM NAME="SizeMode" VALUE="3">
        <PARAM NAME="Size" VALUE="1455;1058">
        <PARAM NAME="PictureAlignment" VALUE="0">
        <PARAM NAME="VariousPropertyBits" VALUE="19">
    </OBJECT>
    <OBJECT ID="shapes10"
     CLASSID="CLSID:D4A97620-8E8F-11CF-93CD-00AA00C08FDF"
➡STYLE="TOP:165pt;LEFT:229pt;WIDTH:30pt;HEIGHT:29pt;ZINDEX:21;">
        <PARAM NAME="PicturePath" VALUE="orangecircle.gif">
        <PARAM NAME="AutoSize" VALUE="-1">
        <PARAM NAME="BorderStyle" VALUE="0">
        <PARAM NAME="SizeMode" VALUE="3">
        <PARAM NAME="Size" VALUE="1058;1032">
        <PARAM NAME="PictureAlignment" VALUE="0">
```

Example 2   293

```
              <PARAM NAME="VariousPropertyBits" VALUE="19">
        </OBJECT>
        <OBJECT ID="Image3"
         CLASSID="CLSID:D4A97620-8E8F-11CF-93CD-00AA00C08FDF"
➡STYLE="TOP:35pt;LEFT:358pt;WIDTH:31pt;HEIGHT:38pt;ZINDEX:22;">
            <PARAM NAME="PicturePath" VALUE="hole2.gif">
            <PARAM NAME="AutoSize" VALUE="-1">
            <PARAM NAME="BorderStyle" VALUE="0">
            <PARAM NAME="SizeMode" VALUE="3">
            <PARAM NAME="Size" VALUE="1085;1323">
            <PARAM NAME="PictureAlignment" VALUE="0">
            <PARAM NAME="VariousPropertyBits" VALUE="19">
        </OBJECT>
        <OBJECT ID="CommandButton1"
         CLASSID="CLSID:D7053240-CE69-11CD-A777-00DD01143C57"
➡STYLE="TOP:214pt;LEFT:338pt;WIDTH:68pt;HEIGHT:30pt;TABINDEX:2;ZINDEX:23;">
            <PARAM NAME="ForeColor" VALUE="65280">
            <PARAM NAME="BackColor" VALUE="16744576">
            <PARAM NAME="Caption" VALUE="START!!">
            <PARAM NAME="Size" VALUE="2399;1058">
            <PARAM NAME="FontEffects" VALUE="1073741825">
            <PARAM NAME="FontHeight" VALUE="240">
            <PARAM NAME="FontCharSet" VALUE="0">
            <PARAM NAME="FontPitchAndFamily" VALUE="2">
            <PARAM NAME="ParagraphAlign" VALUE="3">
            <PARAM NAME="FontWeight" VALUE="700">
        </OBJECT>
</DIV>
```

Example 2

Document title: Qwerty Manufacturing Inc.

Files:

Page files:

- ❏ index.htm
- ❏ tabmenu.htm
- ❏ welcome.htm
- ❏ whatsnew.htm
- ❏ products.htm
- ❏ ordering.htm
- ❏ contacts.htm

Layout file: `tabstrip.alx` (see Figures 16.5 through 16.8)

Images:

- ❏ pencil.gif
- ❏ qwerty.gif
- ❏ bg2.gif

ActiveX control: Tab Strip

NOTE: The Tab Strip control is part of the full installation of Microsoft Internet Explorer 3.x (MSIE 3.x) final version. If you have a beta version of MSIE 3.0 or you did not carry out a full installation, you can also find the control on the CD-ROM in the \SOURCE\CHAPTER16 directory.

Description: The Qwerty Manufacturing example shows the implementation of an ActiveX Tab Strip control as a navigation aid. The tab strip takes the place of hyperlinked or button-controlled menus, allowing the user to quickly and easily navigate between pages. The HTML Layout control containing the tab strip is held in the top frame of a frameset.

Techniques Applied

ActiveX controls: (See Chapters 1, 12, 13, and 14.)

HTML Layout control: (See Chapter 14.)

Use of frames: The Tab Strip control in the top frame changes the HTML page in the bottom frame.

The index page loads as shown in Figure 16.5. As it loads, two frames are created: an upper frame containing the `tabstrip.alx` file and a lower frame containing the first page (`welcome.htm`).

Figure 16.5.
The welcome page.

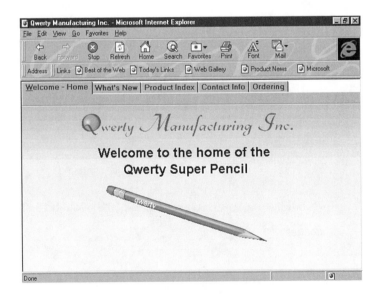

Example 2   295

This example demonstrates the creativity you can use when designing user interfaces with the Layout control. Again, you are making use of controls and functionality that were once the reserve of Windows programmers. As you can see from this example, by simply clicking the tab strip headers, you can navigate around the Web site (shown in Figure 16.6) as if it is a Windows dialog.

Figure 16.6.
Clicking the tab strip loads the next page.

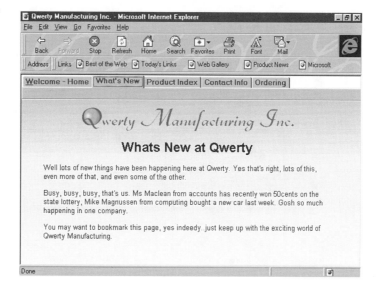

You can make your Web site stand out from the crowd by using the latest ActiveX controls as navigation tools (shown in Figure 16.7), rather than using straightforward hyperlinks.

Figure 16.7.
Another page of the Web site.

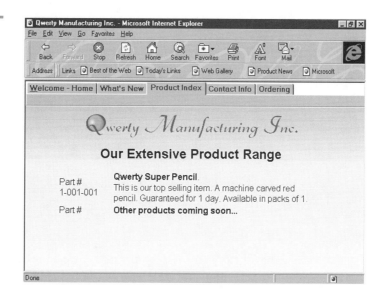

Only two tabs are defined at design time, as shown in Figure 16.8. The rest are added programmatically as the page loads.

Figure 16.8.
The Properties window for tabstrip.alx.

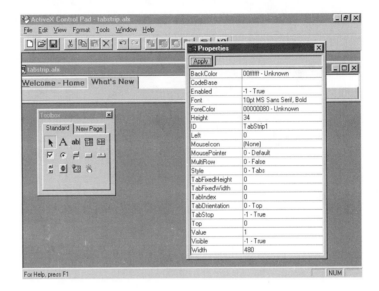

Listing 16.2 shows the complete source code for tabstrip.alx. As the page loads, the OnLoad event handler is executed. This creates three new tabs in positions 2, 3, and 4. When the user clicks a tab, the tab strip's Click event is fired. A straightforward Select Case block is used to execute code that loads a given page based on the tab that was clicked.

Listing 16.2. The tabstrip.alx code.

```
<SCRIPT LANGUAGE="VBScript">
<!--
Sub TabStrip1_Click(Index)
 Select Case Index
 Case 0
  Top.bodyframe.Location.Href = "welcome.htm"
 Case 1
  Top.bodyframe.Location.Href = "whatsnew.htm"
 Case 2
  Top.bodyframe.Location.Href = "products.htm"
 Case 3
  Top.bodyframe.Location.Href = "contacts.htm"
 Case 4
  Top.bodyframe.Location.Href = "ordering.htm"
 End Select

end sub
-->
</SCRIPT>
<SCRIPT LANGUAGE="VBScript">
```

Example 2   297

```
<!--
Sub Layout1_OnLoad()
call TabStrip1.Tabs.Add(thirdTab, "Product Index", 2)
call TabStrip1.Tabs.Add(fourthTab, "Contact Info", 3)
call TabStrip1.Tabs.Add(fifthTab, "Ordering", 4)

end sub
-->
</SCRIPT>
<DIV BACKGROUND="#ffffff" ID="Layout1" STYLE="LAYOUT:FIXED;WIDTH:480pt;
➥HEIGHT:33pt;">
    <OBJECT ID="TabStrip1"
     CLASSID="CLSID:EAE50EB0-4A62-11CE-BED6-00AA00611080"
➥STYLE="TOP:0pt;LEFT:0pt;WIDTH:480pt;HEIGHT:34pt;TABINDEX:0;ZINDEX:0;">
        <PARAM NAME="ListIndex" VALUE="0">
        <PARAM NAME="BackColor" VALUE="16777215">
        <PARAM NAME="ForeColor" VALUE="128">
        <PARAM NAME="Size" VALUE="16933;1199">
        <PARAM NAME="Items" VALUE="Welcome - Home;What's New;">
        <PARAM NAME="TipStrings" VALUE="Our Home Page;News from Qwerty;">
        <PARAM NAME="Names" VALUE="Tab1;Tab2;">
        <PARAM NAME="NewVersion" VALUE="-1">
        <PARAM NAME="TabsAllocated" VALUE="2">
        <PARAM NAME="Tags" VALUE=";;">
        <PARAM NAME="TabData" VALUE="2">
        <PARAM NAME="Accelerator" VALUE="W;P;">
        <PARAM NAME="FontEffects" VALUE="1073741825">
        <PARAM NAME="FontHeight" VALUE="200">
        <PARAM NAME="FontCharSet" VALUE="0">
        <PARAM NAME="FontPitchAndFamily" VALUE="2">
        <PARAM NAME="FontWeight" VALUE="700">
        <PARAM NAME="TabState" VALUE="3;3">
    </OBJECT>
</DIV>
```

PART

IV

Developing Dynamic Web Applications with VBScript

SEVENTEEN

Using Client-Side Image Maps—the Easy Way

Image maps are popular, despite the bandwidth they waste and the time they take to load. Users like using them and Web page designers like designing them—perhaps because image maps are one of the few elements of a Web page that truly distinguish the Web from other media.

Why use client-side image maps? Using client-side image maps means you don't have to create a server-side script and program in CGI. All the processing work is done at the browser; to the server, a page with client-side image maps is just another HTML page. Server-side image maps can operate only by sending a special message to the server that is then interpreted by the image map script file. Only then is the correct page dispatched from the server. As a result, tasks such as displaying varying text when a mouse passes over each area of a map are not possible without client-side scripting.

The client-side image map example I use in this chapter would not usually see the light of day on my computer, because the graphic I use is 27KB—huge in comparison to my usual mean, sub-10KB images. Regardless, client-side image maps are fun to work with, and the one I use in this chapter is also an example of two-dimensional HTML using the HTML layout control. The text box that displays a message as the mouse passes over the image actually sits on top of the image itself. More astute designers can take this concept further and make the message appear to be part of the image.

TASK | Creating a Clickable Image

The following example uses an HTML layout to hold the image and handle the mouse events that give the image map its functionality:

1. First, open the ActiveX Control Pad and select New HTML Layout from the File menu.

2. When the new layout appears, resize it to almost fill the client area of the layout control.

3. You use an ISImage control to hold the image, so click the ISImage icon on the tool box and then click anywhere on the canvas of the layout to add the image control.

4. To add the actual graphic image to the control, you simply set the PicturePath property, as shown in Figure 17.1. You can find the graphic for this example, truck.gif, on the CD-ROM.

NOTE: When you develop layouts that include graphics such as truck.gif, you need to specify an absolute path for the graphic. However when you are ready to put the page, the .ALX HTML layout file, and the graphic online, you can edit the PicturePath property from the source of the .ALX file to make it a relative path on the server.

Figure 17.1.

The `.GIF` *placed in the image control via the* `PicturePath` *property.*

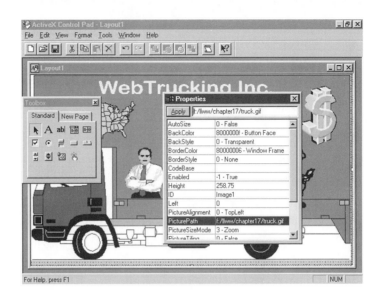

5. Now you can add the text box control that displays a short description of the linked file to the user. Using the Properties window, which you access from the Control Menu (by right-clicking the control), set the following properties (see Figure 17.2):

MultiLine	True
Font	12 pt. Bold
ForeColor	A shade of orange

6. Save the layout as `truck.alx`.

Figure 17.2.

Setting the properties for the layout.

The next stage is to work out which parts of the image are clickable and act as hyperlinks to other pages in the Web site.

Determining Areas Within an Image Map

When dealing with image maps in VBScript, you use rectangles to determine the clickable areas. You specify the virtual rectangles with two coordinates, representing the top, left corner and bottom, right corner.

The two coordinates are known as x1,y1 and x2,y2. X is the horizontal axis, and Y is the vertical axis; both axes have their origins in the top, left corner of the screen.

Therefore, you need to specify four values for each clickable area: x1, y1, x2, and y2. x1 is the number of pixels from the left side of the layout to the left edge of the clickable area. x2 is the number of pixels from the left side of the layout to the right edge of the clickable area. y1 is the number of pixels from the top edge of the layout to the top edge of the clickable area. And finally, y2 is the number of pixels from the top edge of the layout to the bottom edge of the clickable area.

To be sure that I specified values that are understood by the layout control, I found it easiest to use the layout control itself to view the values of x and y. You can do this by adding a very simple line of code to the MouseMove event of the image as follows:

1. With truck.alx open in the layout control, launch the Script Wizard.
2. Select Image1's MouseMove event.
3. Enter the following line of code in the event handler (see Figure 17.3):

   ```
   rem TextBox1.Text = "X=" & X & " Y=" & Y
   ```

   This displays the values of both x and y as you move the mouse pointer around the screen.
4. Save the layout.
5. Open a new HTML document in the ActiveX Control Pad.
6. Amend the <BODY> tag so that the background color is white.
7. Add <CENTER> tags to the page.
8. With the cursor between the open and close <CENTER> tags, select Add HTML Layout from the Edit menu.
9. Choose truck.alx from the file dialog and click OK. The object definition for the layout control is automatically placed in your HTML document, as shown in Figure 17.4.

Figure 17.3.

The temporary event handler to display the X and Y mouse values.

Figure 17.4.

The new HTML document complete with layout object definition.

10. Save the file as truck.htm, and run it with the browser. It should look like what you see in Figure 17.5.

Figure 17.5.

Determining the clickable areas on the image.

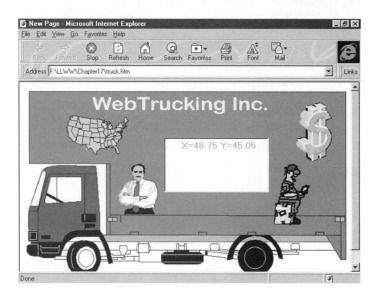

11. With the cursor at the top of a clickable area, make a note of the Y value; this is Y1.

12. With the cursor at the bottom of a clickable area, make a note of the Y value; this is Y2.

13. With the cursor at the left of a clickable area, make a note of the x value; this is x1.

14. With the cursor at the right of a clickable area, make a note of the x value; this is x2.

You then create a table of values like the one shown in Table 17.1, which is your map.

Table 17.1. The X and Y coordinate values.

	X1	Y1	X2	Y2
Area 1	50	29	154	92
Area 2	124	92	190	168
Area 3	375	10	434	96
Area 4	344	97	403	184

You are now ready to add the code that turns your image into an image map.

Adding MouseMove and MouseDown Code to the Image Map

The main functionality of any image map is the capability to click an area of the graphic and have that mouse click translated into an instruction to navigate to a different URL. However, the ActiveX Image control does not include a click event. It does have a MouseDown event, and in reality, a click event is the joining together of two other events—MouseDown and MouseUp. The MouseDown event is fired when the mouse button is pressed, which works just as well as a click for your purposes.

One thing that server-side image maps cannot do is track the mouse as it passes over the image. For this, you need a MouseMove event, which you will program to display relevant messages about the area of the image that the mouse is currently over.

1. If it's not already there, load truck.alx into the layout control.

2. Launch the Script Wizard.

3. Go to the Image1 MouseMove event that you created earlier.

4. Add the word rem to the start of the line you entered earlier. This means "remark" and instructs the VBScript compiler to ignore the line as executable code. You can obviously delete it if you want, but you might want to make further amendments later on.

5. Add the following code to the event handler:
```
If (InArea(x, y,  50, 29, 154, 92)=true) Then
    TextBox1.Text = "Our routes, pick-ups, and drop-offs"
ElseIf (InArea(x, y, 124, 92, 190, 168)=true) Then
    TextBox1.Text = "Meet the management team"
ElseIf (InArea(x, y,  375, 10, 434, 96)=true) Then
    TextBox1.Text = "Our Rates.. the best in the business"
ElseIf (InArea(x, y,  344, 97, 403, 184)=true) Then
    TextBox1.Text = "Job vacancies with Web Trucking"
Else
    TextBox1.Text = "Welcome to the Web Trucking Web Site"
End If
```

What's this little lot doing? Notice that each pair of lines is basically the same; only the numbers and the explicit text are changing.

You are going to call a custom function, InArea, which you create shortly. InArea takes the actual values of x and y that were passed from the MouseMove event. x and y pinpoint the whereabouts of the mouse cursor. InArea is also passed the four coordinates that describe the clickable area. If InArea finds that x and y are within the clickable area, the Text property of TextBox1 is changed to a particular description.

Figure 17.6 shows what your finished MouseMove event handler should look like.

Figure 17.6.

The MouseMove event handler.

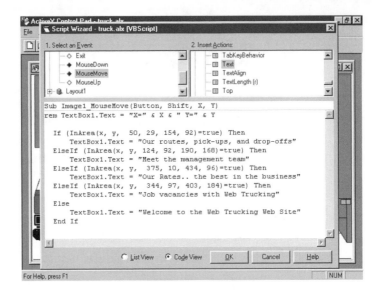

6. Now select the MouseDown event for Image1. Note that an image does not have an explicit OnClick or click event, which is no problem in this case because MouseDown passes the X and Y coordinates that you need to determine whether the mouse is within a clickable area. As the name suggests, MouseDown fires when the mouse button is pressed.

   Add the following code to the MouseDown event handler:

```
If (InArea(x, y,  50, 29, 154, 92)=true) Then
    Window.location.href = "truck2.html"
ElseIf (InArea(x, y, 124, 92, 190, 168)=true) Then
    Window.location.href = "truck3.html"
ElseIf (InArea(x, y,  375, 10, 434, 96)=true) Then
    Window.location.href = "truck1.html"
ElseIf (InArea(x, y,  344, 97, 403, 184)=true) Then
    Window.location.href = "truck4.html"
End If
```

   Notice that the conditional statements are identical to those of the MouseMove event handler. This time, if the mouse is found to be within a clickable area, you change the href property of the Location object, thereby launching a new page, replicating the functionality of a hyperlink. Your MouseDown event handler should now resemble the one in Figure 17.7.

Figure 17.7.

The completed MouseDown *event handler.*

7. Now you need to create the custom function that determines whether the mouse cursor is within a clickable area. With your mouse in the right Actions pane, right-click and select New Procedure from the pop-up menu.

8. Change the word Sub to Function and replace the default name of Procedure1 with InArea.

9. After the word InArea, add the following argument list, which is the list of variables that you want passed into the function:

```
(x, y, ax1, ay1, ax2, ay2)
```

10. In the script window, enter the code for the custom function (shown in Figure 17.8), which is a straightforward one liner:

```
InArea =  x>=ax1 AND x<=ax2 AND y>=ay1 AND y<=ay2
```

11. Click OK, and the Script Wizard generates the required code in the truck.alx source file.

12. Save the layout and try it with the browser.

13. Run truck.htm with the browser. Remember that no amendments are necessary to the HTML file because all the functionality of the page is held within the .ALX file.

Let's look at the image map in action within the browser. Figure 17.9 shows that, as the mouse is moved around the image, the MouseMove event is fired, causing text to be displayed in the text box.

Figure 17.8.
The InArea custom function.

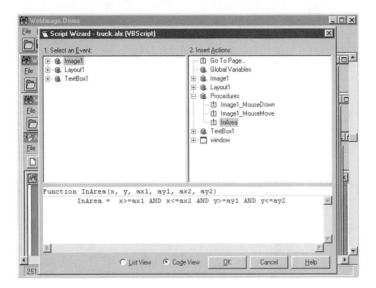

Figure 17.9.
As you pass the cursor over an area, the text changes.

As you move the cursor to another area of the image map, the text in the text box changes, as shown in Figure 17.10.

Figure 17.10.

Move to another area of the image map, and the text changes.

Clicking on an area of the image map causes another page of the Web site to be loaded, as shown in Figure 17.11.

Figure 17.11.

What happens when you click an area? You access other pages in the Web site.

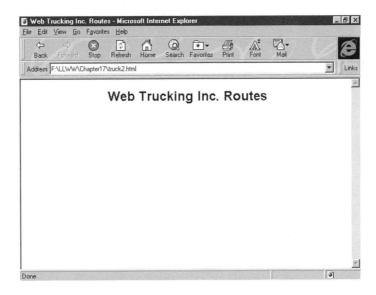

Listing 17.1 contains the complete source code for the image map example, `truck.alx`.

Listing 17.1. The `truck.alx` code.

```
<SCRIPT LANGUAGE="VBScript">
<!--
Sub Image1_MouseMove(Button, Shift, X, Y)
rem TextBox1.Text = "X=" & X & " Y=" & Y

  If (InArea(x, y,  50, 29, 154, 92)=true) Then
     TextBox1.Text = "Our routes, pick-ups, and drop-offs"
  ElseIf (InArea(x, y, 124, 92, 190, 168)=true) Then
     TextBox1.Text = "Meet the management team"
  ElseIf (InArea(x, y,  375, 10, 434, 96)=true) Then
     TextBox1.Text = "Our Rates.. the best in the business"
  ElseIf (InArea(x, y,  344, 97, 403, 184)=true) Then
     TextBox1.Text = "Job vacancies with Web Trucking"
  Else
     TextBox1.Text = "Welcome to the Web Trucking Web Site"
  End If
end sub
Sub Image1_MouseDown(Button, Shift, X, Y)
  If (InArea(x, y,  50, 29, 154, 92)=true) Then
     Window.location.href = "truck2.html"
  ElseIf (InArea(x, y, 124, 92, 190, 168)=true) Then
     Window.location.href = "truck3.html"
  ElseIf (InArea(x, y,  375, 10, 434, 96)=true) Then
     Window.location.href = "truck1.html"
  ElseIf (InArea(x, y,  344, 97, 403, 184)=true) Then
     Window.location.href = "truck4.html"
  End If

end sub
Function InArea(x, y, ax1, ay1, ax2, ay2)
     InArea =  x>=ax1 AND x<=ax2 AND y>=ay1 AND y<=ay2
end function
-->
</SCRIPT>
<DIV ID="Layout1" STYLE="LAYOUT:FIXED;WIDTH:450pt;HEIGHT:254pt;">
    <OBJECT ID="Image1"
     CLASSID="CLSID:D4A97620-8E8F-11CF-93CD-00AA00C08FDF"
➥STYLE="TOP:0pt;LEFT:0pt;WIDTH:450pt;HEIGHT:253pt;ZINDEX:0;">
        <PARAM NAME="PicturePath" VALUE="f:\llww\chapter17\truck.gif">
        <PARAM NAME="BorderStyle" VALUE="0">
        <PARAM NAME="SizeMode" VALUE="3">
        <PARAM NAME="Size" VALUE="15875;8925">
        <PARAM NAME="PictureAlignment" VALUE="0">
        <PARAM NAME="VariousPropertyBits" VALUE="19">
    </OBJECT>
    <OBJECT ID="TextBox1"
     CLASSID="CLSID:8BD21D10-EC42-11CE-9E0D-00AA006002F3"
➥ STYLE="TOP:64pt;LEFT:195pt;WIDTH:146pt;HEIGHT:74pt;TABINDEX:0;ZINDEX:1;">
        <PARAM NAME="VariousPropertyBits" VALUE="2894088219">
        <PARAM NAME="ForeColor" VALUE="4227327">
        <PARAM NAME="Size" VALUE="5151;2611">
        <PARAM NAME="Value" VALUE="Welcome to the Web Trucking Inc. Web Site">
        <PARAM NAME="FontEffects" VALUE="1073741825">
        <PARAM NAME="FontHeight" VALUE="240">
```

```
            <PARAM NAME="FontCharSet" VALUE="0">
            <PARAM NAME="FontPitchAndFamily" VALUE="2">
            <PARAM NAME="ParagraphAlign" VALUE="3">
            <PARAM NAME="FontWeight" VALUE="700">
        </OBJECT>
    </DIV>
```

Workshop Wrap-Up

Creating image maps with VBScript and the HTML layout control is very straightforward and enables you to use techniques that are not available elsewhere. The key is to accurately specify the boundaries of each clickable area, ensuring that they do not overlap.

Next Steps

Now look at these other chapters about the HTML layout control and interacting with the browser itself:

❏ To learn more about the HTML layout control, see Chapter 14, "Using the HTML Layout Control."

❏ To see another graphic example of VBScript and the layout control, consult Chapter 16, "Real-Life Examples II."

❏ Chapter 18, "Interacting with the Browser," shows how you can use VBScript in other ways to interact with the browser.

Q&A

Q: Can any graphic be used as an image map?

A: Yes. The format and type of graphic are unimportant. If you can display it through the image control, you can use it as an image map.

Q: I tried using my exisiting coordinate table with my image map in VBScript with the layout control as described in this chapter, and it didn't work properly. Why is that?

A: The measurement system of the layout control is different from the normal HTML page that your current coordinates relate to. Therefore, you must re-measure your X and Y coordinates.

EIGHTEEN

Interacting with the Browser

A major part of creating interactive Web pages involves interacting directly with the browser. MSIE 3.0 makes this task very easy, exposing many of the browser's own objects, properties, events, and methods, which you can include within your scripts. The MSIE 3.0 browser itself can be thought of as a combination of several main objects (window, document, location, navigator, and history), as well as several objects that can be present in the current window and document (frame, form, script, and link). Each of these objects can be controlled from VBScript. The extent and depth of that control depends upon the object.

In this chapter you will see VBScript used to control some of the browser's objects via their methods and properties. For a complete summary of the objects, properties, events, and methods that form the MSIE Object Model, see Appendix D, "Active Scripting Object Model."

In this chapter, you

- ❏ Learn how to programmatically open a new window to your specifications
- ❏ Learn how to set the browser's built-in timer
- ❏ Learn how to use VBScript to navigate within a Frame document
- ❏ Learn how to call a VBScript procedure in another document
- ❏ Learn how to create a new document on the fly

Tasks in this chapter:

- ❏ Opening a new browser window via VBScript
- ❏ Setting a TimeOut
- ❏ Navigating within frames
- ❏ Calling a script in another frame
- ❏ Creating a Web page with VBScript

Opening a New Browser Window via VBScript

The Window object that is at the top of the browser's hierarchical tree exposes a method called Open, which enables you to create a new window to your own specifications via a series of options that come directly from a script.

The syntax for Window.Open is as follows:

```
Window.Open URL, Target, OptionList
```

URL is the unique resource locator for the document that you want to load into the new window on opening.

Target is the name that you want to give to the new window, which enables you to reference the window from hyperlinks in another document through the Target HTML element.

OptionList is a single complete string made up of a series of comma-delimited option/value pairs, which are listed here:

- ❏ toolbar=*boolean*
- ❏ location=*boolean*
- ❏ directories=*boolean*
- ❏ status=*boolean*
- ❏ menubar=*boolean*
- ❏ scrollbars=*boolean*
- ❏ resizable=*boolean*
- ❏ width=*pixels*
- ❏ height=*pixels*

Not all of the options in the preceding list have to appear in the option list. You pass an option list as a comma-delimited series of options, as in the following example:

```
"toolbar=no, location=no, status=no, width=300, height=200"
```

NOTE: Unlike the boolean data subtype within VBScript, the boolean data type used for the window object evaluates to 1 = yes and 0 = no. Remember that to set a window property to true, you use the literal yes.

NOTE: The complete option list for a new browser window, which is specified in the Active Scripting Object Model, has not been fully implemented in MSIE 3.0. This means that several of the options in the preceding list are ignored and remain true, regardless of whether you specify yes or no. Later releases of MSIE might extend the functionality of Window.Open. You can use the following sample script to determine which options can and cannot be set using the Window.Open method.

Here is a complete example that allows you to experiment with the Window.Open method. You can specify, directly from the Web page, the size of the window, the document to be loaded, and also the elements that will be present in the new window.

1. First, create a simple HTML template like this:

```
<HEAD>
<TITLE>Open a New Window</TITLE>
 <SCRIPT LANGUAGE="vbscript">
 <!--


 -->
 </SCRIPT>
</HEAD>
<BODY BGCOLOR="white">
<FORM NAME="form1">

</FORM>
</BODY>
</HTML>
```

2. Between the <FORM> tags, add the form elements that you will use to specify the look of your new window.

```
New Window Width<INPUT TYPE="text" NAME="WinWidth"><BR>
New Window Height<INPUT TYPE="text" NAME="WinHeight"><BR>
ToolBar <INPUT TYPE="checkbox" NAME="tools"><BR>
Location <INPUT TYPE="checkbox" NAME="loc"><BR>
MenuBar <INPUT TYPE="checkbox" NAME="menu"><BR>
ScrollBars <INPUT TYPE="checkbox" NAME="scrolls"><BR>
ReSizable <INPUT TYPE="checkbox" NAME="resize"><BR>
Directories <INPUT TYPE="checkbox" NAME="dirs"><BR>
Status<INPUT TYPE="checkbox" NAME="stat"><BR>
URL <INPUT TYPE="text" NAME="url"><BR>
New Window Name <INPUT TYPE="text" NAME="WinName"><BR>
<INPUT TYPE="button" NAME="cmdButton1" VALUE="Open Now">
```

3. Save the file as newwin.htm, and run it through the browser just to ensure that everything is correct with the HTML side of things before you progress on the scripting. The file should look like the one in Figure 18.1.

Figure 18.1.

Testing that the HTML part of `newwin.htm` *is bug-free.*

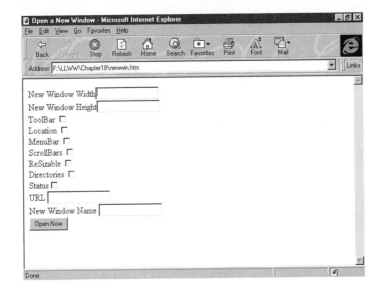

Now for the script. Unfortunately, you cannot directly relate the checkbox's checked property, which is either `True` if checked or `False` if unchecked, to the browser window's option list properties because the browser window's options only understand `yes` and `no`. Even using the numeric equivalent doesn't work: `True = -1` but `yes = 1`. Therefore, each element of the option list must have a conditional statement block written for it, which is somewhat tedious. But when you get your copy (Ctrl+C) and paste (Ctrl+V) fingers working, it doesn't take too long.

1. The first thing to do is create the prototype for the event handler and also declare a variable to hold the option list string.

   ```
   Sub cmdButton1_OnClick
     Dim strNewWin
   ```

2. The first option list element is the toolbar, as you see in the following code. You simply find out whether the checkbox is checked and, if so, concatenate `yes` to the string; otherwise, you concatenate `no`. Don't forget the very important comma after each element.

   ```
   strNewWin = "toolbar="
   If Document.form1.tools.Checked Then
     strNewWin = strNewWin & "yes" & ", "
   Else
     strNewWin = strNewWin & "no" & ", "
   End If
   ```

3. The rest of the elements are very similar:

   ```
   strNewWin = strNewWin & "location="
   If Document.form1.loc.Checked Then
     strNewWin = strNewWin & "yes" & ", "
   Else
     strNewWin = strNewWin & "no" & ", "
   End If
   ```

```
strNewWin = strNewWin & "directories="
If Document.form1.dirs.Checked Then
 strNewWin = strNewWin & "yes" & ", "
Else
 strNewWin = strNewWin & "no" & ", "
End If

strNewWin = strNewWin & "status="
If Document.form1.stat.Checked Then
 strNewWin = strNewWin & "yes" & ", "
Else
 strNewWin = strNewWin & "no" & ", "
End If

strNewWin = strNewWin & "menubar="
If Document.form1.menu.Checked Then
 strNewWin = strNewWin & "yes" & ", "
Else
 strNewWin = strNewWin & "no" & ", "
End If

strNewWin = strNewWin & "scrollbars="
If Document.form1.scrolls.Checked Then
 strNewWin = strNewWin & "yes" & ", "
Else
 strNewWin = strNewWin & "no" & ", "
End If

strNewWin = strNewWin & "resizeable="
If Document.form1.resize.Checked Then
 strNewWin = strNewWin & "yes" & ", "
Else
 strNewWin = strNewWin & "no" & ", "
End If
```

4. The `width` and `height` elements take their values directly from the form.

```
strNewWin = strNewWin & "width="
strNewWin = strNewWin & CStr(Document.form1.WinWidth.Value) & ", "
strNewWin = strNewWin & "height="
strNewWin = strNewWin & CStr(Document.form1.WinHeight.Value)
```

5. Just so you can see what is happening with the option list, add an `Alert` displaying `strNewWin`.

```
Alert strNewWin
```

6. Finally, you add the code to create the new window to your personal specifications. Don't forget to close the procedure with an `End Sub`.

```
Window.Open Document.form1.URL.Value, Document.form1.WinName.Value,
➥strNewWin


End Sub
```

Listing 18.1 shows the complete code for the example.

Listing 18.1. The `newwin.htm` code.

```
<HTML>
<HEAD>
<TITLE>Open a New Window</TITLE>
 <SCRIPT LANGUAGE="vbscript">
 <!--
 Sub cmdButton1_OnClick
  Dim strNewWin

  strNewWin = "toolbar="
  If Document.form1.tools.Checked Then
   strNewWin = strNewWin & "yes" & ", "
  Else
   strNewWin = strNewWin & "no" & ", "
  End If


   strNewWin = strNewWin & "location="
   If Document.form1.loc.Checked Then
    strNewWin = strNewWin & "yes" & ", "
   Else
    strNewWin = strNewWin & "no" & ", "
   End If

   strNewWin = strNewWin & "directories="
   If Document.form1.dirs.Checked Then
    strNewWin = strNewWin & "yes" & ", "
   Else
    strNewWin = strNewWin & "no" & ", "
   End If

   strNewWin = strNewWin & "status="
   If Document.form1.stat.Checked Then
    strNewWin = strNewWin & "yes" & ", "
   Else
    strNewWin = strNewWin & "no" & ", "
   End If

   strNewWin = strNewWin & "menubar="
   If Document.form1.menu.Checked Then
    strNewWin = strNewWin & "yes" & ", "
   Else
    strNewWin = strNewWin & "no" & ", "
   End If

   strNewWin = strNewWin & "scrollbars="
   If Document.form1.scrolls.Checked Then
    strNewWin = strNewWin & "yes" & ", "
   Else
    strNewWin = strNewWin & "no" & ", "
   End If

   strNewWin = strNewWin & "resizeable="
   If Document.form1.resize.Checked Then
    strNewWin = strNewWin & "yes" & ", "
   Else
    strNewWin = strNewWin & "no" & ", "
   End If
 strNewWin = strNewWin & "width="
   strNewWin = strNewWin & CStr(Document.form1.WinWidth.Value) & ", "
```

```
        strNewWin = strNewWin & "height="
        strNewWin = strNewWin & CStr(Document.form1.WinHeight.Value)

        Alert strNewWin


        Window.Open Document.form1.URL.Value, Document.form1.WinName.Value,
        ➥strNewWin


    End Sub
    -->
    </SCRIPT>
    </HEAD>
    <BODY BGCOLOR="white">
    <FORM NAME="form1">
    New Window Width<INPUT TYPE="text" NAME="WinWidth"><BR>
    New Window Height<INPUT TYPE="text" NAME="WinHeight"><BR>
    ToolBar <INPUT TYPE="checkbox" NAME="tools"><BR>
    Location <INPUT TYPE="checkbox" NAME="loc"><BR>
    MenuBar <INPUT TYPE="checkbox" NAME="menu"><BR>
    ScrollBars <INPUT TYPE="checkbox" NAME="scrolls"><BR>
    ReSizable <INPUT TYPE="checkbox" NAME="resize"><BR>
    Directories <INPUT TYPE="checkbox" NAME="dirs"><BR>
    Status<INPUT TYPE="checkbox" NAME="stat"><BR>
    URL <INPUT TYPE="text" NAME="url"><BR>
    New Window Name <INPUT TYPE="text" NAME="WinName"><BR>
    <INPUT TYPE="button" NAME="cmdButton1" VALUE="Open Now">
    </FORM>
    </BODY>
    </HTML>
```

Save the file and run it though the browser. Try different combinations of elements, as shown in Figure 18.2, remembering that the Window.Open method was not fully implemented in the first release of MSIE 3.0.

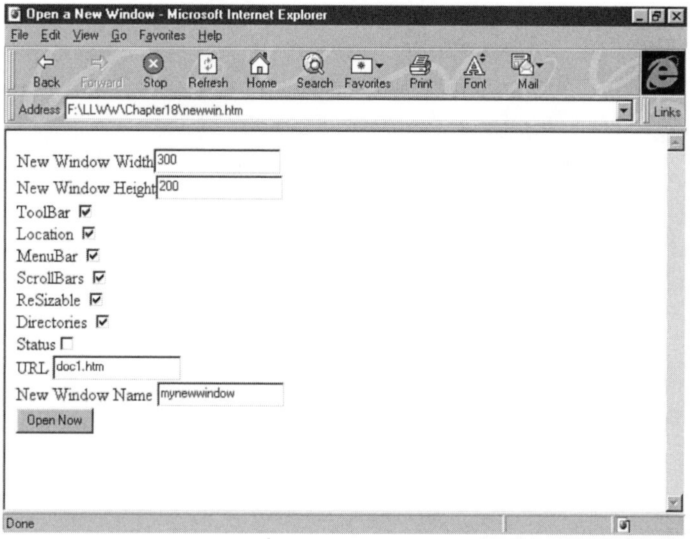

Figure 18.2.

Specifying the new window.

When you click the Open Now button, an alert box shows you the complete option list with values that will be passed to the `Window.Open` method, as shown in Figure 18.3.

Figure 18.3.
So that's what the option list looks like!

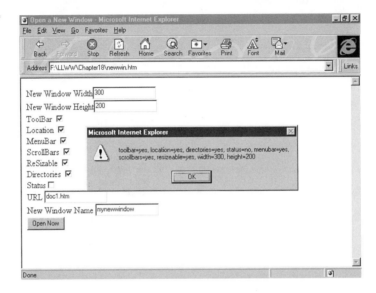

The new window opens and loads the HTML file specified by you in the URL text box, as shown in Figure 18.4.

Figure 18.4.
The tailor-made new window.

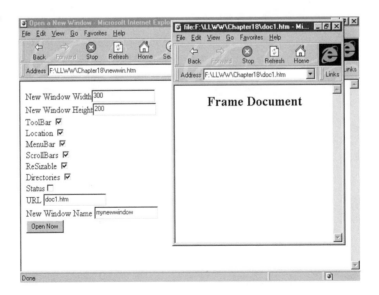

Setting a TimeOut

What's a TimeOut? The `setTimeout` method of the `window` object calls a built-in timer. You simply specify what you want to happen after a certain period of time. For example, you can set the timer to execute one of your scripted procedures, show a message, or clear the status bar. Here's the syntax:

```
Id = SetTimeout("actionstring",milliseconds)
```

`actionstring` is a self-contained string containing a method, procedure, or function. Here is an example:

```
"Status='Hello World'"
```

Notice that if you want to use quotes within the quotes of the action string, you must use single quotes, or build the string using `chr(34)` in place of the double quotes, like this:

```
"Status=" & Chr(34) & "Hello World" Chr(34)
```

The `setTimeout` method returns the ID of the timer, which enables you to reference the timer. For example, you can cancel the timer prior to execution, like this:

```
clearTimeout ID
```

The `setTimeout` method, therefore, lets you create a script that appears to execute automatically. However, don't confuse the browser's built-in timer with the ActiveX Timer Control, which repeatedly executes an event handler at given intervals. The browser's timer executes only once. After it has executed, the ID is cleared, and the timer is reset.

Here's a short and simple example to demonstrate how to add the built-in timer to your script:

1. Start with your normal HTML template.

   ```
   <HTML>
   <HEAD>
   <TITLE>Timeout</TITLE>
    <SCRIPT LANGUAGE="vbscript">
    <!--

    -->
    </SCRIPT>
   </HEAD>
   <BODY BGCOLOR="white">

   </BODY>
   </HTML>
   ```

2. Add a form between the `<BODY>` tags. The form contains two text boxes and a button.

```
<FORM NAME="form1">
Enter Timeout <INPUT TYPE="text" NAME="TimeVal"><BR>
<INPUT TYPE="button" NAME="cmdButton1" VALUE="OK"><P>
<INPUT TYPE="text" NAME="AutoVal">
</FORM>
```

3. Now for the simple script, which is the event handler for the cmdButton1 button.

```
Sub cmdButton1_OnClick
  xID = setTimeout("Document.form1.AutoVal.Value='Hello World'",
CInt(Document.form1.TimeVal.Value))
End Sub
```

Here's the full code:

```
<HTML>
<HEAD>
<TITLE>Timeout</TITLE>
 <SCRIPT LANGUAGE="vbscript">
 <!--
 Sub cmdButton1_OnClick
   xID = setTimeout("Document.form1.AutoVal.Value='Hello World'",
   ➥CInt(Document.form1.TimeVal.Value))
 End Sub
 -->
 </SCRIPT>
</HEAD>
<BODY BGCOLOR="white">
<FORM NAME="form1">
Enter Timeout <INPUT TYPE="text" NAME="TimeVal"><BR>
<INPUT TYPE="button" NAME="cmdButton1" VALUE="OK"><P>
<INPUT TYPE="text" NAME="AutoVal">
</FORM>
</BODY>
</HTML>
```

When you click the button, the value you entered into the first text box (shown in Figure 18.5) is converted to an integer value and used as the TimeOut time value. Remember that this value is in milliseconds. At the end of the TimeOut period, the old chestnut "Hello World" is shown in the second text box, as shown in Figure 18.6.

Figure 18.5.

Enter a value for the timer in milliseconds.

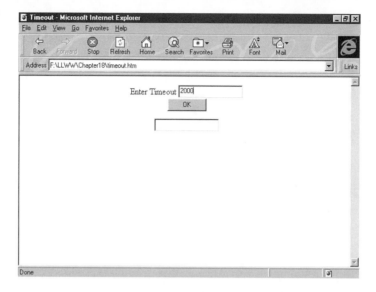

Figure 18.6.

And as if by magic...

TASK Navigating Within Frames

With frame documents becoming so popular—especially with the enhancement of MSIE 3.0 borderless frames—you need to know how to reference more than one document within a window from within your scripts. But, first you need to understand how the browser treats frames internally.

The `Frame` is a subobject whose parent is the `Window` object(often referred to within the script as `top`). Each `Window` object has at least one frame, which means that a non-frame document is held within a frame that is, in fact, the main window (although you would never go to the trouble of referencing it). Where there is more than one frame in a `frameset`, the frames are held within an array called `Frames`, and they can be referenced as such. For example, if you set up a `<FRAMESET>` with two documents in two frames, the first document could be referenced as follows:

```
Top.Frames(0).Document
```

And the second document could be referenced like this:

```
Top.Frames(1).Document
```

A much easier way is to give your frames a name when you create them in the `<FRAMESET>` document:

```
<FRAME NAME="scriptframe" SRC="script.htm">
```

The document in this frame can now be referenced like this:

```
Top.scriptframe.document
```

When you can reference other frames within a frameset, you can create a frameset with one main script document that controls the documents in the other frames, as the following example shows:

1. First, create the frameset document and save it as `vbsframes.htm`.

   ```
   <HTML>
   <HEAD><TITLE>Using VBScript in Frames(1)</TITLE></HEAD>
   <FRAMESET COLS=50%,50%>
    <FRAME NAME="scriptframe" SRC="script.htm">
    <FRAME NAME="docframe" SRC="doc1.htm">
   <FRAMESET>
   </HTML>
   ```

2. Create an HTML template document, which will hold the script.

   ```
   <HTML>
   <HEAD><TITLE>Script</TITLE>
   <SCRIPT LANGUAGE="vbscript">
   <!--

   -->
   </SCRIPT>
   <BODY BGCOLOR="white">

   </BODY>
   </HTML>
   ```

3. Finish the HTML with two Command Buttons on the page, each of which will eventually load a new page in the right frame.

   ```
   <CENTER>
   <H2>Script Document</H2>
   ```

```
<INPUT TYPE="button" NAME="cmdButton1" VALUE="Load Page 2 in Frame">
<P>
<INPUT TYPE="button" NAME="cmdButton2" VALUE="Load Page 3 in Frame">
```

4. Save the file as `script.htm`.

5. Create the two event handlers for the buttons. Simply as a demonstration, the two buttons use a different way of referencing the second frame: one by ordinal number in the `Frames` array, and the other by name.

```
Sub cmdButton1_OnClick
 Top.docframe.Location.href = "doc2.htm"
End Sub

Sub cmdButton2_OnClick
 Top.frames(1).Location.href = "doc3.htm"
End Sub
```

Here's the complete source for `script.htm`:

```
<HTML>
<HEAD><TITLE>Script</TITLE></HEAD>
<SCRIPT LANGUAGE="vbscript">
<!--
Sub cmdButton1_OnClick
 Top.docframe.Location.href = "doc2.htm"
End Sub

Sub cmdButton2_OnClick
 Top.frames(1).Location.href = "doc3.htm"
End Sub
-->
</SCRIPT>
<BODY BGCOLOR="white">
<CENTER>
<H2>Script Document</H2>
<INPUT TYPE="button" NAME="cmdButton1" VALUE="Load Page 2 in Frame">
<P>
<INPUT TYPE="button" NAME="cmdButton2" VALUE="Load Page 3 in Frame">
</BODY>
</HTML>
```

When you load `vbsframes.htm` into the browser, it loads `script.htm` into the left frame and `doc1.htm` into the right frame, as shown in Figure 18.7. When you click the buttons, the appropriate file—either `doc2.htm` or `doc3.htm`—is loaded into the right frame, as shown in Figure 18.8. The files `doc1.htm`, `doc2.htm`, and `doc3.htm` can be found on the CD-ROM that accompanies this book.

Figure 18.7.

The frameset as it loads.

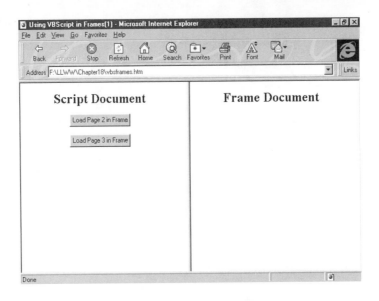

Figure 18.8.

Button 1 clicked.

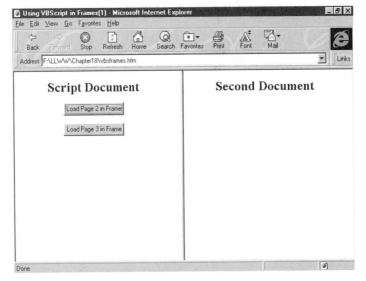

Calling a Script in Another Frame

Let's take the idea of using VBScript within frames a stage further. In this example, you'll see how you can actually call a procedure, which resides in one document, from a script in another unrelated document. The following example uses frames to demonstrate this, but you can translate its functionality to separate windows just as easily—assuming that you know the name of the second window.

The concept of being able to call procedures, functions, and even event handlers in other documents is a powerful one. For example, you can create a frameset in which just one of the documents holds regularly used or common functions that are accessed by the scripts in other documents. It can quite literally present you with unlimited possibilities.

The following example calls the OnClick event handler of a button in the second document, as though the user had clicked that button.

1. Again, create a frameset for the example, and save this one as remote.htm.

```
<HTML>
<HEAD><TITLE>Using a remote script</TITLE></HEAD>
<FRAMESET COLS=50%,50%>
 <FRAME NAME="scriptframe" SRC="script2.htm">
 <FRAME NAME="docframe" SRC="doc4.htm">
<FRAMESET>
</HTML>
```

2. Create an HTML template.

```
<HTML>
<HEAD>
<SCRIPT LANGUAGE="vbscript">

</SCRIPT>
<BODY BGCOLOR="white">

</BODY>
</HTML>
```

3. This page will contain one button and one text box within an HTML form, so your next step is to add the following HTML between the Body tags.

```
<CENTER>
<H2>Remote Script</H2>
</CENTER>
<FORM NAME="Form1">
<INPUT TYPE="text" NAME="Text1" SIZE=30>
<P>
<INPUT TYPE="button" NAME="Command1" VALUE="Click Me">
</FORM>
```

4. Now add the event handler for Command1 between the <SCRIPT> tags.

```
Sub Command1_OnClick
 Document.Form1.Text1.Value = "Hello World"
End Sub
```

5. Save the file as doc4.htm. This file resides in the right frame and can be used on its own, but it will be used as the remote script that is called by the script in the left frame.

6. To create the document for the left frame, you need to create another HTML template as described in step 2.

7. Now add the following button between the body tags.

```
<CENTER>
<H2>Script Document</H2>
```

```
<INPUT TYPE="button" NAME="cmdButton1" VALUE="Put text over there">
<P>
<INPUT TYPE="button" NAME="cmdButton2" VALUE="Execute Remote Script">
```

8. Save this second file as `script2.htm`.

9. The script for the `script2.htm` file performs two tasks. The first button puts the phrase `Where did this come from?` in the text box of the document in the right frame. The second button calls the event handler of the button in the right frame, thereby programmatically replicating a click on the button. Here are the event handlers for the two buttons:

```
Sub cmdButton1_OnClick
 Top.docframe.Form1.Text1.Value = "Where did this come from?"
End Sub

Sub cmdButton2_OnClick
 Call Top.docframe.Command1_OnClick()
End Sub
```

Here's the complete source for the two files:

```
<HTML>
<HEAD>
<SCRIPT LANGUAGE="vbscript">
Sub Command1_OnClick
 Document.Form1.Text1.Value = "Hello World"
End Sub
</SCRIPT>
<BODY BGCOLOR="white">
<CENTER>
<H2>Remote Script</H2>
</CENTER>
<FORM NAME="Form1">
<INPUT TYPE="text" NAME="Text1" SIZE=30>
<P>
<INPUT TYPE="button" NAME="Command1" VALUE="Click Me">
</FORM>
</BODY>
</HTML>

<HTML>
<HEAD><TITLE>Script</TITLE>

<SCRIPT LANGUAGE="vbscript">
<!--
Sub cmdButton1_OnClick
 Top.docframe.Form1.Text1.Value = "Where did this come from?"
End Sub

Sub cmdButton2_OnClick
 Call Top.docframe.Command1_OnClick()
End Sub
-->
</SCRIPT>

<BODY BGCOLOR="white">
<CENTER>
<H2>Script Document</H2>
<INPUT TYPE="button" NAME="cmdButton1" VALUE="Put text over there">
<P>
```

```
<INPUT TYPE="button" NAME="cmdButton2" VALUE="Execute Remote Script">
</BODY>
</HTML>
```

When you run this example through the browser, you can click the top button in the left frame, which automatically enters text in the right frame from the script in the left frame. (See Figure 18.9.) When you click the bottom button in the left frame, you are calling the event handling script that is part of the document in the right frame, thereby programmatically "clicking" the button in the right frame, as shown in Figure 18.10.

Figure 18.9.

Click the "Put text over there" button.

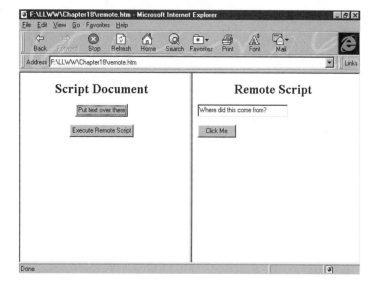

Figure 18.10.

Click the "Execute Remote Script" button.

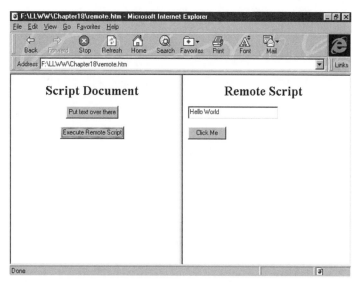

Creating a Web Page with VBScript

What could be more dynamic and interactive than one Web page that has the power to create an almost infinitely variable number of other Web pages without referring back to the server? It sounds almost too good to be true, but that is exactly what you can do with the `Document.Write` method.

The `Write` method of the `Document` object enables you to create variable Web pages at runtime, or it can be used to add variable elements to the Web page as the page is loading. The syntax for `Document.Write` is as follows:

```
Document.Write string
```

The *string* that you pass to the `Write` method can contain any HTML tags and any text you want to place on the page, as in the following example:

```
Document.Write "<H2>This is a heading</H2>"
```

It could also be an expression, like this:

```
Document.Write "The date is " & Date()
```

If you are using `Document.write` to add variable elements to a Web page as it downloads to the browser, you simply place the code in line with the rest of the HTML for the document. Enclose the method within `SCRIPT` tags, without any `sub` or `function`, as shown here:

```
...
<TABLE WIDTH=80%>
<TD>
<SCRIPT LANGUAGE="vbscript">
Document.Write "The date is " & Date()
</SCRIPT>
<TD>
...
```

To create a new document, use `Document.Write` in conjunction with `Document.Open` and `Document.Close`. But remember that if you use the current window or frame to write your new document to, the Web page containing the script that is creating the page will be overwritten in the browser. Therefore, it is wise to create new documents in a second frame or window. The following example shows you how this is done:

1. First, create the `<FRAMESET>` document.

    ```
    <HTML>
    <HEAD><TITLE>Build a Document</TITLE></HEAD>
    <FRAMESET COLS=50%,50%>
     <FRAME NAME="scriptframe" SRC="docscript.htm">
     <FRAME NAME="docframe" SRC="tempdoc.htm">
    <FRAMESET>
    </HTML>
    ```

    Note the `tempdoc.htm` page in the second frame. This is an HTML document that contains only `<HTML>` and `<BODY>` tags.

2. Now create a simple template.

```
<HTML>
<HEAD><TITLE>Script</TITLE>

<SCRIPT LANGUAGE="vbscript">
<!--

-->
</SCRIPT>

<BODY BGCOLOR="white">

</BODY>
</HTML>
```

3. Save the preceding code as `docscript.htm`.

4. Now add an HTML form. The example you are creating here enables you to automatically create a document that displays a heading and body text, the data for which is entered in the form. Here's the rest of the HTML work for the page:

```
<CENTER>
<H2>Build a New Document</H2>
<FORM NAME="form1">
Enter a Heading<INPUT TYPE="text" NAME="heading" SIZE=30><P>
Enter the message
<TEXTAREA NAME="thetext" ROWS=6 COLS=40 WRAP=VIRTUAL></TEXTAREA><P>
<INPUT TYPE="button" NAME="cmdButton1" VALUE="Build Now">
</FORM>
```

5. The script is to be attached to the Event handler for `cmdButton1` and is a series of `Document.Write` methods to build up the new document in the right frame.

```
Sub cmdButton1_OnClick

    top.docframe.Document.Open
    top.docframe.Document.Write "<HTML><BODY BGCOLOR=white>"
    top.docframe.Document.Write "<FONT FACE=arial SIZE=2>"
    top.docframe.Document.Write "<CENTER><H3>"
    top.docframe.Document.Write Document.form1.heading.value
    top.docframe.Document.Write "</H3></CENTER><P><BLOCKQUOTE>"
    top.docframe.Document.Write Document.form1.thetext.value
    top.docframe.Document.Write "</BLOCKQUOTE>"
    top.docframe.Document.Write "</BODY></HTML>"
    top.docframe.Document.Close

End Sub
```

6. Save the file and run it through the browser.

Here's the complete code for this example:

```
<HTML>
<HEAD><TITLE>Script</TITLE>

<SCRIPT LANGUAGE="vbscript">
<!--
Sub cmdButton1_OnClick
```

```
top.docframe.Document.Open
top.docframe.Document.Write "<HTML><BODY BGCOLOR=white>"
top.docframe.Document.Write "<FONT FACE=arial SIZE=2>"
top.docframe.Document.Write "<CENTER><H3>"
top.docframe.Document.Write Document.form1.heading.value
top.docframe.Document.Write "</H3></CENTER><P><BLOCKQUOTE>"
top.docframe.Document.Write Document.form1.thetext.value
top.docframe.Document.Write "</BLOCKQUOTE>"
top.docframe.Document.Write "</BODY></HTML>"
top.docframe.Document.Close

End Sub


-->
</SCRIPT>

<BODY BGCOLOR="white">
<CENTER>
<H2>Build a New Document</H2>
<FORM NAME="form1">
Enter a Heading<INPUT TYPE="text" NAME="heading" SIZE=30><P>
Enter the message
<TEXTAREA NAME="thetext" ROWS=6 COLS=40 WRAP=VIRTUAL></TEXTAREA><P>
<INPUT TYPE="button" NAME="cmdButton1" VALUE="Build Now">
</FORM>
</BODY>
</HTML>
```

When you run this example through the browser, enter a heading and some text to be displayed on the new page, as shown in Figure 18.11. When you click the button, a brand new document is created and shown in the right frame, using the inputs from the left frame, as shown in Figure 18.12.

Figure 18.11.

Enter a heading and some body text.

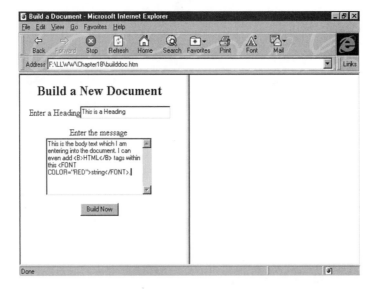

Figure 18.12.

Click the button to create the document in the right frame.

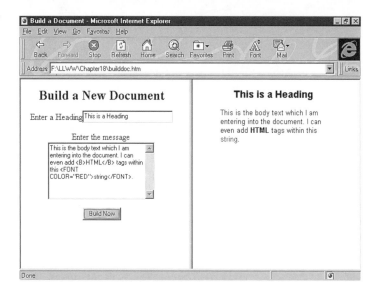

Workshop Wrap-Up

Using the browser's objects within your scripts enables you to perform a wide range of complex windows tasks easily and quickly. The browser's object model creates a flexible working environment that you can exploit to create the most powerful and state-of-the-art Web applications. You now have almost complete control over the document within the browser, as well as over the browser itself.

Controlling the browser, creating new windows, and writing new documents at the client are tasks that are the very essence of interactive and dynamic Web pages. They will set your Web site apart from the rest.

Next Steps

Now that you know how to control the browser, use scripts within frames, and create new documents from within the browser, there should be no stopping you. So off you go to these other chapters:

- ❏ To learn how you can use another of the Document object's properties to create even more neat applications, see Chapter 19, "Baking Cookies with VBScript."
- ❏ To see a cool example of the Document.Write method, check out Chapter 20, "Real-Life Examples III."
- ❏ To learn more about the Window object's methods, see Chapter 3, "Communicating with Your Users."

Q&A

Q: Is it possible to write text into a current document?

A: No, that facility is not available yet. It will undoubtedly be available before very long. You can only use the Document.Write while the HTML page is being loaded into the browser. When it has been loaded, it is fixed.

Q: If I have a document in a frame and then I use the Document.Write method in that frame, does it overwrite the document?

A: Only within the display space. The underlying document is still intact. If you click reload, the original document is redisplayed.

Q: I've tried to use the Document.Write method in a frame that doesn't contain a document, and I get an error message. Why?

A: If a frame doesn't contain a document, there is no document object to use the Write method on. The only way around this is to create a very simple "blank" HTML document that you load into the frame before calling the Document.Write method.

NINETEEN

Baking Cookies with VBScript

Put away your mixing bowl and flour. The cookies you'll learn about here have nothing to do with the edible variety. So what is a cookie? A cookie is a simple text file that is linked to a particular Web document and is stored on the client machine. "Ah," I can hear you say, "but VBScript doesn't allow you to read and write files on the client machine." In the general sense this is true, but cookies are not ordinary files.

A cookie file is a very limited ASCII text; therefore, it cannot contain any potentially harmful binary code. Furthermore, the only way that it can be written to or read from the Web is by the page that originally created it. To see the cookie files you've already collected on your travels around the Web, open your Windows Explorer and open the Cookies subdirectory within the Windows directory.

Security Issues

When cookies were first introduced, some people thought—and some still do—that the humble cookie would be a security risk. So first of all, let me put your mind at ease. Cookies cannot read information from your hard drive, nor can they publicize your personal information to the world. Here's a list of the limitations placed on cookies:

❏ A client machine cannot store more than 300 cookies.

❏ A client machine cannot store more than 20 cookies from a single domain.

❏ Only cookies that have an expiration date associated with them are stored on the client machine. Most cookies are simply lost when the browser is exited.

❏ A cookie is not a program. It is simply an ASCII text file.

❏ Cookies cannot obtain personal information, unless you have given that information to the domain associated with the cookie (for example, in a questionnaire).

❏ A cookie can be read only by the domain that created it.

What Can You Use Cookies For?

Cookies have allowed the creation of a range of new applications, including shopping carts. This is because cookies store variables that can be used from page to page, or written and read every time a user enters a Web site. Here are just a few examples of how you could use cookies:

❏ Maintain a list of selected items, quantities, and colors in a shopping application.

❏ Maintain a record of the number of times a user has visited your site.

❏ Store the date that a user last visited your Web site, and highlight items that have changed since his last visit.

❏ Maintain a user-customized color scheme for your Web site.

❏ Maintain a basic information file for a user—that is, first name, preferences, and so on—to enable you to personalize the site for the user.

Cookie Variables

Cookie values are stored as `name=value` pairs, delimited with a semicolon (`;`). You can create your own variable names and assign values to them, and you can set several standard cookie variables.

domain

syntax: `domain=domain_name;`

When the client searches the list of cookie files, a comparison of the domain name attributes of the cookie file is made with the domain name of the host from which the Web page has been fetched. If the domain name minus the machine name (such as mcp.com) matches the stored domain name—which is known as tail matching—the cookie then performs path matching.

Only hosts within the specified domain can set a cookie for that domain, and domains must have at least two or three periods in them to prevent generic domains such as .com or .net. The default value of domain is the host name of the server that initially generated the cookie file.

A machine name is the first part of the URL: for example, www. or search. as in search.yahoo.com, or home. as in home.netscape.com.

path

syntax: path=*path*;

The path attribute is used to specify the URLs within a domain for which the particular cookie is valid. When the domain matching has been successfully completed, the pathname component of the URL is compared with the path attribute. The path /laura would match /lauralemay and /laura/lemay.html. If a path attribute is not specified, the path is assumed to be that of the document calling the cookie.

secure

syntax: secure;

The secure attribute specifies that the cookie can be transmitted only if the communications channel with the host is a secure one. If secure is not specified, a cookie is considered safe to be sent openly, or "in the clear," over unsecured channels. However, you are dealing with client-side scripting, so the secure attribute is somewhat redundant because your VBScript cookies are never "transmitted" and remain within the client environment.

Expiration Date

syntax: expires=*date*;

The expiration date attribute must be written in a particular format to be recognized.

day, dd-mmm-yy hh:mm:ss GMT

Here is an example:

Thursday, 09-Oct-97 15:01:00 GMT

This poses something of a problem in VBScript, because you don't have access to a GMT date format, like you would in JavaScript. A work-around to this is to hard code an expiration date that is far into the future, say 1999. Otherwise, you will have to resort to mixing JavaScript in your document to calculate the current time offset to GMT at the client.

Baking a Temporary Cookie

A temporary cookie is one that exists only while the browser is open; when the browser is closed, the cookie is gone. This first example demonstrates how to set the value within a temporary cookie and then read back the name/value pair.

1. Start by entering the following HTML into Notepad or your usual HTML editor:

```
<HTML>
<HEAD>
<TITLE>Setting a cookie [1]</TITLE>
<SCRIPT LANGUAGE="vbscript">

</SCRIPT>
<BODY BGCOLOR="white">
<CENTER>
<INPUT TYPE="button" NAME="cmdButton1" VALUE="Show Cookie Value">
</CENTER>
</BODY>
</HTML>
```

2. Now you need to add the VBScript code that writes the cookie value when the page is loaded. The following code goes between the <SCRIPT> tags. Note that it is not within a custom procedure, function, or event handler; therefore, it will execute as the page downloads to the browser.

```
1: Dim VarName
2: Dim VarVal
3:
4: VarName = "mycookie"
5: VarVal = Date()
6:
7: Document.Cookie = VarName & "=" & VarVal & ";"
```

First, in lines 1 and 2, you have declared two variables—one for the name of the cookie variable and the second for the cookie value. Lines 4 and 5 assign values to these variables. The cookie variable has been given the name mycookie. The value is taken from the client machine's date. Finally, in line 7, the Document's Cookie property is set by building a string made up of the Cookie variable's name, an equal sign, the cookie value, and a semicolon.

3. To finish, you need to add an event handler for cmdButton1, which will be used to display the name/value pair from the cookie.

```
Sub cmdButton1_OnClick
  Alert Document.Cookie
End Sub
```

As you can see, it's frighteningly easy. All you have to do in this case is pass the Document.Cookie property to an Alert box.

Here's the complete code for this example. To use this demonstration, you need to load the HTML file onto a Web server and run it from there. Cookies don't appear to like being run from a local drive. Figure 19.1 shows this example running from the test subdirectory of my `vbscripts.com` domain.

```
<HTML>
<HEAD>
<TITLE>Setting a cookie [1]</TITLE>
<SCRIPT LANGUAGE="vbscript">
Dim VarName
Dim VarVal

VarName = "mycookie"
VarVal = Date()

Document.Cookie = VarName & "=" & VarVal & ";"

Sub cmdButton1_OnClick
  Alert Document.Cookie
End Sub

</SCRIPT>
<BODY BGCOLOR="white">
<CENTER>
<INPUT TYPE="button" NAME="cmdButton1" VALUE="Show Cookie Value">
</CENTER>
</BODY>
</HTML>
```

Figure 19.1.

The cookie name/value pair.

When you have run this example, take a look in the `Cookies` subdirectory, just to prove to yourself that the cookie hasn't been written to disk. To write a cookie to disk, all you need to do is add an expiration date.

Baking a Semi-Permanent Cookie

This example demonstrates how to create a semi-permanent cookie file. I use the term semi-permanent because there is no such thing as a permanent cookie file. By its very nature, a cookie can be written to disk only if it has been given an expiration date. However, by setting the date to a time in the distant future, you can give the cookie some semi-permanence.

1. Start again with your HTML template.

```
<HTML>
<HEAD>
<TITLE>Setting a cookie [2]</TITLE>
<SCRIPT LANGUAGE="vbscript">

</SCRIPT>
<BODY BGCOLOR="white">
<CENTER>
<INPUT TYPE="button" NAME="cmdButton1" VALUE="Get Cookie Value">
</CENTER>
</BODY>
</HTML>
```

2. Now add the following code between the <SCRIPT> tags to create the cookie. Notice that it is very similar to the previous example, with the addition of an expiration variable.

```
Dim VarName
Dim VarVal
Dim Exp

Exp = "expires=Wednesday, 09-Nov-1999 23:12:40 GMT"
VarName = "mycookie"
VarVal = Date()

Document.Cookie = VarName & "=" & VarVal & ";" & Exp
```

The easiest way to specify an expiration date is to specify it explicitly, as shown in the preceding code. It must be specified in this format, which involves an awful lot of extra coding if, for example, you want to specify an expiration date based on the current date.

3. Finally, add the same event handler as before to show the cookie's name/value pair.

```
Sub cmdButton1_OnClick
 Alert Document.Cookie
End Sub
```

Here's the completed code:

```
<HTML>
<HEAD>
<TITLE>Setting a cookie [2]</TITLE>
<SCRIPT LANGUAGE="vbscript">
Dim VarName
Dim VarVal
Dim Exp

Exp = "expires=Wednesday, 09-Nov-1999 23:12:40 GMT"
VarName = "mycookie"
VarVal = Date()

Document.Cookie = VarName & "=" & VarVal & ";" & Exp

Sub cmdButton1_OnClick
 Alert Document.Cookie
End Sub

</SCRIPT>
<BODY BGCOLOR="white">
<CENTER>
<INPUT TYPE="button" NAME="cmdButton1" VALUE="Get Cookie Value">
</CENTER>
</BODY>
</HTML>
```

Again, this example executes properly only from a Web server, as shown in Figure 19.2. This time when you have run the page, you should find a new cookie file in your Cookies subdirectory. You can open the file (for what it's worth) in Notepad, as shown in Figure 19.3.

Figure 19.2.

The bake2.htm *file in the browser.*

Figure 19.3.
The resultant cookie file.

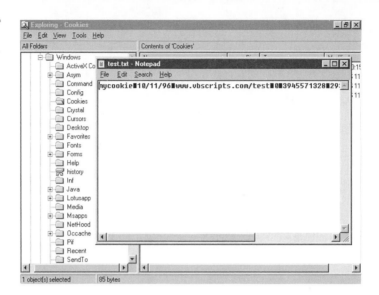

 Baking a Cookie with Multiple Values

The previous two examples have used a single variable. Now you can try creating a cookie file that stores multiple values:

1. Start with the HTML template.

```
<HTML>
<HEAD>
<TITLE>Setting a cookie [3]</TITLE>
<SCRIPT LANGUAGE="vbscript">

</SCRIPT>
<BODY BGCOLOR="white">
<CENTER>
<INPUT TYPE="button" NAME="cmdButton1" VALUE="Get Cookie Value">
</CENTER>
</BODY>
</HTML>
```

2. Add the following code between the <SCRIPT> tags:

```
 1: Dim VarName
 2: Dim VarVal
 3: Dim VarName1
 4: Dim VarVal1
 5: Dim Exp
 6:
 7: Exp = "expires=Wednesday, 09-Nov-1999 23:12:40 GMT"
 8: VarName = "mycookie"
 9: VarVal = Date()
10: VarName1 = "nextname"
11: VarVal1 = "anything;"
12:
13: Document.Cookie = VarName & "=" & VarVal & ";"
➥& VarName1 & "=" & VarVal1 & Exp
```

Notice that in this example the semicolon that delimits the second value is attached to the string as part of the second value.

3. Again, add the event handler for the button, which displays the two name/value pairs as shown in Figure 19.4.

```
Sub cmdButton1_OnClick
 Alert Document.Cookie
End Sub
```

Figure 19.4.

The two name/value pairs are now displayed.

Here's the complete code for the multiple value example. You can add as many name/value pairs as you require, up to a maximum total cookie size of 4KB.

```
<HTML>
<HEAD>
<TITLE>Setting a cookie [3]</TITLE>
<SCRIPT LANGUAGE="vbscript">
Dim VarName
Dim VarVal
Dim VarName1
Dim VarVal1
Dim Exp

Exp = "expires=Wednesday, 09-Nov-1999 23:12:40 GMT"
VarName = "mycookie"
VarVal = Date()
VarName1 = "nextname"
VarVal1 = "anything;"

Document.Cookie = VarName & "=" & VarVal & ";" & VarName1 & "=" & VarVal1 & Exp

Sub cmdButton1_OnClick
 Alert Document.Cookie
End Sub
```

```
</SCRIPT>
<BODY BGCOLOR="white">
<CENTER>
<INPUT TYPE="button" NAME="cmdButton1" VALUE="Get Cookie Value">
</CENTER>
</BODY>
</HTML>
```

TASK

Reading Individual Cookie Values

In the real world, you need to get hold of individual cookie values rather than the complete cookie or a name/value pair. This requires you to get involved in manipulating the string that is returned by `Document.Cookie`.

The string that is returned is the complete cookie—basically, a series of name/value pairs delimited by semicolons. Therefore, you need to find the variable name within the string, and from its position in the string, you can then extract the value associated with that variable. This example shows you how to dissect the cookie string in order to return the value of a specific variable within the cookie.

For more information on string manipulation, see Chapter 7, "Manipulating Strings."

The HTML template for this example is slightly different from the ones used before. For ease of demonstration, each of the two variables within the cookie will be returned by clicking on the appropriate button.

```
<HTML>
<HEAD>
<TITLE>Getting a Cookie</TITLE>
<SCRIPT LANGUAGE="vbscript">

</SCRIPT>
<BODY BGCOLOR="white">
<CENTER>
<INPUT TYPE="button" NAME="cmdButton1" VALUE="Get MyCookie Value">
<P>
<INPUT TYPE="button" NAME="cmdButton2" VALUE="Get NextName Value">
</CENTER>
</BODY>
</HTML>
```

When you've entered the HTML template, between the `<SCRIPT>` tags add the following two event handlers for the two buttons. Note that each one calls the same custom procedure, passing the name of the variable to be returned.

```
Sub cmdButton1_OnClick
 Call GetCookieValue("mycookie")
End Sub

Sub cmdButton2_OnClick
 Call GetCookieValue("nextname")
End Sub
```

Now you can enter the custom procedure. Again, the line numbers are only for ease of explanation.

```
1: Sub GetCookieValue(CkName)
2:
3:  CkNameLen = Len(CkName)
4:
5:  If InStr(Document.Cookie, CkName) = 0 Then
6:   Alert "Cookie value not found"
7:  Else
8:   CkValStart = InStr(Document.Cookie, CkName) + CkNameLen + 1
9:
10:    If InStr(CkValStart, Document.Cookie, ";") = 0 Then
11:     CkVal = Mid(Document.Cookie, CkValStart)
12:    Else
13:     CkValEnd = InStr(CkValStart, Document.Cookie, ";")
14:     CkValLen = CkValEnd - CkValStart
15:     CkVal = Mid(Document.Cookie, CkValStart, CkValLen)
16:    End If
17:
18:    Alert CkVal
19:  End If
20: End Sub
```

The custom procedure prototype is on line 1, and it requires that the name of the cookie variable be passed into the procedure when it is called. The length of the name string is obtained and assigned to the variable CkNameLen in line 3.

Line 5 checks to make sure that the variable name is present within the cookie string. If it is not, a warning message is displayed and the procedure is terminated.

If the variable name is found within the cookie string, execution continues at line 8, where the position of the first character of the variable value is calculated. This is done by adding the length of the variable name to the start position of the variable name to give the end position of the variable name. Then you add one further character to basically jump past the = that sits between the variable name and the variable value.

If the variable value that you are seeking is the last one in the cookie, the semicolon will not appear after the value. Therefore, line 10 checks to see whether a semicolon is present at some point after the start of the variable value. If not, this is the last value of the cookie, and its end point can be taken as the end point of the overall cookie. If there is a semicolon present after the variable value, the position of the semicolon is the end point of the variable value.

The Mid function used in line 11 does not use a string length element and, therefore, Mid returns a string that ends at the last character of the source string. The Mid function in line 15 uses the calculated length of the value string to pluck the value from the source string.

Here's the complete source code for the example. The results of clicking the two buttons are shown in Figures 19.5 and 19.6.

```
<HTML>
<HEAD>
<TITLE>Getting a Cookie</TITLE>
<SCRIPT LANGUAGE="vbscript">

Sub cmdButton1_OnClick
 Call GetCookieValue("mycookie")
End Sub

Sub cmdButton2_OnClick
 Call GetCookieValue("nextname")
End Sub

Sub GetCookieValue(CkName)

 CkNameLen = Len(CkName)

 If InStr(Document.Cookie, CkName) = 0 Then
  Alert "Cookie value not found"
 Else
  CkValStart = InStr(Document.Cookie, CkName) + CkNameLen + 1

   If InStr(CkValStart, Document.Cookie, ";") = 0 Then
    CkVal = Mid(Document.Cookie, CkValStart)
   Else
    CkValEnd = InStr(CkValStart, Document.Cookie, ";")
    CkValLen = CkValEnd - CkValStart
    CkVal = Mid(Document.Cookie, CkValStart, CkValLen)
   End If

  Alert CkVal
 End If
End Sub

</SCRIPT>
<BODY BGCOLOR="white">
<CENTER>
<INPUT TYPE="button" NAME="cmdButton1" VALUE="Get MyCookie Value">
<P>
<INPUT TYPE="button" NAME="cmdButton2" VALUE="Get NextName Value">
</CENTER>
</BODY>
</HTML>
```

Workshop Wrap-Up

Cookies represent an important aspect of interactive Web development. Most people are coming to realize that, far from being a threat to their privacy, cookies have been developed to enhance the surfing experience by allowing site designers to personalize Web sites. The security argument is further diminished with client-side scripting, because the cookie file never leaves the client machine.

Figure 19.5.

Click the MyCookie button to return the value of the mycookie *variable.*

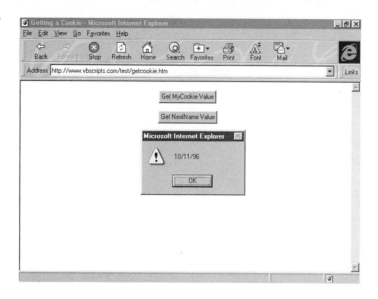

Figure 19.6.

Click the NextName button to return the value of the nextname *variable.*

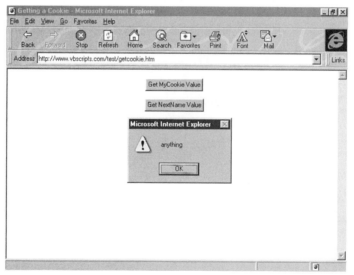

You can find more general information about cookies at this Netscape site:

```
http://home.netscape.com/newsref/std/cookie_spec.html
```

You can also find an excellent Web page, called *Andy's Netscape HTTP Cookie Info,* at this address:

```
http://www.illuminatus.com/cookie.fcgi
```

Next Steps

Now that you've seen how cookies work and how you bake them to create wonderfully tasty Web pages, why not add some of the following VBScript flavorings to your recipe?

❏ To see a real-life working example of cookies, see Chapter 20, "Real-Life Examples III."

❏ To learn more about string manipulation, see Chapter 7, "Manipulating Strings."

❏ To learn more about dates and times within VBScript, see Chapter 8, "Adding Date and Time Functions."

Q&A

Q: Why are cookies called cookies?

A: I've never seen a definitive answer to this one. Cookies were originally referred to as *Magic Cookies*. The most plausible explanation I have read is that they were so named after Dan O'Neill's book, *Hear the Sound of My Feet Walking... Drown the Sound of My Voice Talking...* In the book, Fred gives Hugh and Sam magic cookies and watches their interactive Magic Cookie Land dreams; then Fred uses a magic cookie himself to get into Hugh's dream. (Like you would, I suppose!)

This relates to cookies because Fred symbolizes the webmaster, and dreams represent browsing or surfing. Maybe now you can see where the idea for the name came from, although "watching" would be a gross exaggeration of the purpose and use of cookies.

TWENTY

Real-Life Examples III

This chapter describes two sample Web pages created using VBScript, with techniques introduced in Part IV, "Developing Dynamic Web Applications with VBScript" (Chapters 17 through 19). The following examples are included:

Example 1. A corporate home page that automatically alerts the user to items that have been added or amended since his previous visit.

Example 2. A Web page that launches customized browser windows, the contents of which are customized in accordance with the choices made by the user.

Example 1: Web Software Kings

Document title: Web Software Kings

Files:

Page files:

- ❏ `kings.html` (see Figures 20.1, 20.3, 20.4)
- ❏ `register.html` (see Figure 20.2)

Images:

- ❏ `lcrown.gif`
- ❏ `crown.gif`
- ❏ `new.gif`
- ❏ `updated.gif`

Description: The example demonstrates the use of cookies to personalize a site for a user. The Web page stores a cookie containing only two pieces of information: the user's forename (if given) and the date the user last visited the site.

An array is used to maintain the dates when links on the main page have been added or when the content of the link has been updated. Quite simply, when a user returns to the site, a comparison is made between the date the user last visited the site and the date of the amendment to the site. If the date last visited is prior to the site amendment, a graphic is displayed to alert the user to the change.

Techniques Applied

Cookies: (See Chapter 19, "Baking Cookies with VBScript.") A cookie file is used to store the date when the user last visited the site, and if the user has registered with the site, the cookie also stores the user's first name.

Document.Write: (See Chapter 18, "Interacting with the Browser.") The Document.Write method is used to create the custom HTML based on the values returned by the cookie.

Date and time formatting: (See Chapter 8, "Adding Date and Time Functions.") Various date and time functions are used to compare dates from the cookie file with those stored in the HTML file.

Arrays: (See Chapter 10, "Using the Power of Arrays.") Arrays are used to store the date that a link has been added to the page or the date that the contents of the link have been updated.

Figure 20.1.

*This is what a first-time
visitor to the site sees.*

Figure 20.2.

*A new user can then
register.*

Figure 20.3.

Even if the user doesn't register, this is how the site looks on a subsequent visit.

Figure 20.4.

If the user has registered, he is greeted upon his return.

Listing 20.1 shows the complete source code for `kings.html`, which is the main page of this example. This page contains the scripts that read and write values to the cookie file and hold the data for determining when items have been added or updated.

Listing 20.1. The `kings.html` code.

```
<HTML>
<HEAD>
<TITLE>Web Software Kings</TITLE>
<SCRIPT LANGUAGE="vbscript">
Dim DateLastVisited
Dim LinkType(5)
Dim LinkDate(5)
LinkType(0) = "new"
LinkType(1) = "updated"
LinkType(2) = ""
LinkType(3) = "updated"
LinkType(4) = "updated"
LinkDate(0) = "11/12/96"
LinkDate(1) = "10/12/96"
LinkDate(2) = ""
LinkDate(3) = "09/20/96"
LinkDate(4) = "08/21/96"
DateLastVisited = GetCookieValue("DLV")
Sub window_onUnload()
 dim VarName
 dim VarVal
 dim ExpDate
 ExpDate = "expires=Friday, 01-Jan-1999 23:00:00 GMT"
 VarName = "DLV"
 VarVal = Date()
 Document.Cookie = VarName & "=" & VarVal & ";" & ExpDate
End Sub
Function GetCookieValue(CkName)
 CkNameLen = Len(CkName)

 If InStr(Document.Cookie, CkName) = 0 Then
 GetCookieValue = ""
 Exit Function
 Else
 CkValStart = InStr(Document.Cookie, CkName) + CkNameLen + 1
 If InStr(CkValStart, Document.Cookie, ";") = 0 Then
 CkVal = Mid(Document.Cookie, CkValStart)
 Else
 CkValEnd = InStr(CkValStart, Document.Cookie, ";")
 CkValLen = CkValEnd - CkValStart
 CkVal = Mid(Document.Cookie, CkValStart, CkValLen)
 End If

 GetCookieValue = CkVal
 End If
End Function
Function IsNewOrUpdate(LinkNo)

 LType = LinkType(LinkNo)

 If LType = "" or DateLastVisited = "" Then
   IsNewOrUpdate = "crown.gif"
   Exit Function
 End If
 If DateValue(DateLastVisited) < DateValue(LinkDate(LinkNo)) Then
   IsNewOrUpdate = CStr(LType) + ".gif"
 Else
```

continues

Listing 20.1. continued

```
     IsNewOrUpdate = "crown.gif"
 End If
End Function
Sub DoFName()
 fName = GetCookieValue("ForeName")
 If fName = "" Then
 Exit Sub
 Else
 Document.Write "Hi " & fName & "<BR>"
 End If
End Sub
Sub PreviousVisits()
 If DateLastVisited = "" Then
 Exit Sub
 Else
 Document.Write "back "
 End If
End Sub
Sub FirstTimer()
 If DateLastVisited = "" Then
 Document.Write "As this is your first visit to Web Software Kings "
 Document.Write "please take a moment to register and enhance your "
 Document.Write "future visits to the site..."
 Document.Write "<A HREF=register.html>Click Here to Register</A><P>"
 End If
End Sub
</SCRIPT>
</HEAD>
<BODY BGCOLOR="white">
<FONT FACE="arial" SIZE=3>
<CENTER><B>
<TABLE><TR><TD ALIGN=MIDDLE><IMG SRC="lcrown.gif" ALIGN=LEFT>
</TD>
<TD ALIGN=CENTER>
<H2>
 <SCRIPT LANGUAGE="vbscript">
Call DoFName()
 </SCRIPT>
Welcome
 <SCRIPT LANGUAGE="vbscript">
Call PreviousVisits()
 </SCRIPT>
to the <BR>Web Software Kings</H2>
</TD></TR></TABLE>
<BR><P>
 <SCRIPT LANGUAGE="vbscript">
Call FirstTimer()
 </SCRIPT>
 <SCRIPT LANGUAGE="vbscript">
Document.Write "<IMG SRC="
 Document.Write IsNewOrUpdate(0)
Document.Write ">"
 </SCRIPT>
<A HREF="a.html">WebBase FAQ</A>
<P>
 <SCRIPT LANGUAGE="vbscript">
Document.Write "<IMG SRC="
 Document.Write IsNewOrUpdate(1)
```

```
 Document.Write ">"
 </SCRIPT>
<A HREF="a.html">WebBase Version 65.3</A>
<P>
 <SCRIPT LANGUAGE="vbscript">
Document.Write "<IMG SRC="
 Document.Write IsNewOrUpdate(2)
 Document.Write ">"
 </SCRIPT>
<A HREF="a.html">Dealer Listing</A>
<P>
 <SCRIPT LANGUAGE="vbscript">
Document.Write "<IMG SRC="
 Document.Write IsNewOrUpdate(3)
 Document.Write ">"
 </SCRIPT>
<A HREF="a.html">Pricing Structure</A>
<P>
 <SCRIPT LANGUAGE="vbscript">
Document.Write "<IMG SRC="
 Document.Write IsNewOrUpdate(4)
 Document.Write ">"
 </SCRIPT>
<A HREF="a.html">Order Form</A>
<P>
</BODY>
</HTML>
```

Listing 20.2 shows the complete source code for `register.html`, which is used to create a new cookie file containing the user's name.

Listing 20.2. The `register.html` code.

```
<HTML>
<HEAD>
<TITLE>Web Software Kings - Register</TITLE>
<SCRIPT LANGUAGE="vbscript">
 Sub Register_OnClick
 dim VarName
 dim VarVal
 dim ExpDate
 ExpDate = "expires=Friday, 01-Jan-1999 23:00:00 GMT"
 VarName = "ForeName"
 VarVal = Document.Form1.forename.Value
 Document.Cookie = VarName & "=" & VarVal & ";" & ExpDate

 Location.Href = "kings.html"
 End Sub
</SCRIPT>
</HEAD>
<BODY BGCOLOR="white">
<FONT FACE="arial" SIZE=3>
<CENTER><B>
<TABLE><TR><TD ALIGN=MIDDLE><IMG SRC="lcrown.gif" ALIGN=LEFT>
</TD>
<TD ALIGN=CENTER>
<H2>
```

continues

Listing 20.2. continued

```
Web Software Kings<BR>User Registration</H2>
</TD></TR></TABLE>
<BR><P>
<FORM NAME="form1">
 It's easy to register, just enter your first name here
 <INPUT TYPE="text" NAME="forename"><P>
 <INPUT TYPE="button" NAME="register" VALUE="Register Now">
</FORM>
</BODY>
</HTML>
```

Example 2: A2Z Aluminium Box Co.

Document title: A2Z Aluminium Box Co.

Files:

Page files:

- ❏ specs.htm

- ❏ specification.htm

Images:

- ❏ back.jpg

- ❏ a2z.gif

Description: The main page (specs.htm), shown in Figure 20.5, lists the range of standard products produced by the A2Z Aluminium Box Company. To view the specification for each product, the user clicks the button next to the product name.

The script attached to the buttons launches a new browser window using the Window.Open method. (See Figure 20.6.) The HTML file that is loaded into the new window contains a script that writes the appropriate details depending on which button has been clicked. The name given to the new window is used to pass the product number from one script to the other. More than one new window can be open at any time, as shown in Figure 20.7. The script ensures that the correct details are shown in the window.

Techniques Applied

Window.Open: (See Chapter 18.) The example uses the Window.Open method to launch the new customized windows. It also uses Window.Close from the script within the new window.

Document.Write: (See Chapter 18.) The example uses the `Document.Write` method to create a table of information displayed in the new customized window.

Arrays: (See Chapter 10.) Several arrays, including a multidimension array, are used to store the information that will be displayed in the new window.

Figure 20.5.

The product listing page: `specs.html`.

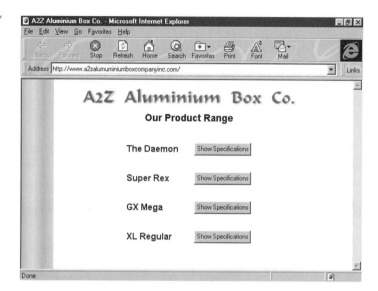

Figure 20.6.

Click a button to launch the specifications window.

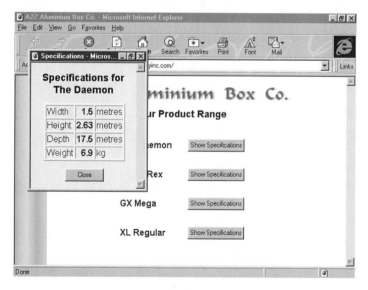

Figure 20.7.

More than one window can be open at any time.

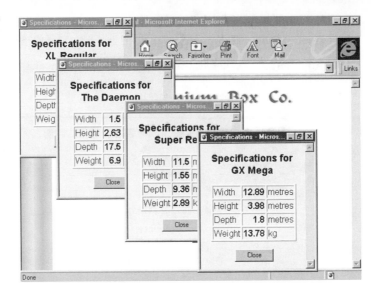

Listing 20.3 shows the complete source code for specs.html, which handles the opening of the new windows. The name of the new window is used to pass the product number value from the main window to the new window.

Listing 20.3. The specs.html code.

```
<HTML>
<HEAD>
<TITLE>A2Z Aluminium Box Co.</TITLE>
<SCRIPT LANGUAGE="vbscript">
Sub DoSpecPage(ProductNo)
 winname = ProductNo
 Window.Open "specification.htm", winname,"toolbar=no, location=no,
➥directories=no, status=no, menubar=no, scrollbars=no, resizable=no,
➥width=200, height=200"
End Sub
</SCRIPT>
<BODY BACKGROUND="back.jpg">
<FONT FACE="arial" SIZE=3>
<CENTER>
<IMG SRC="a2z.gif">
<P>
<H3>Our Product Range</H3>
<P>
<TABLE CELLSPACING=10 CELLPADDING=10>
<TR><TD><B>The Daemon</TD>
<TD><INPUT TYPE="button" NAME="cmdButton1" VALUE="Show Specifications"
➥LANGUAGE="vbscript" OnClick="Call DoSpecPage(0)"></TD></TR>
<TR><TD><B>Super Rex</TD>
<TD><INPUT TYPE="button" NAME="cmdButton2" VALUE="Show Specifications"
➥LANGUAGE="vbscript" OnClick="Call DoSpecPage(1)"></TD></TR>
<TR><TD><B>GX Mega</TD>
<TD><INPUT TYPE="button" NAME="cmdButton3" VALUE="Show Specifications"
➥LANGUAGE="vbscript" OnClick="Call DoSpecPage(2)"></TD></TR>
```

```
<TR><TD><B>XL Regular</TD>
<TD><INPUT TYPE="button" NAME="cmdButton4" VALUE="Show Specifications"
➥LANGUAGE="vbscript" OnClick="Call DoSpecPage(3)"></TD></TR>
</TABLE>
</CENTER>
</BODY>
</HTML>
```

Listing 20.4 shows the complete source code for `specification.htm`, which is the HTML page to be loaded into the newly created windows. This page contains all the variable values for each product within arrays, and it displays the correct values based on the product number that is passed to it from `specs.htm` as the name of the current window.

Listing 20.4. The `specification.htm` code.

```
<HTML>
<HEAD>
<TITLE>Specifications</TITLE>
<SCRIPT LANGUAGE="vbscript">
Dim WinName
Dim ProdNames(3)
ProdNames(0)="The Daemon"
ProdNames(1)="Super Rex"
ProdNames(2)="GX Mega"
ProdNames(3)="XL Regular"
Dim Specs(3)
Specs(0)="Width"
Specs(1)="Height"
Specs(2)="Depth"
Specs(3)="Weight"
Dim Spec(3, 3)
Spec(0,0)=1.5
Spec(0,1)=2.63
Spec(0,2)=17.5
Spec(0,3)=6.9
Spec(1,0)=11.5
Spec(1,1)=1.55
Spec(1,2)=9.36
Spec(1,3)=2.89
Spec(2,0)=12.89
Spec(2,1)=3.98
Spec(2,2)=1.8
Spec(2,3)=13.78
Spec(3,0)=10.5
Spec(3,1)=1.52
Spec(3,2)=16.5
Spec(3,3)=11.5
Dim Units(3)
Units(0)="metres"
Units(1)="metres"
Units(2)="metres"
Units(3)="kg"
WinName = Window.Name
```

continues

Listing 20.4. continued

```
Sub Closeme_OnClick
 Window.Close
End Sub
</SCRIPT>
</HEAD>
<BODY BGCOLOR="yellow">
<FONT FACE="arial">
<CENTER><H3>Specifications for
<SCRIPT LANGUAGE="vbscript">
 Document.Write ProdNames(WinName)
</SCRIPT>
</H3><B>
<TABLE BORDER=1>
<SCRIPT LANGUAGE="vbscript">
 For i = 0 to 3
 Document.Write "<TR><TD>"
 Document.Write Specs(i) & "</TD><TD ALIGN=RIGHT><B>"
 Document.Write Spec(WinName,i) & "</TD><TD>"
 Document.Write Units(i) & "</TD></TR>"
 Next
</SCRIPT>
</TABLE>
<P>
<INPUT TYPE="button" NAME="closeme" VALUE="Close">
</BODY>
</HTML>
```

V

Toward the Seamless Desktop and ActiveX Web

by Rogers Cadenhead & Paul Lomax

TWENTY-ONE

Advanced ActiveX Techniques

The development of ActiveX, Java, and other Internet programming solutions has brought into vogue the idea of software components. Instead of designing computer software as a large, self-contained tool that performs a wide range of tasks, software is broken into smaller modules called components. These components are created to accomplish a specific task, and they are designed to be generic enough to work with a wide range of software. The goal of component-based programming is to make software design simpler, cheaper, faster, and more reusable.

Components make the job of software development more manageable, under the premise that it would be easier to build a fence from a stack of wooden slats, nails, and posts than it would be if someone handed you an ax and pointed to a nearby forest.

ActiveX is the latest and greatest incarnation of the Component Object Model, a standard for software development that Microsoft has developed in the past five years. In this chapter, you'll learn about the Component Object Model and some other advanced topics in regard to ActiveX and VBScript.

In this chapter, you

- ❑ Learn about the Component Object Model
- ❑ Discover how ActiveX was developed
- ❑ Learn about Cabinet (`.cab`) files
- ❑ Find out how to get started with ActiveX control programming
- ❑ Learn how to use VB4 custom controls in place of ActiveX controls

Tasks in this chapter:

- ❑ Downloading the CABARC tool
- ❑ Acquiring and installing the ActiveX SDK
- ❑ Adding a Grid OCX control to a Web page

An Overview of COM Theory

ActiveX is built on the Component Object Model, often abbreviated as COM. Because ActiveX is a refinement of the existing COM standard, thousands of programmers familiar with COM can learn ActiveX much more easily.

COM establishes a standard, structured way for programs on the same desktop to share software components. A component can be set up to perform a task, and any other software that wants to use the component can do so by using methods described in the COM. ActiveX extends this system by making it possible to share components across the Internet.

Software that Doesn't Use COM

Software components—also called *objects*—present a different way to organize a computer program. Most software that is developed without components puts all of its functionality into a single, self-contained program or set of programs. Figure 21.1 shows NerdStar, a fictional example of a word processing program developed without using components.

Figure 21.1.

A program with four self-contained functions and no parts using COM.

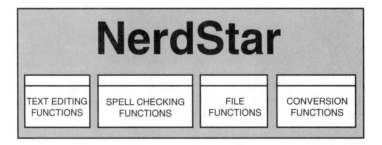

NerdStar is a self-contained program that does all of its own work. It has functions to handle text editing, spell checking, file handling, and document conversion. If NerdStar needs to accomplish one of these tasks, it calls upon its own functions.

One of the biggest reasons to develop a program this way is because everything is fully compatible. Every part of NerdStar works with every other part (or at least it should!), because each part was designed in conjunction with the rest.

Most software that has been developed in the past 20 years is like NerdStar in its approach, containing the functions that it needs inside a single program or set of programs.

This approach has been highly successful for many years, but it can prove costly when software needs to be improved, modified, or used to create other software.

Making Use of COM

After many years of success with NerdStar, the developers invent a new spell-checking program, called Spellvis, that is faster and more comprehensive than the leading brand. The decision is made to replace NerdStar's spell-checking routine by putting Spellvis inside a new version of NerdStar. This is not necessarily an easy task.

The difficulty arises because NerdStar's original spell-checking function is thoroughly entwined with the other parts of NerdStar. In a program that is composed of thousands of lines of code, it will be difficult and time-consuming to find all the lines that will be affected if the original spell-checking function is removed. The rest of NerdStar also must be changed in order to work with the Spellvis code inside it, because Spellvis might not operate in a similar manner to the original spell checker.

In order to make NerdStar easier to maintain, expand, and use with other software, it is rewritten using the Component Object Model. The newly christened NerdStar 95 breaks its text editing, file handling, and document conversion functions into their own components, and it also adds Spellvis as its own component. Figure 21.2 shows NerdStar 95, the new version of the word processing program designed with the Component Object Model. All of its functions have been developed as components (shown here as plugs), and the main NerdStar 95 program is a series of sockets. Each component has the job of accomplishing a specific task or set of tasks. The main job of the central NerdStar 95 program is to enable the components to communicate with each other.

Figure 21.2.

A program with all of its components using COM.

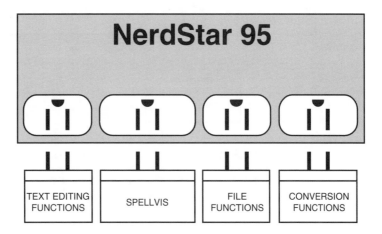

Using Figure 21.2 as a reference, the Component Object Model is the standard that defines what a plug is, what a socket is, and how the two connect to each other. When a component follows the standard and a program follows the standard, they can be used together.

COM is a comprehensive specification, but it does not add any overhead to software. There is no COM interpreter or any kind of controlling routine that must be used between the component and the program.

The Benefits of COM

Developing software using COM is a significant undertaking, but NerdStar 95's programmers have an immediate benefit in regard to Spellvis. The company also has introduced Pagerrific, a Web page editor that can be used to create, modify, and view HTML documents.

Pagerrific has its own special text editing, file handling, and document conversion functions, but the company wants to add Spellvis to this new program. Using the COM model, the same Spellvis component used with NerdStar 95 can be plugged into Pagerrific.

Figure 21.3 shows Pagerrific, a program that uses COM for Spellvis and has self-contained functions for the rest of its tasks.

Figure 21.3.
A program with three self-contained functions and a Spellvis component using COM.

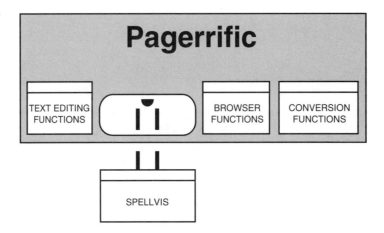

Because they use COM, the NerdStar 95 developers will benefit from the following:

❏ Each of NerdStar 95's components can be used in other software, perhaps even being marketed to other software developers who want to add NerdStar 95 functions to their own products.

❏ Adding new components to NerdStar 95 can be done more easily, because the relationship between existing components is well-defined.

❏ Replacing components with better upgrades is easier: If a new Spellvis is created that is compatible with the old Spellvis, adding it to NerdStar 95 is simply a matter of swapping components.

❏ Maintenance of NerdStar 95 requires less work, because bugs are easier to isolate in the specific component where the problems occur.

These benefits have been discussed in relation to COM, because it is the underlying structure of ActiveX, as you will see in the following section. However, other solutions have been offered for the development of component software. Many of these are focused on the programming language, unlike the Component Object Model, which focuses on the executable programs and can be achieved with many languages. As an example of a component system that differs from COM, object-oriented programming languages such as Java can be used to divide software into self-contained components that can be plugged into other programs as needed.

ActiveX's Connection to COM

Although software components and object-oriented programming have reached a new peak in popularity, ActiveX is the product of years of development at Microsoft. In some ways, it can be considered the fourth step in Microsoft's shift toward component software development.

The four steps Microsoft took toward ActiveX are as follows:

1. First came Dynamic Data Exchange (DDE), which was the original protocol for messages to be sent between Windows programs.

2. Then came Object Linking and Embedding (OLE), a development of DDE, which provided a way to create visual links between programs inside an application.

3. OLE was followed by the Component Object Model, which has become an almost universal industry standard for the use and design of OLE applications.

4. Finally, Microsoft arrived at ActiveX, a modified form of COM that was developed for use in Internet-related software.

COM software components are usable across different languages; a component written with one language can be used in software written with another language. ActiveX components, also called *controls*, can be used by programmers writing with Microsoft Visual Basic, Micro Focus Visual Object COBOL, PowerBuilder, and other popular development tools. COM has been used as the underlying foundation in applications to offer 3D graphics, transaction processing, and compound documents. This last area is one that you might have encountered with word processing software, as shown in the previous NerdStar example.

One of the areas in which components have been used to great advantage is in office suite software, which offers a word processor, spreadsheet, and other software as a unified set—or *suite*—of programs. For instance, COM can be used to put a functional spreadsheet inside a text document. The only new programming required in the word processing software would be to plug in the spreadsheet's component.

ActiveX as an Open Standard

The COM standard was pioneered by Microsoft, and its progress has largely been at the initiative of the company. However, Microsoft announced recently that it was releasing management of COM, the related Distributed Component Object Model, and ActiveX to an international standards body—the ActiveX Working Group.

The standards group—which consists of Microsoft customers, software vendors, and hardware producers—will be in charge of standardizing these tools and fostering future development. You can find out more about the group at the following Web site:

```
http://www.activex.org/
```

The move was made to provide evidence of Microsoft's support for open Internet standards. It could give ActiveX the same kind of push that Java received when Sun Microsystems made the source code of the language publicly available. COM is an open standard, documented from top to bottom for the use of software vendors and other interested parties.

The Component Object Model specification includes a set of standard Application Programming Interfaces (APIs) and network protocols. Software components must follow a standard in binary form, but they can be created with programming languages that can use these APIs to produce components in that binary form.

One advantage of a system such as COM is that it encourages the development of objects that can be used by other programmers. If an application developer needs a special graphics conversion function and a software component is available that can accomplish the task, the developer can plug in the component and avoid the hours required to write new code.

The author of the graphics conversion utility can make the component available easily in binary form, which removes the significant difficulty of making source code available to developers. The focus would be in the right place—developing and enhancing the graphics conversion component—instead of protecting the code from being stolen or used incorrectly.

As shown in ActiveX's use of the OBJECT tag, version control is also possible so that new components are only installed if needed. The following is an example of a CODE attribute in an OBJECT tag:

```
CODE=http://www.ibfake.com/Spellvis.ocx#Version=3
```

When an ActiveX-enabled browser encounters an attribute with a version declared in the HTML code, its component download mechanism only retrieves and installs the component if its version is newer than versions the user already has. If no version is included in the CODE attribute, the presence of any version of the component stops it from being downloaded again.

A new wrinkle on the Component Object Model and ActiveX system is the Distributed Component Object Model. This was introduced by Microsoft as a way for software components to communicate with other components across both the Internet and intranets. Described as "COM with a longer wire" by Microsoft, DCOM is an extension of COM for use on a broader scale of multi-user applications. During an early stage of development, DCOM was called Network OLE.

As an ActiveX technology, DCOM provides native support for Internet protocols such as TCP/IP and HTTP, and for the Java language. Because DCOM is language-neutral, Java applets can use DCOM to communicate with each other and with ActiveX controls.

Object-Oriented Design

Although COM has been described as an approach that is different from object-oriented programming (OOP), a component system such as COM embodies the same principles. An object, according to OOP terminology, is software that includes two things: functions that indicate how the object will behave, and data that is used to perform those functions. When you combine data and programming to do something with the data, an object contains everything it needs to perform a task. Because of this, when you use an object, you can focus on what it does, not how it does it.

This is called *encapsulation*. The users of an object don't need—and don't have access to—the internal structure of an object. They can focus on how the object behaves. Referring back to the NerdStar example, a programmer who wants to use the Spellvis component only needs to know how to make it spell check a document.

COM is a system of communication between an object—a *component*, in other words—and anything that wants to work with the object. Using COM, this communication is done using a request called an interface. A COM interface can be thought of as a contract between two pieces of software. By creating such a strong standard, COM and descendants such as ActiveX provide a method for software to operate together on a large scale.

Using Cab Files

A lot of Microsoft's Internet strategy involves adapting the company's existing solutions to the Internet. The contents of this book are full evidence of this: VBScript is based on the highly successful Visual Basic programming language, and ActiveX is a successor to OCX development. Cabinet files (also called Cab files) are another example of Microsoft adapting one of its tools for the Net.

Cabinet files are a way to archive Java applets or ActiveX controls into a single file. The Cabinet file archive is compressed into a single file, and it can be used to hold all programs, images, and other files that are used by an applet or ActiveX control.

Also, Cab files can be signed using the same code-signing system as ActiveX controls. This is true of Java files in addition to ActiveX controls, providing an extra level of security for Java programs on the World Wide Web.

The Cab file format is based on Lempel-Ziv compression, one of the popular compression systems, and Microsoft has made a set of command-line tools available for use with the Cabinet archival system. The set of tools is called CABARC, the Cabinet Archiver.

The following Web page, located in the Site Builder section of Microsoft's site, is the current address where Cab tools can be downloaded:

http://www.microsoft.com/workshop/java/cab-f.htm

Because Java applets often require the use of several class files, in addition to any image or data files that are required, the Cab system is especially useful with that language.

Using CABARC, a Java program can be assembled into a single Cabinet archive file with a .cab file extension.

This file would be placed on a Web site, and a new parameter is used with the <APPLET> tag to indicate the location of the archive.

The new parameter, cabbase, is shown in the following example of an <APPLET> tag:

```
<APPLET CODE="LearnToPolka.class" WIDTH=220 HEIGHT=500>
<PARAM NAME="cabbase" VALUE="learn2polka.cab">
</APPLET>
```

If the cabbase parameter is found in an <APPLET> tag and the Web browser supports Cabinet files, cabbase will be used when the applet is loaded. If the cabbase parameter is not present, the CODE attribute of the <APPLET> tag will be used to indicate the applet's main class file. At the time of this writing, only Microsoft Internet Explorer 3.0 supports Cabinet files. Using cabbase does not interfere with the use of Java applets on browsers that do not support this archival system. A browser such as Netscape Navigator 2.02 would ignore the cabbase parameter and use the CODE and CODEBASE attribute to find the main Java class file to load.

This .cab file contains one or more files that are all downloaded together as a single compressed file. This Cabinet file should only include files that must be downloaded, and should not include any supporting programs such as dynamic link libraries (DLLs). These DLLs might already be present on the user's system, so they would be redundant to download in a Cabinet archive.

The most recent version of the CABARC tool operates in a manner similar to archival utilities such as PKZIP, LHArc, and others. It also supports the use of an information file that controls how the .cab file will be installed. This file has the .inf file extension, and it is included in the Cabinet archive.

Developing ActiveX Controls

As stated previously, COM software components such as ActiveX controls can be developed with several different programming languages. The most common choice, if Web pages on the subject are any indication, is Microsoft Visual C++. Using Visual C++, COM software can be written using one of three development libraries: the ActiveX Template Library, Microsoft Foundation Class Library, or the BaseCtl framework. ActiveX controls can use a variety of programming languages from Microsoft for component design in addition to Visual C++—Visual Basic, Visual J++, and even Word or Excel's programming languages.

ActiveX control programming is beyond the scope of this book, but if you're interested in developing your own controls, this section provides the information you need to get started.

Developing new controls for ActiveX requires the use of the ActiveX Software Development Kit (SDK) from Microsoft. It can be downloaded from the following Web page:

http://www.microsoft.com/intdev/sdk/

Using the ActiveX SDK requires the following software:

- ❏ The final release of Microsoft Internet Explorer 3.0
- ❏ A compiler that is compatible with the ActiveX SDK, which includes Visual C++ 4.1 or Visual C++ 4.2 with a patch that is being made available from Microsoft
- ❏ Windows 95 or the final version of Windows NT 4.0
- ❏ The Win32 SDK for Windows NT 4.0

After downloading the ActiveX SDK, you end up with a single executable file, `activex.exe`, that will unpack itself. Instead of clicking the mouse to run this file, you need to use a command-line prompt or Run command from the Start menu to add an argument.

After you have moved the `activex.exe` to the root file directory in which you want it to be stored, you can unpack the file by entering the following:

```
activex.exe -d
```

You can then install the SDK by running the `SETUPSDK.EXE` program. Documentation for the development kit can be found in HTML form in the following subdirectory: `\INetSDK\Help\Default.htm`.

Adding a Grid OCX Control to a Web Page

The following example demonstrates the fact that ActiveX technology has been with us for some time. You will take a Grid OCX file, which you can find on the CD-ROM, and add it into a Layout control, just like any other ActiveX control. The Grid control is normally used as a custom control in Visual Basic 4. Figure 21.4 shows the control you will use in the VB4 environment. If you have your own copy of VB4, you can use the `grid32.ocx` file from your `windows/system` directory.

Figure 21.4.

The `grid32.ocx` *control in the VB4 development environment.*

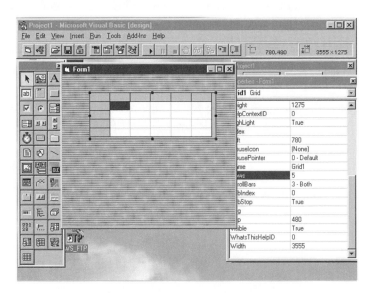

Using VB4 custom controls is not really recommended if you are building a Web page for public consumption. However, you might find that when building intranet applications in which you are trying to mirror the functionality of a current VB application, you could be forced into using specialized OCX files.

For a start, OCX files are somewhat "fatter" than their ActiveX brethren, increasing download time across the Web. OCX files do not have the Authentication and Security certification that ActiveX files have, and as you will see later in this example, this can cause alarm among users faced with what can appear to be a potential virus warning! Finally, although you will see how to include a `CodeBase` variable for the control, OCX files are best used from the local drive—in this case, from `windows/system`. If you are building an intranet application, it is very likely that the users of the application will already have the controls you include loaded onto their machine to enable the windows-based version of the application to operate.

So, now you are ready to start creating an application using a VB4 custom control.

1. The first thing to do is open the ActiveX Control Pad, and select New HTML Layout from the File menu.

2. To add the control to your toolbox, select the second page of the toolbox and right-click anywhere on the page.

3. Select Additional Controls from the pop-up menu. The additional controls dialog is now displayed. (See Figure 21.5.)

4. Scroll down the list until you reach Grid Control, check the box to the left of the name (as shown in Figure 21.5), and click OK to load the control into your toolbox.

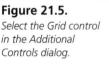

Figure 21.5.

Select the Grid control in the Additional Controls dialog.

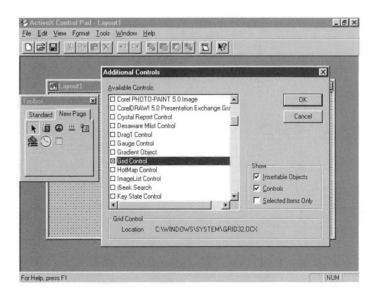

5. Add the Grid control to the layout by selecting it from the toolbox and then clicking on the layout and dragging it to the required size.

6. You need to change only a few properties for this example. First, change the `BackColor` property to `white`.

7. Now change the `Rows` property value to `6`.

8. Change the `Cols` property value to `6`.

9. Optionally, you can set the `CodeBase` property to be that of the Web location of the `.ocx` file, as in the following example:

   ```
   http://www.mydomain.com/subdir/grid32.ocx
   ```

   In any case, during testing it's best to leave this blank so that your local copy is used. This gives you the added advantage of not needing to be online to test and debug the application. Your Layout should now look like the one in Figure 21.6.

Figure 21.6.
The Grid control added to your Layout.

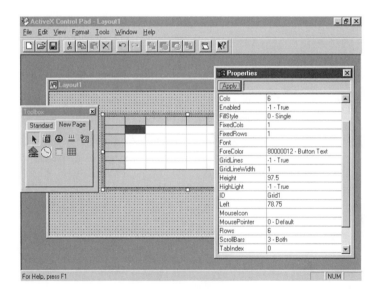

10. Save the layout as `grid.alx`.

11. The next thing you need to do is declare several global constants and arrays. You might remember from previous chapters that the Script Wizard enables you to add Global Variables. So launch the Script Wizard.

12. Right-click anywhere in the right Actions pane.

13. Select New Global Variable from the pop-up menu.

14. Enter `ColHeads(5)` in the New Global Variable dialog box. This declares a Global Single Dimension array.

15. Repeat steps 12 and 13 to add another single-dimension array to store the Row Titles.

```
RowTitles(5)
```

16. Now declare the following multidimension array in the same way:

```
DataVals(5,5)
```

17. Declare the following Global Constants, like this:

```
OFF_RENT
HEAT_LIGHT
SALARIES
VEHICLES
JAN
FEB
MAR
APR
MAY
```

This example simply displays a predefined data set in the array. The arrays you just declared are used to hold the column headers, row titles, and cell data. The arrays are populated and the data is added to the Grid control via the Grid control's `OnLoad` event.

18. In the left events pane, select `Layout1` and then its `OnLoad` event.

19. Enter the following code in the event handler:

```
ColHeads(JAN)="January"
ColHeads(FEB)="February"
ColHeads(MAR)="March"
ColHeads(APR)="April"
ColHeads(MAY)="May"
RowTitles(OFF_RENT)="Office Rent"
RowTitles(HEAT_LIGHT)="Heat & Light"
RowTitles(SALARIES)="Salaries"
RowTitles(VEHICLES)="Vehicles"
RowTitles(5)="TOTAL"
DataVals(JAN,OFF_RENT) = 1000
DataVals(JAN,HEAT_LIGHT) = 70
DataVals(JAN,SALARIES) = 10000
DataVals(JAN,VEHICLES) = 500
DataVals(FEB,OFF_RENT) = 1000
DataVals(FEB,HEAT_LIGHT) = 80
DataVals(FEB,SALARIES) = 11100
DataVals(FEB,VEHICLES) = 500
DataVals(MAR,OFF_RENT) = 1000
DataVals(MAR,HEAT_LIGHT) = 80
DataVals(MAR,SALARIES) = 12000
DataVals(MAR,VEHICLES) = 600
DataVals(APR,OFF_RENT) = 1000
DataVals(APR,HEAT_LIGHT) = 70
DataVals(APR,SALARIES) = 12000
DataVals(APR,VEHICLES) = 600
DataVals(MAY,OFF_RENT) = 1000
DataVals(MAY,HEAT_LIGHT) = 60
DataVals(MAY,SALARIES) = 14000
DataVals(MAY,VEHICLES) = 600
```

```
OFF_RENT = 1
HEAT_LIGHT = 2
SALARIES = 3
VEHICLES = 4
JAN = 1
FEB = 2
MAR = 3
APR = 4
MAY = 5
 Grid1.ColWidth(0) = 1000
 Grid1.Row = 0
 For x = 1 To 5
    Grid1.ColWidth(x) = 700
    Grid1.Col = x
    Grid1.Text = ColHeads(x)
 Next

 Grid1.Col = 0
 For y = 1 To 5
    Grid1.Row = y
    Grid1.Text = RowTitles(y)
 Next

 For x = 1 To 5
 totval = 0
    Grid1.Col = x
    For y = 1 To 4
       Grid1.Row = y
          Grid1.Text = DataVals(x,y)
          totVal = totval + DataVals(x,y)
    Next
    Grid1.Row = 5
    Grid1.Text = totVal
 Next
```

Your event handler should now look like the one in Figure 21.7.

Figure 21.7.

The `Layout1_OnLoad` *event handler in the Script Wizard.*

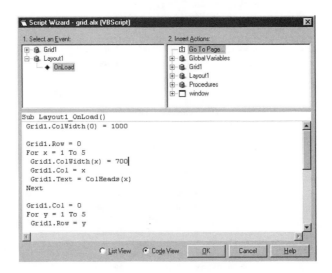

20. Click OK and the Script Wizard generates the appropriate VBScript code.

21. Save the .alx file. Your next step is to create the HTML file that will control the Layout you just built.

22. Open a new HTML template by selecting New HTML from the File menu.

23. Add a bgcolor="white" element to the <BODY> tag.

24. Add a <CENTER> tag under the <BODY> tag.

25. With your cursor directly under the <CENTER> tag, select Insert HTML Layout from the Edit menu.

26. Select grid.alx from the dialog and press OK. The HTML declarations for the Layout are now automatically added to the HTML file, as shown in Figure 21.8.

Figure 21.8.

The Layout control added to the HTML file.

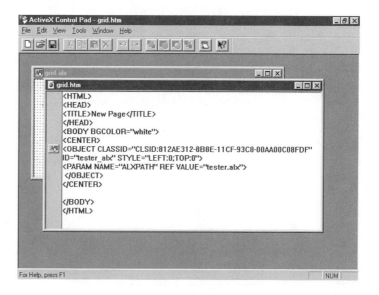

27. Save the HTML file as grid.htm.

As I mentioned earlier, standard .ocx files do not have the code authentication certificate that is present in true ActiveX controls. This can lead to the browser automatically refusing the control on security grounds. However, there is a way to configure your browser to allow certain controls to be downloaded and used at your discretion.

28. Open MSIE3.0 and select View|Options.

29. Click the Security tag (shown in Figure 21.9).

Figure 21.9.
The MSIE3.0 security options.

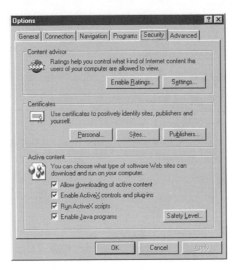

30. Click the Safety Level button in the Active Content section. This displays the range of ActiveX safety options available to you.

31. Check the middle (Medium Security) option, as shown in Figure 21.10.

Figure 21.10.
The MSIE ActiveX options.

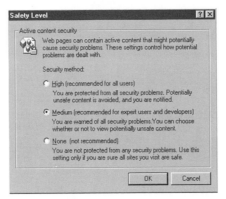

32. Click OK, and click OK again, so that you can run the file. As the file is loading, the warning message shown in Figure 21.11 is displayed. Click OK.

The final result of all the steps is shown in Figure 21.12.

Figure 21.11.
The security warning dialog.

Figure 21.12.

The VB4 Grid OCX control Web page.

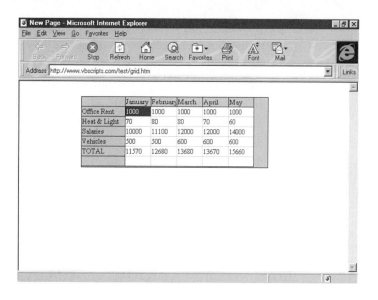

Workshop Wrap-Up

ActiveX controls allow the creation of Web applications that mirror the functionality of Windows applications, with the added advantages of ease of distribution and, eventually, cross-platform usability.

Information Technology departments around the world are already gearing up to face the challenge of converting desktop windows applications into Web applications to be operated via the company's intranet infrastructure.

With the next version of MSIE just around the corner, in which the desktop and Web (whether via an intranet or Internet) become a seamless single platform, it is important that you understand how your Windows applications can be transformed into Web applications.

In this chapter, you have learned the basics of COM and ActiveX, and you've also seen how easy it is to treat OCX custom controls as though they are ActiveX controls—even if this is a stopgap measure until the control you require is made available as a fully Internet-aware ActiveX control.

Next Steps

Unless you feel the need to lie down in a darkened room for awhile, you can read the following chapters and find out how to put your newfound knowledge to good use:

❑ To discover the fundamentals of ActiveX, see Chapter 1, "Getting to Grips with ActiveX."

❑ To learn about how ActiveX controls are used in conjunction with VBScript, see Chapter 12, "Using VBScript with ActiveX Controls."

❑ To learn more about using the ActiveX Control Pad with forms, see Chapter 13, "Implementing an ActiveX Menu Control."

❑ To learn how to use Java applets with VBScript, see Chapter 15, "Using Java Applets with VBScript."

❑ To learn more about converting Visual Basic applications for use on the Web, see Chapter 22, "Converting a Visual Basic Application for the Web."

❑ To learn more about intranet-type business applications, see Chapter 23, "Real-Life Examples IV."

Q&A

Q: I'm not sure what you mean by the statement that software components must follow a standard in binary form. What does this Component Object Model requirement mean by binary compatibility?

A: This means that the executable file (or files) associated with the component must fully support the COM standard. ActiveX controls, and other COM software, can be created with a number of different languages, so the source code of a COM object will vary widely from the source code of another COM object. However, the end result of those two COM objects will be highly similar, because the executable form of these components must follow the COM standard completely. This executable form is also called the binary form of a program, so ActiveX and COM feature binary compatibility.

Q: Does ActiveX replace the Component Object Model?

A: ActiveX is a streamlined form of the COM standard intended for Internet and intranet use. It has several revisions from COM to make it more suitable for Internet programming, such as reduced file size to speed up remote downloading. It does not, however, fully supplant the COM as a component development solution.

Q: Where can I find ActiveX controls to begin working with and learning from?

A: Microsoft maintains a gallery of sample controls, and there is also a CINet Web site that features ActiveX news and a directory of controls. The Web addresses of these two sites are as follows:

```
http://www.microsoft.com/activex/gallery/
http://www.activex.com
```

TWENTY-TWO

Converting a Visual Basic Application for the Web

There are literally millions of applications in use throughout the world that have been written in Visual Basic, and many of these would make excellent Web applications, either for public use on the Internet/WWW or for internal corporate use on an intranet. When linked with the Microsoft Internet Information Server (IIS) and Web-enabled database systems, these become formidable applications. IIS and its use with Web applications is unfortunately beyond the scope of this book, but in this chapter you will see how to convert the "front-end" VB4 application to run on the Web.

Soon it will be common practice in IT departments across the world to create the majority of applications and business solutions for a Web-type environment. The fact that almost every major software house is revamping its product range to be "Internet-aware" is testament to this.

In this chapter, you

❑ See the steps involved in converting a Visual Basic application

❑ Learn which Visual Basic controls can and can't be replaced

❑ Discover which Visual Basic language elements Microsoft left out of VBScript

❑ Learn how to translate a front-end Visual Basic application for use on the Web

Tasks in this chapter:

❑ Translating a Visual Basic Application for the Web

Much of the translation work involved in transferring a desktop VB application to operate on the Web is actually in the mindset of the programmer. Instead of trying to faithfully reproduce the original application, you can let your creative mind wander a little. You have a new and exciting environment in which to fashion your applications. At each stage, think how you can best use the new features and functionality afforded to you by the Web page. In very much the same way that successful Web designers have realized that, rather than trying to replicate traditional media in a Web page, they should treat the Web as its own medium with its own unique set of opportunities and limitations, you too have the chance to improve on the once desktop-bound user interfaces and functionality of legacy applications.

So if you are faced with translating the company's VB application, where do you start? There are several issues that can be treated separately:

- ❑ Forms
- ❑ Controls
- ❑ Event handlers, procedures, and functions
- ❑ The "back end"

Replacing VB Forms

The form will be replaced by either an HTML Web page or preferably an ActiveX Layout. The design and functionality of an ActiveX Layout is very similar to that of a VB form, allowing easy and accurate placement of controls.

For more information on the HTML Layout Control, see Chapter 14, "Using the HTML Layout Control."

Almost any Visual Basic form can be faithfully reproduced as a Web page using the HTML Layout Control, and you have the additional functionality that a Web page can offer, such as hyperlinking and easy multimedia extensions.

Replacing VB Controls

The vast majority of standard controls such as text boxes, combo boxes, and labels can quickly and easily be replaced with an equivalent ActiveX control. Some of the more exotic controls might be available as ActiveX controls, and many more are currently being produced. Table 22.1 gives you a guide to what can and can't be replaced, and the following explanations are used in the second column of the table:

Part of MSIE 3.0: An equivalent ActiveX control should be available to users who have installed the full version of MSIE 3.0. However, some properties, methods, and events might differ slightly from the VB4 equivalent. Many of these controls are part of the Windows 95 install.

Not available: An equivalent ActiveX control is not available at the time of this writing. However, you should check the ActiveX Gallery regularly. It might be possible to use the VB4 OCX control. (See Chapter 21, "Advanced ActiveX Techniques.")

Cannot be used: For reasons of security, it is not possible to use this control in a Web page. This includes controls that deal with file I/O and disk house-keeping.

Table 22.1. Replacing Visual Basic controls.

Visual Basic Control	ActiveX Equivalent
Picture Box	see Image Control
Label	Part of MSIE 3.0
Text Box	Part of MSIE 3.0
Frame	Not available
Command Button	Part of MSIE 3.0
Check Box	Part of MSIE 3.0
Option/Radio Button	Part of MSIE 3.0
Combo Box	Part of MSIE 3.0
List Box	Part of MSIE 3.0
Horizontal Scrollbar	Part of MSIE 3.0
Vertical Scrollbar	Part of MSIE 3.0
Timer	Download from ActiveX Gallery
File List Box	Cannot be used
Directory List Box	Cannot be used
Drive List Box	Cannot be used
Shape	Not available
Line	Not available
Image	Part of MSIE 3.0
Data Control	Cannot be used
OLE	Cannot be used
Common Dialog	Not available
Tab Strip	Part of MSIE 3.0
Rich Text Box	Cannot be used
Toolbar	Not available

continues

Table 22.1. continued

Visual Basic Control	ActiveX Equivalent
Status Bar	Not available
Progress Bar	Not available
Tree View	Not available
Image List	Not available
List View	Not available
Slider	Not available
Grid	Not available
Graph	Not available

Replacing Event Handlers, Procedures, and Functions

Several conversion utilities have started to appear on the market to turn VB applications into Web/VBScript applications, and the resultant files can save you an awful lot of manual recoding. However, they are not a 100-percent translation, and some only convert the form controls into HTML Intrinsic Controls—all of which means that, at some point, you need to roll up your sleeves and do some manual translation work.

There's a very simple rule when it comes to translating a VB program to VBScript. If it deals directly with the computer in terms of disk or file I/O, printer, or monitor, you can't do it. A few other VB functions have been left out of VBScript to save space—for example, `Format` is missing. But, in general, the basic programming functionality has been left intact. Table 22.2 gives you a list of all the language and runtime features that are not available in VBScript at the time of this writing.

Table 22.2. VBA language features not supported in VBScript.

Category	Feature
Array Handling	`Array` function
	`Option Base`
	`Private, Public`
	Declaring arrays with lower bound <> `0`
Collection	`Add, Count, Item, Remove`
	Access to collections using ! character
Conditional Compilation	`#Const`
	`#If...Then...#Else`

Category	Feature
Constants/Literals	`Const`
	All intrinsic constants
	Type-declaration characters (such as `256&`)
Control Flow	`DoEvents`
	`For Each...Next`
	`GoSub...Return, GoTo`
	`On Error GoTo`
	`On...GoSub, On...GoTo`
	Line numbers, line labels
	`With...End With`
Conversion	`CCur, CVar, CVDate`
	`Format`
	`Str, Val`
Data Types	All intrinsic data types except `Variant`
	`Type...End Type`
Date/Time	`Date` statement, `Time` statement
	`Timer`
DDE	`LinkExecute, LinkPoke, LinkRequest, LinkSend`
Debugging	`Debug.Print`
	`End, Stop`
Declaration	`Declare` (for declaring DLLs)
	`Property Get, Property Let, Property Set`
	`Public, Private, Static`
	`ParamArray, Optional`
	`New`
Error Handling	`Erl`
	`Error`
	`On Error...Resume`
	`Resume, Resume Next`
File Input/Output	All
Financial	All financial functions

continues

Table 22.2. continued

Category	Feature
Object Manipulation	`CreateObject`
	`GetObject`
	`TypeOf`
Objects	`Clipboard, Collection`
Operators	`Like`
Options	`Def` *type*
	`Option Base`
	`Option Compare`
	`Option Private`
	`Module`
Strings	Fixed-length strings
	`LSet, RSet`
	`Mid` statement
	`StrConv`
Using Objects	`TypeName`
	Collection access using `!`

The Back End

The conversion of the application's back end is somewhat more complex because it depends on what software or system you are currently using to feed data to the application. The breadth of current back-end database systems to which Visual Basic can be linked makes it impossible to try to cover the subject in this book.

Translating a Visual Basic Application for the Web

The following application shows you how to convert a program written in Visual Basic to run as a Web application or Web page. The application is a very simple one that has been put together to demonstrate the differences and similarities between the two environments. First, you see the Visual Basic Windows 95 version, and then you create the HTML Layout Control version.

The application is for an imaginary auto insurance broker. To use the application, you select several criteria and then press the Quote Now button to receive a quotation.

The Visual Basic Application

First of all, take a look at the Visual Basic application. Figure 22.1 shows the application running within Windows 95. After you have entered the client's details, click the Quote Now button and the program calculates the insurance premium, as shown in Figure 22.2.

The Visual Basic application is made up of three files:

❑ `insure.frm`: The form source code and event handlers within the form

❑ `insure.bas`: The code module, which in this case contains the global variables for the application

❑ `insure.vbp`: The Visual Basic project file

Figure 22.1.
The application running in Windows 95.

Figure 22.2.
Click the button to calculate the quotation.

Figure 22.3.

The insure.vbp *file in the Visual Basic development environment.*

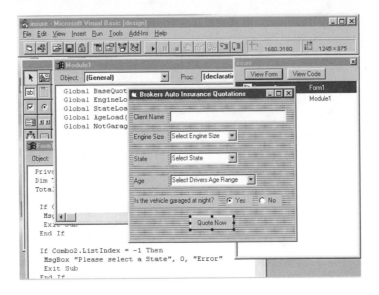

When the project is compiled, the runtime file insure.exe is created. Figure 22.3 shows what the project looks like in the Visual Basic 4 development environment. Listing 22.1 shows the source code for the form module (insure.frm), and Listing 22.2 shows the source code for the code module (insure.bas).

Listing 22.1. The insure.frm code.

```
VERSION 4.00
Begin VB.Form Form1
     Caption = "Brokers Auto Insurance Quotations"
     ClientHeight = 3840
     ClientLeft = 2865
     ClientTop = 1995
     ClientWidth = 4620
     Height = 4245
     Left = 2805
     LinkTopic = "Form1"
     ScaleHeight = 3840
     ScaleWidth = 4620
     Top = 1650
     Width = 4740
     Begin VB.ComboBox Combo3
             Height = 315
             Left = 1140
             TabIndex = 8
             Text = "Select Drivers Age Range"
             Top = 2040
             Width = 2415
     End
     Begin VB.ComboBox Combo2
             Height = 315
             Left = 1140
```

```
                  TabIndex = 7
                  Text = "Select State"
                  Top = 1440
                  Width = 1905
         End
         Begin VB.OptionButton NotIsGaraged
                  Caption = "No"
                  Height = 255
                  Left = 3600
                  TabIndex = 4
                  Top = 2640
                  Width = 645
         End
         Begin VB.OptionButton IsGaraged
                  Caption = "Yes"
                  Height = 255
                  Left = 2700
                  TabIndex = 3
                  Top = 2640
                  Value = -1       'True
                  Width = 735
         End
         Begin VB.ComboBox Combo1
                  Height = 315
                  Left = 1140
                  TabIndex = 2
                  Text = "Select Engine Size"
                  Top = 840
                  Width = 1905
         End
         Begin VB.CommandButton Command1
                  Caption = "Quote Now"
                  Height = 375
                  Left = 1680
                  TabIndex = 1
                  Top = 3180
                  Width = 1245
         End
         Begin VB.TextBox Text1
                  Height = 315
                  Left = 1140
                  TabIndex = 0
                  Top = 300
                  Width = 3255
         End
         Begin VB.Label Label5
                  Caption = "Is the vehicle garaged at night?"
                  Height = 255
                  Left = 120
                  TabIndex = 11
                  Top = 2640
                  Width  = 2355
```

continues

Listing 22.1. continued

```
        End
        Begin VB.Label Label4
                Caption = "Age"
                Height = 255
                Left = 120
                TabIndex =10
                Top = 2100
                Width = 945
        End
        Begin VB.Label Label2
                Caption = "Engine Size"
                Height = 255
                Left = 120
                TabIndex = 9
                Top = 900
                Width = 945
        End
        Begin VB.Label Label3
                Caption = "State"
                Height = 255
                Left = 120
                TabIndex = 6
                Top = 1500
                Width = 945
        End
        Begin VB.Label Label1
                Caption = "Client Name"
                Height = 255
                Left = 120
                TabIndex = 5
                Top = 360
                Width = 945
        End
End
Attribute VB_Name = "Form1"
Attribute VB_Creatable = False
Attribute VB_Exposed = False
Private Sub Command1_Click()
Dim TotalQuote As Double
TotalQuote = 0
 If Combo1.ListIndex = -1 Then
     MsgBox "Please select an Engine Size", 0, "Error"
     Exit Sub
 End If

 If Combo2.ListIndex = -1 Then
     MsgBox "Please select a State", 0, "Error"
     Exit Sub
 End If

 If Combo3.ListIndex = -1 Then
     MsgBox "Please select an Age Range", 0, "Error"
     Exit Sub
 End If

TotalQuote = BaseQuote
TotalQuote = TotalQuote + EngineLoad(Combo1.ListIndex)
TotalQuote = TotalQuote + StateLoad(Combo2.ListIndex)
```

```
TotalQuote = TotalQuote + AgeLoad(Combo3.ListIndex)
If NotIsGaraged.Value = True Then
 TotalQuote = TotalQuote + NotGaraged
End If
MsgBox "Thank-you Your Quote is $" & CStr(TotalQuote) & " per Annum",
➥ 0, "Quotation"

End Sub
Private Sub Form_Load()
 Combo1.AddItem "< 1000 c.c"
 Combo1.AddItem "1000 to 2499 c.c"
 Combo1.AddItem "2500 to 2999 c.c"
 Combo1.AddItem "3000 + c.c"

 Combo2.AddItem "AL"
 Combo2.AddItem "CA"
 Combo2.AddItem "IL"
 Combo2.AddItem "MI"
 Combo2.AddItem "NY"
 Combo2.AddItem "TX"

 Combo3.AddItem "Under 20"
 Combo3.AddItem "21 - 25 Years Old"
 Combo3.AddItem "26 - 35 Years Old"
 Combo3.AddItem "Over 36"

 BaseQuote = 110.5

 EngineLoad(0) = 20
 EngineLoad(1) = 30
 EngineLoad(2) = 40
 EngineLoad(3) = 50

 StateLoad(0) = 0
 StateLoad(1) = 10
 StateLoad(2) = 20
 StateLoad(3) = 0
 StateLoad(4) = 20
 StateLoad(5) = 10

 AgeLoad(0) = 50
 AgeLoad(1) = 40
 AgeLoad(2) = 30
 AgeLoad(3) = 20

 NotGaraged = 30


End Sub
```

Listing 22.2. The `insure.bas` code.

```
Attribute VB_Name = "Module1"
Global BaseQuote As Double
Global EngineLoad(4) As Double
Global StateLoad(5) As Double
Global AgeLoad(4) As Double
Global NotGaraged As Double
```

All three files that make up the `insure.vbp` Visual Basic project are on the CD-ROM, as is `insure.exe`. If you have Visual Basic 4 on your computer, you can open the project to take a closer look within the development environment.

The HTML Conversion

So now you know what it is you're trying to do: to convert a simple, stand-alone Visual Basic application to run as a Web page. The interface can remain almost the same as the original application. All the controls used in the Visual Basic application can be directly translated to the standard ActiveX controls available in the ActiveX Control Pad.

Because this is a Web page creation, you will make a couple of minor additions to the interface. First, you can add a colorful graphic of (what else?) a car. You also add two hyperlinks, which in the real world would be extremely useful in this application. The first link is to the policy conditions, and the next link is to the brokerage's payment terms. Obviously, because this is an exercise, neither of the two links go anywhere.

You will use the HTML Layout Control to create the form section of the application. The form layout will reside in the left side of an HTML page. The right side of the page will contain the graphic and the hyperlinks. A table will be used to divide the page. You can start by designing the form:

1. Open the ActiveX Control Pad.
2. Select New HTML Layout from the File menu.
3. Add the following ActiveX controls to the layout, using the Visual Basic form as a style guide.
    - ❑ One Text Box control
    - ❑ Three Combo Box controls
    - ❑ Two Option Button controls
    - ❑ Five Label controls (next to each of the above controls)
    - ❑ One CommandButton control
4. Now amend the Text property of ComboBox1 to read Select Engine Size.
5. Amend the Text property of ComboBox2 to read Select State.
6. Amend the Text property of ComboBox3 to read Select Age Range.
7. Amend Label1 properties.
    - ❑ BackColor = white
    - ❑ Caption = "Client Name"

8. Amend `Label2` properties.

   ❑ `BackColor = white`

   ❑ `Caption = "Engine Size"`

9. Amend `Label3` properties.

   ❑ `BackColor = white`

   ❑ `Caption = "State"`

10. Amend `Label4` properties.

    ❑ `BackColor = white`

    ❑ `Caption = "Age"`

11. Amend `Label5` properties.

    ❑ `BackColor = white`

    ❑ `Caption = "Is the vehicle garaged overnight?"`

12. Amend `OptionButton1` properties.

    ❑ `BackColor = white`

    ❑ `Caption = "Yes"`

13. Amend `OptionButton2` properties.

    ❑ `BackColor = white`

    ❑ `Caption = "No"`

14. Amend the layout properties.

    ❑ `Width = 250` (approx)

    ❑ `Height = 190` (approx)

    ❑ `BackColor = white`

15. Save as `insure.alx`, and your layout should look like the one shown in Figure 22.4.

16. Launch the Script Wizard.

17. Right-click anywhere in the right Actions pane.

18. Select Global Variable.

19. Type `BaseQuote`.

20. Click OK.

21. Repeat steps 18 through 20 to enter the following global variables:

    ❑ `EngineLoad(4)`

    ❑ `StateLoad(5)`

    ❑ `AgeLoad(4)`

    ❑ `NotGaraged`

Figure 22.4.

`insure.alx`.

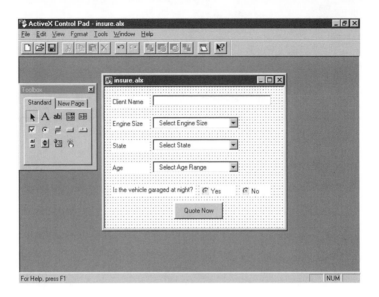

Now you are ready to add the code to populate the combo boxes and arrays as the layout loads:

1. Select Layout in the left events pane.

2. Select the `OnLoad` event.

3. Enter the following code in the event handler:

```
ComboBox1.AddItem "< 1000 c.c"
ComboBox1.AddItem "1000 to 2499 c.c"
ComboBox1.AddItem "2500 to 2999 c.c"
ComboBox1.AddItem "3000 + c.c"

ComboBox2.AddItem "AL"
ComboBox2.AddItem "CA"
ComboBox2.AddItem "IL"
ComboBox2.AddItem "MI"
ComboBox2.AddItem "NY"
ComboBox2.AddItem "TX"

ComboBox3.AddItem "Under 20"
ComboBox3.AddItem "21 - 25 Years Old"
ComboBox3.AddItem "26 - 35 Years Old"
ComboBox3.AddItem "Over 36"

BaseQuote = 110.5

EngineLoad(0) = 20
EngineLoad(1) = 30
EngineLoad(2) = 40
EngineLoad(3) = 50

StateLoad(0) = 0
StateLoad(1) = 10
StateLoad(2) = 20
```

```
StateLoad(3) = 0
StateLoad(4) = 20
StateLoad(5) = 10

AgeLoad(0) = 50
AgeLoad(1) = 40
AgeLoad(2) = 30
AgeLoad(3) = 20

NotGaraged = 30
```

Your event handler should now resemble the one in Figure 22.5.

Figure 22.5.

The OnLoad *event handler.*

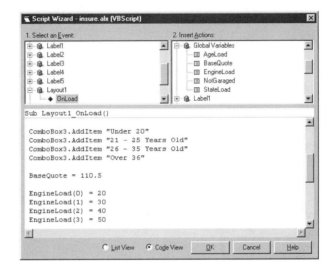

4. Select CommandButton1 in the left events pane.

5. Select the Click event.

6. Enter the following code in the event handler:

```
Dim TotalQuote
TotalQuote = 0
 If ComboBox1.ListIndex = -1 Then
     Alert "Please select an Engine Size"
     Exit Sub
 End If

 If ComboBox2.ListIndex = -1 Then
     Alert "Please select a State"
     Exit Sub
 End If

 If ComboBox3.ListIndex = -1 Then
     Alert "Please select an Age Range"
     Exit Sub
 End If

TotalQuote = BaseQuote
TotalQuote = TotalQuote + EngineLoad(ComboBox1.ListIndex)
```

```
TotalQuote = TotalQuote + StateLoad(ComboBox2.ListIndex)
TotalQuote = TotalQuote + AgeLoad(ComboBox3.ListIndex)
If OptionButton2.Value = True Then
 TotalQuote = TotalQuote + NotGaraged
End If
MsgBox "Thank-you Your Quote is $" & CStr(TotalQuote) & " per Annum", 0,
➥"Quotation"
```

First, the event handler checks each combo box in turn to ensure that the user has made a selection. If no selection has been made, `ListIndex` returns `-1`, in which case a warning message is displayed and the event handler terminates.

The quotation figure commences with the `BaseQuote`, and it adds the loadings for each of the criteria. Note that the list items and array elements correspond to each other, making it a simple job to relate the item chosen from the list to the value held in the array element. Your event handler should look like the one in Figure 22.6.

Figure 22.6.
The `CommandButton1_` `Click` *event.*

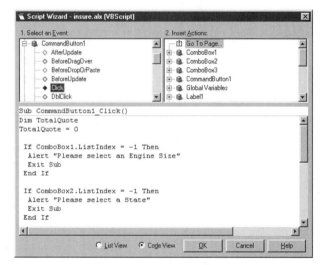

7. Click OK to generate the script.

8. Save the layout, which is now complete.

9. Now you need to create an HTML file to hold the layout. Select New HTML from the File menu.

10. Amend the HTML template to read as follows:

```
<HTML>
<HEAD>
<TITLE>Brokers Auto Insurance Quotation</TITLE>
</HEAD>
<BODY BGCOLOR="white">
<TABLE>
<TR><TD>
```

```
</TD>
<TD ALIGN="CENTER">
<FONT FACE="arial">
<H2>Brokers Auto <BR>Insurance Quotation</H2>
<P>
<IMG SRC="car.gif">
<P>
<A HREF="">View Policy Conditions</A><BR>
<A HREF="">View Payment Terms Guide</A>
</TD></TR>
</TABLE>
</BODY>
</HTML>
```

11. Place your cursor between the first <TD></TD> tags.

12. Select Insert HTML Layout from the Edit menu.

13. Select insure.alx.

14. Save the HTML file as insure.htm, which should look like the file shown in Figure 27.7.

Figure 27.7.

insure.htm.

Finally, run insure.htm through the browser to test. The functionality of the form is the same as for the Visual Basic application, with some added features, as you can see in Figure 22.8. As with the Visual Basic application, a simple message box is used to display the quotation when you press the button, as shown in Figure 22.9.

The complete listing for the source code in insure.alx is shown in Listing 22.3. Listing 22.4 shows the source code for insure.htm.

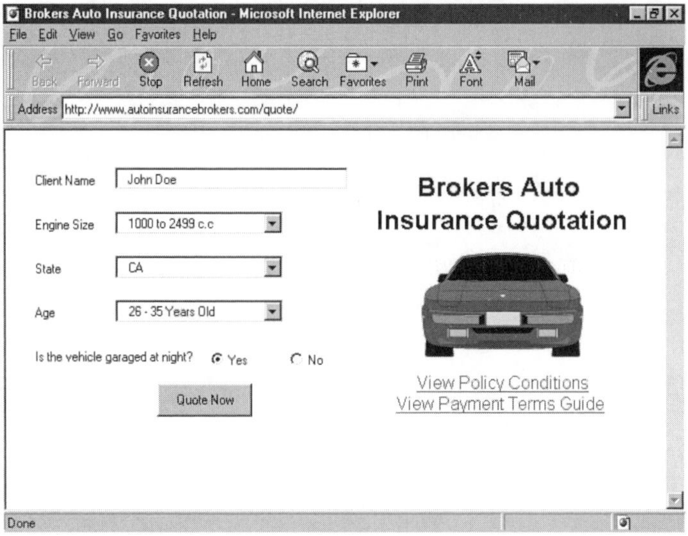

Figure 22.8.

The insure.htm *file in the browser.*

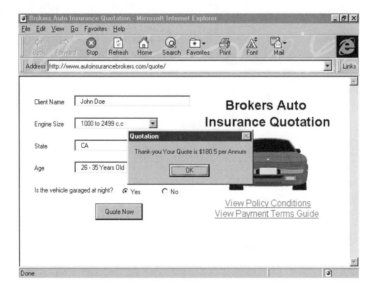

Figure 22.9.

Fill in the form and click the button to obtain a quote.

Listing 22.3. The insure.alx **code.**

```
<SCRIPT LANGUAGE="VBScript">
<!--
dim BaseQuote
dim EngineLoad(4)
dim StateLoad(5)
dim AgeLoad(4)
dim NotGaraged
-->
</SCRIPT>
<SCRIPT LANGUAGE="VBScript">
<!--
Sub CommandButton1_Click()
```

```
Dim TotalQuote
TotalQuote = 0
 If ComboBox1.ListIndex = -1 Then
     Alert "Please select an Engine Size"
     Exit Sub
 End If

 If ComboBox2.ListIndex = -1 Then
     Alert "Please select a State"
     Exit Sub
 End If

 If ComboBox3.ListIndex = -1 Then
     Alert "Please select an Age Range"
     Exit Sub
 End If

TotalQuote = BaseQuote
TotalQuote = TotalQuote + EngineLoad(ComboBox1.ListIndex)
TotalQuote = TotalQuote + StateLoad(ComboBox2.ListIndex)
TotalQuote = TotalQuote + AgeLoad(ComboBox3.ListIndex)
If OptionButton2.Value = True Then
 TotalQuote = TotalQuote + NotGaraged
End If
MsgBox "Thank-you Your Quote is $" & CStr(TotalQuote) & " per Annum",
➥ 0, "Quotation"

end sub
-->
</SCRIPT>
<SCRIPT LANGUAGE="VBScript">
<!--
Sub Layout1_OnLoad()
 ComboBox1.AddItem "< 1000 c.c"
 ComboBox1.AddItem "1000 to 2499 c.c"
 ComboBox1.AddItem "2500 to 2999 c.c"
 ComboBox1.AddItem "3000 + c.c"

 ComboBox2.AddItem "AL"
 ComboBox2.AddItem "CA"
 ComboBox2.AddItem "IL"
 ComboBox2.AddItem "MI"
 ComboBox2.AddItem "NY"
 ComboBox2.AddItem "TX"

 ComboBox3.AddItem "Under 20"
 ComboBox3.AddItem "21 - 25 Years Old"
 ComboBox3.AddItem "26 - 35 Years Old"
 ComboBox3.AddItem "Over 36"

 BaseQuote = 110.5

 EngineLoad(0) = 20
 EngineLoad(1) = 30
 EngineLoad(2) = 40
 EngineLoad(3) = 50

 StateLoad(0) = 0
 StateLoad(1) = 10
 StateLoad(2) = 20
```

continues

Listing 22.3. continued

```
StateLoad(3) = 0
StateLoad(4) = 20
StateLoad(5) = 10

AgeLoad(0) = 50
AgeLoad(1) = 40
AgeLoad(2) = 30
AgeLoad(3) = 20

NotGaraged = 30
end sub
-->
</SCRIPT>
<DIV BACKGROUND="#ffffff" ID="Layout1" STYLE="LAYOUT:FIXED;WIDTH:250pt;
➥HEIGHT:192pt;">
        <OBJECT ID="TextBox1"
         CLASSID="CLSID:8BD21D10-EC42-11CE-9E0D-00AA006002F3"
➥STYLE="TOP:11pt;LEFT:68pt;WIDTH:165pt;HEIGHT:15pt;TABINDEX:0;ZINDEX:0;">
                    <PARAM NAME="VariousPropertyBits" VALUE="746604571">
                    <PARAM NAME="Size" VALUE="5821;529">
                    <PARAM NAME="FontCharSet" VALUE="0">
                    <PARAM NAME="FontPitchAndFamily" VALUE="2">
                    <PARAM NAME="FontWeight" VALUE="0">
        </OBJECT>
        <OBJECT ID="ComboBox1"
         CLASSID="CLSID:8BD21D30-EC42-11CE-9E0D-00AA006002F3"
➥STYLE="TOP:41pt;LEFT:68pt;WIDTH:120pt;HEIGHT:16pt;TABINDEX:1;ZINDEX:1;">
                    <PARAM NAME="VariousPropertyBits" VALUE="746604571">
                    <PARAM NAME="DisplayStyle" VALUE="3">
                    <PARAM NAME="Size" VALUE="4234;556">
                    <PARAM NAME="MatchEntry" VALUE="1">
                    <PARAM NAME="ShowDropButtonWhen" VALUE="2">
                    <PARAM NAME="Value" VALUE="Select Engine Size">
                    <PARAM NAME="FontCharSet" VALUE="0">
                    <PARAM NAME="FontPitchAndFamily" VALUE="2">
                    <PARAM NAME="FontWeight" VALUE="0">
        </OBJECT>
        <OBJECT ID="ComboBox2"
         CLASSID="CLSID:8BD21D30-EC42-11CE-9E0D-00AA006002F3"
➥STYLE="TOP:71pt;LEFT:68pt;WIDTH:120pt;HEIGHT:16pt;TABINDEX:2;ZINDEX:2;">
                    <PARAM NAME="VariousPropertyBits" VALUE="746604571">
                    <PARAM NAME="DisplayStyle" VALUE="3">
                    <PARAM NAME="Size" VALUE="4234;556">
                    <PARAM NAME="MatchEntry" VALUE="1">
                    <PARAM NAME="ShowDropButtonWhen" VALUE="2">
                    <PARAM NAME="Value" VALUE="Select State">
                    <PARAM NAME="FontCharSet" VALUE="0">
                    <PARAM NAME="FontPitchAndFamily" VALUE="2">
                    <PARAM NAME="FontWeight" VALUE="0">
        </OBJECT>
        <OBJECT ID="ComboBox3"
         CLASSID="CLSID:8BD21D30-EC42-11CE-9E0D-00AA006002F3"
➥STYLE="TOP:101pt;LEFT:68pt;WIDTH:120pt;HEIGHT:16pt;TABINDEX:3;ZINDEX:3;">
                    <PARAM NAME="VariousPropertyBits" VALUE="746604571">
                    <PARAM NAME="DisplayStyle" VALUE="3">
                    <PARAM NAME="Size" VALUE="4234;556">
                    <PARAM NAME="MatchEntry" VALUE="1">
                    <PARAM NAME="ShowDropButtonWhen" VALUE="2">
```

```
                <PARAM NAME="Value" VALUE="Select Age Range">
                <PARAM NAME="FontCharSet" VALUE="0">
                <PARAM NAME="FontPitchAndFamily" VALUE="2">
                <PARAM NAME="FontWeight" VALUE="0">
        </OBJECT>
        <OBJECT ID="OptionButton1"
         CLASSID="CLSID:8BD21D50-EC42-11CE-9E0D-00AA006002F3"
➥STYLE="TOP:135pt;LEFT:135pt;WIDTH:49pt;HEIGHT:15pt;TABINDEX:4;ZINDEX:4;">
                <PARAM NAME="BackColor" VALUE="16777215">
                <PARAM NAME="ForeColor" VALUE="2147483666">
                <PARAM NAME="DisplayStyle" VALUE="5">
                <PARAM NAME="Size" VALUE="1720;529">
                <PARAM NAME="Caption" VALUE="Yes">
                <PARAM NAME="FontCharSet" VALUE="0">
                <PARAM NAME="FontPitchAndFamily" VALUE="2">
                <PARAM NAME="FontWeight" VALUE="0">
        </OBJECT>
        <OBJECT ID="OptionButton2"
         CLASSID="CLSID:8BD21D50-EC42-11CE-9E0D-00AA006002F3"
➥STYLE="TOP:135pt;LEFT:191pt;WIDTH:41pt;HEIGHT:15pt;TABINDEX:5;ZINDEX:5;">
                <PARAM NAME="BackColor" VALUE="16777215">
                <PARAM NAME="ForeColor" VALUE="2147483666">
                <PARAM NAME="DisplayStyle" VALUE="5">
                <PARAM NAME="Size" VALUE="1455;529">
                <PARAM NAME="Caption" VALUE="No">
                <PARAM NAME="FontCharSet" VALUE="0">
                <PARAM NAME="FontPitchAndFamily" VALUE="2">
                <PARAM NAME="FontWeight" VALUE="0">
        </OBJECT>
        <OBJECT ID="Label1"
         CLASSID="CLSID:978C9E23-D4B0-11CE-BF2D-00AA003F40D0"
➥STYLE="TOP:15pt;LEFT:11pt;WIDTH:53pt;HEIGHT:15pt;ZINDEX:6;">
                <PARAM NAME="BackColor" VALUE="16777215">
                <PARAM NAME="Caption" VALUE="Client Name">
                <PARAM NAME="Size" VALUE="1853;529">
                <PARAM NAME="FontCharSet" VALUE="0">
                <PARAM NAME="FontPitchAndFamily" VALUE="2">
                <PARAM NAME="FontWeight" VALUE="0">
        </OBJECT>
        <OBJECT ID="Label2"
         CLASSID="CLSID:978C9E23-D4B0-11CE-BF2D-00AA003F40D0"
➥STYLE="TOP:45pt;LEFT:11pt;WIDTH:53pt;HEIGHT:15pt;ZINDEX:7;">
                <PARAM NAME="BackColor" VALUE="16777215">
                <PARAM NAME="Caption" VALUE="Engine Size">
                <PARAM NAME="Size" VALUE="1853;529">
                <PARAM NAME="FontCharSet" VALUE="0">
                <PARAM NAME="FontPitchAndFamily" VALUE="2">
                <PARAM NAME="FontWeight" VALUE="0">
        </OBJECT>
        <OBJECT ID="Label3"
         CLASSID="CLSID:978C9E23-D4B0-11CE-BF2D-00AA003F40D0"
➥STYLE="TOP:75pt;LEFT:11pt;WIDTH:53pt;HEIGHT:15pt;ZINDEX:8;">
                <PARAM NAME="BackColor" VALUE="16777215">
                <PARAM NAME="Caption" VALUE="State">
                <PARAM NAME="Size" VALUE="1853;529">
                <PARAM NAME="FontCharSet" VALUE="0">
                <PARAM NAME="FontPitchAndFamily" VALUE="2">
                <PARAM NAME="FontWeight" VALUE="0">
        </OBJECT>
        <OBJECT ID="Label4"
```

continues

Listing 22.3. continued

```
                CLASSID="CLSID:978C9E23-D4B0-11CE-BF2D-00AA003F40D0"
➥STYLE="TOP:105pt;LEFT:11pt;WIDTH:53pt;HEIGHT:15pt;ZINDEX:9;">
                    <PARAM NAME="BackColor" VALUE="16777215">
                    <PARAM NAME="Caption" VALUE="Age">
                    <PARAM NAME="Size" VALUE="1853;529">
                    <PARAM NAME="FontCharSet" VALUE="0">
                    <PARAM NAME="FontPitchAndFamily" VALUE="2">
                    <PARAM NAME="FontWeight" VALUE="0">
        </OBJECT>
        <OBJECT ID="Label5"
            CLASSID="CLSID:978C9E23-D4B0-11CE-BF2D-00AA003F40D0"
➥STYLE="TOP:135pt;LEFT:11pt;WIDTH:116pt;HEIGHT:15pt;ZINDEX:10;">
                    <PARAM NAME="BackColor" VALUE="16777215">
                    <PARAM NAME="Caption" VALUE="Is the vehicle garaged
➥at night?">
                    <PARAM NAME="Size" VALUE="4101;529">
                    <PARAM NAME="FontCharSet" VALUE="0">
                    <PARAM NAME="FontPitchAndFamily" VALUE="2">
                    <PARAM NAME="FontWeight" VALUE="0">
        </OBJECT>
        <OBJECT ID="CommandButton1"
            CLASSID="CLSID:D7053240-CE69-11CD-A777-00DD01143C57"
➥STYLE="TOP:158pt;LEFT:98pt;WIDTH:68pt;HEIGHT:23pt;TABINDEX:11;ZINDEX:11;">
                    <PARAM NAME="Caption" VALUE="Quote Now">
                    <PARAM NAME="Size" VALUE="2381;794">
                    <PARAM NAME="FontCharSet" VALUE="0">
                    <PARAM NAME="FontPitchAndFamily" VALUE="2">
                    <PARAM NAME="ParagraphAlign" VALUE="3">
                    <PARAM NAME="FontWeight" VALUE="0">
        </OBJECT>
</DIV>
```

Listing 22.4. The `insure.htm` code.

```
<HTML>
<HEAD>
<TITLE>Brokers Auto Insurance Quotation</TITLE>
</HEAD>
<BODY BGCOLOR="white">
<TABLE>
<TR><TD>
<OBJECT CLASSID="CLSID:812AE312-8B8E-11CF-93C8-00AA00C08FDF"
ID="insure_alx" STYLE="LEFT:0;TOP:0">
<PARAM NAME="ALXPATH" REF VALUE="insure.alx">
 </OBJECT>
</TD>
<TD ALIGN="CENTER">
<FONT FACE="arial">
<H2>Brokers Auto <BR>Insurance Quotation</H2>
<P>
<IMG SRC="car.gif">
<P>
<A HREF="">View Policy Conditions</A><BR>
<A HREF="">View Payment Terms Guide</A>
</TD></TR>
</TABLE>
</BODY>
</HTML>
```

Workshop Wrap-Up

As you have seen, converting Visual Basic applications can be very straightforward. If you compare `insure.alx` with `insure.frm`, you will notice that apart from a few name changes, the coding is almost identical. The Web environment affords many advantages to application developers over the window environment, whether the application is destined for use as a corporate intranet or a publicly available Web page. Soon, the conversion of back-end data sources for Visual Basic applications will be as easy as creating the user interface, because Microsoft and other companies will continue the now unstoppable march toward the multiplatform seamless desktop and Web.

We should count ourselves lucky to be an integral part of the development of the next great information medium—a phase in social history that will prove to be just as important as the invention of the first printing press. I sincerely hope that, in the course of reading this book, your imagination has been stirred and your knowledge of client-side scripting increased sufficiently to allow you to venture further into creating new, dynamic, and interactive Web pages using VBScript. We are all part of the World Wide Web, and its continued success is dependent upon us developing and improving both the content and presentation of the information we have to share. Whether your motivation for using VBScript is to increase traffic to your site, to improve the functionality of your Web pages, or to move toward an intranet, I wish you luck and look forward to seeing the results on my travels around the Net.

Next Steps

Now you've seen how to transfer your VB applications to a Web environment using ActiveX controls and the HTML Layout Control. To learn more about these controls, see the following chapters:

- ❏ To learn more about the HTML Layout Control, see Chapter 14, "Using the HTML Layout Control."
- ❏ To see how to use Visual Basic OCX Custom Controls as ActiveX controls, see Chapter 21, "Advanced ActiveX Techniques."

Q&A

Q: How do I convert an application that needs to reference data stored on the user's hard drive?

A: You have to rethink how you are going to access that data, and whether the data must remain on the user's drive. You might find that it is actually more efficient to store the data on the server and access it as needed. If you are in a situation where user-specific information is held on the user's machine, you might again be faced with rethinking the database design.

For example, you can have the user log onto a page with a unique ID, which you then use to retrieve the user's specific data from a general users database on the server. There is no safe method at present—other than the limited text data stored within a cookie file—by which you can read and write data to a user's hard drive.

TWENTY-THREE

Real-Life Examples IV

This chapter describes a sample Web application created using VBScript. The example is

Example 1. XYZ Inc. Corporate Intranet

Example 1: XYZ Inc. Corporate Intranet

Document title: XYZ Corporate Intranet

Files:

Page files:

- ❑ `menudemo.htm`
- ❑ `menu.htm`
- ❑ `welcome.htm`
- ❑ `b.htm`

Images:

- ❑ `file.gif`
- ❑ `cust.gif`
- ❑ `prod.gif`
- ❑ `users.gif`

❏ external.gif

❏ help.gif

❏ leftend.gif

❏ rightend.gif

ActiveX controls used:

❏ IeMenu

❏ Label

❏ IeTimer

Description: This example shows how to implement an ActiveX menu control. To aid maintenance and to speed the addition of further menu items, the text for each menu item and the associated location for each menu item are held within arrays, which are transferred to the menu at runtime. The other method of populating a menu is to specify a menu item as a parameter, <PARAM MenuItem[1]... >, within the <OBJECT> tag. However, the maintenance of these menus can become somewhat confusing when there are a large number of menus and menu items.

The maintenance of the locations that are loaded when a menu item is clicked is also enhanced because the locations are held within arrays, which are specified at the beginning of the script.

The example also demonstrates how to implement a continuous clock within the menu bar, using an ActiveX label and an ActiveX timer control.

The menu bar is displayed within the upper frame of a borderless frameset. The lower frame is used to display the content pages for the Web site.

Techniques Applied

ActiveX controls: (See Chapters 1, 12, 13, and 14.) The example uses a range of ActiveX controls. The example also demonstrates changing properties at runtime—in this case, to populate the menus.

Arrays: (See Chapter 10, "Using the Power of Arrays.") The menu items and the locations, which are loaded when you click a menu item, are held within multidimensional static arrays.

Programming elements: (See Chapter 9, "Making Your Program Flow.") A range of VBScript language elements are used.

The example uses a frameset document (menudemo.htm), which creates an upper frame into which the menu document is loaded (menu.htm) and a lower frame that contains the main pages, as shown in Figure 23.1.

Figure 23.1.
The menu bar and opening page.

When the user clicks on a menu item, the particular menu pops up, as shown in Figures 23.2 and 23.3.

Figure 23.2.
The File menu.

Clicking on a menu item causes the page associated with that menu item to be loaded in the lower frame, as shown in Figure 23.4.

Figure 23.3.
The Customers menu.

Figure 23.4.
One of the Web pages loaded into the lower frame.

A timer control is used to display a clock at the end of the menu bar. At predetermined intervals, the timer event (shown in Figure 23.5) is fired, causing the clock display to be updated.

As the application is loading, the OnLoad event handler (shown in Figure 23.6) creates the menus from the data stored in the arrays.

Figure 23.5.

The script to operate the clock.

Figure 23.6.

The onLoad *event handler.*

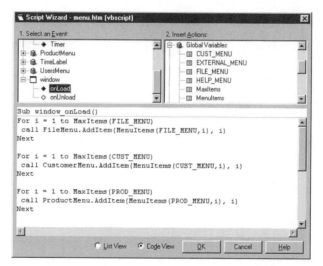

The menu's click event, shown in Figure 23.7, loads the required page into the lower frame. The value of the menu caption is passed to a form and is used in this example to display the correct caption on the page (b.htm) in the lower frame.

The menu objects are defined within the HTML code. They are shown in the ActiveX Control Pad in Figure 23.8.

Figure 23.7.
The menu's `Click`
event handler.

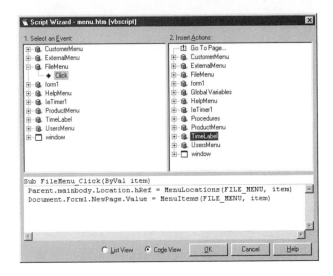

Figure 23.8.
*The menu object
definitions.*

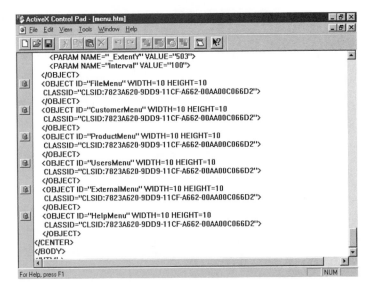

Listing 23.1 shows the HTML code for the frameset document `menudemo.htm`.

Listing 23.1. The `menudemo.htm` code.

```
<HTML>
<HEAD>
<TITLE>XYZ Inc. Intranet</TITLE>
</HEAD>
 <FRAMESET ROWS=8%,92% FRAMEBORDER=0 FRAMESPACING=0>
  <FRAME SRC="menu.htm" NAME="menubar" MARGINWIDTH=0 MARGINHEIGHT=0
➡SCROLLING=No NORESIZE>
  <FRAME SRC="welcome.htm" NAME="mainbody">
 </FRAMESET>
</HTML>
```

Listing 23.2 shows the complete source code for the menu document, `menu.htm`.

Listing 23.2. The `menu.htm` code.

```
<HTML>
<HEAD>

<TITLE>New Page</TITLE>
    <SCRIPT LANGUAGE="vbscript">
<!--
Dim NewPage
Dim MenuItems(6,10)
Dim MenuLocations(6,10)
Dim MaxItems(6)

Dim FILE_MENU, CUST_MENU, PROD_MENU, USERS_MENU, EXTERNAL_MENU, HELP_MENU

FILE_MENU = 0
CUST_MENU = 1
PROD_MENU = 2
USERS_MENU = 3
EXTERNAL_MENU = 4
HELP_MENU = 5

MenuItems(FILE_MENU,1) = "Welcome Page"
MenuItems(FILE_MENU,2) = "Latest Company News"
MenuItems(FILE_MENU,3) = "New and Updated Areas"
MenuLocations(FILE_MENU,1) = "welcome.htm"
MenuLocations(FILE_MENU,2) = "b.htm"
MenuLocations(FILE_MENU,3) = "b.htm"
MaxItems(FILE_MENU) = 3

MenuItems(CUST_MENU,1) = "Search Customer Database"
MenuItems(CUST_MENU ,2) = "Browse Customer Database"
MenuItems(CUST_MENU ,3) = "Add New Customer Record"
MenuItems(CUST_MENU ,4) = "Edit Customer Record"
MenuLocations(CUST_MENU ,1) = "b.htm"
MenuLocations(CUST_MENU ,2) = "b.htm"
MenuLocations(CUST_MENU ,3) = "b.htm"
MenuLocations(CUST_MENU ,4) = "b.htm"
MaxItems(CUST_MENU) = 4

MenuItems(PROD_MENU,1) = "Search Product Database"
MenuItems(PROD_MENU,2) = "Browse Product Database"
MenuItems(PROD_MENU,3) = "Add New Product Record"
MenuItems(PROD_MENU,4) = "View Product Technical Reports"
MenuItems(PROD_MENU,5) = "Add Product Comment"
MenuLocations(PROD_MENU,1) = "b.htm"
MenuLocations(PROD_MENU,2) = "b.htm"
MenuLocations(PROD_MENU,3) = "b.htm"
MenuLocations(PROD_MENU,4) = "b.htm"
MenuLocations(PROD_MENU,5) = "b.htm"
MaxItems(PROD_MENU) = 5

MenuItems(USERS_MENU,1) = "Search User Database"
MenuItems(USERS_MENU,2) = "User EMail Addresses"
MenuItems(USERS_MENU,3) = "Change your password"
MenuItems(USERS_MENU,4) = "Employee Forum"
```

continues

Listing 23.2. continued

```
MenuItems(USERS_MENU,5) = "Technical Forum"
MenuLocations(USERS_MENU,1) = "b.htm"
MenuLocations(USERS_MENU,2) = "b.htm"
MenuLocations(USERS_MENU,3) = "b.htm"
MenuLocations(USERS_MENU,4) = "b.htm"
MenuLocations(USERS_MENU,5) = "b.htm"
MaxItems(USERS_MENU) = 5

MenuItems(EXTERNAL_MENU,1) = "Microsoft"
MenuItems(EXTERNAL_MENU,2) = "SAMS.Net"
MenuItems(EXTERNAL_MENU,3) = "vbscripts.com"
MenuLocations(EXTERNAL_MENU,1) = "http://www.microsoft.com/"
MenuLocations(EXTERNAL_MENU,2) = "http://www.mcp.com/sams/"
MenuLocations(EXTERNAL_MENU,3) = "http://www.vbscripts.com/"
MaxItems(EXTERNAL_MENU) = 3

MenuItems(HELP_MENU,1) = "Search Help Topics"
MenuItems(HELP_MENU,2) = "Contact Support Desk"
MenuItems(HELP_MENU,3) = "Contact Support Desk"
MenuLocations(HELP_MENU,1) = "b.htm"
MenuLocations(HELP_MENU,2) = "b.htm"
MenuLocations(HELP_MENU,3) = "b.htm"
MaxItems(HELP_MENU) = 3

Sub window_onLoad()

For i = 1 to MaxItems(FILE_MENU)
 call FileMenu.AddItem(MenuItems(FILE_MENU,i), i)
Next

For i = 1 to MaxItems(CUST_MENU)
 call CustomerMenu.AddItem(MenuItems(CUST_MENU,i), i)
Next

For i = 1 to MaxItems(PROD_MENU)
 call ProductMenu.AddItem(MenuItems(PROD_MENU,i), i)
Next

For i = 1 to MaxItems(USERS_MENU)
 call UsersMenu.AddItem(MenuItems(USERS_MENU,i), i)
Next

For i = 1 to MaxItems(EXTERNAL_MENU)
 call ExternalMenu.AddItem(MenuItems(EXTERNAL_MENU,i), i)
Next

For i = 1 to MaxItems(HELP_MENU)
 call HelpMenu.AddItem(MenuItems(HELP_MENU,i), i)
Next

End sub

  Sub File_OnClick
    FileMenu.PopUp
  End Sub

  Sub Customers_OnClick
    CustomerMenu.PopUp
  End Sub
```

```
    Sub Products_OnClick
      ProductMenu.PopUp
    End Sub

    Sub Users_OnClick
      UsersMenu.PopUp
    End Sub

    Sub External_OnClick
      ExternalMenu.PopUp
    End Sub

    Sub Help_OnClick
      HelpMenu.PopUp
    End Sub

Sub FileMenu_Click(ByVal item)
 Parent.mainbody.Location.hRef = MenuLocations(FILE_MENU, item)
 Document.Form1.NewPage.Value = MenuItems(FILE_MENU, item)
end sub

Sub CustomerMenu_Click(item)
 Parent.mainbody.Location.hRef = MenuLocations(CUST_MENU, item)
 Document.Form1.NewPage.Value = MenuItems(CUST_MENU, item)
end sub

Sub ProductMenu_Click(item)
 Parent.mainbody.Location.hRef = MenuLocations(PROD_MENU, item)
 Document.Form1.NewPage.Value = MenuItems(PROD_MENU, item)
end sub

Sub UsersMenu_Click(item)
 Parent.mainbody.Location.hRef = MenuLocations(USERS_MENU, item)
 Document.Form1.NewPage.Value = MenuItems(USERS_MENU, item)
end sub

Sub ExternalMenu_Click(ByVal item)
 top.Location.hRef = MenuLocations(EXTERNAL_MENU, item)
end sub

Sub HelpMenu_Click(item)
 Parent.mainbody.Location.hRef = MenuLocations(HELP_MENU, item)
 Document.Form1.NewPage.Value = MenuItems(HELP_MENU, item)
end sub


-->
    </SCRIPT>
</HEAD>
<BODY BGCOLOR="white">
<CENTER>

<IMG SRC="leftend.gif">
<A HREF="menu.htm" ID="File"><IMG SRC="file.gif" BORDER=0></A>
<A HREF="menu.htm" ID="Customers"><IMG SRC="cust.gif" BORDER=0></A>
<A HREF="menu.htm" ID="Products"><IMG SRC="prod.gif" BORDER=0></A>
<A HREF="menu.htm" ID="Users"><IMG SRC="users.gif" BORDER=0></A>
<A HREF="menu.htm" ID="External"><IMG SRC="external.gif" BORDER=0></A>
```

continues

Listing 23.2. continued

```
<A HREF="menu.htm" ID="Help"><IMG SRC="help.gif" BORDER=0></A>
    <OBJECT ID="TimeLabel" WIDTH=95 HEIGHT=22
     CLASSID="CLSID:978C9E23-D4B0-11CE-BF2D-00AA003F40D0">
        <PARAM NAME="BackColor" VALUE="15066597">
        <PARAM NAME="VariousPropertyBits" VALUE="268435483">
        <PARAM NAME="Caption" VALUE="Current Time:">
        <PARAM NAME="Size" VALUE="2505;529">
        <PARAM NAME="BorderColor" VALUE="16711680">
        <PARAM NAME="BorderStyle" VALUE="1">
        <PARAM NAME="FontEffects" VALUE="1073741825">
        <PARAM NAME="FontHeight" VALUE="200">
        <PARAM NAME="FontCharSet" VALUE="0">
        <PARAM NAME="FontPitchAndFamily" VALUE="2">
        <PARAM NAME="FontWeight" VALUE="700">
    </OBJECT>
<IMG SRC="rightend.gif"><BR>
    <FORM NAME="form1">
        <INPUT TYPE=hidden NAME="NewPage">
    </FORM>
    <SCRIPT LANGUAGE="vbscript">
<!--
Sub IeTimer1_Timer()
 TimeLabel.Caption = "Current Time: " & Time()
end sub
-->
    </SCRIPT>
    <OBJECT ID="IeTimer1" WIDTH=19 HEIGHT=19
     CLASSID="CLSID:59CCB4A0-727D-11CF-AC36-00AA00A47DD2">
        <PARAM NAME="_ExtentX" VALUE="503">
        <PARAM NAME="_ExtentY" VALUE="503">
        <PARAM NAME="Interval" VALUE="100">
    </OBJECT>
    <OBJECT ID="FileMenu" WIDTH=10 HEIGHT=10
     CLASSID="CLSID:7823A620-9DD9-11CF-A662-00AA00C066D2">
    </OBJECT>
    <OBJECT ID="CustomerMenu" WIDTH=10 HEIGHT=10
     CLASSID="CLSID:7823A620-9DD9-11CF-A662-00AA00C066D2">
    </OBJECT>
    <OBJECT ID="ProductMenu" WIDTH=10 HEIGHT=10
     CLASSID="CLSID:7823A620-9DD9-11CF-A662-00AA00C066D2">
    </OBJECT>
    <OBJECT ID="UsersMenu" WIDTH=10 HEIGHT=10
     CLASSID="CLSID:7823A620-9DD9-11CF-A662-00AA00C066D2">
    </OBJECT>
    <OBJECT ID="ExternalMenu" WIDTH=10 HEIGHT=10
     CLASSID="CLSID:7823A620-9DD9-11CF-A662-00AA00C066D2">
    </OBJECT>
    <OBJECT ID="HelpMenu" WIDTH=10 HEIGHT=10
     CLASSID="CLSID:7823A620-9DD9-11CF-A662-00AA00C066D2">
    </OBJECT>
</CENTER>
</BODY>
</HTML>
```

PART

VI

Appendixes

by Dick Oliver

HTML Reference/ MSIE Extensions

This appendix is a reference to the HTML tags you can use in your documents. Unless otherwise noted, all of the tags listed here are supported by both Microsoft Explorer 3.0 and Netscape Navigator 3.0. Note that some other browsers do not support all the tags listed, and some of the tags listed as (MS) may also be supported in the final shipping version of Netscape 3.0.

The proposed HTML style sheet specification is also not covered here. Refer to the Netscape (http://home.netscape.com/) or Microsoft (http://www.microsoft.com/) Web sites for details on this and other late-breaking changes to the new HTML 3.2 standard.

HTML Tags

These tags are used to create a basic HTML page with text, headings, and lists. An (MS) beside the attribute indicates Microsoft.

Comments

`<!-- ... -->` Creates a comment. Can also be used to hide JavaScript from browsers that do not support it.

`<COMMENT>...</COMMENT>` The new official way of specifying comments.

Structure Tags

`<HTML>...</HTML>` Encloses the entire HTML document.

`<HEAD>...</HEAD>` Encloses the head of the HTML document.

`<BODY>...</BODY>` Encloses the body (text and tags) of the HTML document.

Attributes:

`BACKGROUND="..."`	The name or URL of the image to tile on the page background.
`BGCOLOR="..."`	The color of the page background.
`TEXT="..."`	The color of the page's text.
`LINK="..."`	The color of unfollowed links.
`ALINK="..."`	The color of activated links.
`VLINK="..."`	The color of followed links.
`BGPROPERTIES="..."`(MS)	Properties of background image. Currently allows only the value FIXED, which prevents the background image from scrolling.
`TOPMARGIN="..."`(MS)	Top margin of the page, in pixels.
`BOTTOMMARGIN="..."`(MS)	Bottom margin of the page, in pixels.

`<BASE>`		Indicates the full URL of the current document. This optional tag is used within `<HEAD>`.
Attributes:		
	`HREF="..."`	The full URL of this document.
`<ISINDEX>`		Indicates that this document is a gateway script that allows searches.
Attributes:		
	`PROMPT="..."`	The prompt for the search field.
	`ACTION="..."`	Gateway program to which the search string should be passed.
`<LINK>`		Indicates a link between this document and some other document. Generally used only by HTML-generating tools. `<LINK>` represents a link from this entire document to another, as opposed to `<A>`, which can create multiple links in the document. Not commonly used.
Attributes:		
	`HREF="..."`	The URL of the document to call when the link is activated.
	`NAME="..."`	If the document is to be considered an anchor, the name of that anchor.
	`REL="..."`	The relationship between the linked-to document and the current document; for example, `"TOC"` or `"Glossary"`.
	`REV="..."`	A reverse relationship between the current document and the linked-to document.
	`URN="..."`	A Uniform Resource Number (URN), a unique identifier different from the URL in `HREF`.

	`TITLE="..."`	The title of the linked-to document.
	`METHODS="..."`	The method with which the document is to be retrieved; for example, FTP, Gopher, and so on.
`<META>`		Indicates meta-information about this document (information about the document itself); for example, keywords for search engines, special HTTP headers to be used for retrieving this document, expiration date, and so on. Meta-information is usually in a key/value pair form. Used in the document `<HEAD>`.

Attributes:

	`HTTP-EQUIV="..."`	Creates a new HTTP header field with the same name as the attribute's value; for example, `HTTP-EQUIV="Expires"`. The value of that header is specified by the `CONTENT` attribute.
	`NAME="..."`	If meta data is usually in the form of key/value pairs, `NAME` indicates the key; for example, `Author` or `ID`.
	`CONTENT="..."`	The content of the key/value pair (or of the HTTP header indicated by `HTTP-EQUIV`).
`<NEXTID>`		Indicates the "next" document to this one (as might be defined by a tool to manage HTML documents in series). `<NEXTID>` is considered obsolete.

Headings and Title

| `<H1>...</H1>` | A first-level heading. |
| `<H2>...</H2>` | A second-level heading. |

`<H3>...</H3>`	A third-level heading.
`<H4>...</H4>`	A fourth-level heading.
`<H5>...</H5>`	A fifth-level heading.
`<H6>...</H6>`	A sixth-level heading.
`<TITLE>...</TITLE>`	Indicates the title of the document. Used within `<HEAD>`.

All heading tags accept the following attribute:

Attributes:

`ALIGN="..."`	Possible values are `CENTER`, `LEFT`, and `RIGHT`.

Paragraphs and Regions

`<P>...</P>`	A plain paragraph. The closing tag (`</P>`) is optional.

Attributes:

`ALIGN="..."`	Align text to `CENTER`, `LEFT`, or `RIGHT`.

`<DIV>...</DIV>`	A region of text to be formatted.

Attributes:

`ALIGN="..."`	Align text to `CENTER`, `LEFT`, or `RIGHT`.

Links

`<A>...</A>`	With the `HREF` attribute, this creates a link to another document or anchor; with the `NAME` attribute, it creates an anchor that can be linked to.

Attributes:

`HREF="..."`	The URL of the document to be called when the link is activated.
`NAME="..."`	The name of the anchor.
`REL="..."`	The relationship between the linked-to document and the current document; for example, `"TOC"` or `"Glossary"` (not commonly used).

`REV="..."`	A reverse relationship between the current document and the linked-to document (not commonly used).
`URN="..."`	A Uniform Resource Number (URN), a unique identifier different from the URL in HREF (not commonly used).
`TITLE="..."`	The title of the linked-to document (not commonly used).
`METHODS="..."`	The method with which the document is to be retrieved; for example, FTP, Gopher, and so on (not commonly used).
`TARGET="..."`	The name of a frame in which the linked document should appear.

Lists

`<OL>...</OL>`	An ordered (numbered) list.
Attributes:	

`TYPE="..."`	The type of numerals to label the list. Possible values are A, a, I, i, 1.
`START="..."`	The value with which to start this list.

`<UL>...</UL>`	An unordered (bulleted) list.
Attributes:	

`TYPE="..."`	The bullet dingbat to use to mark list items. Possible values are DISC, CIRCLE (or ROUND), and SQUARE.

`<MENU>...</MENU>`	A menu list of items.
`<DIR>...</DIR>`	A directory listing; items are generally smaller than 20 characters.
`<LI>`	A list item for use with `<OL>`, `<UL>`, `<MENU>`, or `<DIR>`.

Attributes:

	`TYPE="..."`	The type of bullet or number to label this item with. Possible values are `DISC`, `CIRCLE` (or `ROUND`), `SQUARE`, `A`, `a`, `I`, `i`, `1`.
	`VALUE="..."`	The numeric value this list item should have (affects this item and all below it in `<OL>` lists).

`<DL>...</DL>`	A definition or glossary list.

Attributes:

	`COMPACT`	The `COMPACT` attribute specifies a formatting that takes less whitespace to present.

`<DT>`	A definition term, as part of a definition list.
`<DD>`	The corresponding definition to a definition term, as part of a definition list.

Character Formatting

`<EM>...</EM>`	Emphasis (usually italic).
`<STRONG>...</STRONG>`	Stronger emphasis (usually bold).
`<CODE>...</CODE>`	Code sample (usually Courier).
`<KBD>...</KBD>`	Text to be typed (usually Courier).
`<VAR>...</VAR>`	A variable or placeholder for some other value.
`<SAMP>...</SAMP>`	Sample text (seldom used).
`<DFN>...<DFN>`	A definition of a term.
`<CITE>...</CITE>`	A citation.
`<B>...</B>`	Boldface text.
`<I>...</I>`	Italic text.
`<TT>...</TT>`	Typewriter (monospaced) font.

`<PRE>...</PRE>`	Preformatted text (exact line endings and spacing will be preserved—usually rendered in a monospaced font).
`<BIG>...</BIG>`	Text is slightly larger than normal.
`<SMALL>...</SMALL>`	Text is slightly smaller than normal.
`<SUB>...</SUB>`	Subscript.
`<SUP>...</SUP>`	Superscript.
`<STRIKE>...</STRIKE>`	Puts a strikethrough line in the text.

Other Elements

`<HR>`	A horizontal rule line.
Attributes:	

`SIZE="..."`	The thickness of the rule, in pixels.
`WIDTH="..."`	The width of the rule, in pixels or as a percentage of the document width.
`ALIGN="..."`	How the rule line will be aligned on the page. Possible values are `LEFT`, `RIGHT`, and `CENTER`.
`NOSHADE`	Causes the rule line to be drawn as a solid line instead of a transparent bevel.
`COLOR="..."` (MS)	Color of the horizontal rule.

` `	A line break.
Attributes:	

`CLEAR="..."`	Causes the text to stop flowing around any images. Possible values are `RIGHT`, `LEFT`, and `ALL`.

`<NOBR>...</NOBR>`	Causes the enclosed text not to wrap at the edge of the page.
`<WBR>`	Wraps the text at this point only if necessary.
`<BLOCKQUOTE>...</BLOCKQUOTE>`	Used for long quotes or citations.

`<ADDRESS>...</ADDRESS>`		Used for signatures or general information about a document's author.
`<CENTER>...</CENTER>`		Centers text or images.
`<BLINK>...</BLINK>`		Causes the enclosed text to blink irritatingly.
`<FONT>...</FONT>`		Changes the size of the font for the enclosed text.

Attributes:

	`SIZE="..."`	The size of the font, from 1 to 7. Default is 3. Can also be specified as a value relative to the current size; for example, +2.
	`COLOR="..."`	Changes the color of the text.
	`FACE="..."` (MS)	Name of font to use if it can be found on the user's system. Multiple font names can be separated by commas, and the first font on the list that can be found will be used.
`<BASEFONT>`		Sets the default size of the font for the current page.

Attributes:

	`SIZE="..."`	The default size of the font, from 1 to 7. Default is 3.

Images, Sounds, and Embedded Media

`<IMG>`		Inserts an inline image into the document.

Attributes:

	`ISMAP`	This image is a clickable image map.
	`SRC="..."`	The URL of the image.
	`ALT="..."`	A text string that will be displayed in browsers that cannot support images.

ALIGN="..."	Determines the alignment of the given image. If LEFT or RIGHT (N), the image is aligned to the left or right column, and all following text flows beside that image. All other values such as TOP, MIDDLE, BOTTOM, or the Netscape-only TEXTTOP, ABSMIDDLE, BASELINE, and ABSBOTTOM determine the vertical alignment of this image with other items in the same line.
VSPACE="..."	The space between the image and the text above or below it.
HSPACE="..."	The space between the image and the text to its left or right.
WIDTH="..."	The width, in pixels, of the image. If WIDTH is not the actual width, the image is scaled to fit.
HEIGHT="..."	The height, in pixels, of the image. If HEIGHT is not the actual height, the image is scaled to fit.
BORDER="..."	Draws a border of the specified value in pixels to be drawn around the image. In the case of images that are also links, BORDER changes the size of the default link border.
LOWSRC="..."	The path or URL of an image that will be loaded first, before the image specified in SRC. The value of LOWSRC is usually

		a smaller or lower resolution version of the actual image.
	USEMAP="..."	The name of an image map specification for client-side image mapping. Used with <MAP> and <AREA>.
	DYNSRC="..." (MS)	The address of a video clip or VRML world (dynamic source).
	CONTROLS (MS)	Used with DYNSRC to display a set of playback controls for inline video.
	LOOP="..." (MS)	The number of times a video clip will loop. (-1 or INFINITE means to loop indefinitely.)
	START="..." (MS)	When a DYNSRC video clip should start playing. Valid options are FILEOPEN (play when page is displayed) or MOUSEOVER (play when mouse cursor passes over the video clip).
<BGSOUND> (MS)		Plays a sound file as soon as the page is displayed.
Attributes:		
	SRC="..."	The URL of the WAV, AU, or MIDI sound file to embed.
	LOOP="..." (MS)	The number of times a video clip will loop. (-1 or INFINITE means to loop indefinitely.)
<OBJECT> (MS)		Inserts an image, video, Java applet, or ActiveX OLE control into a document.

NOTE: The full syntax for the `<OBJECT>` tag is not yet completely finalized. Check `http://www.w3.org/pub/WWW/TR/WD-object.html` and `http://www.microsoft.com/intdev/author/` for the latest attributes supported by the HTML 3.2 standard and implemented in Microsoft Internet Explorer.

`<EMBED>` (Netscape only!)	Embeds a file to be read or displayed by a plug-in application.

NOTE: In addition to the following standard attributes, you can specify applet-specific attributes to be interpreted by the plug-in that displays the embedded object.

Attributes:

	`SRC="..."`	The URL of the file to embed.
	`WIDTH="..."`	The width of the embedded object, in pixels.
	`HEIGHT="..."`	The height of the embedded object, in pixels.
	`ALIGN="..."`	Determines the alignment of the media window. Values are the same as for the `<IMG>` tag.
	`VSPACE="..."`	The space between the media and the text above or below it.
	`HSPACE="..."`	The space between the media and the text to its left or right.
	`BORDER="..."`	Draws a border of the specified size in pixels to be drawn around the media.
`<NOEMBED>...</NOEMBED>` (N)		Alternate text or images to be shown to users who do not have a plug-in installed.
`<OBJECT>` (MS)		Inserts an embedded program, control, or other object. (This tag was under revision when this book was printed.)

`<MAP>...</MAP>`	A client-side image map, referenced by `<IMG USEMAP="...">`. Includes one or more `<AREA>` tags.
`<AREA>`	Defines a clickable link within a client-side image map.

Attributes:

`SHAPE="..."`	The shape of the clickable area. Currently, only RECT is supported.
`COORDS="..."`	The left, top, right, and bottom coordinates of the clickable region within an image.
`HREF="..."`	The URL that should be loaded when the area is clicked.
`NOHREF`	Indicates that no action should be taken when this area of the image is clicked.

Forms

`<FORM>...</FORM>`	Indicates an input form.

Attributes:

`ACTION="..."`	The URL of the script to process this form input.
`METHOD="..."`	How the form input will be sent to the gateway on the server side. Possible values are GET and POST.
`ENCTYPE="..."`	Normally has the value `application/x-www-form-urlencoded`. For file uploads, use `multipart/form-data`.
`NAME="..."`	A name by which JavaScript scripts can refer to the form.

`<INPUT>`	An input element for a form.

Attributes:

	`TYPE="..."`	The type for this input widget. Possible values are CHECKBOX, HIDDEN, RADIO, RESET, SUBMIT, TEXT, SEND FILE, or IMAGE.
	`NAME="..."`	The name of this item, as passed to the gateway script as part of a name/value pair.
	`VALUE="..."`	For a text or hidden widget, the default value; for a check box or radio button, the value to be submitted with the form; for Reset or Submit buttons, the label for the button itself.
	`SRC="..."`	The source file for an image.
	`CHECKED`	For check boxes and radio buttons, indicates that the widget is checked.
	`SIZE="..."`	The size, in characters, of a text widget.
	`MAXLENGTH="..."`	The maximum number of characters that can be entered into a text widget.
	`ALIGN="..."`	For images in forms, determines how the text and image will align (same as with the `<IMG>` tag).
`<TEXTAREA>...</TEXTAREA>`		Indicates a multiline text entry form element. Default text can be included.

Attributes:

	NAME="..."	The name to be passed to the gateway script as part of the name/value pair.
	ROWS="..."	The number of rows this text area displays.
	COLS="..."	The number of columns (characters) this text area displays.
	WRAP="..." (N)	Control text wrapping. Possible values are OFF, VIRTUAL, and PHYSICAL.

<SELECT>...</SELECT>	Creates a menu or scrolling list of possible items.

Attributes:

	NAME="..."	The name that is passed to the gateway script as part of the name/value pair.
	SIZE="..."	The number of elements to display. If SIZE is indicated, the selection becomes a scrolling list. If no SIZE is given, the selection is a pop-up menu.
	MULTIPLE	Allows multiple selections from the list.

<OPTION>	Indicates a possible item within a <SELECT> element.

Attributes:

	SELECTED	With this attribute included, the <OPTION> will be selected by default in the list.
	VALUE="..."	The value to submit if this <OPTION> is selected when the form is submitted.

Tables

`<TABLE>...</TABLE>`		Creates a table that can contain a caption (`<CAPTION>`) and any number of rows (`<TR>`).

Attributes:

`BORDER="..."`	Indicates whether the table should be drawn with or without a border. In Netscape, `BORDER` can also have a value indicating the width of the border.
`CELLSPACING="..."`	The amount of space between the cells in the table.
`CELLPADDING="..."`	The amount of space between the edges of the cell and its contents.
`WIDTH="..."`	The width of the table on the page, in either exact pixel values or as a percentage of page width.
`ALIGN="..."` (MS)	Alignment (works like `IMG ALIGN`). Values are `LEFT` or `RIGHT`.
`BACKGROUND="..."` (MS)	Background image to tile within all cells in the table that do not contain their own `BACKGROUND` or `BGCOLOR` attribute.
`BGCOLOR="..."` (MS)	Background color of all cells in the table that do not contain their own `BACKGROUND` or `BGCOLOR` attribute.
`BORDERCOLOR="..."` (MS)	Border color (used with `BORDER="..."`).
`BORDERCOLORLIGHT="..."` (MS)	Color for light part of 3D-look borders (used with `BORDER="..."`).

	`BORDERCOLORDARK="..."` (MS)	Color for dark part of 3D-look borders (used with `BORDER="..."`).
	`VALIGN="..."` (MS)	Alignment of text within the table. Values are `TOP` and `BOTTOM`.
	`FRAME="..."` (MS)	Controls which external borders will appear around a table. Values are `"void"` (no frames), `"above"` (top border only), `"below"` (bottom border only), `"hsides"` (top and bottom), `"lhs"` (left side), `"rhs"` (right side), `"vsides"` (left and right sides), and `"box"` (all sides).
	`RULES="..."` (MS)	Controls which internal borders appear in the table. Values are `"none"`, `"basic"` (rules between `THEAD`, `TBODY`, and `TFOOT` only), `"rows"` (horizontal borders only), `"cols"` (vertical borders only), and `"all"`.
`<CAPTION>...</CAPTION>` *Attributes:*		The caption for the table.
	`ALIGN="..."`	The position of the caption. Possible values are `TOP` and `BOTTOM`.
`<TR>...</TR>` *Attributes:*		Defines a table row, containing headings and data (`<TR>` and `<TH>` tags).
	`ALIGN="..."`	The horizontal alignment of the contents of the cells within this row. Possible values are `LEFT`, `RIGHT`, and `CENTER`.

`VALIGN="..."`	The vertical alignment of the contents of the cells within this row. Possible values are TOP, MIDDLE, BOTTOM, and BASELINE.
`BACKGROUND="..."`(MS)	Background image to tile within all cells in the row that do not contain their own BACKGROUND or BGCOLOR attributes.
`BGCOLOR="..."`	Background color of all cells in the row that do not contain their own BACKGROUND or BGCOLOR attributes.
`BORDERCOLOR="..."`(MS)	Border color (used with BORDER="...").
`BORDERCOLORLIGHT="..."` (MS)	Color for light part of 3D-look borders (used with BORDER="...").
`BORDERCOLORDARK="..."` (MS)	Color for dark part of 3D-look borders (used with BORDER="...").

`<TH>...</TH>`	Defines a table heading cell.

Attributes:

`ALIGN="..."`	The horizontal alignment of the contents of the cell. Possible values are LEFT, RIGHT, and CENTER.
`VALIGN="..."`	The vertical alignment of the contents of the cell. Possible values are TOP, MIDDLE, BOTTOM, and BASELINE.
`ROWSPAN="..."`	The number of rows this cell will span.
`COLSPAN="..."`	The number of columns this cell will span.

	`NOWRAP`	Does not automatically wrap the contents of this cell.
	`WIDTH="..."`	The width of this column of cells, in exact pixel values or as a percentage of the table width.
	`BACKGROUND="..."` (MS)	Background image to tile within the cell.
	`BGCOLOR="..."` (MS)	Background color of the cell.
	`BORDERCOLOR="..."` (MS)	Border color (used with `BORDER="..."`).
	`BORDERCOLORLIGHT="..."` (MS)	Color for light part of 3D-look borders (used with `BORDER="..."`).
	`BORDERCOLORDARK="..."` (MS)	Color for dark part of 3D-look borders (used with `BORDER="..."`).
`<TD>...</TD>`		Defines a table data cell.

Attributes:

	`ALIGN="..."`	The horizontal alignment of the contents of the cell. Possible values are `LEFT`, `RIGHT`, and `CENTER`.
	`VALIGN="..."`	The vertical alignment of the contents of the cell. Possible values are `TOP`, `MIDDLE`, `BOTTOM`, and `BASELINE`.
	`ROWSPAN="..."`	The number of rows this cell will span.
	`COLSPAN="..."`	The number of columns this cell will span.
	`NOWRAP`	Does not automatically wrap the contents of this cell.
	`WIDTH="..."`	The width of this column of cells, in exact pixel values or as a percentage of the table width.

	`BACKGROUND="..."` (MS)	Background image to tile within the cell.
	`BGCOLOR="..."` (MS)	Background color of the cell.
	`BORDERCOLOR="..."` (MS)	Border color (used with `BORDER="..."`).
	`BORDERCOLORLIGHT="..."` (MS)	Color for light part of 3D-look borders (used with `BORDER="..."`).
	`BORDERCOLORDARK="..."` (MS)	Color for dark part of 3D-look borders (used with `BORDER="..."`).
`<THEAD>` (MS)		Begins the header section of a table. The closing `</THEAD>` tag is optional.
`<TBODY>` (MS)		Begins the body section of a table. The closing `</TBODY>` tag is optional.
`<TFOOT>` (MS)		Begins the footer section of a table. The closing `</TFOOT>` tag is optional.
`<COL>...</COL>` (MS)		Sets width and alignment properties for one or more columns.
Attributes:		
	`WIDTH="..."`	Width of column(s) in pixels or relative width followed by a * (`"2*"` columns will be twice as wide as `"1*"` columns, for example).
	`ALIGN="..."`	Text alignment within the column(s). Valid values are `"center"`, `"justify"`, `"left"`, and `"right"`.
	`SPAN="..."`	Number of columns to which the properties specified in this `<COL>` tag apply.
`<COLGROUP>...</COLGROUP>`		Sets properties of a group of columns all at once (should enclose one or more `<COL>` tags).

Attributes:

`ALIGN="..."`	Text alignment within the columns. Valid values are `"center"`, `"justify"`, `"left"`, and `"right"`.
`VALIGN="..."`	Vertical alignment of text within the columns. Valid values are `"baseline"`, `"bottom"`, `"middle"`, and `"top"`.

Frames

`<FRAMESET>...</FRAMESET>`	Divides the main window into a set of frames that can each display a separate document.

Attributes:

`ROWS="..."`	Splits the window or frameset vertically into a number of rows specified by a number (such as 7), a percentage of the total window width (such as 25%), or as an asterisk (*) indicating that a frame should take up all the remaining space or divide the space evenly between frames (if multiple * frames are specified).
`COLS="..."`	Works similar to ROWS, except that the window or frameset is split horizontally into columns.

`<FRAME>`	Defines a single frame within a `<FRAMESET>`.

Attributes:

`SRC="..."`	The URL of the document to be displayed in this frame.

`NAME="..."`	A name to be used for targeting this frame with the `TARGET` attribute in `<A HREF>` links.
`<MARGINWIDTH>`	The amount of space to leave to the left and right side of a document within a frame, in pixels.
`<MARGINHEIGHT>`	The amount of space to leave above and below a document within a frame, in pixels.
`SCROLLING="..."`	Determines whether a frame has scrollbars. Possible values are `YES`, `NO`, and `AUTO`.
`NORESIZE`	Prevents the user from resizing this frame (and possibly adjacent frames) with the mouse.
`FRAMEBORDER="..."` (MS)	Specifies whether to display a border for a frame. Options are `YES` and `NO`.
`FRAMESPACING="..."` (MS)	Space between frames, in pixels.
`</NOFRAME>...</NOFRAMES>`	Provides an alternative document body in `<FRAMESET>` documents for browsers that do not support frames (usually encloses `<BODY>...</BODY>`).

Scripting and Applets

`<APPLET>`	Inserts a self-running Java applet.

NOTE: In addition to the following standard attributes, you can specify applet-specific attributes to be interpreted by the Java applet itself.

Attributes:

	`CLASS="..."`	The name of the applet.
	`SRC="..."`	The URL of the directory where the compiled applet can be found (should end in a slash / as in `"http://mysite/ myapplets/"`). Do not include the actual applet name, which is specified with the `CLASS` attribute.
	`ALIGN="..."`	Indicates how the applet should be aligned with any text that follows it. Current values are `TOP`, `MIDDLE`, and `BOTTOM`.
	`WIDTH="..."`	The width of the applet output area, in pixels.
	`HEIGHT="..."`	The height of the applet output area, in pixels.

`<SCRIPT>`   An interpreted script program.

Attributes:

	`LANGUAGE="..."`	Currently only `JAVASCRIPT` is supported by Netscape. Both `JAVASCRIPT` and `VBSCRIPT` are supported by Microsoft.
	`SRC="..."`	Specifies the URL of a file that includes the script program.

Marquees

`<MARQUEE>...</MARQUEE>` (MS)   Displays text in a scrolling marquee.

Attributes:

	`WIDTH="..."`	The width of the embedded object in pixels or percentage of window width.

`HEIGHT="..."`	The height of the embedded object in pixels or percentage of window height.
`ALIGN="..."`	Determines the alignment of the text outside the marquee. Values are TOP, MIDDLE, and BOTTOM.
`BORDER="..."`	Draws a border of the specified size in pixels to be drawn around the media.
`BEHAVIOR="..."`	How the text inside the marquee should behave. Options are SCROLL (continuous scrolling), SLIDE (slide text in and stop), and ALTERNATE (bounce back and forth).
`BGCOLOR="..."`	Background color for the marquee.
`DIRECTION="..."`	Direction for text to scroll (LEFT or RIGHT).
`VSPACE="..."`	Space above and below the marquee, in pixels.
`HSPACE="..."`	Space on each side of the marquee, in pixels.
`SCROLLAMOUNT="..."`	Number of pixels to move each time text in the marquee is redrawn.
`SCROLLDELAY="..."`	Number of milliseconds between each redraw of marquee text.
`LOOP="..."` (MS)	The number of times marquee will loop. (-1 or INFINITE means to loop indefinitely.)

Character Entities

Table A.1 contains the possible numeric and character entities for the ISO-Latin-1 (ISO8859-1) character set. Where possible, the character is shown.

NOTE: Not all browsers can display all characters, and some browsers may even display characters different from those that appear in the table. Newer browsers seem to have a better track record for handling character entities, but be sure to test your HTML files extensively with multiple browsers if you intend to use these entities.

Table A.1. ISO-Latin-1 character set.

Character	Numeric Entity	Character Entity	Description
	&#00;-&#08;		Unused
	&#09;		Horizontal tab
	&#10;		Line feed
	&#11; &#31;		Unused
	&#32;		Space
!	&#33;		Exclamation mark
"	&#34;	&quot;	Quotation mark
#	&#35;		Number sign
$	&#36;		Dollar sign
%	&#37;		Percent sign
&	&#38;	&amp;	Ampersand
'	&#39;		Apostrophe
(	&#40;		Left parenthesis
)	&#41;		Right parenthesis
*	&#42;		Asterisk
+	&#43;		Plus sign
,	&#44;		Comma
-	&#45;		Hyphen
.	&#46;		Period (fullstop)
/	&#47;		Solidus (slash)
0–9	0 9		Digits 0-9

continues

Table A.1. continued

Character	Numeric Entity	Character Entity	Description
:	&#58;		Colon
;	&#59;		Semicolon
<	&#60;	&lt;	Less than
=	&#61;		Equals sign
>	&#62;	&gt;	Greater than
?	&#63;		Question mark
@	&#64;		Commercial "at"
A–Z	A-Z		Letters A-Z
[	&#91;		Left square bracket
\	&#92;		Reverse solidus (backslash)
]	&#93;		Right square bracket
^	&#94;		Caret
—	&#95;		Horizontal bar
`	&#96;		Grave accent
a–z	a z		Letters a-z
{	&#123;		Left curly brace
		&#124		Vertical bar
}	&#125;		Right curly brace
~	&#126;		Tilde
	&#127;		Unused
¡	&#161;	&iexcl;	Inverted exclamation
¢	&#162;	&cent;	Cent sign
£	&#163;	&pound;	Pound sterling
¤	&#164;	&curren;	General currency sign
¥	&#165;	&yen;	Yen sign
¦	&#166;	¦ or brkbar;	Broken vertical bar
§	&#167;	&sect;	Section sign
¨	&#168;	&uml;	Umlaut (dieresis)
©	&#169;	&copy;	Copyright
ª	&#170;	&ordf;	Feminine ordinal
‹	&#171;	&laquo;	Left angle quote, guillemot left

Character	Numeric Entity	Character Entity	Description
¬	¬	¬	Not sign
-	­	­	Soft hyphen
®	®	®	Registered trademark
¯	¯	&hibar;	Macron accent
°	°	°	Degree sign
±	±	±	Plus or minus
²	²	²	Superscript two
³	³	³	Superscript three
´	´	´	Acute accent
µ	µ	µ	Micro sign
¶	¶	¶	Paragraph sign
·	·	·	Middle dot
¸	¸	¸	Cedilla
¹	¹	¹	Superscript one
º	º	º	Masculine ordinal
›	»	»	Right angle quote, guillemot right
¼	¼	¼	Fraction one-fourth
½	½	½	Fraction one-half
¾	¾	¾	Fraction three-fourths
¿	¿	&iquest	Inverted question mark
À	À	À	Capital A, grave accent
Á	Á	Á	Capital A, acute accent
Â	Â	Â	Capital A, circumflex accent
Ã	Ã	Ã	Capital A, tilde
Ä	Ä	Ä	Capital A, dieresis or umlaut mark
Å	Å	Å	Capital A, ring
Æ	Æ	Æ	Capital AE diphthong (ligature)
Ç	Ç	Ç	Capital C, cedilla
È	È	È	Capital E, grave accent
É	É	É	Capital E, acute accent
Ê	Ê	Ê	Capital E, circumflex accent

continues

Table A.1. continued

Character	Numeric Entity	Character Entity	Description
Ë	&#203;	&Euml;	Capital E, dieresis or umlaut mark
Ì	&#204;	&Igrave;	Capital I, grave accent
Í	&#205;	&Iacute;	Capital I, acute accent
Î	&#206;	&Icirc;	Capital I, circumflex accent
Ï	&#207;	&Iuml;	Capital I, dieresis or umlaut mark
Đ	&#208;	&ETH;	Capital Eth, Icelandic
Ñ	&#209;	&Ntilde;	Capital N, tilde
Ò	&#210;	&Ograve;	Capital O, grave accent
Ó	&#211;	&Oacute;	Capital O, acute accent
Ô	&#212;	&Ocirc;	Capital O, circumflex accent
Õ	&#213;	&Otilde;	Capital O, tilde
Ö	&#214;	&Ouml;	Capital O, dieresis or umlaut mark
×	&#215;		Multiply sign
Ø	&#216;	&Oslash;	Capital O, slash
Ù	&#217;	&Ugrave;	Capital U, grave accent
Ú	&#218;	&Uacute;	Capital U, acute accent
Û	&#219;	&Ucirc;	Capital U, circumflex accent
Ü	&#220;	&Uuml;	Capital U, dieresis or umlaut mark
Ý	&#221;	&Yacute;	Capital Y, acute accent
þ	&#222;	&THORN;	Capital THORN, Icelandic
β	&#223;	&szlig;	Small sharp s, German (sz ligature)
à	&#224;	&agrave;	Small a, grave accent
á	&#225;	&aacute;	Small a, acute accent
â	&#226;	&acirc;	Small a, circumflex accent
ā	&#227;	&atilde;	Small a, tilde
ä	&#228;	&aauml;	Small a, dieresis or umlaut mark
å	&#229;	&aring;	Small a, ring
æ	&#230;	&aelig;	Small ae diphthong (ligature)
ç	&#231;	&ccedil;	Small c, cedilla
è	&#232;	&egrave;	Small e, grave accent

Character	Numeric Entity	Character Entity	Description
é	&#233;	&eacute;	Small e, acute accent
ê	&#234;	&ecirc;	Small e, circumflex accent
ë	&#235;	&euml;	Small e, dieresis or umlaut mark
ì	&#236;	&igrave;	Small i, grave accent
í	&#237;	&iacute;	Small i, acute accent
î	&#238;	&icirc;	Small i, circumflex accent
ï	&#239;	&iuml;	Small i, dieresis or umlaut mark
ð	&#240;	&eth;	Small eth, Icelandic
ñ	&#241;	&ntilde;	Small n, tilde
ò	&#242;	&ograve;	Small o, grave accent
ó	&#243;	&oacute;	Small o, acute accent
ô	&#244;	&ocirc;	Small o, circumflex accent
õ	&#245;	&otilde;	Small o, tilde
ö	&#246;	&ouml;	Small o, dieresis or umlaut mark
÷	&#247;		Division sign
ø	&#248;	&oslash;	Small o, slash
ù	&#249;	&ugrave;	Small u, grave accent
ú	&#250;	&uacute;	Small u, acute accent
û	&#251;	&ucirc;	Small u, circumflex accent
ü	&#252;	&uuml;	Small u, dieresis or umlaut mark
ý	&#253;	&yacute;	Small y, acute accent
þ	&#254;	&thorn;	Small thorn, Icelandic
ÿ	&#255;	&yuml;	Small y, dieresis or umlaut mark

B

HTML Intrinsic Controls: Properties, Events, and Methods

The tables in this appendix summarize the properties, events, and methods for the Elements objects otherwise known as *HTML Intrinsic Controls*.

- ❏ Button
- ❏ Submit
- ❏ Reset
- ❏ CheckBox
- ❏ Radio
- ❏ Password
- ❏ Text
- ❏ TextArea
- ❏ Select
- ❏ Hidden

Table B.1. The Button, Submit, and Reset controls.

Properties	Events	Methods
form	OnClick	click
name	OnFocus	focus
value		
enabled		

Table B.2. The CheckBox control.

Properties	Events	Methods
form	OnClick	click
name	OnFocus	focus
value		
enabled		
checked		
defaultchecked		

Table B.3. The Radio control.

Properties	Events	Methods
form	OnClick	click
name	OnFocus	focus
value		
enabled		
checked		

Table B.4. The Password control.

Properties	Events	Methods
form	OnBlur	blur
name	OnFocus	focus
value		
enabled		

Table B.5. The **Text** and **Textarea** controls.

Properties	Events	Methods
form	OnBlur	blur
name	OnFocus	focus
value		
enabled		

Table B.6. The **Select** control.

Properties	Events	Methods
length	OnBlur	blur
options	OnFocus	focus
selectedIndex	OnChange	

Table B.7. The **Hidden** control.

Properties	Events	Methods
name		
value		

C

VBScript Reference of Syntax, Methods, and Functions

This appendix summarizes the statements, functions, and operators used in the Visual Basic Scripting Edition.

Category / Keyword	Type	Usage
Arithmetic		
Atn	Function	Returns the arctangent of a number Atn(*number*)
Cos	Function	Returns the cosine of an angle Cos(*number*)
Exp	Function	Returns a number raised to a power Exp(*number*)
Log	Function	Returns the logarithm of a number Log(*number*)

continues

Category / Keyword	Type	Usage
		Arithmetic
`Randomize`	Statement	Primes the internal random number generator `Randomize` (See Chapter 11, "Real-Life Examples I")
`Rnd`	Function	Returns a random number `Rnd` (See Chapter 11)
`Sin`	Function	Returns the sine of an angle `Sin(`*number*`)`
`Sqr`	Function	Returns the square root of a number `Sqr(`*number*`)`
`Tan`	Function	Returns the tangent of an angle `Tan(`*number*`)`
		Array handling
`Dim`	Statement	Declares an array `Dim` *arrayname([subscripts])* (See Chapter 4, "Using the VBScript Language")
`Erase`	Statement	Clears the contents of an array `Erase` *arrayname*
`IsArray`	Function	Returns `True` if *var* is an array, and `False` if not. `IsArray(`*var*`)`
`LBound`	Function	In VBScript, always returns `0` `Lbound(`*arrayname*`)`
`Preserve`	Statement	Copies the contents of a dynamic array to a resized dynamic array `Redim Preserve` *arrayname(subscripts)*
`ReDim`	Statement	Declares a dynamic array or redimensions a dynamic array (see `Preserve`) `ReDim` *arrayname()* or `ReDim` *arrayname([subscripts])*
`UBound`	Statement	Returns the largest subscript of an array `Ubound(`*arrayname*`)`

Category / Keyword	Type	Usage

Assignment

=	Operator	Assigns a value to a variable or property `variable = value` (See Chapter 4)
Set	Statement	Assigns an object reference to a variable `Set variable = object`

Comment

Rem	Statement	Declares the following line as a comment to be ignored by the language engine `Rem comment_text`

Constants/Literals

Empty	Literal	Declares a special uninitialized variable value `variable = Empty` (See Chapter 4)
False	Constant	A Boolean value representing `0` `variable = False` (See Chapter 4)
Nothing	Literal	Used to disassociate an object reference from a variable; used in conjunction with `Set` `Set variable = Nothing` (See Chapter 4)
Null	Literal	Represents no valid data `variable = Null` (See Chapter 4)
True	Constant	Boolean value representing `-1` `variable = True` (See Chapter 4)

continues

Category / Keyword	Type	Usage
		Conversions
Abs	Function	Returns the unsigned (absolute) value of a number Abs(*number*)
Asc	Function	Returns the ANSI/ASCII code of a character Asc(*string*) (See Chapter 3, "Communicating with Your Users")
CBool	Function	Returns a Boolean subtype Variant value from any valid expression CBool(*expression*)
CByte	Function	Returns a Byte subtype Variant value from any valid expression CByte(*expression*)
CDate	Function	Returns a Date subtype Variant value from any valid date expression CDate(*expression*)
CDbl	Function	Returns a Double Precision subtype Variant value from any valid numeric expression CDbl(*expression*)
Chr	Function	Returns the character corresponding to the ANSI or ASCII code Chr(*number*)
CInt	Function	Returns an Integer subtype Variant value from any valid numeric expression CInt(*expression*)
CLng	Function	Returns a Long Integer subtype Variant value from any valid numeric expression CLng(*expression*)
CSng	Function	Returns a Single Precision subtype Variant value from any valid numeric expression CSng(*expression*)
CStr	Function	Returns a String subtype Variant value from any valid expression CStr(*expression*)

Category / Keyword	Type	Usage
DateSerial	Function	Returns a Date subtype Variant from valid year, month, and day values DateSerial(*year*,*month*,*day*)
DateValue	Function	Returns a Date subtype Variant value from any valid date expression DateValue(*expression*)
Hex	Function	Returns a String subtype Variant representing the hexadecimal value of a number Hex(*number*)
Int	Function	Returns an Integer subtype Variant rounded down from the number supplied Int(*number*)
Fix	Function	Returns an Integer subtype Variant rounded up from the number supplied Fix(*number*)
Oct	Function	Returns a String subtype Variant representing the octal value of a number Hex(*number*)
Sgn	Function	Returns an Integer subtype Variant representing the sign of a number Sgn(*number*) values > 0 return 1 values = 0 return 0 values < 0 return -1
TimeSerial	Function	Returns a Date subtype Variant from valid hour, minute, and second values TimeSerial(*hour*,*minute*,*second*)
TimeValue	Function	Returns a Date subtype Variant value from any valid time expression TimeValue(*expression*)

Dates and Times

Date	Function	Returns the current system date Date()

continues

Category / Keyword	Type	Usage
		Dates and Times
DateSerial	Function	Returns a Date subtype `Variant` from valid year, month, and day values. `DateSerial(year,month,day)`
DateValue	Function	Returns a Date subtype `Variant` value from any valid date expression. `DateValue(expression)`
Day	Function	Returns an Integer subtype `Variant` representing the day (`1-31`) from a valid date expression `Day(dateexpression)`
Hour	Function	Returns an Integer subtype `Variant` representing the hour (`0-23`) from a valid time expression `Hour(timeexpression)`
Minute	Function	Returns an Integer subtype `Variant` representing the minute (`0-60`) from a valid time expression `Minute(timeexpression)`
Month	Function	Returns an Integer subtype `Variant` representing the month (`1-12`) from a valid date expression `Month(dateexpression)`
Now	Function	Returns the current date and time of the system `Now()`
Second	Function	Returns an Integer subtype `Variant` representing the second (`0-60`) from a valid time expression `Second(timeexpression)`
Time	Function	Returns the current system time `Time()`
TimeSerial	Function	Returns a Date subtype `Variant` from valid hour, minute and second values `TimeSerial(hour,minute,second)`
TimeValue	Function	Returns a Date subtype `Variant` value from any valid time expression `TimeValue(expression)`

Category / Keyword	Type	Usage
Weekday	Function	Returns an Integer subtype `Variant` between 1 and 7 representing the day of the week, starting at Sunday, from a date expression `Weekday(dateexpression)`
Year	Function	Returns an Integer subtype `Variant` representing the year from a valid date expression `Year(dateexpression)`

Declarations

Category / Keyword	Type	Usage
Dim	Statement	Declares a variable `Dim variable`

End	Statement	Declares the end of a `Sub` procedure or function
		`End Sub`
		`End Function`

Exit	Statement	Use with `Do`, `For`, `Function`, or `Sub` to prematurely exit the routine `Exit Do/For/Function/Sub`

Function	Statement	Declares a function and the argument list passed into the function, and declares the end of a function; also used with `Exit` to prematurely end a function
		`Function functionname(argumentlist)`
		`Exit Function`
		`End Function`
		`Public variable`

Sub	Statement	Declares a custom procedure or event handler and the argument list, if any, and declares the end of a custom procedure or event handler; also used with `Exit` to prematurely end a custom procedure or event handler
		`Sub subroutinename([argumentlist])`
		`Exit Sub`
		`End Sub`

continues

Category / Keyword	Type	Usage
		Error Handling
`Clear`	Method	A method of the `Err` object to reset the `Err.Number` property to `0` `Err.Clear`
`Description`	Property	A property of the `Err` object that contains a description of the last error as specified in the `Err.Number` property `Err.Description`
`Err`	Object	An object containing information about the last error `Err.property¦method`
`On Error`	Statement	Used in conjunction with `Resume Next` to continue execution with the line directly following the line in which the error occurred `On Error Resume Next`
`Raise`	Method	A method of the `Err` object used to simulate the occurrence of an error specified by number `Err.Raise(errornumber)`
`Number`	Property	A property of the `Err` object that contains the error code for the last error, or `0` if no error has occurred `Err.Number`
`Source`	Property	Returns the name of the object or application that raised the error `Err.Source`
		Input/Output
`InputBox`	Function	Displays a dialog box to allow user input `InputBox(caption[,title][,value][,x][,y])`
`MsgBox`	Function	Displays a dialog box `MsgBox(prompt[, definition][, title])`
		Operators
`+`	Operator	Addition of two numerical expressions `result = expr1 + expr2`
`And`	Operator	Logical conjunction operator `If expression AND expression Then`

Category / Keyword	Type	Usage
/	Operator	Division operator `result = expression / expression`
=	Operator	Equality operator `If expression = expression Then`
Eqv	Operator	Logical equivalence operator `If expression Eqv expression Then`
^	Operator	Exponentiation operator `result = expression ^ expression`
>	Operator	Greater than comparison `If expression > expression Then`
>=	Operator	Greater than or equal to comparison `If expression >= expression Then`
Imp	Operator	Logical implication `If expression Imp expression Then`
<>	Operator	Inequality comparison `If expression <> expression Then`
\	Operator	Integer division operator `result = expression \ expression`
<	Operator	Less than comparison `If expression < expression Then`
<=	Operator	Less than or equal to comparison `If expression <= expression Then`
Mod	Operator	Modulus arithmetic; returns only the remainder of a division of two numbers `result = expression mod expression`
*	Operator	Multiplication `result = expression * expression`
-	Operator	Subtraction `result = expression - expression`
Or	Operator	Logical disjunction `If expression Or expression Then`
&	Operator	Concatenation of two string values `result = string & string`
Xor	Operator	Logical exclusion `If expression Xor expression Then`

continues

Category / Keyword	Type	Usage
		Options
`Option`	Statement	Forces a compile-time error if an `Explicit` undeclared variable is found
		`Option Explicit`
		Program Flow
`Call`	Statement	Passes execution to a subroutine or event handler; also can be used to replicate the actions of the user
		`Call myroutine()`
		`Call cmdbutton_OnClick()`
`Do...Loop`	Statement	Repeats code while a condition is met or until a condition is met
		`Do While condition`
		`...`
		`Loop`
		`or`
		`Do Until condition`
		`...`
		`Loop`
		`or`
		`Do`
		`...`
		`Loop While condition`
		`or`
		`Do`
		`...`
		`Loop Until condition`
`For...Next`	Statement	Repeats a block of code until the counter reaches a given number
		`For counter = lower to upper [step]`
		`...`
		`Next`
`If...Then...Else`	Statement	Conditional execution of code
		`If condition Then`
		`... (if condition met)`
		`Else`
		`... (if condition not met)`
		`End If`

Category / Keyword	Type	Usage

Select Case	Statement	Selective execution of code, where *testexpression* must match *expression*
		`Select Case testexpression`
		`Case expression`
		`...`
		`Case expression`
		`...`
		`Case Else`
		`End Select`

While...Wend	Statement	Execution of a code block while a condition is met
		`While expression`
		`...`
		`Wend`

Strings

Category / Keyword	Type	Usage
InStr	Function	Returns the starting point of one string within another string, or 0 if not found *result* = `InStr(`*start*`,`*searched*`,`*sought*`)`
LCase	Function	Converts a string to lowercase *result* = `LCase(`*string*`)`
Left	Function	Returns the *n* leftmost characters of a string *result* = `LCase(`*string*`)`
Len	Function	Returns the length of a string *result* = `Len(`*string*`)`
LTrim	Function	Removes all leading spaces *result* = `LTrim(`*string*`)`
Mid	Function	Returns a string of length *L*, starting at *s* within *string* *result* = `Mid(`*string*`, S, L)`
Right	Function	Returns the rightmost *n* characters *result* = `Right(`*string*`, n)`
RTrim	Function	Removes all trailing spaces from a string *result* = `RTrim(`*string*`)`

continues

Category / Keyword	Type	Usage
		Strings
Space	Function	Returns a string consisting of *n* spaces *result* = Space(*n*)
StrComp	Function	Returns an Integer subtype Variant representing the result of a comparison of two strings *result* = StrComp(*string1*, *string2*) *string1* < *string2* returns -1 *string1* < *string2* returns 0 *string1* < *string2* returns 1
String	Function	Returns a string consisting of character *c*, of length *L* *result* = String(*L*, *C*)
Trim	Function	Removes both leading and trailing spaces *result* = Trim(*string*)
UCase	Function	Returns a string as uppercase alphabetical characters *result* = UCase(*string*)
		Variants
IsArray	Function	Returns True (-1) if expression is an array, and False (0) if not *result* = IsArray(*expression*)
IsDate	Function	Returns True (-1) if expression is a valid date and False (0) if not *result* = IsDate(*expression*)
IsEmpty	Function	Returns True (-1) if expression equates to an Empty subtype and False (0) if not *result* = IsEmpty(*expression*)
IsNull	Function	Returns True (-1) if expression equates to a Null subtype and False (0) if not *result* = IsNull(*expression*)
IsNumeric	Function	Returns True (-1) if expression is a valid numeric expression and False (0) if not *result* = IsNumeric(*expression*)
VarType	Function	Returns an integer representing the sub data type of a Variant *result* = VarType(*expression*)

D

Active Scripting Object Model

This appendix summarizes the properties, events, and methods for the objects in the Active Scripting Object Model.

The Active Scripting Object Model consists of the following objects:

- ❏ Window
- ❏ Frame
- ❏ History
- ❏ Navigator
- ❏ Location
- ❏ Script
- ❏ Document
- ❏ Link
- ❏ Anchor
- ❏ Form

See Appendix B, "HTML Intrinsic Controls: Properties, Events, and Methods," for details of the Elements objects (also known as Intrinsic HTML Controls).

Window Object

Window Object Properties

- ❏ Name: Returns the name of the current window
- ❏ Parent: Returns a window object of the current window's parent
- ❏ Self: Returns the window object of the current window
- ❏ Top: Returns the window object of the topmost window
- ❏ Location: Returns the Location object of the current window
- ❏ Status: Gets or sets the text in the browser status bar
- ❏ Frames: Returns the array of frames for the current window
- ❏ History: Returns the History object for the current window
- ❏ Navigator: Returns the Navigator object for the current window
- ❏ Document: Returns the Document object for the current window

Window Object Methods

- ❏ Alert: Displays a simple message box with exclamation icon
- ❏ Confirm: Displays a message box containing Yes and No buttons
- ❏ Prompt: Prompts the user for input
- ❏ Open: Creates a new window
- ❏ Close: Closes the current window
- ❏ SetTimeout: Sets a timer to call a function after a specified number of milliseconds
- ❏ ClearTimeout: Clears the specified timer
- ❏ Navigate: Loads the resource at a URL

Window Object Events

- ❏ OnLoad: Fires when the contents of a window are loaded
- ❏ OnUnload: Fires when the contents of a window are unloaded

Frame Object

The Frame object can be treated as another window. Therefore, you can use the properties, methods, and events of the Window object.

History Object

History Object Properties

- ❏ Length: Returns the number of items in the current history list

History Object Methods

- ❏ `Back`: Moves back *n* items in the history list
- ❏ `Forward`: Moves forward *n* items in the history list
- ❏ `Go`: Moves to item *n* in the history list

There are currently no History object events.

Navigator Object

Navigator Object Properties

- ❏ `appCodeName`: Returns the code name of the browser application
- ❏ `appName`: Returns the name of the browser application
- ❏ `appVersion`: Returns the version of the browser application
- ❏ `userAgent`: Returns the `HTTP_USER_AGENT` string for the browser application

The Navigator object currently has no methods or events.

Location Object

Location Object Properties

- ❏ `href`: Gets or sets the complete URL for the current resource location
- ❏ `protocol`: Gets or sets the protocol section of the URL
- ❏ `host`: Gets or sets the host and port of the URL
- ❏ `hostname`: Gets or sets the hostname section of the URL
- ❏ `port`: Returns the port section of the URL
- ❏ `pathname`: Gets or sets the pathname section of the URL
- ❏ `search`: Gets or sets the search portion (characters following a question mark) of the URL

The Location object currently has no methods or events.

Script Object

The Script object currently has no properties, methods, or events.

Document Object

Document Object Properties

- ❏ `linkColor`: Gets or sets the color of the links
- ❏ `aLinkColor`: Gets or sets the color of the active links

❏ vLinkColor: Gets or sets the color of the visited links

❏ bgColor: Gets or sets the background color

❏ fgColor: Gets or sets the text (foreground) color

❏ anchors: Returns the array of anchors for the current document

❏ links: Returns the array of links for the current document

❏ forms: Returns the array of forms for the current document

❏ location: Returns a read-only location object

❏ lastModified: Returns the date when the current document was last saved

❏ title: Returns the document's title

❏ cookie: Gets or sets a cookie string for the current document

❏ referrer: Gets the URL of the referring document

Document Object Methods

❏ write: Places a string into the document buffer

❏ writeLn: Has the same functionality as the write method, but adds a line feed character to the end of the string

❏ open: Opens the document buffer

❏ close: Closes the document buffer and writes the contents of the buffer to the screen

The Document object currently has no events.

Link Object

Link Object Properties

❏ length: Returns the number of links in the links array

❏ href: Returns the complete URL for the link

❏ protocol: Returns the protocol section of the URL

❏ host: Returns the hostname and port for the URL

❏ hostname: Returns the hostname for the URL

❏ port: Returns the port for the URL

❏ pathname: Returns the pathname for the URL

❏ search: Returns the search portion of the URL

❏ target: Returns the window name for the target

The Link object currently has no methods.

Link Object Events

- ❑ `mouseMove`: Fires as the mouse arrow passes over the link
- ❑ `onMouseOver`: Fires as the mouse arrow passes over the link
- ❑ `OnClick`: Fires as the link is clicked

Anchor Object

Anchor Object Properties

- ❑ `name`: Returns the name of the anchor
- ❑ `count`: Returns the number of anchors in the anchor array

Form Object

Form Object Properties

- ❑ `action`: Gets or sets the form action
- ❑ `encoding`: Gets or sets the form encoding
- ❑ `method`: Gets or sets the form method—either `Get` or `Post`
- ❑ `target`:Gets or sets the name of the window to display the form action (results)
- ❑ `elements`: Returns an array of elements within the form

Form Object Methods

- ❑ `submit`: Submits the form

Form Object Events

- ❑ `onSubmit`: Fires immediately prior to submission of the form

ActiveX Controls: Properties, Events, and Methods

The tables in this appendix summarize the properties, events, and methods for the standard ActiveX controls found in the ActiveX Control Pad:

- ❏ CheckBox
- ❏ ComboBox
- ❏ Command Button
- ❏ HotSpot
- ❏ Image Control
- ❏ Label
- ❏ ListBox
- ❏ Option Button
- ❏ Scroll Bar
- ❏ Spin Button
- ❏ Tab Strip
- ❏ TextBox
- ❏ Toggle Button

Table E.1. The CheckBox control.

Properties	Events	Methods
Accelerator	AfterUpdate	SetFocus
Alignment	BeforeDragOver	ZOrder
AutoSize	BeforeDropOrPaste	
BackColor	BeforeUpdate	
BackStyle	Change	
Caption	Click	
CodeBase	DblClick	
Enabled	Enter	
Font	Exit	
ForeColor	Error	
Height	KeyDown	
Width	KeyUp	
ID	KeyPress	
Left	MouseDown	
Top	MouseUp	
Locked	MouseMove	
MouseIcon		
MousePointer		
Picture		
PicturePosition		
SpecialEffect		
TabIndex		
TabStop		
TripleState		
Value		
Visible		
WordWrap		

Table E.2. The ComboBox control.

Properties	Events	Methods
AutoSize	AfterUpdate	AddItem
AutoTab	BeforeDragOver	Clear
AutoWordSelect	BeforeDropOrPaste	Copy
BackColor	BeforeUpdate	Cut
BackStyle	Change	DropDown
BorderColor	Click	Paste
BorderStyle	DblClick	RemoveItem
BoundColumn	DropButtonClick	SetFocus
CodeBase	Enter	ZOrder
Column	Exit	
ColumnCount	Error	
ColumnHeads	KeyDown	
ColumnWidths	KeyUp	
DragBehaviour	KeyPress	
DropButtonStyle	MouseDown	
Enabled	MouseUp	
EnterFieldBehaviour	MouseMove	
Font		
ForeColor		
Height		
Width		
HideSelection		
ID		
IMEMode		
IntegralHeight		
Left		
Top		
List		
ListCount		
ListIndex		
ListRows		

continues

Table E.2. continued

Properties	Events	Methods
ListStyle		
ListWidth		
Locked		
MatchEntry		
MatchRequired		
MaxLength		
MouseIcon		
MousePointer		
SelectionMargin		
SelLength		
SelStart		
SelText		
ShowDownButtonWhen		
SpecialEffect		
Style		
TabIndex		
TabStop		
Text		
TextAlign		
TextColumn		
Value		
Visible		

Table E.3. The Command Button control.

Properties	Events	Methods
Accelerator	AfterUpdate	SetFocus
AutoSize	BeforeDragOver	ZOrder
BackColor	BeforeDropOrPaste	
BackStyle	BeforeUpdate	
Caption	Click	
CodeBase	DblClick	
Enabled	Enter	

Properties	Events	Methods
Font	Exit	
ForeColor	Error	
Height	KeyDown	
Width	KeyUp	
ID	KeyPress	
Left	MouseDown	
Top	MouseUp	
Locked	MouseMove	
MouseIcon		
MousePointer		
Picture		
PicturePosition		
TabIndex		
TabStop		
Value		
Visible		
WordWrap		

Table E.4. The HotSpot control.

Properties	Events	Methods
CodeBase	Click	Move
Enabled	DblClick	ZOrder
Height	Enter	
Width	Exit	
ID	MouseDown	
Left	MouseEnter	
Top	MouseExit	
MouseIcon	MouseUp	
MousePointer	MouseMove	
TabIndex		
TabStop		
Visible		

Table E.5. The Image control.

Properties	Events	Methods
AutoSize	BeforeDragOver	Move
BackColor	BeforeDropOrPaste	ZOrder
BackStyle	Enter	
BorderColor	Exit	
BorderStyle	MouseDown	
CodeBase	MouseUp	
Enabled	MouseMove	
Height		
Width		
ID		
Left		
Top		
PictureAlignment		
PicturePath		
PictureSizeMode		
PictureTiling		
SpecialEffect		
Visible		

Table E.6. The Label control.

Properties	Events	Methods
Accelerator	AfterUpdate	ZOrder
AutoSize	BeforeDragOver	
BackColor	BeforeDropOrPaste	
BackStyle	BeforeUpdate	
BorderColor	Click	
BorderStyle	DblClick	
Caption	Enter	
CodeBase	Exit	
Enabled	Error	
Font	MouseDown	

Properties	Events	Methods
ForeColor	MouseUp	
Height	MouseMove	
Width		
ID		
Left		
Top		
MouseIcon		
MousePointer		
Picture		
PicturePosition		
Special Effect		
TabIndex		
TextAlign		
Visible		
WordWrap		

Table E.7. The ListBox control.

Properties	Events	Methods
BackColor	AfterUpdate	AddItem
BorderColor	BeforeDragOver	Clear
BorderStyle	BeforeDropOrPaste	RemoveItem
BoundColumn	BeforeUpdate	SetFocus
CodeBase	Change	ZOrder
Column	Click	
ColumnCount	DblClick	
ColumnHeads	Enter	
ColumnWidths	Exit	
Enabled	Error	
Font	KeyDown	
ForeColor	KeyUp	
Height	KeyPress	
Width	MouseDown	

continues

Table E.7. continued

Properties	Events	Methods
ID	MouseUp	
IMEMode	MouseMove	
IntegralHeight		
Left		
Top		
List		
ListIndex		
ListStyle		
Locked		
MatchEntry		
MouseIcon		
MousePointer		
Selected		
SpecialEffect		
TabIndex		
TabStop		
Text		
TextColumn		
Value		
Visible		

Table E.8. The Option Button control.

Properties	Events	Methods
Accelerator	AfterUpdate	SetFocus
Alignment	BeforeDragOver	ZOrder
AutoSize	BeforeDropOrPaste	
BackColor	BeforeUpdate	
BackStyle	Change	
Caption	Click	
CodeBase	DblClick	
Enabled	Enter	

Properties	Events	Methods
Font	Exit	
ForeColor	Error	
GroupName	KeyDown	
Height	KeyUp	
Width	KeyPress	
ID	MouseDown	
Left	MouseUp	
Top	MouseMove	
Locked		
MouseIcon		
MousePointer		
Picture		
PicturePosition		
SpecialEffect		
TabIndex		
TabStop		
TripleState		
Value		
Visible		
WordWrap		

Table E.9. The Scroll Bar control.

Properties	Events	Methods
BackColor	AfterUpdate	Move
CodeBase	BeforeDragOver	SetFocus
Delay	BeforeDropOrPaste	ZOrder
Enabled	BeforeUpdate	
ForeColor	Change	
Height	Enter	
Width	Exit	
ID	Error	

continues

Table E.9. continued

Properties	Events	Methods
LargeChange	KeyDown	
Left	KeyUp	
Top	KeyPress	
Max	Scroll	
Min		
MouseIcon		
MousePointer		
Orientation		
ProportionalThumb		
SmallChange		
TabIndex		
TabStop		
Value		
Visible		

Table E.10. The Spin Button control.

Properties	Events	Methods
BackColor	AfterUpdate	SetFocus
CodeBase	BeforeDragOver	ZOrder
Delay	BeforeDropOrPaste	
Enabled	BeforeUpdate	
ForeColor	Change	
Height	Enter	
Width	Exit	
ID	Error	
Left	KeyDown	
Top	KeyUp	
Max	KeyPress	
Min	SpinDown	
MouseIcon	SpinUp	
MousePointer		
Orientation		

Properties	Events	Methods
SmallChange		
TabIndex		
TabStop		
Value		
Visible		

Table E.11. The Tab Strip control.

Properties	Events	Methods
Accelerator	BeforeDragOver	SetFocus
BackColor	BeforeDropOrPaste	ZOrder
Caption	Change	
CodeBase	Click	
Enabled	DblClick	
Font	Enter	
ForeColor	Exit	
Height	Error	
Width	KeyDown	
ID	KeyUp	
Left	KeyPress	
Top	MouseDown	
MouseIcon	MouseUp	
MousePointer	MouseMove	
MultiRow		
SelectedItem		
Style		
TabFixedHeight		
TabFixedWidth		
TabIndex		
TabOrientation		
TabStop		
Value		
Visible		

Table E.12. The TextBox control.

Properties	Events	Methods
AutoSize	AfterUpdate	Copy
AutoTab	BeforeDragOver	Cut
AutoWordSelect	BeforeDropOrPaste	Paste
BackColor	BeforeUpdate	SetFocus
BackStyle	Change	ZOrder
BorderColor	DblClick	
BorderStyle	Enter	
CodeBase	Exit	
CurLine	Error	
DragBehaviour	KeyDown	
Enabled	KeyUp	
EnterFieldBehaviour	KeyPress	
EnterKeyBehaviour	MouseDown	
Font	MouseUp	
ForeColor	MouseMove	
Height		
Width		
HideSelection		
ID		
IMEMode		
IntegralHeight		
Left		
Top		
LineCount		
Locked		
MaxLength		
MouseIcon		
MousePointer		
MultiLine		
PasswordChar		
ScrollBars		
SelectionMargin		

Properties	Events	Methods
SelLength		
SelStart		
SelText		
Special Effect		
TabIndex		
TabKeyBehaviour		
TabStop		
Text		
TextAlign		
Value		
Visible		
WordWrap		

Table E.13. The Toggle Button control.

Properties	Events	Methods
Accelerator	AfterUpdate	SetFocus
Alignment	BeforeDragOver	ZOrder
AutoSize	BeforeDropOrPaste	
BackColor	BeforeUpdate	
BackStyle	Change	
Caption	Click	
CodeBase	DblClick	
Enabled	Enter	
Font	Exit	
ForeColor	Error	
Height	KeyDown	
Width	KeyUp	
ID	KeyPress	
Left	MouseDown	
Top	MouseUp	
Locked	MouseMove	

continues

Table E.13. continued

Properties	Events	Methods
MouseIcon		
MousePointer		
Picture		
PictureProperty		
SpecialEffect		
TabIndex		
TabStop		
TripleState		
Value		
Visible		
WordWrap		

APPENDIX

F

The ASCII Character Set

This appendix cross-references the characters represented by ASCII and ANSI code. To convert a code into a character, use `Chr(code)`; to convert a character into a code, use `Asc(char)`. ANSI codes lower than 20 should not be used in a Web page environment.

Dec X_{10}	Hex X_{16}	Binary X_2	ASCII Character	ANSI Characters
000	00	0000 0000	null	000-032
001	01	0000 0001	☺	not def.
002	02	0000 0010	☻	
003	03	0000 0011	♥	
004	04	0000 0100	♦	
005	05	0000 0101	♣	
006	06	0000 0110	♠	
007	07	0000 0111	•	
008	08	0000 1000	◘	
009	09	0000 1001	○	
010	0A	0000 1010	◙	
011	0B	0000 1011	♂	
012	0C	0000 1100	♀	
013	0D	0000 1101	♪	
014	0E	0000 1110	♫	
015	0F	0000 1111	☼	
016	10	0001 0000	►	
017	11	0001 0001	◄	
018	12	0001 0010	↕	
019	13	0001 0011	‼	
020	14	0001 0100	¶	
021	15	0001 0101	§	
022	16	0001 0110	▬	
023	17	0001 0111	↨	
024	18	0001 1000	↑	
025	19	0001 1001	↓	
026	1A	0001 1010	→	
027	1B	0001 1011	←	

Dec X_{10}	Hex X_{16}	Binary X_2	ASCII Character	ANSI Characters
028	1C	0001 1100	∟	
029	1D	0001 1101	↔	
030	1E	0001 1110	▲	
031	1F	0001 1111	▼	
032	20	0010 0000	space	
033	21	0010 0001	!	!
034	22	0010 0010	"	"
035	23	0010 0011	#	#
036	24	0010 0100	$	$
037	25	0010 0101	%	%
038	26	0010 0110	&	&
039	27	0010 0111	'	'
040	28	0010 1000	(	(
041	29	0010 1001	)	)
042	2A	0010 1010	*	*
043	2B	0010 1011	+	+
044	2C	0010 1100	,	'
045	2D	0010 1101	-	-
046	2E	0010 1110	.	.
047	2F	0010 1111	/	/
048	30	0011 0000	0	0
049	31	0011 0001	1	1
050	32	0011 0010	2	2
051	33	0011 0011	3	3
052	34	0011 0100	4	4
053	35	0011 0101	5	5
054	36	0011 0110	6	6
055	37	0011 0111	7	7

continues

Dec X_{10}	Hex X_{16}	Binary X_2	ASCII Character	ANSI Characters
056	38	0011 1000	8	8
057	39	0011 1001	9	9
058	3A	0011 1010	:	:
059	3B	0011 1011	;	;
060	3C	0011 1100	<	<
061	3D	0011 1101	=	=
062	3E	0011 1110	>	>
063	3F	0011 1111	?	?
064	40	0100 0000	@	@
065	41	0100 0001	A	A
066	42	0100 0010	B	B
067	43	0100 0011	C	C
068	44	0100 0100	D	D
069	45	0100 0101	E	E
070	46	0100 0110	F	F
071	47	0100 0111	G	G
072	48	0100 1000	H	H
073	49	0100 1001	I	I
074	4A	0100 1010	J	J
075	4B	0100 1011	K	K
076	4C	0100 1100	L	L
077	4D	0100 1101	M	M
078	4E	0100 1110	N	N
079	4F	0100 1111	O	O
080	50	0101 0000	P	P
081	51	0101 0001	Q	Q
082	52	0101 0010	R	R
083	53	0101 0011	S	S

Dec X_{10}	Hex X_{16}	Binary X_2	ASCII Character	ANSI Characters
084	54	0101 0100	T	T
085	55	0101 0101	U	U
086	56	0101 0110	V	V
087	57	0101 0111	W	W
088	58	0101 1000	X	X
089	59	0101 1001	Y	Y
090	5A	0101 1010	Z	Z
091	5B	0101 1011	[	[
092	5C	0101 1100	\	\
093	5D	0101 1101	]	]
094	5E	0101 1110	^	^
095	5F	0101 1111	–	–
096	60	0110 0000	`	`
097	61	0110 0001	a	a
098	62	0110 0010	b	b
099	63	0110 0011	c	c
100	64	0110 0100	d	d
101	65	0110 0101	e	e
102	66	0110 0110	f	f
103	67	0110 0111	g	g
104	68	0110 1000	h	h
105	69	0110 1001	i	i
106	6A	0110 1010	j	j
107	6B	0110 1011	k	k
108	6C	0110 1100	l	l
109	6D	0110 1101	m	m
110	6E	0110 1110	n	n
111	6F	0110 1111	o	o

continues

Dec X_{10}	Hex X_{16}	Binary X_2	ASCII Character	ANSI Characters
112	70	0111 0000	p	p
113	71	0111 0001	q	q
114	72	0111 0010	r	r
115	73	0111 0011	s	s
116	74	0111 0100	t	t
117	75	0111 0101	u	u
118	76	0111 0110	v	v
119	77	0111 0111	w	w
120	78	0111 1000	x	x
121	79	0111 1001	y	y
122	7A	0111 1010	z	z
123	7B	0111 1011	{	{
124	7C	0111 1100	¦	l
125	7D	0111 1101	}	}
126	7E	0111 1110	~	~
127	7F	0111 1111	Δ	□
128	80	1000 0000	Ç	□
129	81	1000 0001	ü	□
130	82	1000 0010	é	,
131	83	1000 0011	â	ƒ
132	84	1000 0100	ä	"
133	85	1000 0101	à	…
134	86	1000 0110	å	†
135	87	1000 0111	ç	‡
136	88	1000 1000	ê	^
137	89	1000 1001	ë	‰
138	8A	1000 1010	è	Š
139	8B	1000 1011	ï	<

Dec X_{10}	Hex X_{16}	Binary X_2	ASCII Character	ANSI Characters
140	8C	1000 1100	î	Œ
141	8D	1000 1101	ì	□
142	8E	1000 1110	Ä	□
143	8F	1000 1111	Å	□
144	90	1001 0000	É	□
145	91	1001 0001	æ	'
146	92	1001 0010	Æ	'
147	93	1001 0011	ô	"
148	94	1001 0100	ö	"
149	95	1001 0101	ò	•
150	96	1001 0110	û	–
151	97	1001 0111	ù	—
152	98	1001 1000	ÿ	~
153	99	1001 1001	Ö	™
154	9A	1001 1010	Ü	š
155	9B	1001 1011	¢	>
156	9C	1001 1100	£	œ
157	9D	1001 1101	¥	□
158	9E	1001 1110	₧	□
159	9F	1001 1111	ƒ	Ÿ
160	A0	1010 0000	á	
161	A1	1010 0001	í	¡
162	A2	1010 0010	ó	¢
163	A3	1010 0011	ú	£
164	A4	1010 0100	ñ	¤
165	A5	1010 0101	Ñ	¥
166	A6	1010 0110	ª	¦
167	A7	1010 0111	º	»

continues

Dec X_{10}	Hex X_{16}	Binary X_2	ASCII Character	ANSI Characters
168	A8	1010 1000	º	··
169	A9	1010 1001	¿	©
170	AA	1010 1010	⌐	ª
171	AB	1010 1011	¬	«
172	AC	1010 1100	½	¬
173	AD	1010 1101	¼	-
174	AE	1010 1110	¡	®
175	AF	1010 1111	«	‾
176	B0	1011 0000	»	°
177	B1	1011 0001	▒	±
178	B2	1011 0010	▓	²
179	B3	1011 0011	█	³
180	B4	1011 0100	│	'
181	B5	1011 0101	┤	µ
182	B6	1011 0110	╡	¶
183	B7	1011 0111	╢	·
184	B8	1011 1000	╖	¸
185	B9	1011 1001	╣	¹
186	BA	1011 1010	║	º
187	BB	1011 1011	╗	»
188	BC	1011 1100	╝	¼
189	BD	1011 1101	╜	½
190	BE	1011 1110	╛	¾
191	BF	1011 1111	┐	¿
192	C0	1100 0000	└	À
193	C1	1100 0001	┴	Á
194	C2	1100 0010	┬	Â
195	C3	1100 0011	├	Ã

Dec X_{10}	Hex X_{16}	Binary X_2	ASCII Character	ANSI Characters
196	C4	1100 0100	├	Ä
197	C5	1100 0101	─	Å
198	C6	1100 0110	+	Æ
199	C7	1100 0111	╞	Ç
200	C8	1100 1000	╟	È
201	C9	1100 1001	╚	É
202	CA	1100 1010	╔	Ê
203	CB	1100 1011	╩	Ë
204	CC	1100 1100	╦	Ì
205	CD	1100 1101	╠	Í
206	CE	1100 1110	=	Î
207	CF	1100 1111	╬	Ï
208	D0	1101 0000	╧	Ð
209	D1	1101 0001	╨	Ñ
210	D2	1101 0010	╤	Ò
211	D3	1101 0011	╥	Ó
212	D4	1101 0100	╙	Ô
213	D5	1101 0101	╘	Õ
214	D6	1101 0110	╒	Ö
215	D7	1101 0111	╓	×
216	D8	1101 1000	╫	Ø
217	D9	1101 1001	╪	Ù
218	DA	1101 1010	┘	Ú
219	DB	1101 1011	┌	Û
220	DC	1101 1100	█	Ü
221	DD	1101 1101	▪	Ý
222	DE	1101 1110	▌	Þ
223	DF	1101 1111	▐	β

continues

Dec X_{10}	Hex X_{16}	Binary X_2	ASCII Character	ANSI Characters
224	E0	1110 0000	■	à
225	E1	1110 0001	α	á
226	E2	1110 0010	β	â
227	E3	1110 0011	Γ	ã
228	E4	1110 0100	π	ä
229	E5	1110 0101	Σ	å
230	E6	1110 0110	σ	æ
231	E7	1110 0111	μ	ç
232	E8	1110 1000	γ	è
233	E9	1110 1001	Φ	é
234	EA	1110 1010	θ	ê
235	EB	1110 1011	Ω	ë
236	EC	1110 1100	δ	ì
237	ED	1110 1101	∞	í
238	EE	1110 1110	ø	î
239	EF	1110 1111	∈	ï
240	F0	1110 0000	∩	ð
241	F1	1111 0001	≡	ñ
242	F2	1111 0010	±	ò
243	F3	1111 0011	≥	ó
244	F4	1111 0100	≤	ô
245	F5	1111 0101	⌠	õ
246	F6	1111 0110	⌡	ö
247	F7	1111 0111	÷	÷
248	F8	1111 1000	≈	ø
249	F9	1111 1001	°	ù
250	FA	1111 1010	•	ú
251	FB	1111 1011	·	û

Dec X_{10}	Hex X_{16}	Binary X_2	ASCII Character	ANSI Characters
252	FC	1111 1100	√	ü
253	FD	1111 1101	ⁿ	ý
254	FE	1111 1110	²	þ
255	FF	1111 1111	■	ÿ

I N D E X

Laura Lemay's Web Workshop: Netscape Navigator Gold 3

—Laura Lemay & Ned Snell *Covers Web Publishing*

Netscape Gold and JavaScript are two powerful tools to create and design effective Web pages. This book details not only design elements, but also how to use the Netscape Gold WYSIWYG editor. The included CD-ROM contains editors and code from the book, making the reader's learning experience a quick and effective one.

The CD-ROM includes editors and all the source code from the book.

Teaches how to program within Navigator Gold's rich Netscape development environment. Explores elementary design principles for effective Web page creation.

$39.99 USA $53.99 CDN *Casual–Accomplished* *Internet/General*
ISBN: 1-57521-128-9 *400 pp.*

Laura Lemay's Web Workshop: 3D Graphics and VRML 2

—Laura Lemay, Kelly Murdock, & Justin Couch *Covers the Internet*

This is the easiest way for readers to learn how to add three-dimensional virtual worlds to Web pages. It describes the new VRML 2 specification, explores the wide array of existing VRML sites on the Web, and steps readers through the process of creating their own 3D Web environments.

The CD-ROM contains the book in HTML format, a hand-picked selection of the best VRML and 3D graphics tools, plus a collection of ready-to-use virtual worlds.

Contains complete coverage of VRML 2!

Teaches how to create 3D worlds on the Web.

$39.99 USA $56.95 CDN *Casual–Accomplished* *Internet/Graphics/Multimedia*
ISBN: 1-57521-143-2 *400 pp.*

Laura Lemay's Web Workshop: Graphics and Web Page Design

—Laura Lemay, Jon M. Duff, & James L. Mohler *Covers the Internet*

With the number of Web pages increasing daily, only the well-designed will stand out and grab the attention of those browsing the Web. This book illustrates, in classic Laura Lemay style, how to design attractive Web pages that will be visited over and over again.

The CD-ROM contains HTML editors, graphics software, and royalty-free graphics and sound files.

Teaches beginning- and advanced-level design principles.

$55.00 USA $77.95 CDN *Accomplished* *Internet/Online/Communications*
ISBN:1-57521-125-4 *500 pp.*

Laura Lemay's Web Workshop: JavaScript

—Laura Lemay & Michael Moncur *Covers JavaScript*

Readers will explore various aspects of Web publishing—whether JavaScripting and interactivity, or graphics design, or Netscape Navigator Gold—in greater depth than with the *Teach Yourself* books.

The CD-ROM includes the complete book in HTML format, publishing tools, templates, graphics, backgrounds, and more.

Provides a clear, hands-on guide to creating sophisticated Web pages.

$39.99 USA $56.95 CDN *Casual–Accomplished* *Communications/Online–Internet*
ISBN: 1-57521-141-6 *400 pp.*

Laura Lemay's Web Workshop: Microsoft FrontPage

—Laura Lemay & Denise Tyler   *Covers FrontPage*

This is a clear, hands-on guide to maintaining Web pages with Microsoft's FrontPage. Written in the clear, conversational style of Laura Lemay, it is packed with many interesting and colorful examples that demonstrate specific tasks of interest to the reader.

CD-ROM included!

Teaches how to maintain Web pages with FrontPage.

Includes all the templates, backgrounds, and materials needed on the CD-ROM!

$39.99 USA $56.95 CDN   *Casual–Accomplished*   *Internet/Web Publishing*
ISBN: 1-57521-149-1   *672 pp.*   *Communications/Online–Internet*

Laura Lemay's Web Workshop: Creating Commercial Web Pages

—Laura Lemay & Brian K. Murphy   *Covers the Web*

This book is filled with sample Web pages that show how to create commercial-grade Web pages using HTML, CGI, and Java. In the classic clear style of Laura Lemay, author of the bestselling *Teach Yourself Java*, this book details not only how to create the page, but how to apply proven principles of design that will make the Web page a marketing tool.

The CD-ROM includes all the templates in the book, plus HTML editors, graphics software, CGI forms, and more.

Teaches how to use HTML, CGI, and Java.

Illustrates the various corporate uses of Web technology: catalogs, customer service, and product ordering.

$39.99 USA $56.95 CDN   *Accomplished*   *Internet/Business*
ISBN: 1-57521-126-2   *528 pp.*

Teach Yourself Web Publishing with HTML 3.2 in 14 Days, Professional Reference Edition

—Laura Lemay   *Covers HTML 3.2*

This is the updated edition of Lemay's previous bestseller, *Teach Yourself Web Publishing with HTML in 14 Days, Premier Edition*. In this edition, readers will find all the advanced topics and updates—including adding audio, video, and animation to Web page creation.

CD-ROM included.

Explores the use of CGI scripts, tables, HTML 3.2, the Netscape and Internet Explorer extensions, Java applets and JavaScript, and VRML.

$59.99 USA $81.95 CDN   *New–Casual–Accomplished*   *Internet/Web Publishing*
ISBN: 1-57521-096-7   *1,104 pp.*

Teach Yourself Java in 21 Days

—Laura Lemay & Charles L. Perkins   *Covers Java*

Introducing the first, best, and most-detailed guide to developing applications with the hot new Java language from Sun Microsystems.

The CD-ROM includes the Java Developer's Kit.

Provides detailed coverage of the hottest new technology on the World Wide Web.

Shows readers how to develop applications using the Java language.

Includes coverage of browsing Java applications with Netscape and other popular Web browsers.

$39.99 USA $53.99 CDN   *Casual–Accomplished–Expert*   *Internet/Programming*
ISBN: 1-57521-030-4   *500 pp.*

Add to Your Sams.net Library Today
with the Best Books for Internet Technologies

ISBN	Quantity	Description of Item	Unit Cost	Total Cost
1-57521-128-9		Laura Lemay's Web Workshop: Netscape Navigator Gold 3 (Book/CD-ROM)	$39.99	
1-57521-125-4		Laura Lemay's Web Workshop: Graphics and Web Page Design (Book/CD-ROM)	$55.00	
1-57521-141-6		Laura Lemay's Web Workshop: JavaScript (Book/CD-ROM)	$39.99	
1-57521-149-1		Laura Lemay's Web Workshop: Microsoft FrontPage (Book/CD-ROM)	$39.99	
1-57521-143-2		Laura Lemay's Web Workshop: 3D Graphics and VRML 2 (Book/CD-ROM)	$39.99	
1-57521-126-2		Laura Lemay's Web Workshop: Creating Commercial Web Pages (Book/CD-ROM)	$39.99	
1-57521-014-2		Teach Yourself Web Publishing with HTML in 14 Days, Premier Edition (Book/CD-ROM)	$39.99	
1-57521-030-4		Teach Yourself Java in 21 Days (Book/CD-ROM)	$39.99	
		Shipping and Handling: See information below.		
		TOTAL		

Shipping and Handling: $4.00 for the first book, and $1.75 for each additional book. If you need to have it NOW, we can ship product to you in 24 hours for an additional charge of approximately $18.00, and you will receive your item overnight or in two days. Overseas shipping and handling adds $2.00. Prices subject to change. Call between 9:00 a.m. and 5:00 p.m. EST for availability and pricing information on latest editions.

201 W. 103rd Street, Indianapolis, Indiana 46290

1-800-428-5331 — Orders   1-800-835-3202 — FAX   1-800-858-7674 — Customer Service

Installing the CD-ROM

The companion CD-ROM contains all the source code and project files developed by the authors, plus an assortment of evaluation versions of third-party products. To install the CD-ROM, please follow these steps.

Windows 95/NT 4 Installation Instructions

1. Insert the CD-ROM into your CD-ROM drive.

2. From the Windows 95 desktop, double-click on the My Computer icon.

3. Double-click on the icon representing your CD-ROM drive.

4. Double-click on the icon titled setup.exe to run the CD-ROM installation program.